THE COLD WAR

THE
COLD
WAR

A NEW HISTORY

JOHN LEWIS GADDIS

THE PENGUIN PRESS

NEW YORK

2005

THE PENGUIN PRESS
Published by the Penguin Group
Penguin Group (USA) Inc., 375 Hudson Street, New York, New York 10014, U.S.A. • Penguin
Group (Canada), 90 Eglinton Avenue East, Suite 700, Toronto, Ontario, Canada M4P 2Y3
(a division of Pearson Penguin Canada Inc.) • Penguin Books Ltd, 80 Strand, London
WC2R 0RL, England • Penguin Ireland, 25 St. Stephen's Green, Dublin 2, Ireland (a division
of Penguin Books Ltd) • Penguin Books Australia Ltd, 250 Camberwell Road, Camberwell,
Victoria 3124, Australia (a division of Pearson Australia Group Pty Ltd) • Penguin Books India Pvt
Ltd, 11 Community Centre, Panchsheel Park, New Delhi–110 017, India • Penguin Group (NZ),
Cnr Airborne and Rosedale Roads, Albany, Auckland 1310, New Zealand (a division of
Pearson New Zealand Ltd) • Penguin Books (South Africa) (Pty) Ltd, 24 Sturdee
Avenue, Rosebank, Johannesburg 2196, South Africa

Penguin Books Ltd, Registered Offices:
80 Strand, London WC2R 0RL, England

First published in 2005 by The Penguin Press,
a member of Penguin Group (USA) Inc.

Photograph credits appear on page 315.

Map sources appear on page 316.

Library of Congress Cataloging-in-Publication Data

Gaddis, John Lewis.
The Cold War : a new history / John Lewis Gaddis.
p.   cm.
Includes bibliographical references and index.
ISBN 1-59420-062-9
1. Cold War.   2. World politics—1945–1989.   I. Title.
D843.G22 2005
909.82'5—dc22   2005053406

Printed in the United States of America
3   5   7   9   10   8   6   4

Designed by Marysarah Quinn
Interior maps by Jeffrey L. Ward

In memory of George F. Kennan

1904–2005

PREFACE

EVERY MONDAY AND WEDNESDAY afternoon each fall semester I lecture to several hundred Yale undergraduates on the subject of Cold War history. As I do this, I have to keep reminding myself that hardly any of them remember any of the events I'm describing. When I talk about Stalin and Truman, even Reagan and Gorbachev, it could as easily be Napoleon, Caesar, or Alexander the Great. Most members of the Class of 2005, for example, were only five years old when the Berlin Wall came down. They know that the Cold War in various ways shaped their lives, because they've been told how it affected their families. Some of them—by no means all—understand that if a few decisions had been made differently at a few critical moments during that conflict, they might not even have had a life. But my students sign up for this course with very little sense of how the Cold War started, what it was about, or why it ended in the way that it did. For them it's history: not all that different from the Peloponnesian War.

And yet, as they learn more about the great rivalry that dominated the last half of the last century, most of my students are fascinated, many are appalled, and a few—usually after the lecture on the Cuban missile crisis—leave class trembling. "Yikes!" they exclaim (I sanitize somewhat). "We had *no* idea that we came *that* close!" And then they invariably add: "Awesome!" For this first post–Cold War generation, then, the Cold War is at once distant and dangerous. What could anyone ever have had to fear, they wonder, from a state that turned out to be as weak, as bumbling, and as *temporary* as the Soviet Union? But they also ask themselves and me: how did we ever make it out of the Cold War alive?

I've written this book to try to answer these questions, but also to respond—at a much less cosmic level—to another my students regularly pose. It has not escaped their attention that I've written several earlier books on Cold War history; indeed, I regularly assign them one that takes almost 300 pages just to get up to 1962. "Can't you cover more years with fewer words?" some of them have politely asked. It's a reasonable question, and it came to seem even more so when my formidably persuasive agent, Andrew Wylie, set out to convince me of the need for a short, comprehensive, and accessible book on the Cold War—a tactful way of suggesting that my previous ones had not been. Since I regard listening to my students and my agent as only slightly less important than listening to my wife (who also liked the idea), the project seemed worth taking on.

The Cold War: A New History is meant chiefly, therefore, for a new generation of readers for whom the Cold War was never "current events." I hope readers who lived through the Cold War will also find the volume useful, because as Marx once said (Groucho, not Karl), "Outside of a dog, a book is a man's best friend. Inside a dog, it's too dark to read." While the Cold War was going on it was hard to know what was happening. Now that it's over—and now that Soviet, East European, and Chinese archives have begun to open—we know much more: so much, in fact, that it's easy to get overwhelmed. That's yet another reason for writing a short book. It's forced me to apply, to all this new information, the simple test of significance made famous by my late Yale colleague Robin Winks: "So what?"

A word as well about what this book is *not* meant to be. It's not a work of original scholarship. Cold War historians will find much of what I say familiar, partly because I've drawn a lot of it from their work, partly because I've repeated some things I've said in my own. Nor does the book attempt to locate roots, within the Cold War, of such post–Cold War phenomena as globalization, ethnic cleansing, religious extremism, terrorism, or the information revolution. Nor does it make any contribution whatever to international relations theory, a field that has troubles enough of its own without my adding to them.

I will be pleased, though, if this view of the Cold War as a whole produces some new ways of looking at its parts. One that has especially struck me is optimism, a quality not generally associated with the Cold War. The world, I am quite sure, is a better place for that conflict having been fought in the way that it was and won by the side that won it. No one today worries about a new global war, or a total triumph of dictators, or the prospect that civilization itself might end. That was not the case when the Cold War began. For all its dangers, atrocities, costs, distractions, and moral compromises, the Cold War—like the American Civil War—was a necessary contest that settled fundamental issues once and for all. We have no reason to miss it. But given the alternatives, we have little reason either to regret its having occurred.

The Cold War was fought at different levels in dissimilar ways in multiple places over a very long time. Any attempt to reduce its history exclusively to the role of great forces, great powers, or great leaders would fail to do it justice. Any effort to capture it within a simple chronological narrative could only produce mush. I've chosen instead to focus each chapter on a significant theme: as a result, they overlap in time and move across space. I've felt free to zoom in from the general to the particular, and then back out again. And I've not hesitated to write from a perspective that takes fully into account how the Cold War came out: I know no other way.

Finally, I want to express my appreciation to the people who inspired, facilitated, and patiently waited for this book. They certainly include my students, whose continuing interest in the Cold War sustains my own. I'm grateful also to Andrew Wylie, as I know future students will be, for having suggested this method of covering more years with fewer words—and for having since helped several of my former students publish their own books. Scott Moyers, Stuart Proffitt, Janie Fleming, Victoria Klose, Maureen Clark, Bruce Giffords, Samantha Johnson, and their colleagues at Penguin showed admirable equanimity in the face of missed deadlines, and exemplary efficiency in producing this overdue book once it was done. It could hardly have been written at all without Christian Ostermann and his colleagues at the Cold War International History Project, whose energy and thoroughness in collecting documents from all over the world (on the day I write this the latest stash from the Albanian archives has arrived) have placed all Cold War historians in their debt. Last, but hardly least, I thank Toni Dorfman, who is the world's best copy editor/proofreader and the world's most loving wife.

The dedication commemorates one of the greatest figures in Cold War history—and a long-time friend—whose biography it will now be my responsibility to write.

J.L.G.
New Haven

CONTENTS

PREFACE *ix*

LIST OF MAPS *xv*

PROLOGUE: THE VIEW FORWARD *1*

I. THE RETURN OF FEAR *5*

II. DEATHBOATS AND LIFEBOATS *48*

III. COMMAND VERSUS SPONTANEITY *83*

IV. THE EMERGENCE OF AUTONOMY *119*

V. THE RECOVERY OF EQUITY *156*

VI. ACTORS *195*

VII. THE TRIUMPH OF HOPE *237*

EPILOGUE: THE VIEW BACK *259*

NOTES *267*

BIBLIOGRAPHY *299*

INDEX *317*

MAPS

European Territorial Changes, 1939–1947 *13*

Divided Germany and Austria *23*

The Korean War, 1950–1953 *44*

U.S. and U.S.S.R. Alliances and Bases, Early 1970s *96*

The Middle East, 1967, 1979 *205*

The Near East in Upheaval, 1980 *209*

A 1980s Soviet View *220*

Post–Cold War Europe *258*

THE COLD WAR

PROLOGUE
THE VIEW FORWARD

In 1946 a forty-three-year-old Englishman named Eric Blair rented a house at the edge of the world—a house in which he expected to die. It was on the northern tip of the Scottish island of Jura, at the end of a dirt track, inaccessible by automobile, with no telephone or electricity. The nearest shop, the only one on the island, was some twenty-five miles to the south. Blair had reasons to want remoteness. Dejected by the recent death of his wife, he was suffering from tuberculosis and would soon begin coughing up blood. His country was reeling from the costs of a military victory that had brought neither security, nor prosperity, nor even the assurance that freedom would survive. Europe was dividing into two hostile camps, and the world seemed set to follow. With atomic bombs likely to be used, any new war would be apocalyptic. And he needed to finish a novel.

Its title was *1984*, an inversion of the year in which he completed it, and it appeared in Great Britain and the United States in 1949 under Blair's pen name, George Orwell. The reviews, the *New York Times* noted, were "overwhelmingly admiring," but "with cries of terror rising above the applause."[1] This was hardly surprising because *1984* evoked an age, only three and a half decades distant, in which totalitarianism has triumphed everywhere. Individuality is smothered, along with law, ethics, creativity, linguistic clarity, honesty about history, and even love—apart, of course, from the love everyone is forced to feel for the Stalin-like dictator "Big Brother" and his counterparts, who run a world permanently at war. "If you want a picture of the future," Orwell's hero Winston Smith is told, as he undergoes yet another session of relentless torture, "imagine a boot stamping on a human face—forever."[2]

Orwell did die early in 1950—in a London hospital, not on his island—knowing only that his book had impressed and frightened its first readers. Subsequent readers responded similarly: *1984* became the single most compelling vision in the post–World War II era of what might follow it. As the real year 1984 approached, therefore, comparisons with Orwell's imaginary year became inescapable. The world was not yet totalitarian, but dictators dominated large parts of it. The danger of war between the United States and the Soviet Union—two superpowers instead of the three Orwell had anticipated—seemed greater than it had for many years. And the apparently permanent conflict known as the "Cold War," which began while Orwell was still alive, showed not the slightest signs of ending.

But then, on the evening of January 16, 1984, an actor Orwell would have recognized from his years as a film reviewer appeared on television in his more recent role as president of the United States. Ronald Reagan's reputation until this moment had been that of an ardent Cold Warrior. Now, though, he envisaged a different future:

> Just suppose with me for a moment that an Ivan and an Anya could find themselves, say, in a waiting room, or sharing a shelter from the rain or a storm with a Jim and Sally, and that there was no language barrier to keep them from getting acquainted. Would they then deliberate the differences between their respective governments? Or would they find themselves

> comparing notes about their children and what each other did
> for a living? . . . They might even have decided that they were
> all going to get together for dinner some evening soon. Above
> all, they would have proven that people don't make wars.[3]

It was an unexpectedly gentle invitation for human faces to prevail over boots, dictators, and the mechanisms of war. It set in motion, in Orwell's year 1984, the sequence of events by which they would do so. Just over a year after Reagan's speech, an ardent enemy of totalitarianism took power in the Soviet Union. Within six years, that country's control over half of Europe had collapsed. Within eight, the Union of Soviet Socialist Republics—the country that had provoked Orwell's great gloomy prophecy in the first place—had itself ceased to exist.

These things did not happen simply because Reagan gave a speech or because Orwell wrote a book: the remainder of this book complicates the causation. It is worth starting with visions, though, because they establish hopes and fears. History then determines which prevail.

CHAPTER ONE
THE RETURN OF FEAR

We waited for them to come ashore. We could see their faces. They looked like ordinary people. We had imagined something different. Well, they were Americans!

—Liubova Kozinchenka,
Red Army, 58th Guards Division

I guess we didn't know what to expect from the Russians, but when you looked at them and examined them, you couldn't tell whether, you know? If you put an American uniform on them, they could have been American!

—Al Aronson,
U.S. Army, 69th Infantry Division[1]

This was the way the war was supposed to end: with cheers, handshakes, dancing, drinking, and hope. The date was April 25, 1945, the place the eastern German city of Torgau on the Elbe, the event the first meeting of the armies, converging from opposite ends of the earth, that had cut Nazi Germany in two. Five days later Adolf Hitler blew his brains out beneath the rubble that was all that was left of Berlin. Just over a week after that, the Germans surrendered unconditionally. The leaders of the victorious Grand Alliance, Franklin D. Roosevelt, Winston Churchill, and Josef Stalin, had already exchanged their own handshakes, toasts, and hopes for a better world at two wartime summits—Teheran in November, 1943, and Yalta in February, 1945. These gestures would have meant little, though, had the troops they commanded not been able to stage their own more boisterous celebration where it really counted: on the front lines of a battlefield from which the enemy was now disappearing.

Why, then, did the armies at Torgau approach one another warily, as if they'd been expecting interplanetary visitors? Why did the resemblances they saw seem so surprising—and so reassuring? Why, despite these, did their commanders insist on separate surrender ceremonies, one for the western front at Reims, in France, on May 7th, another for the eastern front in Berlin on May 8th? Why did the Soviet authorities try to break up spontaneous pro-American demonstrations that erupted in Moscow following the official announcement of the German capitulation? Why did the American authorities, during the week that followed, abruptly suspend critical shipments of Lend-Lease aid to the U.S.S.R., and then resume them? Why did Roosevelt's key aide Harry Hopkins, who had played a decisive role in crafting the Grand Alliance in 1941, have to rush to Moscow six weeks after his boss's death to try to save it? Why for that matter, years later, would Churchill title his memoir of these events *Triumph and Tragedy*?

The answer to all of these questions is much the same: that the war had been won by a coalition whose principal members were already at war—ideologically and geopolitically if not militarily—with one another. Whatever the Grand Alliance's triumphs in the spring of 1945, its success had always depended upon the pursuit of compatible objectives by incompatible systems. The tragedy was this: that victory would require the victors either to cease to be who they were, or to give up much of what they had hoped, by fighting the war, to attain.

I.

HAD THERE really been an alien visitor on the banks of the Elbe in April, 1945, he, she, or it might indeed have detected superficial resemblances in the Russian and American armies that met there, as well as in the societies from which they had come. Both the United States and the Soviet Union had been born in revolution. Both embraced ideologies with global aspirations: what worked at home, their leaders assumed, would also do so for the rest of the world. Both, as continental states, had advanced across vast frontiers: they were at the time the first and third largest countries in the world. And both had entered the war as the result of surprise attack: the German invasion of the Soviet Union, which began on June 22, 1941, and the Japanese strike against Pearl Harbor on December 7, 1941, which Hitler used as an excuse to declare war on the United States four days later. That would have been the extent of the similarities, though. The differences, as any terrestrial observer could have quickly pointed out, were much greater.

The American Revolution, which had happened over a century and a half earlier, reflected a deep distrust of concentrated authority. Liberty and justice, the Founding Fathers had insisted, could come only through constraining power. Thanks to an ingenious constitution, their geographical isolation from potential rivals, and a magnificent endowment of natural resources, the Americans managed to build an extraordinarily powerful state, a fact that became obvious during World War II. They accomplished this, however, by severely restricting their government's capacity to control everyday life, whether through the dissemination of ideas, the organization of the economy, or the conduct of politics. Despite the legacy of slavery, the near extermination of native Americans, and persistent racial, sexual, and social discrimination, the citizens of the United States could plausibly claim, in 1945, to live in the freest society on the face of the earth.

The Bolshevik Revolution, which had happened only a quarter century earlier, had in contrast involved the embrace of concentrated authority as a means of overthrowing class enemies and consolidating a base from which a proletarian revolution would spread throughout the world. Karl Marx claimed, in the *Communist Manifesto* of 1848, that the industrialization capitalists had set in motion was simultaneously expanding and exploiting the working class, which would sooner or later liberate itself. Not content to wait for this to happen, Vladimir Ilyich Lenin sought to accelerate history in 1917 by seizing control of Russia and imposing Marxism on it, even though that state failed to fit Marx's prediction that the revolution could only occur in an advanced industrial society. Stalin in turn fixed that problem by redesigning Russia to fit Marxist-Leninist ideology: he forced a largely agrarian nation with few traditions of liberty to become a heavily industrialized nation with no liberty at all. As a consequence, the Union of Soviet Socialist Republics was, at the end of World War II, the most authoritarian society anywhere on the face of the earth.

If the victorious nations could hardly have been more different, the same was true of the wars they had fought from 1941 to 1945. The United States waged separate wars simultaneously—against the Japanese in the Pacific and the Germans in Europe—but suffered remarkably few casualties: just under 300,000 Americans died in all combat theaters. Geographically distant from where the fighting was taking place, their country experienced no significant attacks apart from the initial one at Pearl Harbor. With its ally Great Britain (which suffered about 357,000 war deaths), the United States was able to choose where, when, and in what circumstances it would fight, a fact that greatly minimized the costs and risks of fighting. But unlike the British, the Americans emerged from the war with their economy thriving: wartime spending had caused their gross domestic product almost to double in less than four years. If there could ever be such a thing as a "good" war, then this one, for the United States, came close.

The Soviet Union enjoyed no such advantages. It waged only one war, but it was arguably the most terrible one in all of history. With its cities, towns, and countryside ravaged, its industries ruined or hurriedly relocated beyond the Urals, the only option apart from surrender was desperate resistance, on terrain and in circumstances chosen by its enemy. Estimates of casualties, civilian and military, are notoriously inexact, but it is likely that some 27 million Soviet citizens died as a direct result of the war—roughly 90 *times* the number of Americans who died. Victory could hardly have been purchased at greater cost: the U.S.S.R. in 1945 was a shattered state, fortunate to have survived. The war, a contemporary observer recalled, was "both the most fearful and the proudest memory of the Russian people."[2]

When it came to shaping the postwar settlement, however, the victors were more evenly matched than these asymmetries might suggest. The United States had made no commitment to reverse its long-standing tradition of remaining aloof from European affairs—Roosevelt had even assured Stalin, at Teheran, that American troops would return home within two years after the end of the war.[3] Nor, given the depressing record of the 1930s, could there be any assurance that the wartime economic boom would continue, or that democracy would again take root beyond the relatively few countries in which it still existed. The stark fact that the Americans and the British could not have defeated Hitler without Stalin's help meant that World War II was a victory over fascism only—not over authoritarianism and its prospects for the future.

Meanwhile, the Soviet Union had significant assets, despite the immense losses it had suffered. Because it was part of Europe, its military forces would not be withdrawing from Europe. Its command economy had shown itself capable of sustaining full employment when the capitalist democracies had failed, during the prewar years, to do so.

Its ideology enjoyed widespread respect in Europe because communists there had largely led the resistance against the Germans. Finally, the disproportionate burden the Red Army had borne in defeating Hitler gave the U.S.S.R. a moral claim to substantial, perhaps even preponderant, influence in shaping the postwar settlement. It was at least as easy to believe, in 1945, that authoritarian communism was the wave of the future as that democratic capitalism was.

The Soviet Union had one other advantage as well, which was that it alone among the victors emerged from the war with tested leadership. Roosevelt's death on April 12, 1945, had catapulted his inexperienced and ill-informed vice president, Harry S. Truman, into the White House. Three months later, Churchill's unexpected defeat in the British general election made the far less formidable Labour Party leader, Clement Attlee, prime minister. The Soviet Union, in contrast, had Stalin, its unchallenged ruler since 1929, the man who remade his country and then led it to victory in World War II. Crafty, formidable, and to all appearances calmly purposeful, the Kremlin dictator knew what he wanted in the postwar era. Truman, Attlee, and the nations they led seemed much less certain.

II.

SO WHAT *did* Stalin want? It makes sense to start with him, because only he of the three postwar leaders had had the time, while retaining the authority, to consider and rank his priorities. Sixty-five at the end of the war, the man who ran the Soviet Union was physically exhausted, surrounded by sycophants, personally lonely—but still firmly, even terrifyingly, in control. His scrawny mustache, discolored teeth, pock-marked face, and yellow eyes, an American diplomat recalled, "gave him the aspect of an old battle-scarred tiger. . . . An unforewarned visitor would never have guessed what depths of calculation, ambition, love of power, jealousy, cruelty, and sly vindictiveness lurked behind this unpretentious façade."[4] Through a series of purges during the 1930s, Stalin had long since eliminated all his rivals. The raising of an eyebrow or the flick of a finger, subordinates knew, could mean the difference between life and death. Strikingly short—only five feet four inches—this paunchy little old man was nonetheless a colossus, bestriding a colossal state.

Stalin's postwar goals were security for himself, his regime, his country, and his ideology, in precisely that order. He sought to make sure that no internal challenges could ever again endanger his personal rule, and that no external threats would ever again place his country at risk. The interests of communists elsewhere in the world, admirable though those might be, would never outweigh the priorities of the Soviet state as he had determined them. Narcissism, paranoia, and absolute power came together in Stalin:[5] he was, within the Soviet Union and the international communist movement, enormously feared—but also widely worshipped.

Wartime expenditures in blood and treasure, Stalin believed, should largely determine who got what after the war: the Soviet Union, therefore, would get a lot.[6] Not only would it regain the territories it had lost to the Germans during World War II; it would also retain the territories it had taken as a result of the opportunistic but shortsighted "non-aggression" pact Stalin had concluded with Hitler in August, 1939—portions of Finland, Poland, and Romania, all of the Baltic States. It would require that states beyond these expanded borders remain within Moscow's sphere of influence. It would seek territorial concessions at the expense of Iran and Turkey (including control of the Turkish Straits), as well as naval bases in the Mediterranean. Finally, it would punish a defeated and devastated Germany through military occupation, property expropriations, reparations payments, and ideological transformation.

Herein there lay, however, a painful dilemma for Stalin. Disproportionate losses during the war may well have entitled the Soviet Union to disproportionate postwar gains, but they had also robbed that country of the power required to secure those benefits unilaterally. The

U.S.S.R. needed peace, economic assistance, and the diplomatic acquiescence of its former allies. There was no choice for the moment, then, but to continue to seek the cooperation of the Americans and the British: just as they had depended on Stalin to defeat Hitler, so Stalin now depended on continued Anglo-American goodwill if he was to obtain his postwar objectives at a reasonable cost. He therefore *wanted* neither a hot war nor a cold war.[7] Whether he would be skillful enough to avoid these alternatives, however, was quite a different matter.

For Stalin's understanding of his wartime allies and *their* postwar objectives was based more on wishful thinking than on an accurate assessment of priorities as seen from Washington and London. It was here that Marxist-Leninist ideology influenced Stalin, because his illusions arose from it. The most important one was the belief, which went back to Lenin, that capitalists would never be able to cooperate with one another for very long. Their inherent greediness—the irresistible urge to place profits above politics—would sooner or later prevail, leaving communists with the need only for patience as they awaited their adversaries' self-destruction. "The alliance between ourselves and the democratic faction of the capitalists succeeds because the latter had an interest in preventing Hitler's domination," Stalin commented as the war was coming to a close. "[I]n the future we shall be against this faction of the capitalists as well."[8]

This idea of a crisis within capitalism did have some plausibility. World War I, after all, had been a war among capitalists; it thereby provided the opportunity for the world's first communist state to emerge. The Great Depression left the remaining capitalist states scrambling to save themselves rather than cooperating to rescue the global economy or to maintain the postwar settlement: Nazi Germany arose as a result. With the end of World War II, Stalin believed, the economic crisis was bound to return. Capitalists would then need the Soviet Union, rather than the other way around. That is why he fully expected the United States to *lend* the Soviet Union several billion dollars for re-

EUROPEAN TERRITORIAL CHANGES
1939–1947

Annexed by Soviet Union
Annexed by Poland
Annexed by Yugoslavia
To Bulgaria

Petsamo
• Murmansk

White Sea

Gulf of Bothnia

FINLAND

Lake Ladoga

NORWAY

Porkkala-udd (leased to Russia)
Helsinki •
• Leningrad

Gulf of Finland

• Oslo

Stockholm •
• Tallinn
ESTONIA

Baltic Sea

SWEDEN

• Moscow

• Riga
LATVIA

DENMARK

Kaliningrad (Koningsberg)
Copenhagen •
LITHUANIA
• Kaunas

Gdansk (Danzig)
• Minsk

Szczecin (Stettin)
EAST PRUSSIA

SOVIET UNION

Berlin •
EASTERN GERMANY
• Warsaw
EASTERN POLAND

GERMANY
POLAND
• Kiev

Wroclaw (Breslau) •

• Prague
• Cracow

CZECHOSLOVAKIA
NORTHERN BUKOVINA

Vienna •
• Bratislava
BESSARABIA

SWITZ.
AUSTRIA
HUNGARY
• Budapest
SUBCARPATHIAN RUTHENIA
• Odessa

Trieste
VENEZIA GIULIA
ROMANIA
Black Sea

ITALY
• Belgrade
• Bucharest

YUGOSLAVIA
Dobruja

Adriatic Sea
BULGARIA

• Sofia

• Rome

Tirana •
• Istanbul

ALBANIA

Mediterranean Sea
GREECE
TURKEY

© 2005 Jeffrey L. Ward

0 Miles   100   200
0 Kilometers   200

construction: because the Americans would otherwise be unable to find markets for their products during the coming global crash.[9]

It followed as well that the other capitalist superpower, Great Britain—whose weakness Stalin consistently underestimated—would sooner or later break with its American ally over economic rivalries: "[T]he inevitability of wars between capitalist countries remains in force," he insisted, as late as 1952.[10] From Stalin's perspective, then, the long-term forces of history would compensate for the catastrophe World War II had inflicted upon the Soviet Union. It would not be necessary to confront the Americans and British directly in order to achieve his objectives. He could simply wait for the capitalists to begin quarreling with one another, and for the disgusted Europeans to embrace communism as an alternative.

Stalin's goal, therefore, was not to restore a balance of power in Europe, but rather to dominate that continent as thoroughly as Hitler had sought to do. He acknowledged, in a wistful but revealing comment in 1947, that "[h]ad Churchill delayed opening the second front in northern France by a year, the Red Army would have come to France. . . . [W]e toyed with the idea of reaching Paris."[11] Unlike Hitler, however, Stalin followed no fixed timetable. He had welcomed the D-Day landings, despite the fact that they would preclude the Red Army from reaching western Europe anytime soon: Germany's defeat was the first priority. Nor would he write off diplomacy in securing his objective, not least because he expected—for a time at least—American cooperation in achieving it. Had not Roosevelt indicated that the United States would refrain from seeking its own sphere of influence in Europe? Stalin's was, therefore, a grand vision: the peacefully accomplished but historically determined domination of Europe. It was also a flawed vision, for it failed to take into account the evolving postwar objectives of the United States.

III.

WHAT DID the Americans want after the war? Unquestionably also security, but in contrast to Stalin, they were much less certain of what they would have to do to obtain it. The reason had to do with the dilemma World War II had posed for them: that the United States could not continue to serve as a model for the rest of the world while remaining apart from the rest of the world.

Throughout most of their history Americans had tried to do just this. They had not had to worry much about security because oceans separated them from all other states that might conceivably do them harm. Their very independence from Great Britain resulted, as Thomas Paine had predicted it would in 1776, from the implausibility that "a Continent [could] be perpetually governed by an island."[12] Despite their naval superiority, the British were never able to project sufficient military power across some 3,000 miles of water to keep the Americans within the empire, or to prevent them from dominating the North American continent. The prospect that other Europeans might do so was even more remote, because successive governments in London came to agree with the Americans that there should be no further colonization in the western hemisphere. The United States enjoyed the luxury, therefore, of maintaining a vast sphere of influence without the risk that by doing so it would challenge the interests of any other great power.

The Americans did seek global influence in the realm of ideas: their Declaration of Independence had, after all, advanced the radical claim that *all men* are created equal. But they made no effort, during their first fourteen decades of independence, to make good on that assertion. The United States would serve as an example; the rest of the world would have to decide how and under what circumstances to embrace it. "She is the well-wisher to the freedom and independence of all," Secretary of State John Quincy Adams proclaimed in 1821, but "[s]he is the champion and vindicator only of her own."[13] Despite an international ideology, therefore, American practices were isolationist: the nation had not yet concluded that its security required transplanting its principles. Its foreign and military policy was much less ambitious than one might have expected from a nation of such size and strength.

Only with World War I did the United States break out of this pattern. Worried that Imperial Germany might defeat Great Britain and France, Woodrow Wilson persuaded his countrymen that American military might was needed to restore the European balance of power—but even he justified this geopolitical objective in ideological terms. The world, he insisted, had to be made "safe for democracy."[14] Wilson went on to propose, as the basis for a peace settlement, a League of Nations that would impose on states something like the rule of law that states—at least enlightened ones—imposed on individuals. The idea that might alone makes right would, he hoped, disappear.

Both the vision and the restored balance, however, proved premature. Victory in World War I did not make the United States a global power; instead it confirmed, for most Americans, the dangers of overcommitment. Wilson's plans for a postwar collective security organization went well beyond where his countrymen were ready to go. Meanwhile, disillusionment with allies—together with Wilson's ill-conceived and half-hearted military intervention against the Bolsheviks in Siberia and North Russia in 1918–20—turned the fruits of victory sour. Conditions abroad encouraged a return to isolationism: the perceived inequities of the Versailles peace treaty, the onset of a global depression, and then the rise of aggressor states in Europe and East Asia all had the effect of convincing Americans that they would be better off avoiding international involvements altogether. It was a rare *withdrawal* of a powerful state from responsibilities beyond its borders.

After entering the White House in 1933, Franklin D. Roosevelt worked persistently—if often circuitously—to bring the United States into a more active role in world politics. It was not easy: "I feel very much as if I were groping for a door in a blank wall."[15] Even after Japan had gone to war with China in 1937 and World War II had broken out in Europe in 1939, F.D.R. had made only minimal progress in persuading the nation that Wilson had been right: that its security could be threatened by what happened halfway around the world. It would take the shattering events of 1940–41—the fall of France, the battle of Britain, and ultimately the Japanese attack on Pearl Harbor—to bring about an American recommitment to the task of restoring a balance of power beyond the western hemisphere. "We have profited by our past mistakes," the president promised in 1942. "This time we shall know how to make full use of victory."[16]

Roosevelt had four great wartime priorities. The first was to sustain allies—chiefly Great Britain, the Soviet Union, and (less successfully) Nationalist China—because there was no other way to achieve victory: the United States could not fight Germany and Japan alone. The second was to secure allied cooperation in shaping the postwar settlement, for without it there would be little prospect for lasting peace. The third had to do with the nature of that settlement. Roosevelt expected his allies to endorse one that would remove the most probable causes of future wars. That meant a new collective security organization with the power to deter and if necessary punish aggression, as well as a revived global economic system equipped to prevent a new global depression. Finally, the settlement would have to be "sellable" to the American people: F.D.R. was not about to repeat Wilson's mistake of taking the nation beyond where it was prepared to go. There would be no reversion to isolationism, then, after World War II. But the United States would not be prepared either—any more than the Soviet Union would be—to accept a postwar world that resembled its prewar predecessor.

Finally, a word about British objectives. They were, as Churchill defined them, much simpler: to survive at all costs, even if this meant relinquishing leadership of the Anglo-American coalition to Washington, even if it meant weakening the British empire, even if it also meant collaborating with the Soviet Union, a regime the younger

Churchill had hoped, in the aftermath of the Bolshevik Revolution, to crush.[17] The British would attempt to influence the Americans as much as possible—they aspired to the role of Greeks, tutoring the new Romans—but under no circumstances would they get at odds with the Americans. Stalin's expectation of an independent Britain, capable of resisting the United States and even going to war with it, would have seemed strange indeed to those who actually shaped British wartime and postwar grand strategy.

IV.

WITH THESE PRIORITIES, what prospects were there for a World War II settlement that would preserve the Grand Alliance? Roosevelt, Churchill, and Stalin no doubt hoped for such an outcome: nobody wanted new enemies so soon after having overcome their old ones. But their coalition had been, from the start, *both* a means of cooperating to defeat the Axis *and* an instrument through which each of the victors sought to position itself for maximum influence in the postwar world. It could hardly be otherwise: despite public claims by the Big Three that politics were adjourned while the war was going on, none of them believed in or sought to practice this principle. What they did do—in communications and conferences mostly shrouded from public view—was to try to reconcile divergent political objectives even as they pursued a common military task. For the most part, they failed, and it was in that failure that the roots of the Cold War lay. The major issues were as follows:

THE SECOND FRONT AND A SEPARATE PEACE. Apart from defeat itself, the greatest Anglo-American fear had been that the Soviet Union might again cut a deal with Nazi Germany, as it had in 1939, which would leave large portions of Europe in authoritarian hands—hence the importance Roosevelt and Churchill attached to keeping the

Soviet Union in the war. This meant providing all possible assistance in food, clothing, and armaments, even if by desperate means and at great cost: running convoys to Murmansk and Archangel while avoiding German submarines was no easy thing to do. It also meant not contesting Stalin's demands for the restoration of lost territories, despite the awkward fact that some of these—the Baltic States, eastern Poland, parts of Finland and Romania—had fallen under Soviet control only as a result of his pact with Hitler. Finally, forestalling a separate peace meant creating a second front on the European continent as soon as was militarily feasible, although in London and Washington that was understood to require postponement until success seemed likely at an acceptable cost.

As a consequence, the second front—more accurately second *fronts*—materialized slowly, a fact which angered the embattled Russians, who lacked the luxury of minimizing casualties. The first came in Vichy-occupied North Africa, where American and British forces landed in November, 1942; invasions of Sicily and southern Italy followed in the summer of 1943. Not until the June, 1944, landings in Normandy, however, did Anglo-American military operations begin to take significant pressure off the Red Army, which had long since turned the tide of battle on the eastern front and was now pushing the Germans out of the Soviet Union altogether. Stalin congratulated his allies on the success of D-Day, but suspicions remained that the delay had been deliberate, with a view to leaving the burden of fighting disproportionately to the U.S.S.R.[18] The plan, as one Soviet analyst later put it, had been for the United States to participate "only at the last minute, when it could easily affect the outcome of the war, completely ensuring its interests."[19]

The political importance of second fronts was at least as great as their military significance, for they meant that the Americans and the British would participate, along with the Soviet Union, in the surrender and occupation of Germany and its satellites. More for reasons of convenience than anything else, the Anglo-American military command excluded the Russians from this process when Italy capitulated in September, 1943. This provided Stalin with an excuse for something he probably would have done in any event, which was to deny the Americans and British any meaningful role in the occupation of Romania, Bulgaria, and Hungary when the Red Army moved into those territories in 1944–45.

Stalin and Churchill had agreed easily enough in October, 1944, that the Soviet Union should have a predominant influence in those countries, in return for an acknowledgment of British preponderance in Greece. Beneath the surface, though, concerns persisted. Roosevelt protested not having been consulted on the Stalin-Churchill deal, and when the British and Americans began negotiating for the surrender of German armies in northern Italy in the spring of 1945, Stalin's own reaction came close to panic: there might be an arrangement, he warned his military commanders, by which the Germans would stop fighting in the west while continuing to resist in the east.[20] He thereby revealed the depths of his own fears about a separate peace. That he thought his allies capable of making one at this late date showed how little reassurance the second fronts had provided him—and how little trust he was prepared to extend.

SPHERES OF INFLUENCE. A division of Europe into spheres of influence—as implied by the Churchill-Stalin agreement—would leave little room for the Europeans to determine their future: that is why Roosevelt worried about it. However much he might have justified the war to himself in balance of power terms, he had explained it to the American people as Wilson might have done—as a fight for self-determination. Churchill had gone along with this in 1941 by accepting the Atlantic Charter, F.D.R.'s restatement of Wilsonian principles. A major Anglo-American objective, therefore, was to reconcile these ideals with Stalin's territorial demands, as well as his insistence on a sphere of influence that would ensure the presence of "friendly" nations along the Soviet Union's postwar borders. Roosevelt and Churchill repeatedly pressed Stalin to allow free elections in the Baltic States, Poland, and elsewhere in Eastern Europe. At the Yalta Conference he agreed to do so, but without the slightest intention of honoring his commitment. "Do not worry," he reassured his foreign minister, Vyacheslav Molotov. "We can implement it in our own way later. The heart of the matter is the correlation of forces."[21]

So Stalin got the territorial acquisitions and the sphere of influence he wanted: the Soviet Union's borders were moved several hundred miles to the west, and the Red Army installed subservient regimes throughout the rest of Eastern Europe. Not all of them were as yet communist—the Kremlin leader was, for the moment, flexible on that point—but none would challenge the projection of Soviet influence into the center of Europe. The Americans and British had hoped for a different outcome: one in which the Eastern Europeans, especially the Poles—Germany's first victim in World War II—would choose their own governments. The two positions might have been reconciled had all the Eastern Europeans been prepared to elect leaders who would meet Moscow's requirements, something Finland and Czechoslovakia did indeed do. Poland, however, could hardly follow this path, because Stalin's own actions had long since eliminated any possibility that a Polish government subservient to the Soviet Union could sustain popular support.

The offenses included the 1939 Nazi-Soviet Pact, which had extinguished Polish independence, together with the subsequent discovery that the Russians had massacred some 4,000 Polish officers at Katyn Wood in 1940—another 11,000 remained unaccounted for. Stalin broke with the Polish government-in-exile in London over this issue in 1943, shifting his support to a group of Polish communists based in Lublin. He then did nothing when the Nazis brutally suppressed the 1944 Warsaw uprising, organized by the London Poles, despite the fact that the Red Army was on the outskirts of the Polish capital at the time.

Stalin's insistence on taking a third of Poland's territory after the war further embittered the nation; his promise of compensation at the expense of Germany did little to repair the damage.

Because Poles would never elect a pro-Soviet government, Stalin imposed one—the cost, though, was a permanently resentful Poland, as well as a growing sense among his American and British allies that they could no longer trust him. As a disillusioned Roosevelt put it two weeks before his death: "[Stalin] has broken every one of the promises he made at Yalta."[22]

DEFEATED ENEMIES. In contrast to unilateral Soviet control in Eastern Europe, there was never any doubt—at least not after D-Day— that Germany would be jointly occupied. The way in which this happened, however, left the Russians with a sense of having been cheated. The United States, Great Britain, and (through Anglo-American generosity) France wound up controlling two-thirds of Germany, not as a result of the amount of blood they had shed during the war, but because of geographical proximity to their advancing armies, along with the fact that Stalin had given a substantial part of eastern Germany to the Poles. Although the Soviet zone of occupation surrounded the jointly occupied capital, Berlin, it contained only about a third of Germany's population and an even smaller percentage of its industrial facilities.

Why did Stalin accept this arrangement? Probably because of his belief that the Marxist-Leninist government he planned to install in eastern Germany would become a "magnet" for Germans in the western occupation zones, causing them to choose leaders who would eventually unify the entire country under Soviet control. The long-delayed proletarian revolution that Marx had foreseen in Germany would then take place. "All of Germany must be ours, that is, Soviet, communist," Stalin commented in 1946.[23] There were, however, two big problems with this strategy.

The first had to do with the brutality with which the Red Army occupied eastern Germany. Not only did Soviet troops expropriate prop-

North Sea

DENMARK

Baltic Sea

SOVIET UNION

EAST PRUSSIA

Danzig

Hamburg

Bremen (U.S.)

Berlin

BRITISH ZONE

SOVIET ZONE

Oder

FORMERLY GERMAN TERRITORY— UNDER U.S.S.R. AND POLISH ADMINISTRATION

NETHERLANDS

Cologne

POLAND

Warsaw

BELGIUM

WEST GERMANY

Leipzig

EAST GERMANY

LUX.

FRENCH ZONE

Dresden

SAAR

Nuremberg

Prague

UNITED STATES ZONE

CZECHOSLOVAKIA

FRANCE

Stuttgart

Rhine

Danube

Fribourg

Vienna

(U.S.)

(U.S.S.R.)

Munich

HUNGARY

(FR.)

AUSTRIA

SWITZERLAND

(BR.)

Graz

Danube

ITALY

YUGOSLAVIA

0 Miles 100 200

0 Kilometers 200

DIVIDED GERMANY AND AUSTRIA

North Sea

Baltic Sea

Hamburg

Elbe

EAST GERMANY

Stettin

WEST GERMANY

Weser

Berlin (Joint Occupation)

POLAND

Oder

Hannover

Potsdam

Helmstedt

Elbe

Leipzig

DIVIDED GREATER BERLIN

0 Miles 5

0 Km 10

FRENCH SECTOR

Tegel Airfield

BRITISH SECTOR

SOVIET SECTOR

Gatow Airfield

Tempelhof Airfield

UNITED STATES SECTOR

0 Miles 50 100

0 Kilometers 100

Schönefeld Airfield

Frankfurt

CZECHOSLOVAKIA

© 2005 Jeffrey L. Ward

erty and extract reparations on an indiscriminate scale, but they also indulged in mass rape—some 2 million German women suffered this fate between 1945 and 1947.[24] The effect was to alienate almost all Germans, and thus to set up an asymmetry that would persist throughout the Cold War: the regime Stalin installed in the east lacked the legitimacy its counterpart in the west would quickly gain.

The second problem had to do with allies. The unilateralism with which the Soviets had handled their affairs in Germany and Eastern Europe made the British and Americans wary of relying on cooperation with Moscow in occupying the rest of Germany. Accordingly, they seized such opportunities as arose to consolidate their own zones, along with that of the French, with a view to accepting the division of the country. The idea was to preserve as much of Germany as possible under western rule rather than to risk the danger that all of it might come under Soviet control. Most Germans, as they became aware of what Stalin's rule would mean, reluctantly supported this Anglo-American policy.

What had happened in Germany and Eastern Europe, in turn, left the United States with little incentive to include the Soviet Union in the occupation of Japan. The U.S.S.R. had not declared war on that country after Pearl Harbor, nor had its allies expected it to at a time when the German army was on the outskirts of Moscow. Stalin had, however, promised to enter the Pacific war three months after Germany's surrender, in return for which Roosevelt and Churchill had agreed to transfer the Japanese-owned Kurile Islands to Soviet control, as well as to restore the southern half of Sakhalin Island along with territorial rights and naval bases in Manchuria, all of which Russia had lost as a result of its defeat in the Russo-Japanese War of 1904–5.

The prevailing view in Washington and London had been that the Red Army's assistance—especially an invasion of Japanese-occupied Manchuria—would be vital in hastening victory. But that was before the United States successfully tested its first atomic bomb in July, 1945. Once it became clear that the Americans possessed such a weapon, the need for Soviet military assistance vanished.[25] With the precedents of Soviet unilateralism in Europe all too clearly in mind, there was no desire within the new Truman administration to see something similar repeated in Northeast Asia. Here, then, the Americans embraced Stalin's own equation of blood with influence. They had done most of the fighting in the Pacific War. They alone, therefore, would occupy the nation that had started it.

THE ATOMIC BOMB. Meanwhile, the bomb itself was intensifying Soviet-American distrust. The Americans and the British had secretly developed the weapon for use against Germany, but the Nazis surrendered before it was ready. The Manhattan Project had not been secret enough, though, to keep Soviet intelligence from discovering a lot about it through espionage: there were at least *three* separate and successful Soviet efforts to penetrate security at Los Alamos, where the bomb was being built.[26] The fact that Stalin mounted a major operation to spy on his allies in the middle of a war he and they were waging together is another strong indication of his lack of trust in them—although it has to be acknowledged, as well, that the Anglo-Americans themselves did not choose to tell Stalin about the bomb until after the first successful test in the New Mexico desert.

The Soviet leader showed little surprise, therefore, when Truman gave him the news at the Potsdam Conference—he had learned about the bomb long before the new American president had done so. But Stalin reacted strongly when the United States went ahead and used the weapon against the Japanese three weeks later. A test in the desert was one thing. An actual weapon actually employed was something else again. "War is barbaric, but using the A-bomb is a superbarbarity," Stalin complained after learning how Hiroshima had been destroyed. The American breakthrough was yet another challenge to his insistence that blood expended should equal influence gained: all at once, the United States had obtained a military capability that did not depend upon the deployment of armies on a battlefield. Brains—and the military technology they could produce—now counted for just as much. "Hiroshima has shaken the whole world," Stalin told his scientists, in authorizing a crash Soviet program to catch up. "The balance has been destroyed. . . . That cannot be."[27]

In addition to seeing the bomb as shortening the war and thus denying the Russians any significant role in defeating and occupying Japan, Stalin also saw the bomb as a means by which the United States would seek to extract postwar concessions from the Soviet Union: "A-bomb blackmail is American policy."[28] There was something in this. Truman had used the bomb chiefly to end the war, but he and his advisers did indeed expect their new weapon to induce a more conciliatory attitude on the part of the U.S.S.R. They devised no strategy to produce this result, however, while Stalin quickly devised a strategy to deny it to them. He took an even harder line than before in pushing Soviet objectives, if only to demonstrate that he could not be intimidated. "It is obvious," he told his top advisers late in 1945, "that . . . we cannot achieve anything serious if we begin to give in to intimidation or betray uncertainty."[29]

The Cold War's roots in the world war, therefore, help to explain why this new conflict emerged so quickly after the old one had come to an end. But great power rivalries had long been at least as normal a pattern in the behavior of nations as had great power alliances. An interplanetary visitor, aware of this, might well have expected exactly what took place. Certainly a theorist of international relations would have. The interesting question is why the wartime leaders themselves were surprised, even alarmed, by the breakdown of the Grand Alliance. Their hopes for a different outcome were real enough; otherwise they would hardly have made the efforts they did while the fighting was going on to agree on what was to happen when it stopped. Their hopes were parallel—but their visions were not.

To frame the issue in its most basic terms, Roosevelt and Churchill envisaged a postwar settlement which would balance power while embracing principles. The idea was to prevent any new war by avoiding the mistakes that had led to World War II: they would ensure cooperation among the great powers, revive Wilson's League in the form of a new United Nations collective security organization, and encourage the maximum possible political self-determination and economic integration, so that the causes of war as they understood them would in time disappear. Stalin's was a very different vision: a settlement that would secure his own and his country's security while simultaneously encouraging the rivalries among capitalists that he believed would bring about a new war. Capitalist fratricide, in turn, would ensure the eventual Soviet domination of Europe. The first was a multilateral vision that assumed the possibility of compatible interests, even among incompatible systems. The second assumed no such thing.

V.

POLITICAL SCIENTISTS like to speak of "security dilemmas": situations in which one state acts to make itself safer, but in doing so diminishes the security of one or more other states, which in turn try to repair the damage through measures that diminish the security of the first state. The result is an ever-deepening whirlpool of distrust from which even the best-intentioned and most far-sighted leaders find it difficult to extricate themselves: their suspicions become self-reinforcing.[30] Because the Anglo-American relationship with the Soviet Union had fallen into this pattern well before World War II ended, it is difficult to say precisely when the Cold War began. There were no surprise attacks, no declarations of war, no severing even of diplomatic ties. There was, however, a growing sense of insecurity at the highest levels in Washington, London, and Moscow, generated by the efforts the wartime allies were making to ensure their own postwar security. With their enemies defeated, there was less of an incentive for these *former* allies, as they were coming to think of themselves, to keep their anxieties under control. Each crisis that arose fed the next one, with the result that a divided Europe became a reality.

IRAN, TURKEY, THE MEDITERRANEAN—AND CONTAINMENT. Having already obtained the territorial concessions he wanted in Eastern Europe and Northeast Asia, Stalin's first priority after the war was to remove what he regarded as vulnerabilities in the south. One account describes him expressing satisfaction with a map showing the Soviet Union's new boundaries, but pointing to the Caucasus and complaining: "I don't like our border right here!"[31] Three initiatives followed: Stalin delayed the withdrawal of Soviet troops from northern Iran, where they had been stationed since 1942 as part of an Anglo-Soviet arrangement to keep that country's oil supplies out of German hands. He demanded territorial concessions from Turkey as well as bases that would have given the U.S.S.R. effective control of the Turkish Straits. And he requested a role in the administration of former Italian colonies in North Africa with a view to securing one or more additional naval bases in the eastern Mediterranean.

It became clear almost at once, though, that Stalin had gone too far. "They won't allow it," his normally complaisant foreign minister Molotov warned, regarding the Straits. "Go ahead, press them for joint possession!" his irritated boss replied. "Demand it!"[32] Molotov did, but he got nowhere. Truman and Attlee flatly rejected the Soviet bid for boundary adjustments at Turkey's expense, as well as for Turkish and Mediterranean naval bases. They surprised Stalin by taking the continued Soviet occupation of northern Iran to the United Nations Security Council early in 1946, in the first significant use of the new world organization to deal with an international crisis. Finding his military overstretched and his ambitions exposed, Stalin ordered a quiet withdrawal from Iran several months later. By that time, though, Truman had reinforced his own position by deploying the American Sixth Fleet—indefinitely—in the eastern Mediterranean. It was an unmistakable signal that Stalin had reached the limit of what he could expect to achieve by invoking the tradition of wartime cooperation.[33]

This new firmness in Washington coincided with a search for explanations of Soviet behavior: why had the Grand Alliance broken apart? What else did Stalin want? The best answer came from George F. Kennan, a respected but still junior Foreign Service officer serving in the American embassy in Moscow. In what he subsequently acknowledged was an "outrageous encumberment of the telegraphic process," Kennan responded to the latest in a long series of State Department queries with a hastily composed 8,000-word cable, dispatched on February 22, 1946. To say that it made an impact in Washington would be to put it mildly: Kennan's "long telegram" became the basis for United States strategy toward the Soviet Union throughout the rest of the Cold War.[34]

Moscow's intransigence, Kennan insisted, resulted from nothing the West had done: instead it reflected the internal necessities of the Stalinist regime, and nothing the West could do within the foreseeable future would alter that fact. Soviet leaders *had* to treat the outside world as hostile because this provided the only excuse "for the dictatorship without which they did not know how to rule, for cruelties they did not dare not to inflict, for sacrifices they felt bound to demand." To expect concessions to be reciprocated was to be naïve: there would be no change in the Soviet Union's strategy until it encountered a sufficiently long string of failures to convince some future Kremlin leader— Kennan held out little hope that Stalin would ever see this—that his nation's behavior was not advancing its interests. War would not be necessary to produce this result. What would be needed, as Kennan put it in a published version of his argument the following year, was a "long-term, patient but firm and vigilant *containment* of Russian expansive tendencies."[35]

Kennan could not have known at the time that one of his most careful readers was Stalin himself. Soviet intelligence quickly got access to the "long telegram"—a relatively easy task because the document, though classified, was widely circulated.[36] Not to be outdone, Stalin ordered his ambassador in Washington, Nikolai Novikov, to prepare a "telegram" of his own, which he sent to Moscow on September 27, 1946. "The foreign policy of the United States," Novikov claimed, "reflects the imperialistic tendencies of American monopolistic capitalism, [and] is characterized . . . by a striving for world supremacy." As a consequence, the United States was increasing its military spending "colossally," establishing bases far beyond its borders, and had reached an agreement with Great Britain to divide the world into spheres of influence. But Anglo-American cooperation was "plagued with great internal contradictions and cannot be lasting. . . . It is quite possible that the Near East will become a center of Anglo-American contradictions that will explode the agreements now reached between the United States and England."[37]

Novikov's assessment—which reflected Stalin's thinking and which Molotov himself ghost-authored[38]—may well account for the relaxed self-confidence with which the Kremlin leader received Truman's recently appointed secretary of state, George C. Marshall, when the American, British, French, and Soviet foreign ministers met in Moscow in April, 1947. It had long been Stalin's habit, while hosting important visitors, to doodle wolves' heads on a pad in red pencil, and this he did as he assured Marshall that the failure to settle the future of postwar Europe was no great problem: there was no urgency. Marshall, the quiet, laconic, but shrewd former general who more than anyone else had shaped American military strategy during World War II, was not reassured. "All the way back to Washington," an aide later recalled, he talked "of the importance of finding some initiative to prevent the complete breakdown of Western Europe."[39]

THE TRUMAN DOCTRINE AND THE MARSHALL PLAN.
Had Stalin been as attentive to intelligence reports on the foreign ministers' conference as he was to those on the atomic bomb and the Ken-

nan "long telegram," he might have anticipated what was about to happen. Marshall and his British and French counterparts spent many hours in Moscow—when not in fruitless meetings with Molotov—discussing the need for cooperation in the reconstruction of Europe. The rooms in which they did so were no doubt bugged. And yet, ideology overrode eavesdropping in Stalin's mind. Had not Lenin shown that capitalists could never cooperate for very long? Had not Novikov's "telegram" confirmed this? The Kremlin boss had his reasons to be self-confident.

They were not, however, good ones. Truman had already announced, on March 12, 1947, a program of military and economic assistance to Greece and Turkey, occasioned by the British government's unexpected announcement, just two weeks earlier, that it could no longer bear the costs of supporting those countries. He had done so in strikingly broad terms, insisting that it now "must be the policy of the United States to support free peoples who are resisting attempted subjugation by armed minorities or by outside pressures. . . . [W]e must assist free peoples to work out their own destinies in their own way."[40] Stalin paid little attention to Truman's speech, although he did take time that spring to insist that a recently published history of philosophy be rewritten to minimize the deference it had shown to the West.[41]

While Stalin was undertaking that task, Marshall—following Truman's lead—was constructing a Cold War grand strategy. Kennan's "long telegram" had identified the problem: the Soviet Union's internally driven hostility toward the outside world. It had, however, suggested no solution. Now Marshall told Kennan to come up with one: the only guideline was "avoid trivia."[42] The instruction, it is fair to say, was met. The European Recovery Program, which Marshall announced in June, 1947, committed the United States to nothing less than the reconstruction of Europe. The Marshall Plan, as it instantly came to be known, did not at that point distinguish between those parts of the continent that were under Soviet control and those that were not—but the thinking that lay behind it certainly did.

Several premises shaped the Marshall Plan: that the gravest threat to western interests in Europe was not the prospect of Soviet military intervention, but rather the risk that hunger, poverty, and despair might cause Europeans to vote their own communists into office, who would then obediently serve Moscow's wishes; that American economic assistance would produce immediate psychological benefits and later material ones that would reverse this trend; that the Soviet Union would not itself accept such aid or allow its satellites to, thereby straining its relationship with them; and that the United States could then seize both the geopolitical and the moral initiative in the emerging Cold War.

Stalin fell into the trap the Marshall Plan laid for him, which was to get *him* to build the wall that would divide Europe. Caught off guard by Marshall's proposal, he sent a large delegation to Paris to discuss Soviet participation, then withdrew it while allowing the East Europeans to stay, then forbade them—most dramatically the Czechs, whose leaders were flown to Moscow to get the word—from receiving such assistance.[43] It was an unusually uneven performance from the normally self-confident Kremlin dictator, and it suggested the extent to which the strategy of containment, with the Marshall Plan at its center, was already disrupting his own set of priorities. Further revisions of philosophy texts would have to wait.

CZECHOSLOVAKIA, YUGOSLAVIA, AND THE BERLIN BLOCKADE. Stalin responded to the Marshall Plan just as Kennan had predicted he would: by tightening his grip wherever he could. In September, 1947, he announced the formation of the Cominform, a latter-day version of the old prewar Comintern, whose task had been to enforce orthodoxy within the international communist movement. "Don't start throwing your weight around," Andrei Zhdanov, Stalin's spokesman within the new organization, told a protesting Pole. "In Moscow we know better how to apply Marxism-Leninism."[44] What that meant became clear in February, 1948, when Stalin approved a plan by Czechoslovak commu-

nists to seize power in the only Eastern European state that had retained a democratic government. Shortly after the coup, the broken
body of Foreign Minister Jan Masaryk—the son of Thomas Masaryk,
the founder of the country after World War I—was discovered in a
Prague courtyard: whether he jumped or was pushed has never been
established.[45] It made little difference, though, because the prospects
for *any* independence within Stalin's sphere of influence, it appeared,
had perished with Masaryk.

Not all communists, however, fell within that sphere. Yugoslavia
had been one of the Soviet Union's most reliable allies since the end of
World War II, but its leader, Josip Broz Tito, had come to power on his
own. He and his partisans, not the Red Army, had driven the Nazis
out; unlike any of his other East European counterparts, Tito did not
depend upon Stalin's support to remain in power. Efforts to subject
him to Cominform orthodoxy caused Tito to bristle, and by the end of
June, 1948, he had openly broken with Moscow. Stalin professed not to
be worried. "I will shake my little finger, and there will be no more
Tito."[46] Much more than a finger shook within the Soviet Union and
the international communist movement over this first act of defiance
by a communist against the Kremlin, but Tito survived—and was soon
receiving economic assistance from the United States. The Yugoslav
dictator might be a "son-of-a-bitch," the new American secretary of
state, Dean Acheson, acknowledged astringently in 1949, but he was
now "our son-of-a-bitch."[47]

Meanwhile, Stalin had undertaken an even less promising venture:
a blockade of Berlin. His reasons, even now, are not clear. He may have
hoped to force the Americans, British, and French out of their respective sectors of the divided city, taking advantage of their dependence on
supply lines running through the Soviet occupation zone. Or he may
have sought to slow their efforts to consolidate their own zones, which
seemed likely to produce a powerful west German state within which
Moscow would have no influence. Whatever its purposes, Stalin's
blockade backfired as badly as his attempt to discipline Tito. The west-

ern allies improvised an airlift for the beleaguered city, thereby winning the emphatic gratitude of the Berliners, the respect of most Germans, and a global public relations triumph that made Stalin look both brutal and incompetent. "Scoundrels," the old man noted defensively, on a diplomatic dispatch reporting these developments. "It is all lies. . . . It is not a blockade, but a defensive measure."[48]

Defensive it may have been, but the offensive character of this and the other measures Stalin took in response to the Marshall Plan wound up increasing, not decreasing, the Soviet Union's security problems. The Czech coup persuaded the Congress of the United States—which had not yet approved Truman's program for European recovery—to do so quickly. The events in Prague, together with the Berlin blockade, convinced the European recipients of American economic assistance that they needed military protection as well: that led them to request the creation of a North Atlantic Treaty Organization, which committed the United States for the first time ever to the peacetime defense of Western Europe. By the time Stalin grudgingly lifted the Berlin blockade in May, 1949, the North Atlantic Treaty had been signed in Washington and the Federal Republic of Germany had been proclaimed in Bonn—another result that Stalin had not wanted. Tito's heresy remained unpunished, thereby demonstrating that it was possible for communists themselves to achieve a degree of independence from Moscow. And there were no signs whatever of the disagreements among capitalists—or of the Anglo-American war—that Stalin's ideological illusions had led him to expect. His strategy for gaining control of postwar Europe lay in ruins, and he had largely himself to blame.

VI.

OR SO IT appears in retrospect. It did not seem so, however, at the time. Instead the years 1949–50 saw a series of *apparent* setbacks to the West, none of which was substantial enough to reverse the process by which the United States and its allies had seized the initiative in Europe, where it really counted. Those who lived through these events, however, had no way of knowing this: to them, it looked as though the European victories the West had won had been outweighed by an unexpected expansion of the Cold War, almost simultaneously, onto several broader fronts—in none of which the prospects seemed favorable.

The first of these lay within the realm of military technology. The Americans had expected their monopoly over the atomic bomb to last for some six to eight years: hence, the Red Army's disproportionate conventional force advantage in Europe had not greatly worried them. "As long as we can outproduce the world, can control the sea and can strike inland with the atomic bomb," Secretary of Defense James Forrestal observed late in 1947, "we can assume certain risks otherwise unacceptable."[49] The fundamental premise of the Marshall Plan had been that the United States could safely concentrate on European economic reconstruction, while deferring any significant military buildup that would match Soviet capabilities. The bomb would deter the Russians while the Americans revived—and reassured—the Europeans.

But on August 29, 1949, the Soviet Union got its own bomb. Stalin authorized no public announcement of the successful test, which took place in the Kazakhstan desert, but within days airborne sampling flights the Americans had only recently begun flying began detecting radioactive fallout—an unmistakable indicator that an atomic bomb had exploded in Soviet territory. Surprised that this had happened so soon but fearing leaks if he tried to suppress the evidence, Truman himself revealed the existence of the first Soviet nuclear weapon on September 23rd. The Kremlin then confirmed it.

The implications, for the Americans, were daunting. Without its atomic monopoly, the Truman administration would have to consider upgrading conventional forces, possibly even stationing some of them permanently in Europe, a contingency not provided for in the North Atlantic Treaty. It would have to build more atomic bombs if it was to maintain a quantitative and qualitative lead over the U.S.S.R. And it found itself pondering a third and more draconian option, the existence of which American scientists revealed to Truman only at this moment: attempting to build what was then called a "super-bomb"—a thermonuclear or "hydrogen" bomb, in today's terminology—that would be at least a thousand times more powerful than the weapons that had devastated Hiroshima and Nagasaki.

In the end, Truman approved all three alternatives. He quietly authorized an accelerated production of atomic bombs: at the time of the Soviet test, the United States had fewer than 200 in its arsenal, not enough, a Pentagon study had pointed out, to be sure of defeating the Soviet Union if a real war came.[50] He then announced, on January 31, 1950, that the United States would go ahead with the "super-bomb" project. The option Truman resisted the longest was a buildup in American conventional forces, chiefly because of its cost. Producing more atomic bombs, even hydrogen bombs, would still be cheaper than what it would take to bring the army, navy, and air force back to anything approximating World War II levels. Truman, who had hoped for a "peace dividend" that would allow him to balance the federal budget after years of deficits, had taken a major risk with the Marshall Plan, which committed the United States to invest almost 10 percent of annual government expenditures in the reconstruction of Europe. Clearly something—fiscal solvency, an upgraded military, the revival of Europe—was going to have to give: it would not be possible to meet all of those priorities and still cope with the new insecurities created by the Soviet atomic breakthrough.

A second but simultaneous expansion of the Cold War occurred in East Asia, where on October 1, 1949—a week after Truman's announcement of the Soviet atomic bomb—a victorious Mao Zedong proclaimed the formation of the People's Republic of China. The celebration he staged in Beijing's Tiananmen Square marked the end of a civil war between the Chinese nationalists and the Chinese communists that had been going on for almost a quarter of a century. Mao's triumph surprised both Truman and Stalin: they had assumed that the nationalists, under their long-time leader Chiang Kai-shek, would continue to run China after World War II. Neither had anticipated the possibility that, within four years of Japan's surrender, the nationalists would be fleeing to the island of Taiwan, and the communists would be preparing to govern the most populous nation in the world.

Did this mean that China would now become a Soviet satellite? Impressed by what had happened in Yugoslavia, Truman and his advisers thought not. "Moscow faces a considerable task in seeking to bring the Chinese Communists under its complete control," a State Department analysis concluded late in 1948, "if for no other reason than that Mao Tse-tung has been entrenched in power for nearly ten times the length of time that Tito has."[51] Both Mao and Tito had long dominated their respective communist parties, both had led them to victory in civil wars that had overlapped a world war, both had achieved their victories without the Soviet Union's help. Mindful of the unexpected advantages Tito's break with Stalin had provided, American officials consoled themselves with the argument that the "loss" of China to communism would not amount to a "gain" for the Soviet Union. Mao, they thought, might well turn out to be the "Asian Tito": hence, the administration made no commitment to the defense of Taiwan, despite the fact that the powerful pro-Chiang "China Lobby" in Congress was demanding that it do so. The United States, as Secretary of State Acheson put it, would simply "wait until the dust settles."[52]

The comment was unwise because Mao had no intention of following Tito's example. Despite having built his own movement with little help from Moscow, the new Chinese leader was a dedicated Marxist-Leninist who was more than ready to defer to Stalin as the head of the international communist movement. The new China, he announced in June, 1949, must ally "with the Soviet Union, . . . and with the proletariat and broad masses of the people in all other countries, and form an international united front. . . . We must lean to one side."[53]

Mao's reasons had to do first with ideology: Marxism-Leninism gave him a way to link his revolution with the one he regarded as the most successful in all of history—the Bolshevik Revolution of 1917. Stalin's dictatorship provided another useful precedent, for that was how Mao intended to run China. Mao also felt betrayed by the Americans. He had welcomed wartime contacts with them, but soon decided that they themselves were "leaning" to the side of Chiang Kai-shek by continuing to provide him with military and economic assistance—Mao failed to understand that the Truman administration was doing this reluctantly, under pressure from the China Lobby, long after it had convinced itself that Chiang could not prevail. The new Chinese communist leader concluded that Truman was preparing an invasion of the mainland to place the nationalists back in power. Preoccupied with European reconstruction, beset with anxieties over their own conventional military weakness, the overstretched Americans were planning no such thing. But Mao's fears that they might be—together with his determination to prove his revolutionary credentials and to emulate Stalin's dictatorship—were enough to bring him down firmly on the Soviet side.[54]

The "lean to one side" announcement in turn fed fears within the United States that—Tito to the contrary notwithstanding—international communism really was a monolithic movement directed from Moscow. Perhaps Stalin had intended the Chinese communist victory all along as his own "second front" in the Cold War, in the event that his strategy in Europe did not work out. "[T]his Chinese government is really a tool of Russian Imperialism," Acheson admitted shortly after Mao took power.[55] There is no evidence that Stalin had such a long-term grand strategy in Asia, but he was quick to see opportunities in Mao's success and to seek ways in which he might exploit them.

Stalin's first move, uncharacteristically, was to apologize to the Chinese comrades for having underestimated them: "Our opinions are not always correct," he told a visiting delegation from Beijing in July, 1949. He then went on, however, to propose the "second front" the Americans had feared:

[T]here should be some division of labor between us. . . . The Soviet Union cannot . . . have the same influence [in Asia] as China is in a position to do. . . . By the same token, China cannot have the same influence as the Soviet Union has in Europe. So, for the interests of the international revolution, . . . you may take more responsibility in working in the East, . . . and we will take more responsibility in the West. . . . In a word, this is our unshirkable duty.[56]

Mao was amenable, and so in December, 1949, he made the long trip to Moscow—his first ever outside of China—to meet the leader of the world communist movement, and to work out a common strategy. The visit lasted for two months, and in the end produced a Sino-Soviet Treaty—roughly analogous to the North Atlantic Treaty signed almost a year earlier—in which the two communist states pledged to come to the assistance of the other in case of attack.

It was just at this point—while Mao was in Moscow and Truman was making his decision to build a hydrogen bomb—that two major espionage cases broke, one in the United States and the other in Great Britain. On January 21st, former State Department official Alger Hiss was convicted of perjury for having denied under oath that he had been a Soviet agent during the late 1930s and early 1940s. Three days later, the British government revealed that an émigré German scientist, Klaus Fuchs, had confessed to having spied for the Russians while working on the wartime Manhattan Project.

Worries about espionage were nothing new: allegations of Soviet spying had surfaced throughout the war, and by 1947 Truman had become sufficiently concerned to begin a program of "loyalty" checks within his administration. There had been no clear confirmation of espionage, though, until the almost simultaneous announcements of the Hiss conviction and the Fuchs confession. It required no great leap to conclude—accurately enough, as it turned out—that the spies had made it possible for the Soviet Union to succeed so quickly in building its own atomic bomb.[57] Had they also facilitated Mao's victory in China? The course of events seemed too disastrous to have taken place simply by coincidence. A disturbing number of dots, in the minds of administration critics, were beginning to connect.

The most visible dot connector was Senator Joseph McCarthy, a hitherto-obscure Wisconsin Republican, who in February, 1950, began raising the question of how the Soviet Union could have gotten the atomic bomb so quickly at a time when the communists were equally quickly taking over China. The answer, he charged—before the improbable forum of the Women's Republican Club of Wheeling, West Virginia—was "not because the enemy has sent men to invade our shores, but rather because of the traitorous actions of those . . . who have had all the benefits that the wealthiest nation on earth has had to offer—the finest homes, the finest college educations, and the finest jobs in Government [that] we can give."[58] The Truman administration spent the next several months fending off McCarthy's charges, which were themselves beginning to strain credulity as the senator scrambled desperately to substantiate them. However bad things were, an explanation alleging treason in high places seemed beyond the realm of plausibility—until, on June 25, 1950, North Korea launched an invasion of South Korea.

VII.

KOREA, like Germany, had been jointly occupied by Soviet and American forces at the end of World War II. The nation had been part of the Japanese empire since 1910, and when Japanese resistance suddenly collapsed in the summer of 1945, the Red Army, which had been planning to invade Manchuria, found the way open into northern Korea as well. The way was also open, in southern Korea, for some of the American troops whose original mission had been to invade the Japanese home islands. The peninsula was occupied, therefore, more by accident than by design: that probably accounts for the fact that Moscow and Washington were able to agree without difficulty that the 38th parallel, which split the peninsula in half, would serve as a line of demarcation pending the creation of a single Korean government and the subsequent withdrawal of occupation forces.

Those withdrawals did take place, in 1948–49, but there was no agreement on who would run the country. Instead it remained divided, with the American-supported Republic of Korea in control of the south by virtue of an election sanctioned by the United Nations, while the Soviet-supported Democratic Republic of Korea ruled the north, where elections were not held. The only thing unifying the country by then was a civil war, with each side claiming to be the legitimate government and threatening to invade the other.

Neither could do so, however, without superpower support. This the Americans denied to their South Korean allies, chiefly because the Truman administration had decided to liquidate all positions on the Asian mainland and concentrate on the defense of island strongpoints like Japan, Okinawa, and the Philippines—though not Taiwan. The South Korean president, Syngman Rhee, repeatedly sought support for his ambitions to liberate the north from officials in Washington, as well as from General Douglas MacArthur, the commander of United States occupation forces in Japan, but he never got it. One of the reasons the Americans withdrew their troops from South Korea, indeed, was their fear that the unpredictable Rhee might "march north," and thus drag them into a war they did not want.[59]

Rhee's North Korean counterpart, Kim Il-sung, had similar designs on the south, and for a time a similar experience with his superpower sponsor. He had repeatedly sought support in Moscow for a military campaign to unify Korea, and had been repeatedly turned down—until January, 1950, when yet another request got a more encouraging response. What made the difference, it appears, was Stalin's conviction that a "second front" was now feasible in East Asia, that it could be created by proxies, thus minimizing the risk to the U.S.S.R., and that the Americans would not respond. They had done nothing, after all, to save the Chinese nationalists, and on January 12, 1950, Secretary of State Acheson had even announced publicly that the American "defensive perimeter" did not extend to South Korea. Stalin read the speech carefully—as well as (courtesy of British spies) the top-secret National Security Council study upon which it was based—and authorized his foreign minister, Molotov, to discuss it with Mao Zedong. The Soviet leader then informed Kim Il-sung that "[a]ccording to information coming from the United States, . . . [t]he prevailing mood is not to interfere." Kim in turn assured Stalin that "[t]he attack will be swift and the war will be won in three days."[60]

Stalin's "green light" to Kim Il-sung was part of the larger strategy for seizing opportunities in East Asia that he had discussed with the Chinese: shortly after endorsing the invasion of South Korea, he also encouraged Ho Chi Minh to intensify the Viet Minh offensive against the French in Indochina. Victories in both locations would maintain the momentum generated by Mao's victory the previous year. They would compensate for the setbacks the Soviet Union had encountered in Europe, and they would counter increasingly obvious American efforts to bring Japan within its system of postwar military alliances. A particular advantage of this strategy was that it would not require direct Soviet involvement: the North Koreans and the Viet Minh would take the initiative, operating under the pretext of unifying their respective countries. And the Chinese, still eager to legitimize their revolution by winning Stalin's approval, were more than willing to provide backup support, if and when needed.[61]

These were the events, then, that led to the North Korean invasion of South Korea. What Stalin had not anticipated was the effect it would have on the Americans: this unexpected attack was almost as

great a shock as the one on Pearl Harbor nine years earlier, and its consequences for Washington's strategy were at least as profound. South
Korea in and of itself was of little importance to the global balance of
power, but the fact that it had been invaded so blatantly—across the
38th parallel, a boundary sanctioned by the United Nations—appeared
to challenge the entire structure of postwar collective security. It had
been just this sort of thing that had led to the collapse of international
order during the 1930s, and to the subsequent outbreak of World
War II. Truman hardly needed to think about what to do: "We can't let
the UN down," he repeatedly told his advisers.[62] It took his administration only hours to decide that the United States would come to the
defense of South Korea, and that it would do so not just on its own authority, but under that of the United Nations as well.

It was able to do so quickly for two reasons. The first was that an
American army was conveniently stationed nearby, occupying Japan—
a fact Stalin seems to have overlooked. The second—another oversight
on Stalin's part—was that there was no Soviet representative present in
the Security Council to veto United Nations action: he had been with-
drawn, some months earlier, as a protest against the organization's re-
fusal to seat the Chinese communists. With U.N. approval, then, the
international community mobilized within days to counter this new
threat to international security, yet another response that Moscow had
not anticipated.

The response, to be sure, almost failed: American and South Korean troops were forced to retreat to the southeastern tip of the Korean
peninsula and might have had to evacuate it altogether had it not been
for a brilliant military maneuver by the United Nations commander,
General MacArthur, who surprised the North Koreans with a daring
amphibious landing at Inchon, near Seoul, in mid-September. Soon he
had trapped the North Korean army below the 38th parallel, and his
forces were advancing almost unopposed into North Korea. Shocked
by this sequence of events, Stalin was on the verge of accepting a lost

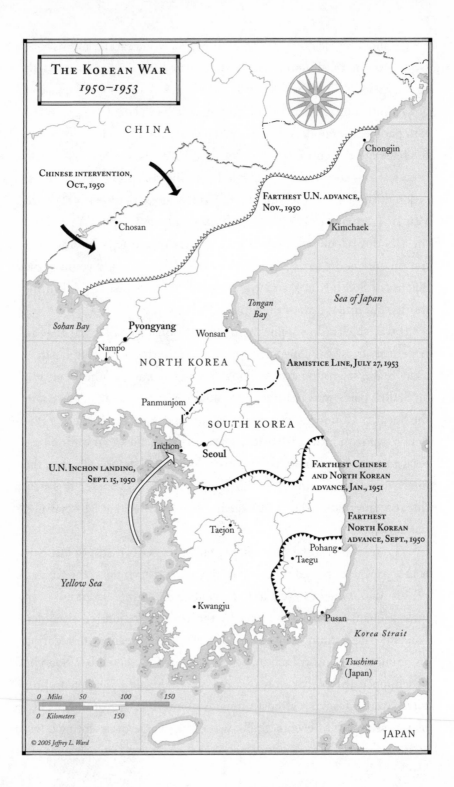

THE KOREAN WAR
1950–1953

CHINA

Chongjin

CHINESE INTERVENTION,
OCT., 1950

FARTHEST U.N. ADVANCE,
NOV., 1950

Chosan

Kimchaek

Sohan Bay

Tongan
Bay

Sea of Japan

Pyongyang

Wonsan

Nampo

NORTH KOREA

ARMISTICE LINE, JULY 27, 1953

Panmunjom

SOUTH KOREA

Inchon

Seoul

U.N. INCHON LANDING,
SEPT. 15, 1950

FARTHEST CHINESE
AND NORTH KOREAN
ADVANCE, JAN., 1951

FARTHEST
NORTH KOREAN
ADVANCE, SEPT., 1950

Taejon

Pohang

Taegu

Yellow Sea

Kwangju

Pusan

Korea Strait

Tsushima
(Japan)

0 Miles   50   100   150

0 Kilometers   150

© 2005 Jeffrey L. Ward

JAPAN

war, even the prospect of the Americans occupying North Korea itself, which directly bordered on China and the Soviet Union: "So what," he commented wearily. "Let it be. Let the Americans be our neighbors."[63]

There remained, though, the question of what the Chinese would do. Mao had supported the invasion of South Korea, and even before the Inchon landing—which he anticipated and warned Kim Il-sung to be ready for—he had begun moving troops from the China coast opposite Taiwan up to the North Korean border. "We should not fail to assist the Koreans," he told his advisers early in August. "We must lend them our hands in the form of sending our military volunteers there."[64] There was concern in Washington about the possibility of Chinese intervention, and for that reason Truman ordered MacArthur not to advance all the way to the Yalu River, which formed the Sino-Korean border. Meanwhile the State Department, through various intermediaries, was seeking to deter the Chinese by raising the prospect of horrendous casualties. Mao for a time had difficulty convincing his own advisers that it would be necessary to intervene, a fact that led Stalin, early in October, to tell Kim Il-sung that he would have to evacuate North Korea altogether. Shortly thereafter, though, Mao prevailed, and so was able to inform the Russians and the North Koreans that the Chinese would be soon coming to the rescue.[65]

Thus it happened that, at the end of November, 1950, two armies once again confronted one another across a river—with a wariness that this time failed to dissolve into cheers, handshakes, drinking, dancing, and hope. "I thought we'd won the war!" an American army officer recalled. "Thanksgiving Day came and we had all of the food . . . that Thanksgiving had meant when we were at home. . . . [A]t that time [we] were nearing the Yalu River and that meant going home."[66] In this case, though, the army on the other side of the river had other ideas. "[W]e shall aim," its commander, Mao Zedong, had explained to Stalin, "at resolving the [Korean] conflict, that is, to eliminate the U.S. troops within Korea or to drive them and other countries' aggressive forces out."[67] On November 26th, some 300,000 Chinese began to make good on this pledge with bugles blowing, human wave attacks, and all the advantages of surprise. Two days later MacArthur informed the Joint Chiefs of Staff: "We face an entirely new war."[68]

VIII.

VICTORY IN World War II brought no sense of security, therefore, to the victors. Neither the United States, nor Great Britain, nor the Soviet Union at the end of 1950 could regard the lives and treasure they had expended in defeating Germany and Japan as having made them safer: the members of the Grand Alliance were now Cold War adversaries. Interests had turned out not to be compatible; ideologies remained at least as polarizing as they had been before the war; fears of surprise attack continued to haunt military establishments in Washington, London, and Moscow. A contest that began over the fate of postwar Europe had now spread to Asia. Stalin's dictatorship remained as harsh—and as reliant on purges—as it had always been; but with the onset of McCarthyism in the United States and with irrefutable evidence that espionage had taken place on both sides of the Atlantic, it was not at all clear that the western democracies themselves could retain the tolerance for dissent and the respect for civil liberties that distinguished them from the dictators, whether of the fascist or the communist variety.

"The fact of the matter is that there is a little bit of the totalitarian buried somewhere, way down deep, in each and every one of us," Kennan told students at the National War College in 1947. "It is only the cheerful light of confidence and security which keeps this evil genius down. . . . If confidence and security were to disappear, don't think that he would not be waiting to take their place."[69] This warning from the founder of containment—that the enemy to be contained might as easily lie within the beneficiaries of freedom as among its enemies—showed how pervasive fear had become in a postwar international order for which there had been so much hope. It helps to explain why Orwell's *1984*, when it appeared in 1949, became an instant literary triumph.[70]

Orwell's vision, however, did at least assume a future, however bleak it might be. Kennan, by early 1950, was worrying that there might not *be* a future. In a top-secret memorandum prepared for, but ignored by, the Truman administration, he pointed out that the use of force had historically been "a means to an end other than warfare, . . . an end which at least did not negate the principle of life itself." Atomic and hydrogen bombs, however, did not have this quality:

> They reach backward beyond the frontiers of western civiliza-
> tion, to the concepts of warfare which were once familiar to
> the Asiatic hordes. They cannot really be reconciled with a
> political purpose directed to shaping, rather than destroying,
> the lives of the adversary. They fail to take into account the ul-
> timate responsibility of men for one another, and even for
> each other's errors and mistakes. They imply the admission
> that man not only can be but is his own worst and most terri-
> ble enemy.

The lesson, Kennan insisted, was a Shakespearean one:

> *Power into will, will into appetite*
> *And appetite, a universal wolf,*
> *So doubly seconded with will and power,*
> *Must make perforce a universal prey*
> *And last eat himself up.*[71]

CHAPTER TWO
DEATHBOATS AND LIFEBOATS

PRESIDENT TRUMAN: *We will take whatever steps are necessary to meet the military situation, just as we always have.*

REPORTER: *Will that include the atomic bomb?*

PRESIDENT TRUMAN: *That includes every weapon we have. . . . The military commander in the field will have charge of the use of the weapons, as he always has.*

—PRESIDENTIAL PRESS CONFERENCE,
November 30, 1950[1]

THE CHINESE PEOPLE'S Volunteer Army—to use its official but inaccurate title—had begun crossing the Yalu River surreptitiously in mid-October. By late November it was ready, and as United Nations forces, made up chiefly of American and South Korean troops, approached the North Korean border, the Chinese suddenly struck, with devastating results. On the day of Truman's press conference, General MacArthur's armies were retreating in the face of an overwhelming enemy onslaught, and desperate measures to save the situation were under consideration in Washington.

On December 2nd, acting under the authority Truman had delegated, MacArthur ordered the United States Air Force to drop five Hiroshima-sized atomic bombs on Chinese columns advancing down the Korean peninsula. Although not as effective as they had been against Japanese cities at the end of World War II, the resulting blasts and firestorms did stop the offensive. Some 150,000 Chinese troops were killed in the attacks, along with an unknown number of American and South Korean prisoners-of-war. NATO allies were quick to condemn MacArthur's action, which he had taken without consulting them, and only an American veto prevented the United Nations Security Council from immediately reversing that body's decision, made six months earlier, to authorize military action in defense of South Korea. The Soviet Union, under intense pressure from its Chinese ally to retaliate with its own atomic weapons, gave the United States a forty-eight-hour ultimatum to halt all military operations on the Korean peninsula or face "the most severe consequences."

When, on December 4th, that deadline passed, two Soviet bombers took off from Vladivostok, each equipped with a primitive but fully operational atomic bomb. Their targets were the South Korean cities of Pusan and Inchon, both of them critical ports supplying United Nations forces. Little was left after the bombs fell. Faced with twice the number of casualties inflicted in the attacks he had ordered against the Chinese together with an almost complete severing of his logistical chain, MacArthur ordered American bombers based in Japan to drop atomic bombs on Vladivostok, as well as the Chinese cities of Shenyang and Harbin. The news of these strikes caused anti-American riots to break out all over Japan—itself within range of Soviet bombers—just as Great Britain, France, and the Benelux countries were announcing their formal withdrawal from the NATO alliance. Not, however, before mushroom clouds were reported over the West German cities of Frankfurt and Hamburg—and so, to paraphrase Kurt Vonnegut, it might have gone.[2]

But it didn't. Only the press conference exchange and the events described in the first paragraph actually happened. The next two are fiction. The Truman administration in fact rushed to reassure the press, the country, its allies, and even its enemies that the president's words had been ill-chosen, that it had *no* plans to use atomic weapons in Korea, and that any decision to reverse those plans would be made only by the commander-in-chief. Despite the shock of its most humiliating military reversal since the Civil War, the United States resolved to keep the Korean War limited, even if that meant an indefinite stalemate. When, in April, 1951, it became clear that MacArthur did not agree with this policy, Truman promptly sacked him.

The fighting in Korea dragged on for another two years, under conditions approximating World War I trench warfare. By the time the Chinese, the Americans, and their respective Korean allies at last managed to agree on an armistice, in July, 1953, the war had left the peninsula devastated, with no clear victory for either side: the boundary between the two Koreas had hardly shifted from where it was in 1950. According to official statistics, 36,568 Americans died in combat. No such specificity is possible in calculating other losses, but it is likely that some 600,000 Chinese troops and well over 2 million Koreans, civilians and military personnel, perished during the three years of fighting.[3] The only decisive outcome of the war was the precedent it set: that there could be a bloody and protracted conflict involving nations armed with nuclear weapons—and that they could choose not to use them.

I.

TOTALITARIANISM was by no means the only thing the world had to fear as the global war came to an end in 1945. The very weapons that brought about the Japanese surrender—the American atomic bombs that really were dropped on Hiroshima and Nagasaki—caused as much concern as they did exhilaration, for if it was now possible for a single bomb to devastate an entire city, what might that imply for future wars? There had been few examples in the past of weapons being developed but held back: the only significant precedent had been the non-use of gas in World War II, a consequence of its extensive but imperfectly controlled use in World War I. In virtually all other instances in which new weapons had been invented, from bows and arrows through gunpowder and artillery to submarines and bombers, occasions had been found upon which to unleash them.

Atomic bombs, however, were unlike any earlier weapon. They were, as the American strategist Bernard Brodie pointed out in 1946, "several million times more potent on a pound-for-pound basis than the most powerful explosives previously known."[4] Any widespread reliance on them could, quite literally, change the nature of warfare by placing at risk not only front lines but supply lines, as well as the urban and industrial complexes that sustained them. Everything would be on the battlefield.

Wars had been fought for as far back as anyone could see. They accompanied the first tribes and settlements, and they persisted through the creation of cities, nations, empires, and modern states. They varied only in the means available with which to fight them: as technology advanced so too did lethality, with the unsurprising result that as wars became bigger their costs became greater. The first war of which we know the details—the Peloponnesian War between Athens and Sparta during the 5th century BCE—probably brought about the deaths of some 250,000 people. The two world wars of the 20th century may well have killed 300 times that number. The propensity for violence that drove these conflicts and all those in between remained much the same, as Thucydides had predicted it would, "human nature being what it is."[5] What made the difference were the "improvements" in weaponry that inflated the body count.

This grim trend led the great Prussian strategist Carl von Clausewitz, writing in the aftermath of the Napoleonic wars, to warn that states resorting to unlimited violence could be consumed by it. If the object of war was to secure the state—how could it not be?—then wars *had* to be limited: that is what Clausewitz meant when he insisted that war is "a continuation of political activity by other means. . . . The political object is the goal, war is the means of reaching it, and means can never be considered in isolation from their purposes."[6] States themselves could become the victims of war if weapons ever became so destructive that they placed at risk the purposes for which wars were being fought. Any resort to force, under such circumstances, could destroy what it was meant to defend.

Something like this happened during the first half of the 20th century. The German, Russian, Austro-Hungarian, and Ottoman empires disappeared as a result of defeat in World War I. Two other empires, the British and the French, emerged victorious, but severely weakened. World War II produced even more catastrophic results: not just the political disappearance of entire states but also their physical devastation and, in the case of the Jews, the near annihilation of an entire people. Well before the Americans dropped atomic bombs on Hiroshima and Nagasaki, Clausewitz's warnings about the dangers of total war had been amply confirmed.

Despite their revolutionary character those bombs were built under an old and familiar set of assumptions: that if they worked, they would be used. Few of the thousands of people employed in the wartime Manhattan Project saw their jobs as differing from the design and production of conventional weapons. Atomic bombs were meant to be dropped, as soon as they were ready, on whatever enemy targets yet remained.[7] Technology might have changed, but the human habit of escalating violence had not.

The bombs' builders would have been surprised to learn, therefore, that the first military uses of nuclear weapons, on August 6 and 9, 1945, would be the last for the rest of the 20th century. As the means of fighting great wars became exponentially more devastating, the likelihood of such wars diminished, and ultimately disappeared altogether. Contrary to the lesson Thucydides drew from the greatest war of his time, human nature did change—and the shock of Hiroshima and Nagasaki began the process by which it did so.

II.

IT TOOK leadership to make this happen, and the most important first steps came from the only individual so far ever to have ordered that nuclear weapons be used to kill people. Harry S. Truman claimed, for the rest of his life, to have lost no sleep over his decision, but his behavior suggests otherwise. On the day the bomb was first tested in the New Mexico desert he wrote a note to himself speculating that "machines are ahead of morals by some centuries, and when morals catch up perhaps there'll be no reason for any of it." A year later he placed his concerns in a broader context: "[T]he human animal and his emotions change not much from age to age. He must change now or he faces absolute and complete destruction and maybe the insect age or an atmosphereless planet will succeed him."[8] "It is a terrible thing," he told a group of advisers in 1948, "to order the use of something that . . . is so terribly destructive, destructive beyond anything we have ever had. . . . So we have got to treat this differently from rifles and cannon and ordinary things like that."[9]

The words were prosaic—Truman was a matter-of-fact man—but the implications were revolutionary. Political leaders had almost always in the past left it to their military chiefs to decide the weapons to be used in fighting wars, regardless of how much destruction they might cause. Clausewitz's warnings had done little over the years to alter this tendency. Lincoln gave his generals a free hand to do whatever it took to defeat the Confederacy: well over 600,000 Americans died before their Civil War came to an end. Civilians imposed few constraints on militaries in World War I, with devastating consequences: some 21,000 British troops died in a single day—most of them in a single hour—at the Battle of the Somme. Anglo-American strategic bombing produced civilian casualties running into the tens of thousands on many nights during World War II, without anyone awakening Churchill or Roosevelt each time this happened. And Truman himself had left it to the Army Air Force to determine when and where the first atomic weapons would be dropped: the names "Hiroshima" and "Nagasaki" were no more familiar to him, before the bombs fell, than they were to anyone else.[10]

After that happened, though, Truman demanded a sharp break from past practice. He insisted that a civilian agency, not the military, control access to atomic bombs and their further development. He also proposed, in 1946, turning all such weapons and the means of producing them over to the newly established United Nations—although under the Baruch Plan (named for elder statesman Bernard Baruch, who presented it) the Americans would not relinquish their monopoly until a foolproof system of international inspections was in place. In the meantime, and despite repeated requests from his increasingly frustrated war planners, Truman refused to clarify the circumstances in which they could count on using atomic bombs in any future war. That decision would remain a presidential prerogative: he did not want "some dashing lieutenant colonel decid[ing] when would be the proper time to drop one."[11]

There were elements of illogic in Truman's position. It made integrating nuclear weapons into existing armed forces impossible. It left unclear how the American atomic monopoly might be used to induce greater political cooperation from the Soviet Union. It impeded attempts to make deterrence work: the administration expected its new weapons to keep Stalin from exploiting the Red Army's manpower advantage in Europe, but with the Pentagon excluded from even basic information about the number and capabilities of these devices, it was not at all apparent how this was to happen. It is likely, indeed, that during the first few years of the postwar era, Soviet intelligence knew more about American atomic bombs than the United States Joint Chiefs of Staff did. Moscow's spies—having penetrated the top levels of the British intelligence establishment—were that good, while Truman's determination to maintain civilian supremacy over his own military establishment was that strong.[12]

In the long run, these lapses proved less important than the precedent Truman set. For by denying the military control over atomic weapons, he reasserted civilian authority over how wars were to be fought. Without ever having read Clausewitz—at least as far as we know—the president revived that strategist's great principle that war must be the instrument of politics, rather than the other way around. Little in Truman's background would have predicted this outcome. His military experience was that of a World War I artillery captain. He had been a failed businessman, and a successful but unremarkable politician. He would never have reached the presidency had Roosevelt not plucked him from the Senate to be his vice-presidential running mate in 1944, and then died.

But Truman did have one unique qualification for demanding a return to Clausewitz: after August, 1945, he had the ability, by issuing a single order, to bring about more death and destruction than any other individual in history had ever been able to accomplish. That stark fact caused this ordinary man to do an extraordinary thing. He reversed a pattern in human behavior so ancient that its origins lay shrouded in the mists of time: that when weapons are developed, they will be used.

III.

THE DURABILITY of this reversal, however, would not depend on Truman alone. Alarmed by how many troops the Red Army had in Europe and how few were available to the United States and its allies, Pentagon planners had no choice but to assume that their commander-in-chief would authorize the use of atomic weapons if the Soviet Union should seek to occupy the rest of the continent. They were probably right in doing so: Truman himself acknowledged in 1949 that had it not been for the bomb, "the Russians would have taken over Europe a long time ago."[13] What that meant, then, was that Stalin's response would have a lot to do with determining what the future of warfare would be.

Truman and his advisers had hoped that Stalin would sense the power of the atomic bomb and moderate his ambitions accordingly. They encouraged Soviet military officers to tour the ruins of Hiroshima, and allowed them to witness the first postwar tests of the bomb, held in the Pacific in the summer of 1946. The president himself remained convinced that "[i]f we could just have Stalin and his boys see one of these things, there wouldn't be any question about another war."[14] This faith in the power of visual demonstrations underestimated the old dictator, who knew from long experience the importance of *showing* no fear, whatever the fears he may have felt.

That there were such fears is now obvious: the atomic bomb was "a powerful thing, pow-er-ful!" Stalin admitted privately.[15] His anxieties led him to launch a massive program to build a Soviet bomb that imposed a considerably greater burden on his country's shattered economy than the Manhattan Project had on the United States—the use of forced labor and the wholesale neglect of health and environmental hazards were routine. He rejected the Baruch Plan, Truman's offer to turn the American atomic arsenal over to the United Nations, because it would have required inspections of Soviet territory. He worried about an American preemptive strike to take out Soviet bomb-making facilities before they could produce their product—an unnecessary concern, as it turned out, for there was little confidence in Washington that the United States could win the war that would have followed, even with an atomic monopoly.[16]

Stalin's fears may also have induced him to allow the Anglo-American airlift during the Berlin blockade to proceed without interference. He probably knew, from espionage, that the B-29s Truman sent to Europe during this crisis were not equipped to carry atomic weapons; but he also knew that shooting down any American plane might cause genuinely atomic-capable bombers to retaliate. And he was pessimistic about the effects of such an attack. The Americans had wiped out Dresden without atomic weapons in 1945. What could they do, with such weapons, to Moscow?[17] "If we, the leaders," should allow a third world war to break out, he told a visiting Chinese delegation shortly before the first Soviet atomic bomb test, "the Russian people would not understand us. Moreover, they could chase us away. For underestimating all the wartime and postwar efforts and suffering. For taking it too lightly."[18]

The point, though, was to hide these fears, lest the Americans learn how much they haunted him. "Atomic bombs are meant to frighten those with weak nerves," Stalin scoffed in a 1946 interview he knew Truman and his advisers would read.[19] The next several years saw far more intransigence than cooperation in Soviet diplomacy: the operative word, in almost all negotiations, seemed to be "*nyet!*" Apart from the single instance of the Berlin blockade, it is difficult to see that the United States got *any* political advantages from its nuclear monopoly. "They frighten [us] with the atomic bomb, but we are not afraid of it," Stalin assured the same Chinese he had warned about the dangers of risking war.[20] The claim may not have been true, but Stalin's strategy made sense: he had shrewdly calculated that, short of war itself, the atomic bomb was an almost unusable weapon.

That conclusion did not diminish Stalin's relief, however, when in August, 1949, Soviet scientists provided him with a bomb of his own. "If we had been late with the atomic bomb [test] by a year or a year and a half," he admitted, "then we perhaps would have gotten it 'tested' against ourselves." Another observation Stalin made at the time was even more intriguing: "If war broke out, the use of A-bombs would depend on Trumans and Hitlers being in power. The people won't allow such people to be in power. Atomic weapons can hardly be used without spelling the end of the world."[21]

The misunderstanding of Truman here is understandable: the president kept his doubts about atomic weapons as quiet as Stalin did his fears. The aging dictator's expression of faith in the American people, however, is surprising—although it parallels his concern that the people of the Soviet Union would "chase us away" if he too casually risked war. And Stalin's vision of how the world might end is even more remarkable, for had Truman known of it, he would have agreed wholeheartedly with it. The "boys" in Moscow, it appears, really did think similarly.

But maybe that is what possessing an atomic bomb does: it causes its owners, whoever they are, to become Clausewitzians. War *has* to become an instrument of policy, regardless of differences in culture, ideology, nationality, and personal morality, because with weapons that powerful the alternative could be annihilation.

IV.

WHAT WORRIED the Truman administration in the dismal winter of 1950–51, however, was not so much the prospect of national or global annihilation, but rather the possibility that American and South Korean forces could be wiped out by the hundreds of thousands of Chinese troops who were chasing them—there is no other word for it—back down the Korean peninsula. The United States at the end of 1950 had 369 operational atomic bombs, all of them easily deliverable on Korean battlefields or on Chinese supply lines from bases in Japan and Okinawa. The Soviet Union probably had no more than five such weapons at the time, and they could hardly have been as reliable as their American counterparts.[22] Why then, with this 74–1 advantage, did the United States not use its nuclear supremacy to reverse the worst military setback it had suffered in almost a hundred years?

Truman's conviction that atomic bombs differed from all other weapons established a *presumption* against such use, but military necessity could have overridden this: had there been a Soviet invasion of Europe, it almost certainly would have done so. There were, however, practical difficulties that discouraged the Americans from using nuclear weapons in Korea. One of these was the simple problem of what to target. The atomic bomb had been developed for use against cities, industrial complexes, military bases, and transportation networks. Few of these existed on the Korean peninsula, where United Nations forces were confronting an army that advanced mostly on foot, carrying its own supplies, along primitive roads and even improvised mountain paths. "What would it be dropped on?" one American general wanted to know. The answer was not clear, nor was the evidence that dropping one, several, or even many bombs under these circumstances would be decisive.[23]

It would, of course, have been possible to bomb Chinese cities, industries, and military facilities north of the Yalu River, and the Truman administration did undertake planning for such an operation, even to the point, in the spring of 1951, of transferring unassembled atomic weapons to western Pacific bases. The political costs, however, would have been severe. As one historian has put it: "Washington's European allies were scared out of their wits at the thought of an expanded war."[24] One reason was that if an atomic attack on China brought the Soviet Union into the war—there was, after all, now a Sino-Soviet mutual defense treaty—the United States would need Western European bases to strike Soviet targets, a requirement that could leave the NATO countries vulnerable in turn to retaliatory airstrikes, or even a full-scale ground invasion. Given the alliance's minimal military capabilities at the time, using the bomb in Korea could ultimately mean a retreat to, or even across, the English Channel.

Another reason for nuclear non-use in Korea had to do with the military situation there. By the spring of 1951 Chinese forces had outrun their supply lines, and United Nations troops—now under the command of General Matthew B. Ridgway—were taking the offensive. It regained little ground, but it did stabilize the fighting front slightly north of the 38th parallel. This paved the way for quiet diplomacy, through Soviet channels, which made it possible to begin armistice negotiations in July. They produced no results—the war would drag on, at great cost to all combatants and to the Korean people, for another two years. But the principle had at least been established that the war would not expand, and that atomic weapons probably would not be used.

Stalin's role in all of this was ambiguous. He had, of course, started the Korean War by authorizing the North Korean invasion. He had been surprised by the decisiveness of the American response, and when it looked as though MacArthur's forces were going to reach the Yalu, he had pushed hard for Chinese intervention—but he would have abandoned North Korea if that had not taken place.[25] He accepted the likelihood of a military stalemate when he approved talks to end the war, but he also saw advantages in keeping the United States tied down militarily in East Asia: the negotiations, therefore, should proceed slowly. "[A] drawn out war," he explained to Mao, "gives the possibility to the Chinese troops to study contemporary warfare on the field of battle and in the second place shakes up the Truman regime in America and harms the military prestige of the Anglo-American troops."[26] Exhausted by the war, the Chinese and the North Koreans were ready to end it by the fall of 1952, but Stalin insisted that they continue fighting. Only after Stalin's death did his successors approve a cease-fire, which took place in July, 1953.

There was, thus, no direct Soviet-American military confrontation over Korea—or so it appeared for many years. Recent evidence, however, has required revising this conclusion, for one other thing Stalin did was to authorize the use of Soviet fighter planes, manned by Soviet pilots, over the Korean peninsula—where they encountered American fighters flown by American pilots. And so there was, after all, a shooting war between the United States and the Soviet Union: it was the only time this happened during the Cold War. Both sides, however, kept it quiet. The Soviet Union never publicized its involvement in these air battles, and the United States, which was well aware of it, chose not to do so either.[27] The two superpowers had found it necessary but also dangerous to be in combat with one another. They tacitly agreed, therefore, on a cover-up.

V.

THE UNFAMILIAR IDEA that weapons could be developed and not used did little, however, to challenge the familiar assumption that the military applications of new technologies should be explored. That was what led a group of American atomic scientists, in the wake of the August, 1949, Soviet bomb test, to brief Truman on something they had known about but he had not: the possibility of constructing a thermonuclear or super-bomb. The device would work not by splitting atoms—the method the atomic bomb had relied upon—but by fusing them. Estimates projected a blast so great that no one could tell Truman what its uses in fighting a war might be. That had been the basis for Kennan's opposition, as well as that of J. Robert Oppenheimer, who had run the Manhattan Project, and several other top advisers who failed to see how such an apocalyptic device could ever meet the Clausewitzian standard that military operations must not destroy what they were meant to defend.[28]

Warfighting, however, was not the basis upon which supporters of the "super" made their case. Thermonuclear weapons, they argued, would be *psychologically*, not militarily, necessary. Not having them would induce panic throughout the West if the Soviet Union got them. Having them would produce reassurance and deterrence: whatever advantages Stalin might have obtained from his atomic bomb would be canceled, and the United States would remain ahead in the nuclear arms race. And what if both sides developed "supers"? That would be better, Truman concluded, than for the Soviet Union to have a "super" monopoly.

In the end, as the president saw it, if the United States *could* build what was now coming to be called a "hydrogen" bomb, then it *must* build one. To be behind in any category of weaponry—or even to appear to be—would risk disaster. The problem now was not so much how to defeat an adversary as how to convince him not to go to war in the first place. Paradoxically, that seemed to require the development of weapons so powerful that no one on the American side knew what their military uses might be, while simultaneously persuading everyone on the Soviet side that if the war did come those weapons would without doubt be employed. Irrationality, by this logic, was the only way to hang on to rationality: an absolute weapon of war could become the means by which war remained an instrument of politics. Truman put it more simply early in 1950: "[W]e had got to do it—make the bomb—though no one wants to use it. But . . . we have got to have it if only for bargaining purposes with the Russians."[29]

As it happened, Soviet scientists had been working on their own "super" since 1946. They never focused, to the extent that American bomb developers did, on the distinction between fission and fusion weapons. Nor did they see, in the fact that hydrogen bombs would be so much more powerful than atomic bombs, anything that would make them less morally justifiable. Because of their head start, the race to develop thermonuclear weapons was much closer than the one to build the atomic bomb had been: the Russians relied less on espionage this time, and more on their own expertise. The first American test of a hydrogen bomb obliterated a Pacific island on November 1, 1952. The first Soviet test followed in a Central Asian desert on August 12, 1953. Both explosions blew blinded and burned birds out of the sky. And that, though bad for the birds, turned out to be a small but significant sign of hope for the human race.

Struck by the phenomenon, American and Soviet observers of these tests recorded it in almost identical terms: since the "supers" could not be tried out on people, as the first atomic bombs had been, it was left to birds to suggest what the human effects might be. They were canaries in the most dangerous mineshaft ever. The witnesses also confirmed what the designers of thermonuclear devices already suspected: that there could be no rational use, in war, for a weapon of this size. "It looked as though it blotted out the whole horizon," an American physicist recalled. A Soviet scientist found that the explosion "transcended some kind of psychological barrier."[30] It was as if they had witnessed the *same* event, not tests separated by nine months, some nine thousand miles, and a geopolitical rivalry that was well on the way to polarizing the world. The laws of physics were the same, whatever the other differences that now divided the planet.

VI.

ALL OF THIS caused Soviet and American scientists to see what Truman and Stalin had already begun to sense—even though neither was aware of the other's concerns—that the new weapons could make real Clausewitz's vision of a total and therefore purposeless war. But Truman left office in January, 1953, and Stalin left life two months later. New leaders came to power in Washington and Moscow who had yet to experience the nightmares that came with nuclear responsibility—or the task of avoiding the abyss about which Clausewitz had warned.

Unlike his predecessor in the White House, Dwight D. Eisenhower had read Clausewitz several times, as a young army officer during the 1920s. He did not doubt that military means must be subordinated to political ends, but he thought that it ought to be possible to include nuclear weapons among those means. He came to the presidency unpersuaded that the nature of warfare had fundamentally changed, and during the final months of the Korean War he repeatedly pushed his military advisers to find ways in which the United States might use both strategic and recently developed "tactical" nuclear weapons to bring the fighting to an end. He also allowed his new secretary of state, John Foster Dulles, to convey hints that such planning was under way. There would of course be objections from allies, Eisenhower acknowledged, but "somehow or other the tabu which surrounds the use of atomic weapons would have to be destroyed."[31]

The reason, from the president's point of view, was simple: the United States could not allow itself to get into any more Korea-like limited wars. To do so would relinquish the initiative to adversaries, who would then choose the most advantageous times, places, and methods of military confrontation. That would give *them* control over the deployment of American resources, with results that could only deplete American economic strength and demoralize the American people. The solution was to reverse the strategy: to make it clear that the United States would henceforth respond to aggression at times, in places, and by means *it* would choose. Those could well involve the use of nuclear weapons. As the president himself put it in 1955, "in any combat when these things can be used on strictly military targets and for strictly military purposes, I can see no reason why they shouldn't be used just exactly as you would use a bullet or anything else."[32]

But by the time Eisenhower made that statement, the physics of thermonuclear explosions had shattered its logic. The critical event was BRAVO, an American test conducted in the Pacific on March 1, 1954, that got out of control. The yield turned out to be fifteen megatons, three times the expected five, or 750 times the size of the Hiroshima atomic bomb. The blast spread radioactive fallout hundreds of miles downwind, contaminating a Japanese fishing boat and killing a member of its crew. Less dangerous debris set off radiation detectors around the world. The question posed for nuclear warfighting was a stark one: if a single thermonuclear blast could have global ecological consequences, what would be the effects of using tens, hundreds, or even thousands of nuclear weapons?

The first answer came, curiously enough, from Georgii Malenkov, an oily *apparatchik* with an odious record who had wound up, more by luck than skill, as one of the triumvirate that succeeded Stalin. Twelve days after the BRAVO test Malenkov surprised his own colleagues, as well as western observers of the Soviet Union, by publicly warning that a new world war fought with "modern weapons" would mean "the end of world civilization." Soviet scientists quickly confirmed, in a top-secret report to the Kremlin leadership, that the detonation of just a hundred hydrogen bombs could "create on the whole globe conditions impossible for life."[33]

Meanwhile, a similar conclusion was forming in the mind of a far more distinguished statesman not previously known for his pacifist tendencies. Winston Churchill, once again British prime minister, had only a few years earlier encouraged the Americans to provoke a military confrontation with the Soviet Union while their atomic monopoly remained in place.[34] But now, in the aftermath of BRAVO, he completely reversed this position, pointing out to his wartime ally Eisenhower that only a few such explosions on British soil would leave his country uninhabitable. This was not, however, necessarily bad news. "[T]he new terror," the old warrior told the House of Commons, "brings a certain element of equality in annihilation. Strange as it may seem, it is to the universality of potential destruction that I think we may look with hope and even confidence."[35]

It was indeed strange that leaders as dissimilar as Malenkov and Churchill said much the same thing at almost the same time. For them, though, the implications of "equality in annihilation" were clear: because a war fought with nuclear weapons could destroy what it was intended to defend, such a war must never be fought. Once again, a common sense of nuclear danger had transcended differences in culture, nationality, ideology, morality, and in this instance also character. But neither of these leaders was in a position to shape Cold War strategy: Malenkov's Kremlin colleagues promptly demoted him for defeatism, while Churchill was forced by age and impatient subordinates to step down as prime minister early in 1955. It would be left to Eisenhower and the man who deposed Malenkov, Nikita Khrushchev, to balance the fears and the hopes that now resided within the thermonuclear revolution.

VII.

EISENHOWER did so exquisitely but terrifyingly: he was at once the most subtle and brutal strategist of the nuclear age. The *physical* effects of thermonuclear explosions appalled him at least as much as they did Malenkov and Churchill: "Atomic war will destroy civilization," he insisted several months after the BRAVO test. "There will be millions of people dead. . . . If the Kremlin and Washington ever lock up in a war, the results are too horrible to contemplate."[36] When told, early in 1956, that a Soviet attack on the United States could wipe out the entire government and kill 65 percent of the American people, he acknowledged that it "would literally be a business of digging ourselves out of the ashes, starting again." Shortly thereafter he reminded a friend that "[w]ar implies a contest." But what kind of a contest would it be when "the outlook comes close to destruction of the enemy and suicide for ourselves"? By 1959, he was insisting gloomily that if war came "you might as well go out and shoot everyone you see and then shoot yourself."[37]

These comments seem completely at odds with Eisenhower's earlier assertion that the United States should fight wars with nuclear weapons "exactly as you would use a bullet or anything else." Now, he appeared to be saying, anyone foolish enough to fire a nuclear "bullet" at an enemy would also be aiming it at himself. Eisenhower's position paralleled those of Malenkov and Churchill—except for one thing: he also insisted that the United States prepare *only* for an all-out nuclear war.

This view alarmed even Eisenhower's closest advisers. They agreed that a war fought with nuclear weapons would be catastrophic, but they worried that the United States and its allies would never match the military manpower available to the Soviet Union, China, and their allies. To rule out nuclear use altogether would be to invite a nonnuclear war that the West could not win. The solution, most of them believed, was to find ways to fight a *limited* nuclear war: to devise strategies that would apply American technological superiority against the manpower advantage of the communist world, so that the certainty of a credible military response would exist at whatever level adversaries chose to fight—without the risk of committing suicide.

By the beginning of Eisenhower's second term in 1957, this consensus extended from Secretary of State Dulles through most of the Joint Chiefs of Staff and into the emerging strategic studies community, where the young Henry Kissinger made the case for what would come to be called "flexible response" in an influential book, *Nuclear Weapons and Foreign Policy.* The critical assumption, in all of this thinking, was that despite their destructiveness nuclear weapons could still be a rational instrument of both diplomacy and warfighting. They could yet be made to fit the Clausewitzian principle that the use of force—or even threats of such use—must reflect political objectives, not annihilate them.

It was all the more startling, then, that Eisenhower so emphatically rejected this concept of limited nuclear war. Assuming even a "nice, sweet World War II type of war," he snapped at one point, would be absurd.[38] If war came in *any* form, the United States would fight it with *every* weapon in its arsenal because the Soviet Union would surely do the same. The president stuck to this argument, even as he acknowledged the moral costs of striking first with nuclear weapons, the ecological damage that would result from their use, and the fact that the United States and its allies could not expect to avoid devastating retaliation. It was as if Eisenhower was in denial: that a kind of nuclear autism had set in, in which he refused to listen to the advice he got from the best minds available.

In retrospect, though, it appears that Eisenhower's may have been the best mind available, for he understood better than his advisers what war is really like. None of them, after all, had organized the first successful invasion across the English Channel since 1688, or led the armies that had liberated Western Europe. None of them, either, had read Clausewitz as carefully as he had. That great strategist had indeed insisted that war had to be the rational instrument of policy, but only because he knew how easily the irrationalities of emotion, friction, and fear can cause wars to escalate into meaningless violence. He had therefore invoked the abstraction of total war to scare statesmen into limiting wars in order that the states they ran might survive.

Eisenhower had the same purpose in mind; but unlike Clausewitz, he lived in an age in which nuclear weapons had transformed total war from an abstraction into an all-too-real possibility. Because no one could be sure that emotions, frictions, and fears would not cause even limited wars to escalate, it was necessary to make such wars difficult to fight: that meant *not* preparing to fight them. That is why Eisenhower—the ultimate Clausewitzian—insisted on planning *only* for total war. His purpose was to make sure that no war at all would take place.[39]

VIII.

THERE WAS every reason to worry, now, about the influence of emotion, friction, and fear in Cold War strategy. The Soviet Union had tested its first air-dropped thermonuclear bomb in November, 1955, by which time it already had long-range bombers capable of reaching American targets. In August, 1957, it successfully launched the world's first intercontinental ballistic missile, and on October 4th, it used another such missile to orbit *Sputnik,* the first artificial earth satellite. It required no rocket scientist to predict the next step: placing nuclear warheads atop similar missiles, which could then reach any target within the United States in only half an hour. Predicting the behavior of the Kremlin's new leader, however, was quite another matter.

Nikita Khrushchev was a poorly educated peasant, coal miner, and factory worker who had become a Stalin protégé and then, after deposing Malenkov and other rivals, Stalin's successor. He came into power knowing little about the nuclear weapons he now controlled, but he learned quickly. Like Eisenhower, he was appalled by the prospect of their military use: he too had seen enough carnage in World War II to know the fragility of rationality on a battlefield.[40] He was no more prepared than Eisenhower had been, however, to declare himself a pacifist. He was convinced, as was the American president, that whatever their impracticalities in fighting wars, nuclear weapons could be made to compensate for national weaknesses in situations short of war.

There, though, the similarities ended. The supremely self-confident Eisenhower was always in command of himself, his administration, and certainly the military forces of the United States. Khrushchev, in contrast, was excess personified: he could be boisterously clownish, belligerently cloying, aggressively insecure. Dignified he never was, and the volatilities of post-Stalin politics were such that he could never be sure of his own authority. There was one other difference as well. The weakness for which Eisenhower sought to compensate with nuclear strength was the manpower deficit of the United States and its NATO allies. The vulnerability Khrushchev hoped to correct with his nuclear capabilities was his own absence of nuclear capabilities.

He faced the need to do this because although the Soviet Union's thermonuclear weapons worked well enough, its long-range bombers were few, primitive, and capable of reaching most American targets only on one-way missions. And despite his claims to be turning out missiles "like sausages," there were far fewer of them than his boasts suggested and they lacked sufficiently precise guidance to place their warheads where they were supposed to go. "It always sounded good to say in public speeches that we could hit a fly at any distance with our missiles," Khrushchev later admitted. "I exaggerated a little." His son Sergei, himself a rocket engineer, put it more bluntly: "We threatened with missiles we didn't have."[41]

Khrushchev first tried this trick in November, 1956. Soviet troops were crushing a rebellion in Hungary just as the British, the French, and the Israelis—without informing the Americans—had seized the Suez Canal in an abortive effort to overthrow the anti-colonial Egyptian leader Gamal Abdel Nasser. On the spur of the moment, with a view to deflecting attention from the bloodbath in Budapest, Khrushchev threatened Britain and France with "rocket weapons" if they did not immediately withdraw their forces from the canal. They immediately did so, but not in response to Khrushchev's warning. Eisenhower, furious at not having been consulted, had ordered them to evacuate Suez or face severe economic sanctions. Because Khrushchev's threats were public and Eisenhower's were not, however, the new Kremlin leader concluded that his own huffing and puffing had produced the withdrawal—and that this practice could become a strategy.[42]

From 1957 through 1961, Khrushchev openly, repeatedly, and blood-curdlingly threatened the West with nuclear annihilation. Soviet missile capabilities were so far superior to those of the United States, he insisted, that he could wipe out any American or European city. He would even specify how many missiles and warheads each target might require. But he also tried to be nice about it: at one point, while bullying an American visitor, Hubert Humphrey, he paused to ask where his guest was from. When Humphrey pointed out Minneapolis on the map, Khrushchev circled it with a big blue pencil. "That's so I don't forget to order them to spare the city when the rockets fly," he explained amiably.[43]

It was a logical observation, at least in Khrushchev's mind, because amiability was part of his strategy as well. He had rejected Stalin's belief in the inevitability of war: the new goal was to be "peaceful coexistence." He took seriously what his scientists told him about the dangers of continuing to test nuclear weapons in the atmosphere. In May, 1958, he even announced a unilateral moratorium on such experiments—admittedly with crafty timing, since the Americans were about to begin a new round of nuclear tests.[44]

Khrushchev shifted back to his belligerent mode in November, when he gave the United States, Great Britain, and France six months to withdraw their troops from the sectors they still occupied in West Berlin, or he would transfer control of western access rights—always a touchy issue after Stalin's 1948 blockade—to the East Germans. He hoped thereby to resolve the increasingly inconvenient problem of having a capitalist enclave in the middle of communist East Germany, and he was convinced that Soviet missile strength would make this possible. "Now, that we have the transcontinental missile," he had earlier explained to Mao, "we hold America by the throat as well. They thought America was beyond reach. But that is not true." Berlin, he told his advisers, was "[t]he Achilles heel of the West." It was "the American foot in Europe [that] had a sore blister on it." Later, he would use a more startling anatomical metaphor: "Berlin is the testicles of the West. Every time I want to make the West scream, I squeeze on Berlin."[45]

Only up to a point, though, because Khrushchev also wanted a more stable superpower relationship, respectability for himself and his country—and an opportunity to visit the United States. When Eisenhower refused to yield on Berlin but reluctantly extended the long-sought invitation, Khrushchev jumped at the opportunity to tour the country he had threatened to incinerate. "This is incredible," he told his son Sergei. "Today they *have* to take us into account. It's our strength that led to this—they have to recognize our existence and our power. Who would have thought that the capitalists would invite me, a worker?"[46]

Khrushchev's September, 1959, visit to the United States was a surreal extravaganza. Worried about behaving appropriately, but also about being treated inappropriately, he was determined not to be impressed by what he saw, but equally determined to convince the Americans that his country would soon catch up. He insisted on flying to Washington in a new and untested airplane so that its size would intimidate his hosts. He acknowledged the richness of the country in a White House toast, but predicted that "tomorrow we shall be as rich as

you are. The next day? Even richer!" He held court for leading capitalists while sitting under a Picasso in a New York town house; he
visited—and purported to be shocked by what he saw there—a Holly-
wood soundstage; he pouted over being denied the opportunity, for
security reasons, to visit Disneyland; he got into a shouting match
with the mayor of Los Angeles; he inspected corn on an Iowa farm;
and he discussed war and peace with Eisenhower at Camp David—
after being assured that an invitation to this *dacha* was an honor and
not an insult.[47]

No substantive agreements came out of Khrushchev's meetings
with Eisenhower, but the trip did confirm that the Soviet Union had a
new kind of leader, very unlike Stalin. Whether that made him more or
less dangerous remained to be seen.

IX.

POTEMKIN VILLAGES work as long as no one peeks behind the
façade. The only way for the United States and its allies to do that in
Stalin's day had been to send reconnaissance planes along the borders
of the Soviet Union, or to release balloons with cameras to drift over it,
or to infiltrate spies into it. None of these measures worked: the planes
got shot at and sometimes shot down, the balloons got blown in the
wrong direction, and the spies got arrested, imprisoned, and often executed because a Soviet agent, Kim Philby, happened to be the British
liaison officer with the American Central Intelligence Agency.[48] Stalin's
U.S.S.R. remained a closed society, opaque to anyone from the outside
who tried to see into it.

Khrushchev's strategy of rattling rockets he did not have required
sustaining this situation. That is why he rejected a proposal from
Eisenhower, at their first summit conference in Geneva in 1955, to allow the United States and the Soviet Union to fly reconnaissance missions over each other's territory: it would have been, he complained,

like "seeing into our bedrooms."[49] What Khrushchev had not known was that Eisenhower had a secret backup for his "open skies" inspection plan that would soon accomplish precisely its purposes.

On July 4, 1956, a new American spy plane, the U-2, made its maiden flight directly over Moscow and Leningrad, snapping excellent photographs from a height well above the range of Soviet fighters and anti-aircraft missiles. That same day Khrushchev was enjoying the annual Independence Day reception in the garden of Spaso House, the American ambassador's residence in Moscow: whether he was visible in the photos has never been made clear.[50] The flights continued at regular intervals over the next four years. The Russians, who could detect them on radar but could not shoot them down, confined themselves to perfunctory protests, not wanting to advertise their inability to control their airspace. The Americans, aware that the flights violated international law, said nothing at all while reaping an intelligence bonanza.

The U-2 photographs quickly confirmed the limited size and inferior capabilities of the Soviet long-range bomber force. Determining Soviet missile capabilities took longer, however, because the missiles themselves—in the quantities that Khrushchev had claimed—did not exist. By the end of 1959 his engineers had only six long-range missile launch sites operational. Because each missile took almost twenty hours to fuel, leaving them vulnerable to attack by American bombers, this meant that the *total* number Khrushchev could count on launching was precisely that: six.[51]

What the Soviet Union did have by then, however, was an improved anti-aircraft missile. "The way to teach these smart-alecks a lesson," Khrushchev told his son, "is with a fist. . . . Just let them poke their nose in here again."[52] On May 1, 1960, they did: the Russians shot down what might well have been the last U-2 flight Eisenhower would have authorized, captured the pilot, Francis Gary Powers, and threatened to put him on trial for espionage. The president had become convinced that Khrushchev's missile claims were fraudulent, but he had also begun to worry about U-2 vulnerability. The first American reconnaissance satellite was about to go into orbit, and Eisenhower expected—correctly—that it would render the U-2 obsolete. So the plane went down at the end of its usefulness, but Khrushchev turned the crash into a crisis nonetheless.

The next summit conference with Eisenhower was to convene in Paris two weeks later. Khrushchev showed up for it, but only for the purpose of wrecking it. He had decided, just before leaving Moscow, that the U-2 incident made further cooperation with the lame-duck Eisenhower administration impossible. "I became more and more convinced that our pride and dignity would be damaged if we went ahead with the conference as if nothing had happened."[53] He would wait, therefore, for Eisenhower's successor. It was an impulsive decision, but it reflected an awkward reality: having seen the quality of the photographs from the downed plane, Khrushchev had to know that his Potemkin strategy was in trouble.

John F. Kennedy took his time in taking advantage of this. He had made much, during the 1960 campaign, of the alleged "missile gap" that Eisenhower had allowed to develop. To acknowledge its absence too soon after taking office would be embarrassing. There followed, though, a string of setbacks that made Kennedy's first months in the White House themselves an embarrassment: the failed Bay of Pigs landings against Fidel Castro's Cuba in April, 1961; the Soviet Union's success that same month in putting the first man into orbit around the earth; a badly handled summit conference at Vienna in June at which Khrushchev renewed his Berlin ultimatum; and in August East Germany's unopposed construction of the Berlin Wall. When Khrushchev announced shortly thereafter that the Soviet Union would soon resume nuclear weapons testing with a 100-megaton blast—almost seven times the size of BRAVO—Kennedy had had enough.

Drawing on new, copious, and convincing evidence from reconnaissance satellites, he called Khrushchev's bluff. He let it be known through a spokesman that the Soviet Union's nuclear and missile capabilities had never come close to surpassing those of the United States:

"[W]e have a second strike capability which is at least as extensive as what the Soviets can deliver by striking first. Therefore, we are confident that the Soviets will not provoke a major nuclear conflict."[54] Khrushchev responded by going ahead with his big-bomb test—he did show some ecological responsibility by cutting the megatonnage by half—but this was thermonuclear posturing and nothing more. "Given Khrushchev's assumption that even a seeming strategic superiority could be decisive," his biographer has pointed out, "the actual American advantage was doubly damaging: not only had he lost the kind of atomic leverage he had been employing for four years, but the Americans had gained it."[55]

X.

HISTORIANS ASSUMED, for many years, that it was this—having his Potemkin façade ripped away—that drove Khrushchev into a desperate attempt to recover by sending intermediate- and medium-range missiles, which he did have in abundance, to Cuba in 1962. "Why not throw a hedgehog at Uncle Sam's pants?" he asked in April, noting that it would take a decade for the Soviet Union to equal American long-range missile capabilities.[56] It is clear now, though, that this was not Khrushchev's principal reason for acting as he did, which suggests how easily historians can jump to premature conclusions. More significantly, the Cuban missile crisis also shows how badly great powers can miscalculate when tensions are high and the stakes are great. The consequences, as they did in this instance, can surprise everyone.

Khrushchev intended his missile deployment chiefly as an effort, improbable as this might seem, to spread revolution throughout Latin America. He and his advisers had been surprised, but then excited, and finally exhilarated when a Marxist-Leninist insurgency seized power in Cuba on its own, without all the pushing and prodding the Soviets had had to do to install communist regimes in Eastern Europe. Never mind that Marx himself would never have predicted this—there being few proletarians in Cuba—or that Fidel Castro and his unruly followers hardly fit Lenin's model of a disciplined revolutionary "vanguard." It was enough that Cuba had gone communist *spontaneously*, without assistance from Moscow, in a way that seemed to confirm Marx's prophecy about the direction in which history was going. "Yes, he is a genuine revolutionary," the old Bolshevik Anastas Mikoyan exclaimed, after meeting Castro. "Completely like us. I felt as though I had returned to my childhood!"[57]

But Castro's revolution was in peril. Before it left office, the Eisenhower administration had broken diplomatic relations with Cuba, imposed economic sanctions, and begun plotting Castro's overthrow. Kennedy allowed these plans to go forward with the unsuccessful Bay of Pigs landing of anti-Castro Cuban exiles, an event that gave Khrushchev little reason for complacency or congratulation. Rather, as he saw it, the attempted invasion reflected counter-revolutionary resolve in Washington, and it would surely be repeated, the next time with much greater force. "The fate of Cuba and the maintenance of Soviet prestige in that part of the world preoccupied me," Khrushchev recalled. "We had to think up some way of confronting America with more than words. We had to establish a tangible and effective deterrent to American interference in the Caribbean. But what exactly? The logical answer was missiles."[58]

The United States could hardly object, because during the late 1950s the Eisenhower administration—before it had convinced itself that the "missile gap" did not exist—had placed its own intermediate-range missiles in Britain, Italy, and Turkey, all aimed at the Soviet Union. The Americans would learn, Khrushchev promised, "just what it feels like to have enemy missiles pointing at you; we'd be doing nothing more than giving them a little of their own medicine."[59]

But Kennedy and his advisers knew nothing of Khrushchev's reasoning, and those who survived were surprised to learn of it a quarter century later when the opening of Soviet archives began to reveal it.[60]

They saw the missile deployment in Cuba—about which they learned only in mid-October, 1962, from the new mission the U-2s had been given of overflying the island—as the most dangerous in a long sequence of provocations, extending all the way back to the Kremlin leader's threats against Britain and France during the Suez crisis six years earlier. And this one, unlike the others, would at least double the number of Soviet missiles capable of reaching the United States. "Offensive missiles in Cuba have a very different psychological and political effect in this hemisphere than missiles in the U.S.S.R. pointed at us," Kennedy warned. "Communism and Castroism are going to be spread . . . as governments frightened by this new evidence of power [topple]. . . . All this represents a provocative change in the delicate status quo both countries have maintained."[61]

Just what Khrushchev intended to do with his Cuban missiles is, even now, unclear: it was characteristic of him not to think things through.[62] He could hardly have expected Americans not to respond, since he had sent the missiles secretly while lying to Kennedy about his intentions to do so. He might have meant the intermediate-range missiles solely for deterrence, but he also dispatched short-range missiles equipped with nuclear warheads that could only have been used to repel a landing by American troops—who would not have known that these weapons awaited them. Nor had Khrushchev placed his nuclear weapons under tight control: local commanders could, in response to an invasion, have authorized their use.[63]

The best explanation, in the end, is that Khrushchev allowed his ideological romanticism to overrun whatever capacity he had for strategic analysis. He was so emotionally committed to the Castro revolution that he risked his own revolution, his country, and possibly the world on its behalf. "Nikita loved Cuba very much," Castro himself later acknowledged. "He had a weakness for Cuba, you might say— emotionally, and so on—because he was a man of political conviction."[64] But so too, of course, were Lenin and Stalin, who rarely allowed their emotions to determine their revolutionary priorities.

Khrushchev wielded a far greater capacity for destruction than they ever did, but he behaved with far less responsibility. He was like a petulant child playing with a loaded gun.

As children sometimes do, though, he wound up getting some of what he wanted. Despite what was still an overwhelming American advantage in nuclear warheads and delivery systems—depending on how the figure is calculated, the United States had between eight and seventeen times the number of usable nuclear weapons that the Soviet Union did[65]—the prospect of even one or two Soviet missiles hitting American targets was sufficient to persuade Kennedy to pledge publicly, in return for Khrushchev's agreement to remove his weapons from Cuba, that he would make no further attempts to invade the island. Kennedy also promised, secretly, to dismantle the American intermediate-range missiles in Turkey that Khrushchev had hoped to make a visible part of the deal. And long after Kennedy, Khrushchev, and even the Soviet Union itself had passed from the scene, Fidel Castro, whom the missiles had been sent to protect, was still alive, well, and in power in Havana.

But the Cuban missile crisis, in a larger sense, served much the same function that blinded and burned birds did for the American and Soviet observers of the first thermonuclear bomb tests a decade earlier. It persuaded everyone who was involved in it—with the possible exception of Castro, who claimed, even years afterward, to have been willing to die in a nuclear conflagration[66]—that the weapons each side had developed during the Cold War posed a greater threat to *both* sides than the United States and the Soviet Union did to one another. This improbable series of events, universally regarded now as the closest the world came, during the second half of the 20th century, to a third world war, provided a glimpse of a future no one wanted: of a conflict projected beyond restraint, reason, and the likelihood of survival.

XI.

THE KENNEDY administration had by no means anticipated such an outcome: indeed it had entered office in 1961 determined to rationalize the conduct of nuclear war. Shocked to discover that the only war plan Eisenhower had left behind would have required the *simultaneous* use of well over 3,000 nuclear weapons against *all* communist countries, Kennedy instructed his strategists to expand the options. The task fell to Secretary of Defense Robert S. McNamara, who insisted that it ought to be possible, not only to devise a spectrum of possibilities for how a nuclear war might be fought, but also to get the Russians to *agree* on what the rules for such combat might be. The basic idea, he suggested in the summer of 1962, would be to fight a nuclear war "in much the same way that more conventional military operations have been regarded in the past." The objective would be "the destruction of the enemy's military forces, not of his civilian population."[67]

There were, however, certain problems with this strategy. For one thing, the conduct of wars had long since blurred the distinction between combatants and non-combatants. In World War II at least as many civilians had died as military personnel, and in a nuclear war the situation would be much worse. McNamara's own planners estimated that 10 million Americans would be killed in such a conflict, even if only military forces and facilities, not civilians, were targeted.[68] Second, there was no assurance such precise targeting would be possible. Most bombs dropped in World War II had missed their targets, and missile guidance systems—especially on the Soviet side—were still primitive. Moreover, most military facilities in the United States, as well as in the Soviet Union and Europe, were located in and around cities, not apart from them. Finally, McNamara's "no cities" doctrine

would work only if the Russians followed the "rules" and did not themselves target cities. But that depended on getting Khrushchev to think
like McNamara, a highly unlikely possibility.

The Cuban missile crisis confirmed how difficult that task would
be: one lesson that came out of it was the extent to which Russians and
Americans had failed to think similarly going into it. What had
appeared to be "rational" behavior in Moscow had come across as
dangerously "irrational" behavior in Washington, and vice versa. If a
common rationality could be so elusive in peacetime, what prospects
would there be for it in the chaos of a nuclear war? McNamara himself
recalls wondering, as he watched the sun set on the most critical day of
the crisis, whether he would survive to see it do so again.[69] He did survive, but his conviction that there could be a limited, controlled, *rational* nuclear war did not.

What kept war from breaking out, in the fall of 1962, was the irrationality, on both sides, of sheer terror. That is what Churchill had
foreseen when he saw hope in an "equality of annihilation." It is what
Eisenhower had understood when he ruled out fighting limited nuclear wars: his strategy left no option other than an assurance of total
destruction, on the assumption that this, rather than trying to orches-
trate levels of destruction while a war was going on, would best prevent
any war at all from breaking out.

McNamara, characteristically, transformed this reliance on irrationality into a new kind of rationality in the aftermath of the Cuban
missile crisis. He now repudiated his earlier idea of targeting only military facilities: instead each side should target the other's cities, with a
view to causing the *maximum* number of casualties possible.[70] The new
strategy became known as "Mutual Assured Destruction"—its acronym,
with wicked appropriateness, was MAD. The assumption behind it was
that if no one could be sure of surviving a nuclear war, there would not
be one. That, however, was simply a restatement of what Eisenhower
had long since concluded: that the advent of thermonuclear weapons

meant that war could no longer be an instrument of statecraft—rather, the survival of states required that there be no war at all.

Nuclear alarms—even alerts—occurred after 1962, but there were no more nuclear crises of the kind that had dominated the superpower relationship since the late 1940s. Instead a series of Soviet-American agreements began to emerge, at first tacit, later explicit, acknowledging the danger nuclear weapons posed to the capitalist and communist worlds alike. These included an unwritten understanding that both sides would tolerate satellite reconnaissance, the vindication of another Eisenhower insight, which was that by learning to live with transparency—"open skies"—the United States and the Soviet Union could minimize the possibility of surprise attack.[71]

There was also the realization that the time had come, if not for the international control of nuclear weapons, then at least for agreements on how to manage them. The first of these came in 1963 with the Limited Test Ban Treaty, which abolished nuclear tests in the atmosphere. There followed, in 1968, the Nuclear Non-Proliferation Treaty, requiring nations possessing nuclear weapons not to help other states acquire them. And in 1972, the Strategic Arms Limitation Interim Agreement restricted the number of land- and sea-based ballistic missiles to be allowed to each side—with verification of compliance to take place by means of reconnaissance satellites.

Most intriguingly, though, the Soviet Union and the United States also signed, in 1972, an Anti-Ballistic Missile Treaty that banned *defenses* against long-range missiles. This was the first formal acknowledgment, by both sides, of Churchill's—and Eisenhower's—idea that the vulnerability that came with the prospect of instant annihilation could become the basis for a stable, long-term, Soviet-American relationship. It also reflected Moscow's acceptance, not easily arrived at, of Mutual Assured Destruction: persuading the Russians that it was a *bad* idea to try to defend themselves had been a negotiating challenge of the first order. The success of the effort—that American officials could now be educating their Soviet counterparts on how to think about national security—suggests how far things had come since each side's development of nuclear weapons, in the first years of the Cold War, had terrified the other.

And so, to paraphrase Kurt Vonnegut, it did indeed go. The Cold War could have produced a hot war that might have ended human life on the planet. But because the *fear* of such a war turned out to be greater than all of the differences that separated the United States, the Soviet Union, and their respective allies, there was now reason for *hope* that it would never take place.

XII.

FOUR DECADES after the Cuban missile crisis, another novelist, Yann Martel, published *Life of Pi*, an improbable story about a lifeboat that could have become a deathboat.[72] The major characters were a boy and a Bengal tiger, both victims of a shipwreck, stranded together on an uncomfortably small vessel drifting across the Pacific Ocean. There being no common language, there could be no rational discussion between them. But there was, nonetheless, a compatibility of interest: the tiger's in having the boy catch fish for him to eat, the boy's in not himself being eaten. Both somehow figured this out, and both survived.

A Cold War fable? Whether Martel intended it as one hardly matters, for the sign of a good novel is what it can cause its readers to see, even if this lies beyond the author's own vision. What nuclear weapons did was to make states see—even in the absence of a common language, ideology, or set of interests—that they shared a stake in each other's survival, given the tiger they themselves had created but now had to learn to live with.

CHAPTER THREE
COMMAND VERSUS SPONTANEITY

Two nations, between whom there is no intercourse and no sympathy; who are as ignorant of each other's habits, thoughts, and feelings, as if they were dwellers in different zones, or inhabitants of different planets; who are formed by a different breeding, are fed by a different food, are ordered by different manners, and are not governed by the same laws.

—BENJAMIN DISRAELI,
1845[1]

Instead of unity among the great powers—both political and economic—after the war, there is complete disunity between the Soviet Union and the satellites on one side and the rest of the world on the other. There are, in short, two worlds instead of one.

—CHARLES E. BOHLEN,
1947[2]

A SINGLE PLANET shared by superpowers who shared the means of wiping each other out—but who now also shared an interest in each other's survival. So far, so good. What *kind* of survival, though? What would life be like under each system? How much room would there be for economic well-being? For social justice? For the freedom to make one's own choices about how to live one's life? The Cold War was not just a geopolitical rivalry or a nuclear arms race; it was a competition, as well, to answer these questions. The issue at stake was almost as big as that of human survival: how best to organize human society.

"Whether you like it or not, history is on our side," Nikita Khrushchev once boasted before a group of western diplomats. "We will bury you." He spent the rest of his life explaining what he meant by this. He had not been talking about nuclear war, Khrushchev claimed, but rather about the historically determined victory of communism over capitalism. The Soviet Union might indeed be behind the West, he acknowledged in 1961. Within a decade, however, its housing shortage would disappear, consumer goods would be abundant, and its population would be "materially provided for." Within two decades, the Soviet Union "would rise to such a great height that, by comparison, the main capitalist countries will remain far below and way behind."[3] Communism, quite simply, was the wave of the future.

It didn't quite work out that way. By 1971, the Soviet Union's economy and those of its East European satellites were stagnating. By 1981, living standards inside the U.S.S.R. had deteriorated to such an extent that life expectancy was *declining*—an unprecedented phenomenon in an advanced industrial society. By the end of 1991, the Soviet Union itself, the model for communism everywhere else, had ceased to exist.

Khrushchev's predictions, it is now clear, had been based on wishful thinking, not hard-headed analysis. What is striking, though, is how many people took them seriously at the time—by no means all of them communists. John F. Kennedy, for example, found the Soviet leader's ideological self-confidence thoroughly intimidating when he encountered Khrushchev at the 1961 Vienna summit: "He just beat hell out of me," the new president admitted. Kennedy had "seemed rather stunned," British Prime Minister Harold Macmillan noted shortly thereafter, "like somebody meeting Napoleon (at the height of his power) for the first time."[4] J.F.K. was hardly alone: communism had been intimidating statesmen and the states they ran for well over a century. The reason was that it had inspired—and aroused—so many of their own citizens, who saw in Marxism-Leninism the promise of a better life. The early Cold War saw the intimidation and the inspiration peak. By the end of the Cold War, there was little left to hope for from communism, and nothing left to fear.

I.

THE BEST PLACE to start, in seeking to understand the respect communism commanded and the anxieties it caused, is with another novel. Its title was *Sybil*, it appeared in 1845, and its author, Benjamin Disraeli, would also become a British prime minister. Its subtitle was *The Two Nations*, by which Disraeli meant the rich and the poor, who co-existed uneasily within a society in which an industrial revolution—Great Britain's crowning achievement over the preceding half century—was widening the gap between them. "The capitalist flourishes," one character complained,

> he amasses immense wealth; we sink, lower and lower, lower than the beasts of burthen; for they are fed better than we are, cared for more. And it is just, for according to the present system they are more precious. And yet they tell us that the interests of Capital and of Labour are identical.[5]

Sybil was a warning: that a state whose economic progress depended on exploiting some of its citizens for the benefit of others was headed for trouble.

Karl Marx, living in England at the time, witnessed and warned of the same phenomenon, but he did so by means of a theory, not a novel. Because capitalism distributes wealth unevenly, he claimed, it produces its own executioners. The social alienation generated by economic inequalities could only result in revolution: "[N]ot only has the bourgeoisie forged the weapons that bring death to itself; it has also called into existence the men who are to wield those weapons—the modern working class—the proletarians." Capitalism's grave-diggers would sooner or later replace it with communism, a more equitable method of organizing society in which there would be common ownership of the means of production, and in which extremes of wealth and poverty would no longer exist. Neither, therefore, would resentment, so the happiness of the human race would follow. Communism, Marx's collaborator Friedrich Engels claimed, would mark "the ascent of man from the kingdom of necessity to the kingdom of freedom."[6]

This was not just a profession of faith: Marx and Engels also saw it as science. The linkage Marx established between technological progress, social consciousness, and revolutionary consequences, they believed, revealed the engine that drove history forward. This was the class struggle—and because industrialization and the alienation it produced were irreversible, this engine had no reverse gear.

Marxism brought hope to the poor, fear to the rich, and left governments somewhere in between. To rule solely on behalf of the bourgeoisie seemed likely to ensure revolution, thereby confirming Marx's prophecy; but to do so only for the proletariat would mean that Marx's revolution had already arrived. Most political leaders therefore fudged: whether in Disraeli's Britain, or Bismarck's Germany, or the most rapidly industrializing country of all, the United States, they set out to preserve capitalism by mitigating its harshness. The result was the social welfare state, the basic structure of which was in place throughout much of the industrialized world by the time several of its most prominent representatives went to war with one another in August, 1914.

Whatever progress capitalists had made in easing the brutalities of industrialization, World War I showed that they had not yet learned how to preserve peace. Despite unprecedented economic development and the interdependence that had accompanied it, the great powers of Europe—some of them the most socially progressive governments anywhere—blundered into the worst war the world had ever seen. The vast quantities of weaponry their industries were producing made it possible to continue the fighting far longer than anyone had expected. The bourgeoisie, it now appeared, was digging its own grave.

That, at least, was the argument Lenin put forward, at first from exile, and then after the overthrow of Tsar Nicholas II early in 1917, from within Russia itself. Lenin differed from Marx and Engels, however, in his determination to move from theory to action: his *coup d'état* in November—for that is what it was—remains as striking an example as exists of the extent to which one person can change the course of history. Or, as Lenin would have put it, drawing on Marx, by which the "conscious vanguard of the proletariat" can *accelerate* history toward its scientifically predetermined conclusion. What the Bolshevik "revolution" meant was that one state had gone beyond trying to save capitalism: it had, in the middle of a war capitalists had started, declared war on capitalism itself. And if the expectations of Lenin and his followers were correct, the citizens of other states—themselves embittered by capitalism and battered by war—would soon seize power and do the same. The irreversible engine of history guaranteed it.

No one sensed the significance of this moment more clearly than the president of the United States at the time, Woodrow Wilson. He understood, as did Lenin, the extent to which ideas could move nations: had he not brought the United States into the war in April, 1917, by calling for a "world safe for democracy"? But as Wilson conceived it, such a world would not be safe for proletarian revolution, nor would the reverse be true. He quickly found himself waging two wars, one with military might against Imperial Germany and its allies, the other with words against the Bolsheviks. Wilson's Fourteen Points speech of January, 1918, the single most influential statement of an *American* ideology in the 20th century, was a direct response to the ideological challenge Lenin had posed. There began at this point, then, a war of ideas—a contest among visions—that would extend through the rest of World War I, the interwar years, World War II, and most of the Cold War.[7] At stake was the issue that had divided Disraeli's two nations: how best to govern industrializing societies in such a way as to benefit *all* of the people who lived within them.

II.

LENIN'S POSITION was an extension of Marx's: that because capitalists caused inequality and war, neither justice nor peace could prevail until capitalism had been overthrown. Marx had been vague about how that would happen, but Lenin had provided a demonstration. The communist party would lead the way, and a single individual, as he had done in Russia, would lead the party. A *dictatorship* of the proletariat would *free* the proletariat. Because the enemies of the revolution would never yield power voluntarily, that dictatorship would use all the methods available to it—propaganda, subversion, surveillance, informants, covert action, conventional and unconventional military operations, and even terror—in accomplishing its objectives. Its ends would justify its means. This would be, then, an *authoritarian* revolution that would liberate those on the bottom by commanding them from the top.

Wilson's objective, like Disraeli's, was to reform capitalism, not destroy it. The way to do this, he believed, was to encourage spontaneity: the problem with capitalism was that it had left people too little freedom to manage their own lives. It had collaborated with empires that denied their inhabitants the right to choose their leaders. It had limited the efficiency of markets through protectionism, price-fixing, and recurring cycles of booms and busts. And of course—here Wilson agreed with Lenin—capitalism had failed to prevent war, the ultimate denial of freedom. Wilson's plan for the postwar world would promote political self-determination, economic liberalization, and the formation of an international collective security organization with the power to ensure that the rivalries of nations—which would never entirely disappear—would henceforth be peacefully managed. This would be a *democratic* revolution that would open the way for those on the bottom to liberate themselves.

Lenin, following Marx, assumed the incompatibility of class interests: because the rich would always exploit the poor, the poor had no choice but to supplant the rich. Wilson, following Adam Smith, assumed the opposite: that the pursuit of individual interests would advance everyone's interests, thereby eroding class differences while benefiting both the rich and the poor. These were, therefore, radically different solutions to the problem of achieving social justice within modern industrial societies. At the time the Cold War began it would not have been at all clear which was going to prevail. To see why, track the legacies of Lenin and Wilson, both of whom died in 1924, over the next two decades.

Wilson, at the end of World War II, would have looked like a failed idealist. He had compromised so often in negotiating the 1919 Versailles settlement—by accepting its harsh treatment of Germany, its deference to the territorial claims of victorious allies, and its thinly disguised perpetuation of colonialism—that it had hardly been an endorsement of political self-determination and economic liberalization.[8] His own countrymen had refused to join his proudest creation, the League of Nations, thereby severely weakening it. Capitalism had revived precariously after the war, only to crash in 1929, setting off the worst global depression ever. Authoritarianism, meanwhile, was on the rise, first in Italy under Benito Mussolini, then in Imperial Japan, and finally—most ominously—in Germany, where, having come to power constitutionally in 1933, Adolf Hitler immediately abolished the constitution by which he had done so.

The United States and the other remaining democracies made no serious effort to prevent Japanese aggression in Manchuria in 1931, or the Italian seizure of Ethiopia in 1935, or the rapid rearmament of what was now Nazi Germany—a process that by the end of the decade had made that country the dominant power on the European continent. And when, as a predictable result, World War II broke out, the Americans and the British found themselves depending on Stalin's Soviet Union—which had itself collaborated with Hitler between 1939 and 1941—in order to win it. Victory was certain by 1945, but the nature of the postwar world was not. To have expected vindication for Wilson, given this record, would have seemed at best naïve: as a pioneering theorist of international relations had put it at the beginning of the war, "[t]he liberal democracies scattered throughout the world by the peace settlement of 1919 were the product of abstract theory, stuck no roots in the soil, and quickly shrivelled away."[9]

Lenin, at the end of World War II, would have looked like a successful realist. Stalin, his successor, had carried out a revolution from above in the Soviet Union, first by collectivizing agriculture, then by launching a program of rapid industrialization, and finally by ruthlessly purging potential rivals, real and imagined. The international proletarian revolution Lenin expected had not come, but the U.S.S.R. was nonetheless, by the end of the 1930s, the world's most powerful proletarian state. And unlike its capitalist counterparts, it had maintained full production and therefore full employment throughout the Great Depression. The rise of Nazi Germany posed a serious challenge, to be sure, but Stalin's pact with Hitler had bought time and territory, so that when the invasion came in 1941 the Soviet Union not only survived but eventually hurled it back. As the end of the fighting approached, the U.S.S.R. was poised, physically and politically, to dominate half of Europe. Its ideological influence—given these demonstrations of what an authoritarian system could achieve—might well go much farther.

For Marxism-Leninism at that time had millions of supporters in Europe. Spanish, French, Italian, and German communists had led the resistance against fascism. The idea of social revolution—that those on the bottom might wind up on top—had widespread appeal, even in a country like Poland, with its long history of antagonism toward Russia.[10] And given the devastation the war had caused, together with the deprivation the prewar depression had brought about, it was not at all clear that democratic capitalism would be up to the task of postwar reconstruction—not least since the greatest capitalist democracy, the United States, had shown so little willingness in the past to take responsibility for what happened beyond its borders.

Even among the Americans there was self-doubt. Roosevelt's New Deal had patched, but not healed, the nation's economic problems: only wartime spending had done that, and there was no assurance, as federal budgets shrank to normal after the war, that the depression would not return. The power of government had expanded dramatically under F.D.R., but the future of markets, spontaneity, and even—in the eyes of his many critics—freedom itself was much less clear. "We have, on the whole, more liberty and less equality than Russia has," one observer wrote in 1943. "Russia has less liberty and more equality. Whether democracy should be defined primarily in terms of liberty or of equality is a source of unending debate."[11]

The comment could have come from Roosevelt's well-meaning but guileless vice president at the time, Henry A. Wallace, who always had trouble making up his mind about such matters. In fact, though, its author was the tough-minded theologian Reinhold Niebuhr, remembered now for his staunch resistance to communism during the Cold War. That Niebuhr during World War II could wonder whether liberty or equality should primarily define democracy is as good an illustration as any of how clouded the prospects for Wilson's vision then appeared to be.

III.

THE COLD WAR changed all of that, with the result that Wilson is remembered today as a prophetic realist, while Lenin's statues molder in garbage dumps throughout the former communist world. Like the nuclear war that never came, the revival and eventual triumph of democratic capitalism was a surprising development that few people on either side of the ideological divide in 1945 would have foreseen. Circumstances during the first half of the 20th century had provided physical strength and political authority to dictatorships. Why should the second half have been different?

The reasons had less to do with any fundamental shift in the means of production, as a Marxist historian might have argued, than with a striking shift in the attitude of the United States toward the international system. Despite having built the world's most powerful and diversified economy, Americans had shown remarkably little interest, prior to 1941, in how the rest of the world was governed. Repressive regimes elsewhere might be regrettable, but they could hardly harm the United States. Even involvement in World War I had failed to alter this attitude, as Wilson discovered to his embarrassment and chagrin.

What did change it, immediately and irrevocably, was the Japanese attack on Pearl Harbor. That event shattered the illusion that distance ensured safety: that it did not matter who ran what on the other side of the ocean. The nation's security was now at risk, and because future aggressors with air and naval power could well follow the Japanese example, the problem was not likely to go away. There was little choice, then, but for the United States to assume global responsibilities. Those required winning the war against Japan and Germany—Hitler having declared war on the United States four days after Pearl Harbor—but they also meant planning a postwar world in which democracy and capitalism would be secure.

It was here that Wilson became relevant once again, because there was so much to learn from what had gone wrong since the end of World War I. Behind his call to make the world safe for democracy had been the implied claim that democracies do not start wars. The interwar years seemed to confirm that assertion, but what was it that caused nations to cease to be democracies? Germany, Italy, and Japan had once had parliamentary governments; the economic crises of the 1920s and 1930s, however, had discredited them. They and too many other states had embraced authoritarian solutions, which then led to military aggression. Not only had capitalism generated social inequality, as Marx had predicted it would. By this line of reasoning, it had also produced *two* world wars.

How, then, to prevent a third? The answer seemed obvious to the Roosevelt administration: it was to build an international order in which capitalism would be safe from its own self-destructive tendencies; in which people would be safe from the inequities these produced and from the temptations that then arose to flee from freedom; in which nations would be safe from the aggression to which the resulting authoritarianism tended to lead. "A world in economic chaos," Secretary of State Cordell Hull warned in 1944, "would be forever a breeding ground for trouble and war."[12] F.D.R. and his advisers would hardly have admitted it, but they were drawing as much on the Marxist-Leninist critique of capitalism as on Wilson's. Where, though, did this leave Stalin?

The ever-pragmatic Roosevelt had welcomed the Soviet Union as an ally during the war: "I can't take communism nor can you," he told a friend, "but to cross this bridge I would hold hands with the Devil."[13] He understood as well as anyone that cooperation with Moscow might cease once victory had been achieved; but he wanted the responsibility for that to reside there, not in Washington. To that end, he offered the U.S.S.R. membership in three new international organizations behind which he proposed to put the full support of the United States: the International Monetary Fund, the World Bank, and the United Nations.

Together, these institutions were intended to lessen the possibility of future depressions by lowering tariff barriers, stabilizing currencies, and coordinating government planning with the workings of markets, while providing the means by which the international community would contain and if necessary defeat future aggressors. They pulled together two parts of Wilson's program: economic liberalization and collective security. The third, political self-determination, would have to wait, F.D.R. believed, at least for those nations and peoples who had fallen, or were likely to fall, under Soviet rule. The important thing was to win the war, secure the peace, and ensure recovery. Then, he hoped, there would be room for democracy.

Stalin was happy to have the Soviet Union a founding member of the United Nations: the veto in the Security Council would make that organization only what the wartime victors wanted it to be. The Fund and the Bank, however, were quite another matter. Once he understood that their purpose was to *save capitalism*—and not, as he had initially thought, to provide the structures through which the Soviet Union could extract reconstruction assistance from the United States[14]—Stalin wanted no part of them. That decision, together with his increasingly obvious determination to impose authoritarian regimes in Eastern Europe, meant that F.D.R.'s effort to bridge the gap between Wilson and Lenin had clearly failed. But Wilson's vision, at least, had been revived: the contest of ideas that he and Lenin had begun during World War I would continue now within the emerging Cold War. That became apparent in three important speeches, given within thirteen months of one another in 1946–47.

Stalin made the first one in Moscow on February 9, 1946, and in it he went back to basics. He restated Marx's condemnation of capitalism for distributing wealth unevenly. He reiterated Lenin's claim that, as a result, capitalists were likely to go to war with one another. He drew from this the conclusion that peace could come only when communism had triumphed throughout the world. He emphasized that the Soviet Union's industrialization prior to World War II had allowed it to prevail in that conflict, and he said nothing about assistance received from the United States and Great Britain. Finally, he called for equally arduous sacrifices on the part of the Soviet people to recover from the damage the last war had caused, and to prepare for the next war that the contradictions of capitalism were sure to bring about.[15]

Winston Churchill, recently turned out of office, gave the second speech in the improbable setting of Fulton, Missouri, on March 5, with President Truman sitting at his side. In characteristically portentous cadences, the former prime minister warned:

> From Stettin in the Baltic to Trieste in the Adriatic, an iron
> curtain has descended across the Continent. Behind that line
> lie all the capitals of ancient states of central and eastern Eu-
> rope. . . . [A]ll these famous cities and the populations around
> them . . . are subject in one form or another, not only to So-
> viet influence, but to a very high and increasing measure of
> control from Moscow.

The Russians did not want war, Churchill acknowledged, but they did want "the fruits of war and indefinite expansion of their power and doctrines." Only strength could deter them: "If the Western Democracies stand together . . . no one is likely to molest them. If however they become divided or falter in their duty and if these all-important years are allowed to slip away, then indeed catastrophe may overwhelm us all."[16]

Truman himself gave the third speech a year later, on March 12, 1947, in which he asked Congress for aid to Greece and Turkey and announced the Truman Doctrine, with its implied American commitment to assist victims of aggression and intimidation throughout the world. His ideological justification for these measures was Wilsonian: the world was now divided between "two ways of life"—not communism versus capitalism, but democracy versus authoritarianism, a distinction that allowed him to link this new American involvement in European affairs with the ones that had preceded it in 1917 and in 1941. His decision to do so was deliberate: it had been necessary to show the world, one of the drafters of Truman's speech later recalled, "that we have something positive and attractive to offer, and not just anti-communism."[17]

That became the point of the Marshall Plan, as well as the decisions, taken at the same time, to begin the rehabilitation of occupied Germany and Japan. These were Disraeli-like efforts, which Wilson and Roosevelt would have applauded, to salvage capitalism and secure democracy in circumstances so unpromising that authoritarian alternatives—despite their obvious dangers to human liberty—could easily have taken hold. The idea was not to brand "as a Communist

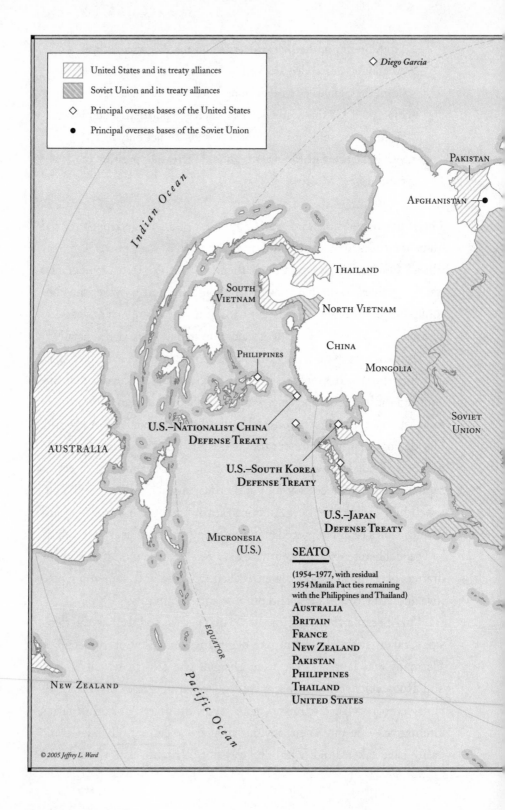

◇ *Diego Garcia*

United States and its treaty alliances

Soviet Union and its treaty alliances

◇ Principal overseas bases of the United States

● Principal overseas bases of the Soviet Union

PAKISTAN

AFGHANISTAN ●

Indian Ocean

THAILAND

SOUTH VIETNAM

NORTH VIETNAM

CHINA

MONGOLIA

PHILIPPINES

SOVIET UNION

AUSTRALIA

U.S.–NATIONALIST CHINA DEFENSE TREATY

U.S.–SOUTH KOREA DEFENSE TREATY

U.S.–JAPAN DEFENSE TREATY

MICRONESIA (U.S.)

EQUATOR

Pacific Ocean

NEW ZEALAND

SEATO

(1954–1977, with residual 1954 Manila Pact ties remaining with the Philippines and Thailand)

AUSTRALIA
BRITAIN
FRANCE
NEW ZEALAND
PAKISTAN
PHILIPPINES
THAILAND
UNITED STATES

© 2005 Jeffrey L. Ward

U.S. AND U.S.S.R. ALLIANCES AND BASES
Early 1970s

AFRICA

Atlantic Ocean

EQUATOR

EGYPT

SYRIA

IRAQ

TURKEY

GREECE

ALBANIA

YUGOSLAVIA

ITALY

WEST GERMANY

GUINEA

BULGARIA

ROMANIA

HUNGARY

CZECHOSLOVAKIA

POLAND

EAST GERMANY

SPAIN

PORTUGAL

FRANCE

BELGIUM

BRITAIN

DENMARK

NETHERLANDS

NORWAY

ICELAND

WARSAW PACT

BULGARIA
CZECHOSLOVAKIA
EAST GERMANY
HUNGARY
POLAND
ROMANIA
SOVIET UNION

✕
North Pole

NATO

BELGIUM
BRITAIN
CANADA
DENMARK
WEST GERMANY
GREECE
ICELAND
ITALY
LUXEMBOURG
SPAIN
NETHERLANDS
PORTUGAL
TURKEY
UNITED STATES

ALASKA

CANADA

SOUTH
AMERICA

UNITED STATES

CUBA

PANAMA

MEXICO

INTER-AMERICAN TREATY

24 NATIONS

anyone who used the language of Marx and Lenin," Marshall's aide
Charles E. Bohlen commented, "since there is much in Marxism . . .
which in no sense reflects a belief in Communist theory or involvement in modern day Communist organization."[18] It was rather to create an alternative to communism, within the framework of democracy
and capitalism, which would remove the economic and social desperation that drove people to communism in the first place. This could only
have happened because the United States, after World War II, assumed peacetime responsibilities beyond its hemisphere. Stalin's challenge had helped to bring that about.

"[T]he gulf is impassable," one of Disraeli's characters acknowledged in *Sybil*, "utterly impassable."[19] A century later the gap between
the rich and the poor—between the few who had the means to live
well and the many who did not—had taken on global geopolitical significance, with two competing visions for how to close it. As Bohlen
put it in the summer of 1947: "There are, in short, two worlds instead
of one."[20]

IV.

BOTH OF the ideologies that defined those worlds were meant to offer hope: that is why one has an ideology in the first place. One of
them, however, had come to depend, for its functioning, upon the creation of fear. The other had no need to do so. Therein lay the basic ideological asymmetry of the Cold War.

It has never been clear how far Lenin intended his dictatorship of
the proletariat to extend. He certainly saw the ends of revolution as
justifying its means, including the use of terror.[21] But would he have
favored concentrating *all* authority in the hands of a single individual,
who would then retain it by imprisoning, exiling, or executing anyone
who questioned—or who he thought *might* question—this process?
Whatever Lenin would have done, that is what Stalin did.

By the end of 1930, his agents had arrested or killed some 63,000 opponents of collectivization. By 1932, they had deported over 1.2 million "kulaks"—Stalin's term for "wealthy" peasants—to remote regions within the U.S.S.R. By 1934 at least 5 million Ukrainians had starved to death from the resulting famine. Stalin then began purging government and party officials, producing the imprisonment of another 3.6 million people and the execution, in just 1937–38, of almost 700,000. They included many of Lenin's surviving associates: the most prominent exception was Leon Trotsky, whom Stalin then hunted down and had murdered in Mexico in 1940. By that time, one historian has estimated, the Stalinist dictatorship had either ended or wrecked the lives of between 10 and 11 million Soviet citizens—all for the purpose of maintaining itself in power.[22]

The full scope of this tragedy could not be known at the end of the war: Stalin had censored his own 1937 census, which would have revealed much of it, by arresting all of its top administrators and shooting many of them.[23] Enough was clear, however, to instill fear as well as hope in the minds of Europeans as they awaited liberation from Nazi oppression by a state whose record seemed almost as bad. The Red Army's behavior as it fought its way into Germany intensified these anxieties: armies are rarely gentle in occupying a defeated enemy's territory, but the Russians were particularly harsh in their looting, physical assaults, and mass rapes.[24] A culture of brutality within the Soviet Union, it appeared, had spawned one beyond its borders.

This was, in one sense, understandable: the Germans had been even more brutal in occupying the U.S.S.R. during the war. But Stalin's objective now was not just retribution. He hoped to spread Marxism-Leninism throughout as much of Europe as possible. He knew he could not do this, however, solely through the use of force and the cultivation of fear, the methods he had employed with such ruthlessness at home. Communists in Poland, Czechoslovakia, Hungary, Romania, Bulgaria, and, after 1949, East Germany would be governing ostensibly independent states. Stalin could certainly control them—Tito and the

Yugoslavs to the contrary notwithstanding, most communists in those days followed Moscow's orders. But his hand could not be *too* heavy, lest it give the appearance of a revolution that required repression to keep it going. It was important, therefore, for communists to gain popular support. "With good agitation and a proper attitude," Stalin told the Polish communist leader Wladyslaw Gomulka in 1945, "you may win a considerable number of votes."[25]

If the Kremlin boss thought this about the *Poles,* of all people, then it would not have seemed unreasonable to him that Germans and other Europeans who lived beyond his sphere of military and political influence might also support local communists, whether by electing them to office or including them within governing coalitions. This would be preferable to confronting the Americans and the British directly; moreover, as Leninist doctrine suggested, the capitalists would be confronting each other soon enough.[26] The proletarian dictatorship, if it was to spread into these regions, could not do so by the means with which Stalin had installed it in the Soviet Union and Eastern Europe. A *majority* of Western Europeans would have to *choose* it.

Stalin's strategy had a certain logic, except for one thing. It required that he cease to be who he was: a tyrant who had come to power and remained there through terror. When the slightest intimations of independence emerged among his East European satellites—as when the Czechs sought permission to participate in the Marshall Plan—he dealt with those responsible in the same way he had handled his real and imagined prewar rivals within the Soviet Union: they were removed from power, frequently put on trial, usually imprisoned, and in several instances executed. He would surely have done the same to Tito, had Yugoslavia not been beyond his reach. By one estimate, a million East European communists were purged in some way between 1949 and 1953.[27] Much the same thing was happening within the U.S.S.R.: Stalin's last years saw an ever-widening circle of arrests, trials, executions, and where these were not easily justified, arranged "accidents." At the time of his death, Soviet prisons were fuller than they had ever been.[28]

"Let the ruling classes tremble at a Communistic revolution," Marx had proclaimed in 1848. "The proletarians have nothing to lose but their chains."[29] A century later, however, proletarians who had not yet fallen under Stalin's dictatorship had every reason to tremble at the chains with which he had bound those who had already suffered that misfortune. It was no accident that Orwell's Big Brother had a Stalin-like mustache.

V.

IF CHAINS were required to control Stalin's proletarians, then it is hard today to see how such an arrangement could ever have attracted support elsewhere. Privation does lead to desperation, however, and when the choice is between starvation and repression it is not always easy to make. To succeed as an alternative, the American ideology could not simply show that communism suppressed freedom. It would also have to demonstrate that capitalism could sustain it.

There was never a plan, worked out in advance in Washington, for how to do this. Instead there had been conflicting objectives at the end of World War II: punishing defeated enemies; cooperating with the Soviet Union; reviving democracy and capitalism; strengthening the United Nations. It had to become clear that not all of these were possible before a realignment and ranking of priorities could take place. By the end of 1947 that had happened: the new goal, best articulated by Kennan, now Marshall's top policy planner, would be to keep the industrial-military facilities of former adversaries—chiefly those of western Germany and Japan—from falling under the rule of the current and future adversary, the U.S.S.R.[30]

This could have been done by destroying what remained of those facilities, but that would have driven the Germans and the Japanese toward starvation while precluding the economic revival of nearby American allies. It could have been done by restoring and then collaborating with German and Japanese authoritarianism, but that would have compromised the purposes for which the war had been fought. So the Americans came up with a third alternative. They would revive the German and Japanese economies, thereby securing the future of capitalism in those and surrounding regions. But they would also transform the Germans and the Japanese into democrats.

It was an ambitious, even audacious, strategy, so much so that if anyone had announced it publicly, alongside the Truman Doctrine and the Marshall Plan, it would have sounded wildly improbable. For while Germany and Japan had indeed had parliamentary systems before succumbing to dictatorships in the 1930s, the *culture* of democracy had never taken root in those countries: that was one reason they had succumbed so easily. Those dictatorships themselves, however, had now been discredited by defeat in war. That gave the Americans a clean slate and, through their military occupations, a free hand. They responded in just the way that Stalin had done: by relying abroad on what had worked at home. But because the domestic institutions of the United States could hardly have been more different from those of the Soviet Union, the Americans' objectives in running their occupation could hardly have been less similar.

The function of government, as they saw it, was to facilitate freedom. That might require regulating the economy, but never, as in the Soviet Union, commanding it in all respects. People could still be trusted to own property, markets could be trusted to allocate resources, and the results could be trusted to advance everyone's interests. Leaders would lead only by consent; laws, administered impartially, would ensure fairness; and a free press would provide transparency and therefore accountability. The underlying basis of government would be hope, not fear. None of these conditions existed within the U.S.S.R., its satellites, or the occupied territories it administered.

All of this would mean little, however, without performance. This is where the Marshall Plan came in. The idea here was to jump-start the European economies—and, simultaneously, that of Japan as well—through a substantial infusion of American assistance, but to involve the recipients from the start in determining how it would be used. The only requirement was that they work together: that old antagonisms fade in the face of new dangers. The goal was to restore self-confidence, prosperity, and social peace by *democratic* means: to show that while there might now be two ideological worlds, there need not be, within the one that was capitalist, the separate nations of rich and poor that had given rise to Marxism in the first place. Nor need there be the wars among capitalists that Lenin had insisted must happen.

Only the United States had the economic resources—perhaps also the naiveté—to attempt this task. The Soviet Union was in no position to compete: that is why Stalin responded by cracking down in those parts of Europe he could control. The Americans had another advantage over the Russians, however, that had nothing to do with their material capabilities: it was their pragmatic reliance on spontaneity. Whatever its roots—whether in market economics or democratic politics or simply national culture—they never accepted the idea that wisdom, or even common sense, could be found only at the top. They were impatient with hierarchy, at ease with flexibility, and profoundly distrustful of the notion that theory should determine practice rather than the other way around.

It did not unduly disturb Truman and his advisers, therefore, when the American military authorities in Germany and Japan rewrote their own directives for the occupation of those countries to accommodate the realities that confronted them. The deficiencies of a "one size fits all" model did not have to be explained. Nor, staunch capitalists though they were, did Washington officials object to working with European socialists to contain European communists. Results were more important than ideological consistency. And when several recipients of Marshall Plan aid pointed out that self-confidence could hardly be attained without military protection, the Americans agreed to provide this too in the form of the North Atlantic Treaty Organization, the first peacetime military alliance the United States had entered into since the termination, in 1800, of the one with France that had secured American independence.

The Soviet Union under Stalin, in striking contrast, suppressed spontaneity wherever it appeared, lest it challenge the basis for his rule. But that meant accepting the proposition that Stalin himself was the font of all wisdom and common sense, claims his acolytes made frequently during the final years of his life. Whether he believed them or not, the "greatest genius of mankind" was in fact a lonely, deluded, and fearful old man, addicted to ill-informed pontifications on genetics, economics, philosophy, and linguistics, to long drunken dinners with terrified subordinates, and—oddly—to American movies. "I'm finished," he acknowledged in a moment of candor shortly before his death. "I don't even trust myself."[31]

So this was what the aspirations of Marx and the ambitions of Lenin had come down to: a system that perverted reason, smothered trust, and functioned by fear—but that now competed with capitalists who offered hope.

VI.

WHAT IF Stalin himself was the problem, though, and communism might be salvaged with different leadership? The men who sought to succeed him all believed the diagnosis to be accurate and the prescription to be appropriate. Each of them set out to liberate Marxism-Leninism from the legacy of Stalinism. They found, though, that the two were inextricably intertwined: that to try to separate one from another risked killing both.

The first post-Stalinist leader who tried to do this wound up getting killed himself. Lavrentii Beria, Stalin's secret police chief since 1938, was a member of the triumvirate which assumed power upon his death—the others were Molotov and Malenkov. A serial murderer and a sexual predator, Beria was also an impressive administrator who more than anyone else deserved credit for building the Soviet atomic bomb. He was surprisingly critical of the system that had given him such power. He could scarcely conceal his delight at Stalin's demise—some historians suggest that he even arranged it[32]—and he moved immediately afterward to try to undo some of the worst aspects of Stalin's rule.

Beria suspended the latest round of purges, which Stalin had launched, most unwisely, against his own doctors. With his colleagues, Beria then instructed the North Koreans and the Chinese to end the long stalemated armistice negotiations and bring the Korean War to a close; they also placed an article in *Pravda* expressing hope for better relations with the United States. Beria then went beyond his colleagues with a proposal to grant the non-Russian nationalities of the Soviet Union much greater autonomy than Stalin had been willing to allow them.[33] His most controversial move, however, was to try to resolve the dilemma Stalin had left behind over the future of Germany.

The formation of the Federal Republic of Germany (West Germany) in May, 1949, frustrated whatever hopes Stalin may have had that communism would spread there on its own. Reunification was less important, for the new government of Konrad Adenauer, than remaining independent of the Soviet Union while closely linked to the United States. This left Stalin little choice but to authorize the formation of the German Democratic Republic (East Germany) in October, but he did so with little enthusiasm. He remained prepared to sacrifice that regime, headed by the veteran German communist Walter Ulbricht, if there was any way to prevent West Germany's incorporation into NATO. In March, 1952, with this goal in mind, Stalin offered reunification in return for neutralization.[34]

The proposal went nowhere: Stalin's motives were too transparent. East Germany then set about transforming itself into a proletarian state, no easy task since it had always been chiefly an agricultural region—and because the Russians had removed much of what industry there was for reparations. However, Ulbricht, a good Stalinist, insisted that East Germans could fix this problem by simply working harder: he instituted a program of rapid industrialization similar to what Stalin had undertaken in the Soviet Union. It quickly became clear, though, that this was deepening the economic crisis, provoking unrest, and driving thousands of East Germans to emigrate to West Germany, which was still possible through the open border that separated East from West Berlin.

The new Kremlin leaders ordered the reluctant Ulbricht to slow down his program—which he only partially did—and in May, 1953, Beria put forward a truly radical proposal: that in return for neutralization, the Soviet Union accept a reunified *capitalist* German state. Ulbricht and the East German communists would simply be abandoned. Before this plan could get anywhere, though, riots broke out the following month in East Berlin and elsewhere.[35] The rioters were chiefly *proletarians*, the very people whose dictatorship, in theory at least, was supposed to have brought them freedom. In practice, it had denied them freedom, and that posed a dilemma for Stalin's successors because at least one communist regime was sitting on a powder keg of resentment, fueled by the failure of Marxism-Leninism to keep its promises. What if there were others?

Beria's colleagues solved the immediate problem by using Soviet troops to crush the East German uprising—a highly embarrassing admission of failure for them and Ulbricht. They next arrested Beria himself, charged him with having been an agent of Anglo-American imperialism, put him on trial, convicted him, and had him shot. Khrushchev, who orchestrated these events, then aligned the Soviet Union closely with Ulbricht's repressive regime, something Stalin had never done.[36] It was not an auspicious beginning for those who sought to liberate communism from Stalinism—but it would not be the last such attempt.

VII.

IT WAS Khrushchev himself who made the next one. Having deposed and executed Beria, he then over the next two years pushed aside Malenkov and Molotov—he did not, however, kill them—so that by mid-1955 he was the dominant leader of the post-Stalinist U.S.S.R. Quite unlike Stalin in his personal qualities, Khrushchev was also sincere—and fundamentally humane—in his determination to return Marxism to its original objective: a better life than that provided by capitalism. The path he chose, once he had consolidated his authority in the Kremlin, was to take on the legacy of Stalin himself.

On February 25, 1956, Khrushchev shocked delegates to the 20th Congress of the Soviet Communist Party by candidly cataloging, and then denouncing, Stalin's crimes. In doing so, he pulled down the façade—the product of both terror and denial—that had concealed the true nature of the Stalinist regime from the Soviet people and from practitioners of communism throughout the world. He did so with a view to preserving communism: reform could only take place by acknowledging error. "I was obliged to tell the truth about the past," he later recalled, "whatever the risks to me."[37] But the system he was trying to preserve had itself been based, since the time of Marx and Engels, on the claim to be error-free. That was what it meant to have discovered the engine that drove history forward. A movement based on science had little place for confession, contrition, and the possibility of redemption. The problems Khrushchev created for himself and for the international communist movement, therefore, began almost from the moment he finished speaking.

One was simple shock. Communists were not used to having mistakes admitted at the top, and certainly not on this scale. It was, as Sec-

retary of State Dulles commented at the time, "the most damning indictment of despotism ever made by a despot."[38] The Polish party
leader, Boleslaw Bierut, had a heart attack when he read Khrushchev's
speech, and promptly died. The effect on other communists was almost
as devastating, for the new Soviet leader seemed to be telling them that
it was not enough now to assert, as a theoretical proposition, that they
had history behind them. It was also necessary to have their people behind them. "I'm absolutely sure of it," Khrushchev announced at
Bierut's funeral. "[W]e will achieve an unprecedented closing of ranks
within our own party, and of the people around our party."[39]

The Polish Communist Party took the lesson to heart, and in the
wake of Bierut's death began to release political prisoners and remove
Stalinists from positions of authority—only to have riots break out, as
had happened under similar circumstances in East Germany. In this
case, though, the hard-liners did not regain power: instead the Poles
brought back Gomulka, who had fallen victim to one of Stalin's purges,
and installed him in the leadership without Khrushchev's approval.
Furious, he flew uninvited to Warsaw, threw a tantrum, threatened to
send in Soviet troops, but in the end quietly accepted the new Polish
government, which had after all only promised what he himself had
said he wanted to do: to give "socialism"—meaning communism—"a
human face."

But the problem with powder kegs—even those that do not blow
up—is that there are often others nearby. Hoping to ward off further
disturbances, Khrushchev had arranged the removal from power of
the Hungarian Stalinist leader Mátyás Rákosi in July, 1956: Rákosi
was told that he was "ill," and needed "treatment" in Moscow.[40] This
only provoked demands for further concessions, and by the end of
October—inspired by the events in Poland—the Hungarians were
mounting a full-scale rebellion, not just against their own communists,
but against the Soviet Union itself. Confronted with bloody fighting in
the streets of Budapest, Red Army forces withdrew, and for a few days
it appeared as though Hungary might be allowed to withdraw from the

Warsaw Pact, the military alliance set up by the Russians the previous year as a counterweight to NATO. Khrushchev agonized over what to do; but in the end, under pressure from Mao Zedong, he ordered Soviet troops to re-enter Hungary and crush the rebellion.

This they promptly did, but not before some 1,500 Soviet soldiers and 20,000 Hungarians had been killed. Imre Nagy, who as premier had reluctantly led the rebel regime, was arrested and later executed. Hundreds of thousands of other Hungarians who survived tried desperately to escape to the West. Those who could not faced a return of repression, which seemed—such was the lesson of Hungary—to be the only way in which Marxist-Leninists knew how to rule. Being a communist was "inseparable from being a Stalinist," Khrushchev told a group of Chinese early in 1957. "[M]ay God grant that every Communist will be able to fight for the interests of the working class as Stalin fought."[41] Whatever God thought about it, the old dictator's ghost was not so easily exorcized after all.

VIII.

IT WAS fitting that the Chinese played such an important role in Khrushchev's decision to suppress the Hungarian uprising, because Mao Zedong himself was another post-Stalinist leader with ideas about how to salvage communism. His solution all along, though, had been to go *back* to Stalin.

Mao had not been consulted in advance about Khrushchev's February, 1956, de-Stalinization speech—no foreign communist had been. He respected Stalin and deferred to him, but never found him easy to deal with. Stalin had been slow to support the Chinese communist revolution, and surprised by its success. He had been less than generous in setting the terms of the 1950 Sino-Soviet Treaty, and in providing military support to the Chinese during the Korean War. He had insisted that the war be continued when Mao and Kim Il-sung were ready to end it. Was Chairman Mao sad to hear of Stalin's death, his translator, Shi Zhe, was once asked. "I don't think the Chairman was sad," he replied.[42]

But Stalin was useful to Mao in another way: as a model for how to consolidate a communist revolution. It fell to Mao to play the role, in China, of both Lenin and Stalin. He had followed Lenin's example in making the leap from Marxist theory to revolutionary action, reversing only the sequence of events so that in China the civil war preceded the seizure of power rather than following it. He was also, however—unlike Lenin—robustly healthy, and so he lived to take on the task that Lenin never had to confront: how to turn a country in which Marxist theory had said the revolution could never take hold into one in which it would. Stalin had done that, in Russia, by *proletarianizing* the country. He built up a huge industrial base, even to the point of attempting to turn agriculture into an industry by collectivizing it. There were not supposed to be any peasants left in Russia by the time he finished, and he came close to achieving that objective.

Mao took a different path. His principal theoretical innovation was to claim that peasants *were* proletarians: that they did not have to be transformed. A revolutionary consciousness resided within them, needing only to be awakened. That was very different from Stalin's approach, and it accounts for some of the uneasiness that existed between them—although the elderly Stalin, frustrated by the failure of workers in Europe to arise, did take some solace in the prospect that peasants outside Europe might do so.[43] Where Mao did follow the Soviet model was on the question of what to do with a revolution once it had gained control of a country. The one in China would fail, he believed, if it did not replicate, with mechanical precision, the steps by which Lenin and especially Stalin had consolidated the one in Russia.

Recalling Lenin's New Economic Policy, Mao allowed a brief period of experimentation with market capitalism during the early 1950s, only to reverse that with a Five-Year Plan for crash industrialization and collectivized agriculture along Stalinist lines. After Stalin's death—

unimpressed with his successors in Moscow—Mao encouraged a "cult of personality" centered around himself, not just as the head of the Chinese Communist Party, but as the most experienced and respected leader, now, of the international communist movement.

It was, therefore, an unwelcome surprise for Mao when Khrushchev, without warning, denounced the Stalinist "cult of personality" early in 1956 and insisted that communists everywhere disassociate themselves from it. "He's just handing the sword to others," Mao grumbled, "helping the tigers harm us. If they don't want the sword, we do. . . . The Soviet Union may attack Stalin, but we will not."[44] Mao would stick to his plan of following Stalin's example, but—perhaps inspired by Khrushchev's ambitions to overtake the West in both missile strength and material goods—he resolved to compress and accelerate the process. The U.S.S.R., he argued, was losing its revolutionary edge. The *truly* revolutionary country, China, would not make that mistake.

Accordingly, Mao added to his industrialization and collectivization campaigns his own purge of potential dissidents. "Let a hundred flowers bloom, let a hundred schools of thought contend," he proclaimed; but then he arrested as "rightists" those critics unwise enough to have taken him at his word. It was a strategy designed to "coax the snakes out of their holes, . . . to let the poisonous weeds grow first and then destroy them one by one. Let them become fertilizer."[45] Then he decided on something even more dramatic: he would *merge* the industrialization and collectivization campaigns by transforming peasants into proletarians after all, but by means that went beyond anything Stalin had ever considered. He ordered farmers throughout China to abandon their crops, build furnaces in their backyards, throw in their own furniture as fuel, melt down their agricultural implements—and produce steel.

The result of Mao's "Great Leap Forward" was the greatest single human calamity of the 20th century. Stalin's campaign to collectivize agriculture had caused between 5 and 7 million people to starve to death during the early 1930s. Mao now *sextupled* that record, producing a famine that between 1958 and 1961 took the lives of over 30 million people, by far the worst on record anywhere ever.[46] So Mao did wind up surpassing the Soviet Union and everyone else in at least one category. But it was not one of which the ideologists of Marxism, Leninism, Stalinism, or Maoism could be proud.

IX.

THE REST of the world, at the time, was hardly aware of what was happening in China. Mao kept his country at least as opaque to the outside as Stalin's U.S.S.R. had been, and the Chinese ever since have censored their censuses almost as carefully as Stalin did his own. It would take many years for the costs of the Maoist version of Marxism-Leninism to become apparent. That ideology's deficiencies were much clearer, at the time, in the one transparent arena where communism and capitalism competed: the divided city of Berlin.

Only the Cold War's peculiarities—the way it froze in place what were meant to be temporary arrangements at the end of World War II—could have produced a city separated into American, British, French, and Soviet sectors, lying more than a hundred miles inside the East German state Stalin had created in 1949, surrounded by several hundred thousand Soviet troops. Thanks to Marshall Plan aid, together with generous subsidies from the West German government as well as support for universities, libraries, cultural centers, and broadcasting facilities from the United States—some of them quietly funded through the Central Intelligence Agency—the western-occupied parts of Berlin became a permanent advertisement for the virtues of capitalism and democracy in the middle of communist East Germany. West Berlin led a precarious existence, though, for there was nothing to prevent the Russians—or the East Germans, if given permission—from cutting off land access to the city, as Stalin had done a decade earlier. It was clear this time that an airlift would not work: there was no way to sustain, by air, a city that was considerably more populous—and far more prosperous—than it had been in 1948. West Berlin's very success had made it vulnerable. It survived only through forbearance in Moscow.

Soviet-occupied East Berlin, however, had its own vulnerabilities, as the riots that broke out there in 1953 had made clear. The discontent had arisen, in large part, because Berliners were then allowed to travel freely between the eastern and western portions of the city. "[I]t was really a crazy system," one East Berliner recalled. "All you had to do [was] board a subway or [a] surface train, . . . and you were in another world. . . . [Y]ou could go from socialism . . . to capitalism in two minutes."[47] From West Berlin in turn, emigration to West Germany was easy. The obvious differences in living standards had caused "great dissatisfaction" within the Soviet zone, Kremlin leader Georgii Malenkov admitted in the immediate aftermath of the riots, "which is particularly obvious, since the population has begun to flee from East Germany to West Germany."[48]

The figure Malenkov cited was 500,000 over the previous two years, but by the end of 1956 Soviet statistics showed that well over a million more East Germans had departed. It soon became clear as well that the refugees were disproportionately well-educated and highly trained, and their motives for abandoning communism had as much to do with the absence of political freedoms as with economic shortcomings. Choosing his words carefully, the Soviet ambassador to East Germany, Mikhail Pervukhin, summed up the situation in 1959: "The presence in Berlin of an open and essentially uncontrolled border between the socialist and capitalist worlds unwittingly prompts the population to make a comparison between both parts of the city, which, unfortunately, does not always turn out in favor of Democratic [East] Berlin."[49]

Khrushchev had tried to solve this problem with his 1958 ultimatum, through which he had threatened either to end the four-power occupation of the city, or to transfer control over access rights to the East Germans, who could then presumably "squeeze" the American, British, and French sectors—as his various anatomical metaphors suggested vividly—with impunity. But that initiative had fallen victim to the Eisenhower administration's firmness, together with Khrushchev's own insatiable desire to visit the United States. After his return, the Soviet leader promised a disappointed Ulbricht that by 1961 "the GDR [East Germany] will start to surpass the FRG [West Germany] in standard of living. This will be a bomb for them. Therefore, our position is to gain time."[50] Instead, time was lost: by 1961 some 2.7 million East Germans had fled through the open border to West Berlin and then on to West Germany. The overall population of the German Democratic Republic had *declined*, since 1949, from 19 million to 17 million.[51]

This was a major crisis for communism itself, as Soviet Vice Premier Anastas Mikoyan warned the East Germans in July, 1961: "Our Marxist-Leninist theory must prove itself in the GDR. It must be demonstrated . . . that what the capitalists and the renegades say is wrong." After all, "Marxism was born in Germany. . . . If socialism does not win in the GDR, if communism does not prove itself as superior and vital here, then we have not won. The issue is this fundamental to us."[52] This was the same Mikoyan who had so emotionally welcomed, the year before, the surprising but historically determined revolution in Castro's Cuba. Now, though, the revolution in Marx's Germany was in peril. The forces of history, it seemed, were not proceeding in the right direction after all.

Ulbricht had had plans in place since at least 1952 to stop the flow of emigrants by walling West Berlin off from East Berlin and the rest of East Germany. Soviet and other East European leaders, however, had always resisted this idea. Molotov warned in 1953 that it would "call forth bitterness and dissatisfaction from the Berliners with regard to the government of the GDR and the Soviet forces in Germany." Khrushchev insisted that the better way to fight the West German challenge would be "to try to win the minds of the people by using culture and policies to create better living conditions." The Hungarian leader János Kádár—who had himself forced a dissatisfied population into line after the 1956 uprising—predicted early in 1961 that the construction of a wall in Berlin would "cause serious harm to the reputation of the entire communist movement." The wall was a "hateful thing," Khrushchev admitted, but "[w]hat should I have done? More than 30,000 people, in fact the best and most qualified people from the GDR, left the country in July. . . . [T]he East German economy would have collapsed if we hadn't done something soon against the mass flight. . . . So the Wall was the only remaining option."[53]

It went up on the night of August 12–13, 1961, first as a barbed wire barrier, but then as a concrete block wall some twelve feet high and almost a hundred miles long, protected by guard towers, minefields, police dogs, and orders to shoot to kill anyone who tried to cross it. Khrushchev's decision did stabilize the Berlin situation as far as the Cold War superpower relationship was concerned. With West Berlin isolated from East Berlin and East Germany, he had no further need to try to force the western powers out of the city, with all the risks of nuclear war that such an effort would have entailed. He could breathe more easily now, and so too—if truth be told—could western leaders. "It's not a very nice solution," Kennedy acknowledged, "but a wall is a hell of a lot better than a war."[54] The president could not resist observing, though, when he himself visited the Berlin Wall in June, 1963, that "we have never had to put a wall up to keep our people in, to prevent them from leaving us." The ugly structure Khrushchev had erected was "the most obvious and vivid demonstration of the failures of the Communist system, for all the world to see."[55]

X.

AND ON the other side of the wall, capitalism was succeeding. No single event, date, or statistic marks the point at which that became clear: what was significant instead was what had *not* happened since the end of World War II. For contrary to the fears of capitalists based on history and the hopes of communists based on theory, the Great Depression had not returned. And any possibility that capitalists might fight another great war with one another—as Stalin, drawing on Lenin, had predicted they would—had become ludicrous.

It was left, years later, to one of the last great Marxist historians, Eric Hobsbawm, to give the early postwar era a name: he called it the "Golden Age." What he meant by this was that "[a]ll the problems which had haunted capitalism . . . appeared to dissolve and disappear." World manufacturing output quadrupled between the early 1950s and the early 1970s. Trade in manufactured products increased by a factor of ten. Food production rose faster than population growth. Consumer goods once considered luxuries—automobiles, refrigerators, telephones, radios, televisions, washing machines—became standard equipment. Unemployment, in Western Europe, almost disappeared. "Of course most of humanity remained poor," Hobsbawm acknowledged, "but in the old heartlands of industrial labor what meaning could the [communist] *Internationale*'s 'Arise, ye starvelings from your slumbers' have for workers who now expected to have their car and spend their annual paid vacation on the beaches of Spain?"[56]

Hobsbawm found it easier to catalog this phenomenon than to account for it, however: "[T]here really are no satisfactory explanations for the sheer scale of this 'Great Leap Forward' of the capitalist world economy, and consequently for its unprecedented social consequences." It might, he thought, have reflected an upturn in the long cycles of economic boom and bust that extended back several hundred years, but this did not explain "the extraordinary scale and depth of the secular boom," which contrasted so strikingly with that of "the preceding era of crises and depressions." It might have resulted from technological advances, but these were more important with the advent of computers in the 1970s and 1980s than in the immediate post–World War II years. What really did the trick, he finally decided, was that "capitalism was deliberately reformed, largely by the men who were in a position to do so in the USA and Britain, during the last war years. It is a mistake to suppose that people never learn from history."[57]

If that was correct, though, then what remained of Marx, who insisted that capitalism produces, in an angry and resentful proletariat, its own executioners? Or of Lenin, who claimed that the greed of capitalists would, in the end, breed war? Or of Stalin, Khrushchev, and Mao, who promised their people a better life under communism than capitalism could ever provide? The fundamental premise of all of them was that capitalists could *never* learn from history. Only communists, who had discovered in the class struggle the engine of history, could do that. Only theory, which cut through complexity while abolishing ambiguity, could point the way. And only dictators, who provided the necessary discipline, could ensure arrival at the intended destination. But a lot depended on getting the history, the theory, and the dictators right. If any of them turned out to be wrong, all bets were off.

This is where the capitalists got it right: they were better than the communists at learning from history, because they never bought into any single, sacrosanct, and therefore unchallengeable theory of history. Instead they were, over the century that separated Disraeli's two nations from Bohlen's two worlds, pragmatic, adaptable, and given to seeking truth in results produced rather than in dogmas advanced. They made mistakes, but they corrected them. "[T]he prospects of socialism as a world alternative depended on its ability to compete with the world capitalist economy, as reformed after the Great Slump and the Second World War," Hobsbawm concluded. "That socialism was falling behind at an accelerating rate was patent after 1960. It was no longer competitive."[58]

That is putting it rather narrowly, for Marxism and its successors, Leninism, Stalinism, and Maoism, cannot be judged on their economic performance alone. The human costs were far more horrendous. These ideologies, when put into practice, may well have brought about the premature deaths, during the 20th century, of almost 100 million people.[59] The number who survived but whose lives were stunted by these ideas and the repression they justified is beyond estimation. There can be few examples in history in which greater misery resulted from better intentions. The sign that went up on an East German factory wall just after the Berlin Wall came down was entirely appropriate—if long overdue: "To the workers of the world: I am sorry." There hardly needed to be a signature.

CHAPTER FOUR
THE EMERGENCE OF AUTONOMY

*The military power deployed at the top of the system ran into . . .
even greater power based on popular will at the bottom. As in
Alice in Wonderland's croquet game, in which the mallets were
flamingos and the balls were hedgehogs, the pawns in the [Cold
War] game, mistaken for inanimate objects by the [superpowers],
came alive in their hands and began, universally and unstop-
pably, to pursue their own plans and ambitions.*

—JONATHAN SCHELL[1]

*Could anyone have dreamed of telling Stalin that he didn't suit
us anymore and suggesting he retire? Not even a wet spot would
have remained where we had been standing. Now everything is
different. The fear is gone, and we can talk as equals. That's my
contribution.*

—NIKITA S. KHRUSHCHEV,
October 13, 1964

KHRUSHCHEV WAS GRASPING for straws when he made this comment, on the day his Kremlin colleagues announced their intention to
depose him. "I'm . . . glad that the party has gotten to the point that it
can rein in even its first secretary," he added. "You smeared me all over
with shit, and I say, 'You're right.'"

The charges made against Khrushchev more than merited his characterization of them. He was accused of rudeness, distraction, arrogance, incompetence, nepotism, megalomania, depression, unpredictability, and growing old. He had allowed his own cult of personality to develop, and no longer listened to his advisers. He had ruined Soviet agriculture while bringing the world to the brink of nuclear war. He had authorized the construction of the Berlin Wall, a public humiliation for Marxism-Leninism. He had long since become an embarrassment to the country he had tried to lead, and to the international communist movement he had sought to inspire. And as his successor, Leonid Brezhnev, felt it necessary to add, Khrushchev had once described members of the Central Committee as "dogs peeing against curbstones."[2]

It was a crude and undignified way to remove the leader of the world's second most powerful state, but no blood was shed, no one was sent to prison, no one went into exile. Khrushchev was allowed a peaceful—if painfully obscure—retirement. Always the optimist, he came to see as his most significant accomplishment the fact that he had *not* been able to keep his job. During his years in power, constraints had developed on the wielding of power. It was no longer possible for a single leader to demand, and to expect to receive, unquestioning obedience.

Khrushchev's fate reflected, in microcosm, that of the Soviet Union and the United States during the late 1950s, the 1960s, and the early 1970s. The international system during those years *appeared* to be one of bipolarity in which, like iron filings attracted by magnets, all power gravitated to Moscow and Washington. In fact, though, the superpowers were finding it increasingly difficult to manage the smaller powers, whether allies or neutrals in the Cold War, while at the same time they were losing the authority they had once taken for granted at home. The weak were discovering opportunities to confront the strong. The nature of power was changing because the fear of power, as traditionally conceived, was diminishing. Mallets were indeed beginning to turn into flamingos, and balls into hedgehogs.

I.

THE FIRST signs that this was happening came with the decline and eventual demise of European colonialism, a process that began before the Cold War started, paralleled its early development, and only gradually affected its subsequent evolution. The European domination of the world dated from the 15th century, when Portugal and Spain first perfected the means of transporting men, weapons, and—without realizing it—germs across the oceans that had hitherto kept human societies apart.[3] By the end of the 19th century, there was little territory left that was not controlled by Europeans or their descendants. But in 1905, Japan, a rising non-European power, won a war it had started with Russia, one of the weakest of the European empires: that victory shattered the illusion that the Europeans, if challenged, would always win.

The Europeans themselves then shattered another illusion—that of unity among themselves—by going to war in 1914. World War I, in turn, produced two compelling justifications for an end to colonial rule. One came out of the Bolshevik Revolution, when Lenin called for an end to "imperialism" in all its forms. The other came from the United States. When Woodrow Wilson made the principle of self-determination one of his Fourteen Points his intent had been to undercut the appeal of Bolshevism, but the effect was to excite opponents of imperialism throughout Asia, the Middle East, and Africa. Among those excited were Mohandas Gandhi in British India, Ho Chi Minh in French Indochina, Syngman Rhee in Japanese-occupied Korea, and an obscure young librarian in China named Mao Zedong.[4]

It took World War II, however, to exhaust colonialism once and for all: the war set in motion processes that would, over the next two decades, end the age of European empires that had begun five centuries earlier. The collapse of colonialism coincided, therefore, with the onset of the Cold War, but the Cold War did not cause that development—its roots lay elsewhere. For just as Thomas Paine had pointed out, in 1776, the illogic of an island indefinitely ruling a continent,[5] so it was also highly improbable, in 1945, that a continent devastated by war could continue indefinitely to rule most of the rest of the world. That would have been the case even if the wartime Grand Alliance had never broken up.

Nor did decolonization become a significant issue during the early Cold War. The Soviet Union remained anti-imperialist—how could it not be?—but advancing revolution in what was coming to be called the "third world" was less important to Stalin in the immediate postwar years than recovering from the war and attempting to spread his influence as widely as possible in Europe. The United States, for its part, was not about to defend European colonialism either. Its own history had begun in rebellion against an empire, and although the Americans had taken colonies of their own at the end of the 19th century—the Philippines being the most significant—they had never been comfortable with colonialism, preferring instead to exert their influence abroad by economic and cultural means. Neither Moscow nor Washington lamented the decline of European empires, therefore, nor did the power vacuums that were developing outside of Europe, as a result, at first preoccupy them.

That situation, however, could hardly last. By the end of 1949, the Soviet-American contest for Europe had become a stalemate, and that created temptations to exploit opportunities elsewhere. Stalin had succumbed to these when he allowed Kim Il-sung to attack South Korea, while simultaneously encouraging Ho Chi Minh's war against the French in Indochina. The old dictator knew little about the "third world," however, and undertook no sustained effort to project Soviet influence into it. Khrushchev was more energetic: unlike Stalin, he loved to travel abroad and rarely missed a chance to do so. Among his favored destinations were the newly independent countries that were emerging from European colonial rule. "I'm not an adventurer," Khrushchev explained, "but we must aid national liberation movements."[6]

The Americans feared precisely this. Colonialism, they believed, was an antiquated institution that could only discredit the West in the regions where it had existed, while weakening its practitioners in Europe, where they needed to be strong. But the United States could not detach itself from its British, French, Dutch, and Portuguese allies just because they still maintained colonial possessions: restoring security and prosperity in postwar Europe was too important. The risk that "third world" nationalists would associate the Americans with imperialism was thus high. Nor was there assurance that the resentments colonialism had generated over so long a period would not make communism an attractive alternative. Marx might have exaggerated capitalism's contradictions, but the self-destructiveness of imperialism was plain for all to see. It was awkward for the United States—even dangerous—that colonialism was ending as the Cold War was intensifying, for the sins of allies in the past could easily create vulnerabilities in the future. Certainly that was Khrushchev's hope.

What all of this meant, then, was that the choices newly independent states made could yet tip the balance of power in the Cold War. One of the most shocking things for the Americans about the Korean War had been the rapidity with which a peripheral interest—the defense of South Korea—had suddenly become vital. To allow even an underdeveloped country with no industrial-military capacity to fall under communist control could shake self-confidence throughout the non-communist world. This was what Eisenhower had in mind when, in 1954, he invoked the most famous of all Cold War metaphors: "You have a row of dominos set up, you knock over the first one, and . . . the last one . . . will go over very quickly. So you could have . . . a disintegration that would have the most profound influences."[7]

"Dominos" could topple as a result of external aggression, as in Korea, or internal subversion, as was happening in Indochina. But they could also do so if states emerging from colonialism *chose* to tilt toward the Soviet Union or China. That put decolonization in a new context: the emergence of nationalism, from Washington's perspective, could cause as much trouble as the persistence of colonialism. The Cold War was becoming global in scope; but the paradoxical effect was to empower the people—only recently without any power at all—over whom it would now be fought. Their method was "non-alignment."

II.

"NON-ALIGNMENT" provided a way in which the leaders of "third world" states could tilt without toppling: the idea was to commit to neither side in the Cold War, but to leave open the possibility of such commitment. That way, if pressure from one superpower became too great, a smaller power could defend itself by *threatening* to align with the other superpower.

Yugoslavia—not a "third world" state—pioneered the process. Tito had not sought Stalin's condemnation in 1948: he was, and remained, a dedicated communist. But he was determined not to sacrifice sovereignty for the sake of ideological solidarity, and unlike most other East European leaders at the time, he had no need to do so. Noting how quickly the Americans offered him economic assistance after his break with Stalin, Tito saw the possibility of a lifeline: would the Russians risk using force against the Yugoslavs if this might lead to war with the Americans? With the United States Sixth Fleet operating just off the long Yugoslav coast, there were good reasons for Stalin to think twice about attempting an invasion, and there is evidence that he did so, contenting himself instead with assassination plots—all of them unsuccessful.[8]

At the same time, though, Tito saw that it would not do to become *too* dependent on the United States. Could he be sure that NATO would defend him? Or that the Americans would not seek, as the price for their aid, to restore capitalism? It made sense, therefore, to leave the way open for reconciliation with the Soviet Union, and when, after Stalin's death, Khrushchev traveled to Belgrade to apologize for his predecessor's behavior, the Yugoslav leader received him with respect—

but also as an equal. From this time on, Khrushchev felt obliged to *consult:* the most striking example came during the 1956 Hungarian crisis, when he and Malenkov made a hair-raising flight in a small plane in horrendous weather and then a sickening voyage in a small boat through rough seas, all to secure Tito's approval of the Soviet decision to suppress the uprising. Tito had been "vacationing" on his island in the Adriatic, and could not be bothered himself to come to Belgrade or to Moscow. "Khrushchev and Malenkov looked very exhausted," one of Tito's advisers recalled, "especially Malenkov who could hardly stand up."[9] It was a vivid demonstration of the leverage "non-alignment" could provide.

Tito's interest in "non-alignment" went well beyond Eastern Europe, however. Sensing the rising tide of nationalism in Asia, he had already associated himself by then with two leaders from that part of the world, Jawaharlal Nehru of India, and Zhou Enlai of China—each of whom had his own reasons for resisting superpower hegemony.

Nehru's had to do with the United States and Pakistan. The British had granted India and Pakistan independence in 1947, and Nehru had hoped to keep the subcontinent they shared out of the Cold War. The Pakistanis, however—concerned about Indian ambitions—had sought support from the Americans by portraying themselves as tough anticommunists with a British-trained military who could provide bases along the sensitive southern border of the U.S.S.R. The contrast with Nehru—also British-trained, but socialist, pacifist, and determined not to take sides in the Cold War—could hardly have been greater. By the end of 1954, Pakistan had maneuvered its way into the Central Treaty Organization (CENTO) *and* the Southeast Asian Treaty Organization (SEATO), both designed by Secretary of State Dulles to surround the Soviet Union with American-sponsored military alliances. For Nehru, aligning India with "non-alignment" was a way to rebuke the Americans and the Pakistanis, while also making the point, to the rest of the "third world," that there were alternatives to taking sides in the Cold War.[10]

Zhou Enlai's reasons for supporting "non-alignment"—they were, of course, those of Mao Zedong—also had to do with the fear of hegemony, which from China's perspective could come from either the U.S. or the U.S.S.R. Washington had continued to support Chiang Kai-shek and the Chinese Nationalists after they had fled to Taiwan in 1949: the threat of a Nationalist effort to retake the mainland, supported by the Americans, could not be written off in Beijing. But Mao was not prepared to rely, for deterrence against this danger, solely on the 1950 Sino-Soviet alliance. It made sense, therefore, for China to align itself with nationalists in former colonial and dependent regions: "[T]heir victory," Zhou wrote Mao, "would be in the interest of the socialist camp and . . . would thwart all attempts of the western imperialists to complete their encirclement of the eastern camp."[11]

It was this convergence of interests, if not ultimate objectives, that led Tito, Nehru, and Zhou to convene the first conference of "non-aligned" nations at Bandung in Indonesia, in April, 1955: its purpose was to expand autonomy by encouraging neutrality in the Cold War. Among those invited was Colonel Gamal Abdel Nasser of Egypt, who would soon prove to be the most skillful of all the practitioners of "non-alignment."

Egypt had never formally been a colony, but Great Britain had controlled it since the 1880s: the Suez Canal, which lay wholly within Egyptian territory, was a critical link to the Middle East, India, and Southeast Asia. A nationalist revolution in 1952 had deposed the notoriously complaisant King Farouk, however, and two years later the British agreed to dismantle their remaining military bases in Egypt, reserving the right to reintroduce their forces to protect the canal if it should ever be in danger. Nasser, by this time, had seized power in Cairo, with aspirations to become the principal nationalist leader in the Arab world.

He could hardly do that by aligning Egypt with the United States, for although the Americans had supported him, they were too visibly tied to the Europeans and therefore fearful, as Nasser put it, "of annoying some colonial power."[12] He resolved, in the spirit of Bandung, to remain neutral, but he would also exploit the hopes held among leaders in both Washington and Moscow that they might bring him within their respective spheres of influence. He persuaded the Americans to fund the construction, on the Nile, of the Aswan High Dam, a project crucial to Egyptian economic development. He also decided, though, to buy arms from Czechoslovakia. These two decisions set off the first great Middle East crisis of the Cold War.

Already uneasy over Nasser's presence at Bandung, Dulles worried that the Czech arms deal might make Nasser "a tool of the Russians," in which case "we might have to consider a revision of our whole policy." Then Egypt extended diplomatic recognition to the People's Republic of China. Nasser had "made a bargain with the Devil with the hope of . . . establishing an empire stretching from the Persian Gulf to the Atlantic Ocean," Dulles fumed: shortly thereafter the Americans canceled financing for the Aswan Dam. But Nasser had already arranged, by then, to have the Soviet Union fund the project, leaving him free to retaliate against the United States by nationalizing the Suez Canal.[13] This in turn alarmed the British and the French, who, without consulting Washington, hatched a plot with the Israelis to have them attack the canal, thereby giving London and Paris the right to "protect" it—the real intention was to depose Nasser altogether. As Prime Minister Anthony Eden put it, "we shall never have a better pretext for intervention against him than we have now."[14] The Anglo-French-Israeli invasion took place at the end of October, 1956, just at the height of the crisis over Poland and Hungary.

Ill-conceived, badly timed, and incompetently managed, the invasion almost broke up the NATO alliance. Eisenhower was furious: at having been surprised, at the distraction from what was happening in Eastern Europe, and at the appearance, at least, of a resurgent European colonialism. "How could we possibly support Britain and France," he demanded, "if in doing so we lose the whole Arab world?"[15] The president insisted on the withdrawal of British and French forces from the canal, as well as the Israeli evacuation of the Sinai, or the United States would apply severe economic sanctions.[16] Khrushchev, by then, had already threatened to attack the invaders with nuclear missiles if they did not immediately cease military operations. The real winner, though, was Nasser, who kept the canal, humiliated the colonialists, and balanced Cold War superpowers against one another, while securing his position as the undisputed leader of Arab nationalism.

The Americans then gave him even more power through their own incompetence. Eisenhower announced, in January, 1957, that the United States would work with the states of that region to keep it free from communism. Given this implied lack of confidence in the staying power of nationalism, the "Eisenhower Doctrine" won little support. As the Central Intelligence Agency noted several months later, it was "probably believed by almost all Arabs to indicate American preoccupation with Communism to the exclusion of what they consider to be the more pressing problems of the area."[17] The United States made one final attempt to contain Arab nationalism through a hastily organized landing of Marines in Lebanon in July, 1958, following the unexpected overthrow of a pro-western government in Iraq. It too achieved little, though, and Eisenhower shortly thereafter drew the appropriate conclusion: "Since we are about to get thrown out of the [Middle East], we might as well believe in Arab nationalism."[18]

What Nasser showed, then—along with Tito, Nehru, and Zhou Enlai—was that being a Cold War superpower did not always ensure that one got one's way. There were limits to how much either Moscow or Washington could order smaller powers around, because they could always defect to the other side, or at least threaten to do so. The very compulsiveness with which the Soviet Union and the United States sought to bring such states within their orbits wound up giving those states the means of escape. Autonomy, in what might have seemed to be inhospitable circumstances, was becoming attainable. Tails were beginning to wag dogs.

III.

"Non-alignment" was not the only weapon available to small powers seeking to expand their autonomy while living in the shadow of superpowers: so too was the possibility of collapse. There was no way that staunch anti-communists like Syngman Rhee in South Korea, Chiang Kai-shek on Taiwan, or Ngo Dinh Diem in South Vietnam could plausibly threaten to defect to the other side (although Diem, desperate to hang on to power as the Americans were abandoning him in 1963, did implausibly attempt to open negotiations with the North Vietnamese).[19] Nor could such dedicated anti-capitalists as Kim Il-sung in North Korea or Ho Chi Minh in North Vietnam credibly raise the prospect of alignment with the United States. What they could do, though, was encourage fears that their regimes might fall if their re-spective superpower sponsors did not support them. The "dominos" found it useful, from time to time, to *advertise* a propensity to topple.

Korea's history after the Korean War provides a clear example. Rhee had adamantly opposed the 1953 armistice that left his country divided, and in an effort to sabotage it, had released thousands of North Korean prisoners-of-war so that they could not be sent home against their will. Washington was as outraged by this as was Pyongyang, for Rhee acted on his own. He did not succeed in scrapping the armistice, but he did signal the Eisenhower administration that being a dependent ally would not necessarily make him an obedient ally.[20] His most effective argument was that if the United States did not support him—and the repressive regime he was imposing on South Korea—that country would collapse, and the Americans would be in far worse shape on the Korean peninsula than if they had swallowed their scruples and as-sisted him.

It was a persuasive case, because there was no obvious alternative to

Rhee. The United States could "*do* all sorts of things to suggest . . . that we might very well be prepared to leave Korea," Eisenhower noted gloomily, "but the truth of the matter was, of course, that we couldn't actually leave."[21] And so Rhee got a bilateral security treaty, together with a commitment from Washington to keep American troops in South Korea for as long as they were needed to ensure that country's safety. This meant that the United States was defending an authoritarian regime, because Rhee had little patience with, or interest in, democratic procedures. South Korea was what he, not the Americans, wanted it to be, and to get his way Rhee devised a compelling form of Cold War blackmail: if you push me too hard, my government will fall, and you'll be sorry.

The Soviet Union, it is now clear, had a similar experience with Kim Il-sung in North Korea. He was allowed to build a Stalinist state, with its own cult of personality centered on himself, at just the time when Khrushchev was condemning such perversions of Marxism-Leninism elsewhere. That country became, as a result, increasingly isolated, authoritarian—and yet totally dependent on economic and military support from the rest of the communist world. It was hardly the result Khrushchev or his successors would have designed, had they had the opportunity. They did not, however, because Kim could counter each suggestion for reform with the claim that it would destabilize his government, and thereby hand victory to the South Koreans and the Americans. "[I]n the interests of our common tasks, we must sometimes overlook their stupidities," one Soviet official explained in 1973.[22] Both Washington and Moscow therefore wound up supporting Korean allies who were embarrassments to them. It was a curious outcome to the Korean War, and another reminder of the extent to which the weak, during the Cold War, managed to obtain power over the strong.

Nor were the Americans and the Russians successful in controlling their respective Chinese allies. Chiang Kai-shek had insisted on retaining several small islands just off the Chinese coast when he evacuated the mainland in 1949: they would be, he claimed, staging areas for an eventual effort to retake all of China. The Truman administration was skeptical, having made no commitment even to defend Taiwan. But when Mao began shelling the offshore islands in September, 1954—apparently as a show of force following Chinese and North Vietnamese concessions at the Geneva Conference on Indochina— Chiang insisted that the psychological effects of losing them would be so severe that his own regime on Taiwan might collapse. Eisenhower and Dulles responded as they had to Rhee: Chiang got a mutual defense treaty that bound the United States to the defense of Taiwan. But it left open the question of defending the offshore islands.

This provided an opening to Mao, who responded by taking one of the islands and building up his military forces across from the others. Convinced that their own credibility as well as Chiang's was now at risk, Eisenhower and Dulles let it be known early in 1955 that they were now prepared to defend the most important islands, Quemoy and Matsu, if necessary with nuclear weapons. Mao then moved to defuse the crisis, but two significant points had been made. One was that another ally had extracted a security commitment from the United States by advertising its weakness. The other was that Washington had relinquished the initiative to Mao, for as the Chinese leader later explained, by sticking their necks out over Quemoy and Matsu, the Americans had handed him a noose, which he could relax—or tighten—at will.[23]

Mao chose to tighten the noose again in August, 1958, in an apparent effort to deflect attention from domestic economic failures and, curiously, to protest the American military landing in Lebanon the previous month.[24] As he began shelling the offshore islands, Chiang reinforced them, and the United States found itself again threatening the use of nuclear weapons in order to defend, as an irritated Dulles had earlier put it, a "bunch of rocks."[25] But it was not just the Americans who found this crisis alarming. Mao had neglected to consult the Russians, who were thoroughly rattled when he casually suggested to them that a war with the United States might not be such a bad thing: the Chinese could lure the Americans deep into their own territory, and then Moscow could hit them "with everything you've got." The offshore islands, Mao later boasted, "are two batons that keep Eisenhower and Khrushchev dancing, scurrying this way and that. Don't you see how wonderful they are?"[26]

Khrushchev, in the end, responded to the American nuclear threats over Quemoy and Matsu with one of his own, but not until he was certain that the crisis was about to be resolved.[27] The offshore islands confrontations of 1954–55 and 1958 gave the Americans, as well as the Russians, yet another lesson in the limits of superpower authority. No one in either Washington or Moscow had instigated these events: Chiang and Mao had done that. Nor did any American or Soviet leader think the offshore islands worth a war in which nuclear weapons might be used. They were, however, unable to avoid threatening each other with just such a result, because they lacked the means of controlling their own "allies." On Taiwan and the offshore islands, as in Korea, tails had again wagged dogs.

Much the same thing happened, with far more devastating results, in yet another East Asian country the Cold War had left divided, Vietnam. After Ho Chi Minh's victory over the French in 1954, they, together with the Americans, the British, the Russians, and the Chinese Communists, had agreed at Geneva that the country should be partitioned at the 17th parallel. Ho then established a communist state in the north, while the Americans took over the search for an anticommunist alternative in the south. They finally settled, in 1955, on Ngo Dinh Diem, an exile untainted by cooperation with France whose Catholicism, they expected, would make him a reliable ally. But Diem, like Rhee, was also an authoritarian, and by the beginning of the 1960s his South Vietnamese government had become an embarrassment to the Americans—and a target for renewed insurgency from North Vietnam. Aware that Washington's credibility was on the line once again, Diem—following the examples of Rhee and Chiang—warned that his regime might collapse if the Americans failed to increase their support for it. "We still have to find the technique," Kennedy adviser

Walt Rostow commented in 1961, "for bringing our great bargaining power to bear on leaders of client states to do things they ought to do but don't want to do."[28]

In South Vietnam, though, there turned out to be limits on how far threats to collapse could go. Diem's regime had become so brutal—but at the same time so ineffective—that the Kennedy administration eventually convinced itself that he had to be removed. Accordingly, it cooperated with a group of South Vietnamese colonels who overthrew the South Vietnamese president, but then murdered him, early in November, 1963. Shocked by this unexpected outcome, and then by Kennedy's own assassination three weeks later, American officials had given little thought to what to do next. They were left with a deteriorating situation in South Vietnam whose importance their own rhetoric had elevated to one of global significance—but which they had no strategy for resolving.

The administration of Lyndon B. Johnson gradually improvised such a strategy over the next year: it obtained Congressional authorization to take whatever measures were necessary to save South Vietnam, and then—after Johnson's landslide victory over Barry Goldwater in the 1964 election—it began a major military escalation. This took the form, first, of bombing North Vietnamese port facilities and supply lines, but by the summer of 1965 it also involved the dispatch of American ground forces to South Vietnam. By the end of the year, 184,000 were in place with many more on the way.[29] "If we are driven from the field in Viet-Nam," Johnson proclaimed, "then no nation can ever again have the same confidence in . . . American protection."[30]

The very *weakness* of an ally had driven the United States—with reluctance and, on the part of the president, deep foreboding—into making an all-out commitment to its defense. By July, 1965, as his wife Lady Bird recorded, Johnson was talking in his sleep: "I don't want to get in a war and I don't see any way out of it. I've got to call up 600,000 boys, [and] make them leave their homes and families." And he knew the consequences: "If this [war] winds up bad, and we get in a land war

[in] Asia," he told her a few days later, "there's only one address they will look for. . . . Mine."[31]

Curiously, though, Soviet leaders were no happier with this development. Khrushchev had sought to improve relations with the United States in the aftermath of the Cuban missile crisis—which had itself grown out of *his* fear that an ally might collapse—and his successors, Leonid Brezhnev and Alexei Kosygin, had hoped to continue that process. Once the war in Vietnam began, though, they felt obliged to support the North Vietnamese, partly for reasons of ideological solidarity, but also because they knew that if they did not do so, the Chinese communists, who were by now hurling open polemics at them, would make the most of it. As Tito, a close observer of the situation, explained: "The Soviet Union cannot fail in its stand of solidarity with Hanoi since it would otherwise expose itself to the danger of isolating itself in Southeast Asia and [with] Communist parties elsewhere."[32]

And so this early effort to relax Cold War tensions failed—despite the fact that Washington and Moscow wanted it to succeed—because the actions of smaller powers locked the superpowers into a confrontation from which they lacked the means, or the resolve, to escape. "The situation was absurd," Soviet ambassador to the United States Anatoly Dobrynin later acknowledged: "[T]he behavior of our allies . . . systematically blocked any rational discussion of other problems that were really of key importance to both of us."[33]

IV.

THAT WAS true enough, but the frustrations of the superpowers were by no means confined to their relations with Asian and Latin American allies. The United States and the Soviet Union possessed disproportionate military and economic power within NATO and the Warsaw Pact—and yet they did not find it easy to control these alliances either.

The problems the Americans and the Russians faced in dealing with their respective German clients best illustrate the pattern.

Postwar Germany had been both strong and weak at the same time. Because it had been the strongest nation in Europe prior to 1945, neither the United States nor the Soviet Union was ready to run the risk that a reunified Germany might align with its principal adversary. The division of the country, in this sense, was imposed from without and became unavoidable once the Cold War was under way. But once their country was divided, the Germans' weakness itself became a strength. By being on the verge of collapse—and, as time went on, by simply *appearing* to be—West and East Germans could raise the specter of a former enemy falling under the control of a future enemy anytime they wanted to do so.[34]

In West Germany, the danger lay, from Washington's perspective, in the possible defeat at the polls of Chancellor Konrad Adenauer's Christian Democratic government. Adenauer had made it clear, since taking office in 1949, that he preferred the continued division of Germany to its possible reunification, since there seemed to be no way that could happen without detaching West Germany from NATO and hence from its guarantee of American protection. It was far better, he claimed, to have a prosperous, democratic portion of Germany closely tied to the United States and to the other democracies of Western Europe than to risk the uncertainties that any effort to unify Germany would surely involve. Adenauer would not reject negotiations with the Soviet Union looking toward unification—to do so would risk losing domestic support—but he would see to it that they did not succeed. He would, as one of his aides put it, "feign flexibility in order to be free to go with the West."[35]

Adenauer's chief rival, the Social Democratic leader Kurt Schumacher, argued strongly for such talks, even if the price for success turned out to be withdrawal from NATO and neutrality in the Cold War. That prospect was sufficiently alarming to the Americans that Adenauer was able to use it to obtain leverage for himself: by 1955, he had gained a virtual veto over whatever negotiating positions the

United States and his other NATO allies might put forward on the German question in general, and on Berlin in particular. Eisenhower speculated after Khrushchev's 1959 visit to the United States that he could probably "strike a bargain" with the Soviet leader, "but our allies would not accept [our] acting unilaterally. . . . [W]e could not, even though tempted to accept, give it consideration, because it would be death to Adenauer."[36]

A similar pattern developed in East Germany, although here the threatened collapse was not of a political party—for there was effectively only one—but of an entire regime. Soviet intervention had saved Ulbricht in June, 1953: paradoxically, though, that demonstration of weakness had given him strength, because the near collapse had been sufficiently frightening in Moscow that the post-Stalin (and post-Beria) Kremlin leadership felt that it had no choice but to do whatever was necessary to prop Ulbricht up. The East German leader therefore had the capacity, whenever he wanted, to blackmail his Soviet counterparts.

Ulbricht was playing this card as early as 1956. Taking advantage of growing unrest in Poland and Hungary, he warned Khrushchev that insufficient economic assistance from the Soviet Union "would have very serious consequences for us," and "would . . . facilitate the work of the enemy." The raw materials and consumer goods Ulbricht requested, which the U.S.S.R. could ill afford to provide, were nonetheless forthcoming.[37] By the fall of 1958, he was pressing Khrushchev to resolve the problem of the East German refugee flow through West Berlin, to the point of citing with approval Mao Zedong's recent shelling of Chinese offshore islands:

> Quemoy and West Berlin are not only misused as centers of provocation by those forces which currently exercise force over them, but are simultaneously developing as areas . . . unjustifiably separated from their hinterland. . . . Both positions have not only the same goals, but also the same weaknesses.

> Both are islands and have to carry all the consequences of an
> island location.[38]

Khrushchev, who was already worrying about controlling Mao, cannot
have found this analogy reassuring. Nevertheless, he issued his November, 1958, ultimatum on Berlin largely in response to Ulbricht's
urgings—perhaps also because he feared that a failure to tighten the
"noose" around Berlin might elicit contempt from the increasingly critical Chinese. What good were Khrushchev's missiles, Mao was beginning to ask, if they could not extract western concessions somewhere?[39]

The same thought had occurred to Ulbricht, who found Khrushchev's subsequent unwillingness to enforce his own demand for a
Berlin settlement exasperating: "[Y]ou only talk about a peace treaty,"
he told the Kremlin leader bluntly in November, 1960, "but [you]
don't do anything about it."[40] Ulbricht had by then begun doing some
things himself: he protested Anglo-American-French policies in West
Berlin without consulting Moscow; he unilaterally modified procedures for crossing into East Berlin; and in January, 1961, he sent an official delegation to China—the Russians found out about it only when
the East Germans stopped over at the Moscow airport. Whether deliberately or not, he also managed to *increase* the refugee flow in June
by publicly acknowledging for the first time the possibility of building
a wall—even though he insisted that no one had any intention of doing so. "[O]ur friends . . . sometimes exercise impatience and a somewhat one-sided approach," the Soviet ambassador in East Berlin
acknowledged shortly before this happened, "not always studying the
interests of the entire socialist camp or the international situation at
the given moment."[41]

Khrushchev concluded, as a result, that he had little choice but to
confront Kennedy with a new Berlin ultimatum at the Vienna summit. And after Kennedy made it clear that he, like Eisenhower, was
prepared to defend West Berlin, even at the risk of nuclear war,
Khrushchev became convinced that the only way out was to allow Ul-

bricht to do what the East German leader had promised not to do: to wall East Germany off from the capitalist enclave in its midst. Khrushchev's hope had been to detach West Berlin from West Germany, not East Germany from West Berlin. Now, though, there were no options left: the wall dramatized the extent to which the Soviet Union had chained itself to a weak ally—who was able to use that weakness to get its way.

What allowed German weakness to become German strength was, of course, the preoccupation with credibility that dominated thinking in Washington and Moscow. Having installed their respective clients and then attached their own reputations to them, neither American nor Soviet leaders found it easy to disengage when those clients began pursuing their own priorities. The United States and the Soviet Union therefore fell into the habit of letting their German allies determine their German interests, and hence their German policies.

V.

ADENAUER AND ULBRICHT were not the most difficult allies, though: that distinction belonged to Charles de Gaulle and Mao Zedong. France and China had both benefited from their relationships with the superpowers. The United States financed French reconstruction after the war, ensured French security through NATO, and quietly supported the development of a French nuclear weapons capability.[42] The Soviet Union had provided the ideological inspiration for China's revolution, and after Stalin's death, it generously sent economic and military aid as well as technical assistance for Mao's efforts, beginning in 1955, to build a Chinese atomic bomb.[43] And yet, during the late 1950s and early 1960s, de Gaulle and Mao set out to dismantle the alliances that had nurtured their states and embraced their regimes. Their goal was nothing less than to break up the bipolar Cold War international system.

The Fourth French Republic, formed after France's defeat and occupation by the Germans in World War II, had been an economic success but a political basket case. Unstable coalitions shuffled in and out
of office with such depressing frequency that constitutional reform became unavoidable: only de Gaulle, the wartime leader of the Free
French, had the authority and the prestige to bring it about. The new
Fifth Republic, established in 1958, gave de Gaulle the power he
needed—with the blessing of the Americans, who hoped for firmer
and more predictable leadership in Paris. "France presents a twelve year
history of almost unbroken moral, political, and military deteriora-
tion," Eisenhower commented at the time. The record "almost demanded the presence of a 'strong man'—in the person of de Gaulle."[44]

The new French president certainly brought firmness, but not pre-
dictability. There were few objections in Washington as de Gaulle
skillfully liquidated France's long but futile effort to retain its last large
colony, Algeria. The war there, the Americans believed, was draining
French resources, fueling Arab nationalism, and could never be won.
That was all Washington found to approve of, though, because de
Gaulle soon made it clear that his next objective would be to thwart
United States policy in Europe wherever he could. The fact that he did
this while expecting the continued protection of the NATO alliance
only added to the Americans' exasperation; but exasperation, it seemed,
was precisely what de Gaulle had intended. It was as if he was determined to show the United States that, in an age of muscle-bound
superpowers, there was room for France not only to assert its autonomy, but to flaunt it. By the middle of 1959, Eisenhower was fuming
over de Gaulle's "Messiah complex": he was a "cross between Napoleon
and Joan of Arc."[45]

The list of de Gaulle's offenses was long. He refused to coordinate
France's nuclear strategy—the French tested their first atomic bomb in
1960—with that of the United States and Great Britain: rather, the
small French *force de frappe* would be designed for "defense in all directions," with the apparent intent of unsettling both adversaries and al-

lies.[46] He vetoed British membership in the European Economic Community, thereby humiliating a close American ally and setting back the movement toward European integration by at least a decade. He tried to persuade the aging Adenauer to loosen West Germany's ties to NATO by arguing that the Americans could not be relied upon to resist Soviet pressure on Berlin. He then proclaimed a vision of Europe that would extend "from the Atlantic to the Urals": where that would leave the Americans—or for that matter the West Germans—was left uncomfortably unclear. De Gaulle extended diplomatic recognition to Mao Zedong's China in 1964, while vociferously criticizing American escalation in Vietnam. And in 1966, he withdrew France altogether from military cooperation with the NATO alliance, forcing the relocation of NATO headquarters from Paris to Brussels, as well as the withdrawal of American troops from the country they had helped liberate in World War II. President Johnson ordered his secretary of state, Dean Rusk, to ask de Gaulle: "Do you want us to move American cemeteries out of France as well?"[47]

Washington's response to these provocations was on all counts ineffective. De Gaulle rebuffed repeated efforts at reconciliation, while remaining impervious to pressure: he had shrewdly calculated that he could detach France from NATO, but that the United States and its other allies could not detach themselves from the need to defend France. He was the ultimate free rider, a "highly egocentric" leader "with touches indeed of megalomania," as one American diplomat put it, who welcomed confrontation with the United States as a way to regain France's identity as a great power.[48] In the end, Johnson concluded, there was nothing the United States could do: it would just have to put up with de Gaulle. "We've really got no control over their foreign policy," Senator Richard Russell told the president in 1964. "That's right," Johnson acknowledged, "none whatever."[49]

The Americans' difficulties in dealing with de Gaulle, however, paled in comparison to those Khrushchev encountered in trying to manage Mao Zedong. The sources of Sino-Soviet tension lay, first, in the long history of hostility between Russia and China, which commitment to a common ideology had only partially overcome: Khrushchev and Mao had all the instincts and prejudices of nationalists, however much they might be communists. Stalin's legacy also posed problems. Mao had defended the dead dictator when Khrushchev attacked him in 1956, but the Chinese leader also cultivated—and frequently displayed—his memory of each of Stalin's slights, affronts, or insults. It was as if Stalin had become a tool for Mao, to be used when necessary to bolster his own authority, but also to be rejected when required to invoke the dangers of Soviet hegemony. At the same time, Mao treated Khrushchev as a superficial upstart, neglecting no opportunity to confound him with petty humiliations, cryptic pronouncements, and veiled provocations. Khrushchev could "never be sure what Mao meant. . . . I believed in him and he was playing with me."[50]

Mao did so, at least in part, because picking fights abroad—whether with adversaries or allies—was a way to maintain unity at home, a major priority as he launched the Great Leap Forward.[51] That had been one of the reasons for the second offshore island crisis, which had brought China to the brink of war with the United States during the summer of 1958. But Mao had already by then picked a separate fight with the Soviet Union. The Russians had made the mistake of proposing the construction of a long-wave radio station on the China coast, together with the establishment of a joint Sino-Soviet submarine flotilla. Mao responded furiously. "You never trust the Chinese!" he complained to the Soviet ambassador. Moscow might as well be demanding joint ownership of "our army, navy, air force, industry, agriculture, culture, education. . . . With a few atomic bombs, you think you are in a position to control us."[52]

When Khrushchev hastened to Beijing to try to smooth things over, Mao accused him of having lost his revolutionary edge. "[W]e obviously have the advantage over our enemies," Mao told him, having already put the imperfectly aquatic Khrushchev at a disadvantage by receiving him in a swimming pool. "All you have to do is provoke the Americans into military action, and I'll give you as many divisions as you need to crush them." Struggling to remain afloat, Khrushchev tried to explain "that one or two missiles could turn all the divisions in China to dust." But Mao "wouldn't even listen to my arguments and obviously regarded me as a coward."[53]

Defying the logic of balancing power within the international system, Mao sought a different kind of equilibrium: a world filled with danger, whether from the United States or the Soviet Union or both, could minimize the risk that rivals within China might challenge his rule.[54] The strategy succeeded brilliantly. Despite a degree of mismanagement unparalleled in modern history—if such a euphemism can characterize policies that caused so many of his countrymen to starve to death during the Great Leap Forward—Mao survived as China's "great helmsman." What did not survive was the Sino-Soviet alliance, which had, as far as Mao was concerned, outlived its usefulness. Khrushchev, fearing the implications, tried desperately to reconstitute it right up to the moment he was deposed in 1964, despite repeated insults, rebuffs, and even instances of deliberate sabotage from Mao.[55] But in the end even he had to admit—revealingly—that "it was getting harder and harder to view China through the eager and innocent eyes of a child."[56]

How was it, then, that de Gaulle and Mao, the leaders of medium powers, were able to treat the superpowers in this way? Why were the traditional forms of power itself—military strength, economic capacity, geographical reach—so useless in this situation? Part of the answer has to do with the new kind of power balancing that was taking place here: de Gaulle's strategy of "defense in all directions" was not that different from Mao's of giving offense in all directions. Both saw in the defiance of external authority a way to enhance their own internal legitimacy. Both sought to rebuild national self-esteem: that required, they believed, the thumbing of noses, even the biting of hands that had previously provided food and other forms of sustenance.

Part of the answer as well, though, involved the disappearance of fear. By the 1960s France and China had become sufficiently strong within the framework of their respective alliances that they no longer suffered from the insecurities that had led them to seek such alliances in the first place. In both the North Atlantic Treaty of 1949 and the Sino-Soviet Treaty of 1950 superpowers had sought to reassure smaller powers: by this standard, at least, the behavior of de Gaulle and Mao a decade later meant that the alliances had achieved their purposes. Distinctive personalities played a role in all of this as well: not every leader would have used reassurance as a foundation for arrogance to the extent that they did. The French and Chinese leaders were very much alike in understanding the uses of *chutzpa,* a word with no precise equivalents in either of their languages. It might well be defined as doing high-wire acrobatics without a net. It required—de Gaulle and Mao were masters of this art—not looking down.[57]

VI.

EVENTUALLY, though, they did look down, and what they saw shook them badly. In July, 1967, Zhongnanhai, Mao's leadership compound in central Beijing, came under siege from thousands of youthful Red Guards. Several of his closest associates were publicly humiliated, even assaulted, and Mao himself had to flee from the city of Wuhan, where he had gone to try to quell growing unrest. "They just don't listen to me," he complained incredulously. "They ignored me."[58] De Gaulle had a similar experience in May, 1968, when, fearing that growing street protests by university students might overthrow his government, he abruptly flew from Paris to a French military base in West Germany. France, he admitted, was suffering from "total paralysis." He was "not in charge of anything anymore."[59]

Both Mao and de Gaulle recovered their authority, but never again their high-wire *chutzpa.* Nor were they alone in feeling beleaguered.

During that same summer of 1968, Brezhnev and his advisers were preparing the invasion of a fraternal socialist state, Czechoslovakia, for the purpose of reversing reforms they themselves had encouraged: as in East Germany in 1953 as well as Poland and Hungary in 1956, these had gone beyond what Moscow had intended, with results that threatened to destabilize Eastern Europe, possibly even the U.S.S.R. itself. "What we are talking about," Ukrainian party chief Petr Shelest warned, "is the fate of socialism in one of the socialist countries, as well as the fate of socialism in the socialist camp." Ulbricht, an experienced hand in assessing the possibility of collapse, was even more emphatic: "If Czechoslovakia continues to follow [this] line, all of us here will run a serious risk which may well lead to our downfall."[60]

West German leaders could take little comfort in Ulbricht's discomfort, though, because they were also under siege. Their universities had been in an uproar for over a year, with the biggest disruptions—directed chiefly against United States involvement in Vietnam—centered in the city so long defended by the American military, West Berlin. The Free University, established with Washington's support in the midst of the 1948 Berlin blockade, had become a beehive of revolutionary activity, while America House, created to encourage cultural contacts with the United States, was now the regular target of hostile demonstrations, often physical attacks. The United States and its West European allies had become "imperialists," student leader Rudi Dutschke announced. It was necessary now for German students to join with Vietnamese villagers—in the spirit of Mao Zedong and Fidel Castro—to "revolutionize the masses."[61]

In the United States that summer, opposition to the Vietnam War had grown so intense that all sources of authority—governmental, military, corporate, educational—were under siege. There were, by then, some 550,000 American troops fighting the war. Most were draftees, and more would soon be needed. Young Americans had both principled and personal reasons for protesting the war: it was, many of them believed, unjust and unwinnable, but they were still expected to fight it.

Student deferments offered some protection, but only at the price of watching the less fortunate fill the resulting vacancies. Meanwhile, race riots were breaking out at home, and assassinations had taken the lives of Martin Luther King, Jr., and Robert F. Kennedy—two leaders especially admired by the young.

President Johnson, having decided not to seek re-election, was virtually a prisoner inside his own White House, surrounded by noisy demonstrators day and night, unable to make public appearances outside of carefully protected military bases. The Democratic Party convention in August turned into a riot, with the Chicago police battling thousands of angry, disillusioned, and—by then—thoroughly cynical young people who could hardly have been less moved by the ill-conceived campaign slogan of Johnson's hand-picked nominee Hubert Humphrey: "the politics of joy."[62]

Richard M. Nixon, who defeated Humphrey for the presidency that fall, inherited a world in which the traditional instruments of state power seemed to be disappearing. It was as if the United States had reached the point, Nixon's national security adviser Henry Kissinger later recalled, "when the seemingly limitless possibilities of youth suddenly narrow, and one must come to grips with the fact that not every option is open any longer."[63] The president put it more bluntly. "We live in an age of anarchy," he told the nation on April 30, 1970:

> We see mindless attacks on all the great institutions which have been created by free civilizations in the last 500 years. Even here in the United States, great universities are being systematically destroyed. . . . If, when the chips are down, the United States of America acts like a pitiful, helpless giant, the forces of totalitarianism and anarchy will threaten free nations and free institutions throughout the world.[64]

Nixon used that speech to announce an American and South Vietnamese invasion of Cambodia, one of several measures he had undertaken to try to break the Vietnam military stalemate. But this expansion of the war set off new waves of domestic protest and, for the first time as a result, the loss of life: on May 4th, Ohio National Guardsmen shot four students dead at Kent State University. The nation itself, along with its universities, seemed about to come apart.

Five nights later, unable to sleep, the president of the United States, accompanied only by his valet and a driver, slipped out of the White House to try to reason with students maintaining a vigil in front of the Lincoln Memorial. Nixon was nervous to the point of incoherence, rambling on about Churchill, appeasement, surfing, football, his own environmental policies, and the advantages of traveling while young. The students, surprised by this unexpected nocturnal apparition, were nonetheless polite, self-confident, and focused: "I hope you understand," one of them told the most "powerful" man in the world, "that we are willing to die for what we believe in."[65]

So what was going on here? How was it that *kids* managed to treat the leaders of most of the major Cold War powers as if they had been *parents:* that is, by reducing them to sputtering ineffectiveness, pointless fury, frequent panic, and the unsettling realization that their authority was no longer what it once had been? How did the young—with so little coordination among themselves—accumulate such strength at the expense of the old?

One explanation is simply that there were more young people than ever before. The post–World War II "baby boom" was an international phenomenon that stretched well beyond the United States. As birth rates rose, mortality rates declined—partly because peace had returned, but also because health care had improved.[66] By the late 1960s and the early 1970s, the postwar generation was in its late teens and early twenties: old enough to make trouble if it wanted to do so.

Paradoxically, governments had given it means and motives. States had long considered education a worthy end in itself, but the Cold War placed a particular premium on *higher* education: it was necessary to stay competitive in a geopolitical contest that relied increasingly on advanced science and technology. Enrollments in American colleges and universities tripled between 1955 and 1970, with much of the expansion financed by the federal government. In the Soviet Union the number of students grew by a factor of two and a half. In France it quadrupled, and even China saw university enrollments more than double by 1965, before plummeting in the wake of Mao's Cultural Revolution, which wrecked Chinese education for well over a decade.[67]

What governments failed to foresee was that more young people plus more education, when combined with a stalemated Cold War, could be a prescription for insurrection. Learning does not easily compartmentalize: how do you prepare students to think for purposes approved by the state—or by their parents—without also equipping them to think for themselves? Youths throughout history had often wished to question their elders' values, but now with university educations their elders had handed them the training to do so. The result was discontent with the world as it was, whether that meant the nuclear arms race, social and economic injustice, the war in Vietnam, repression in Eastern Europe, or even the belief that universities themselves had become the tools of an old order that had to be overthrown. This was something never before seen: a revolution transcending nationality, directed against establishments whatever their ideology.

Only in China did it happen by design: Mao had launched the Cultural Revolution, in the summer of 1966, as yet another of his periodic maneuvers to eliminate potential rivals. "I love great upheavals," he chuckled at the time.[68] This time, though, the upheaval was domestic rather than international—and having set it in motion, Mao had great difficulty shutting it down. With his encouragement, Red Guards attacked the very institutions of government, party, and education that he had put in place: his purpose, Mao claimed, was to prevent bureaucratic ossification, and the consequent loss of revolutionary zeal. But somewhere between 400,000 and a million people died in the resulting violence, his government for the most part ceased to function, and China conveyed the appearance, to the outside world, of a state that had gone completely mad.[69] It was as if, in an effort to relieve stiff joints, Mao had prescribed the most potent chemotherapy available: the cure quickly became worse than the disease.

From as early as 1967, then, he was seeking to regain control of the movement he had unleashed. The nation must "resolutely overcome lack of discipline, or even, in many places, anarchy," he insisted early in 1968. By the end of 1969, he had mostly restored order, but only through the drastic expedient of sending several million former Red Guards—the educated elite of China—to the countryside. It was "absolutely necessary," the *People's Daily* explained, for "young people to ... be re-educated by workers, peasants, and soldiers under the guidance of the correct line [so that] *their* old thinking may be reformed thoroughly."[70]

It is all the more curious, then, that youthful radicals throughout Western Europe and the United States—themselves safe from re-education at the hands of workers, peasants, and soldiers—regarded Mao as a hero, a distinction he shared with Fidel Castro and his fellow revolutionary Che Guevara, who had bungled an attempt to start a Cuba-like insurgency in central Africa and then gotten himself captured and killed, in Bolivia in 1967, by the Central Intelligence Agency.[71] Competence, however, was not the quality admired here. Revolutionary romanticism was, and for that, Mao, Fidel, and Che provided potent symbols.

That helps to explain why the revolutionaries of 1967–68 accomplished so little. To be sure, they shook establishments everywhere. But, in the end, they overthrew none of them: instead they convinced those establishments that they had better cooperate to ward off such challenges in the future. Among those persuaded were the governments of the United States, the Soviet Union, West Germany, East Germany—and also that of the ever-flexible Mao Zedong.

VII.

IN MARCH, 1969, fighting broke out between Soviet and Chinese troops along the Ussuri River, the border their nations shared in Northeast Asia. Soon it spread to the Amur River, and to the Xinjiang-Kazakhstan boundary. By August, there were rumors of all-out war between the world's most powerful *communist* states, possibly involving the use of nuclear weapons. Mao ordered that tunnels be dug and supplies stored in preparation for a Soviet attack. And then he called in his personal physician, Li Zhisui, and presented him with a problem.

"Think about this. . . . We have the Soviet Union to the north and the west, India to the south, and Japan to the east. If all our enemies were to unite, attacking us from the north, south, east, and west, what do you think we should do?" Li confessed that he did not know. "Think again," Mao told him. "Beyond Japan is the United States. Didn't our ancestors counsel negotiating with faraway countries while fighting with those that are near?" Li was shocked, recalling the long history of Sino-American hostility: "How could we negotiate with the United States?" Mao replied:

> The United States and the Soviet Union are different. . . .
> America's new president, Richard Nixon, is a longtime right-
> ist, a leader of the anti-communists there. I like to deal with
> rightists. They say what they really think—not like the left-
> ists, who say one thing and mean another.[72]

One wonders what Mao's youthful admirers in the United States and Europe would have made of this conversation, had they known about it. But this was not the only surprising conversation that took place in the summer of 1969.

Another occurred in Washington, where a mid-level Soviet embassy official posed a question of his own, over lunch, to a State Department counterpart: what might the American response be if the U.S.S.R. were to attack Chinese nuclear facilities? The query could only have been made on instructions from Moscow, and its recipient, having no answer, could only pass it up the line to his superiors, who passed it on to the White House—where it had already been answered. Several days earlier, President Nixon had startled his Cabinet by announcing that the United States could not let China be "smashed" in a Sino-Soviet war. "It was a major event in American foreign policy," Kissinger later commented, "when a President declared that we had a strategic interest in the survival of a major Communist country, long an enemy, and with which we had no contact."[73]

It is unlikely that Mao had highly placed spies in Washington that summer, or that Nixon had them in Beijing: there was as yet little communication between them. What they did have, however, was a convergence of several interests. One, obviously, was concern about the Soviet Union, which appeared to both of them to be increasingly threatening. Its August, 1968, invasion of Czechoslovakia seemed to have been a ruthlessly successful operation, an impression reinforced in November when Brezhnev claimed the right to violate the sovereignty of *any* country in which an effort was under way to replace Marxism-Leninism with capitalism: "[T]his is no longer merely a problem for that country's people, but a common problem, the concern of all socialist countries."[74] Meanwhile, the U.S.S.R. had at last achieved strategic parity with the United States: if there was to be a "missile gap" now, the Americans were likely to find themselves at the short end of it. Finally, there was Moscow's saber-rattling against China, which suggested that the Brezhnev Doctrine, together with Soviet nuclear capabilities, might actually be put to use.

Another shared Sino-American interest had to do with the war in Vietnam. Nixon wanted out of it, but on terms that would not humiliate the United States: that would be the point of his "pitiful, helpless giant" speech the following spring. North Vietnam could not be expected to help, but China—until now a major supplier of military and economic assistance to Hanoi—had a different perspective. It could hardly wish to see fighting drag on along its southern border while facing the prospect of a larger and more dangerous conflict with the Soviet Union. Early in 1970 Kissinger pointedly reminded Hanoi's chief negotiator, Le Duc Tho, that North Vietnam might not continue to enjoy "the undivided support of countries which now support it."[75] The Chinese had already signaled their diminished enthusiasm for the war, and with the passage of time the messages became more direct. "As our broom is too short to sweep the Americans out of Taiwan," Mao told the North Vietnamese late in 1971, "so yours is too short to do the same in South Vietnam."[76]

Nixon and Mao had one other interest in common at the time: it was to restore order in their respective countries. Zhou Enlai, Mao's foreign minister, hinted at this when Kissinger made his first—and highly secret—visit to Beijing in July, 1971. Zhou went out of his way to assure Kissinger that the Cultural Revolution was over. He also promised that China would try to help Nixon improve his own position at home: no other western leader, and certainly no other American politician, would be received in Beijing prior to the president himself.[77] Nixon did come to China in February, 1972, and immediately established a meeting of minds, not only with Zhou, but also with Mao Zedong.

"I voted for you," Mao joked, "when your country was in havoc, during your last electoral campaign. . . . I am comparatively happy when these people on the right come to power." "[T]hose on the right," Nixon acknowledged, "can do what those on the left talk about." When Kissinger suggested that those on the left might also oppose Nixon's visit, Mao agreed: "Exactly that. . . . In our country also there is a reactionary group which is opposed to our contact with you." The following exchange then took place:

MAO: I think that, generally speaking, people like me sound a
lot of big cannons. That is, things like "the whole world
should unite and defeat imperialism, revisionism, and all
reactionaries . . ."

NIXON: Like me. . . .

MAO: But perhaps you as an individual may not be among
those to be overthrown. . . . [Kissinger] is also among
those not to be overthrown personally. And if all of you are
overthrown we wouldn't have any more friends left.

"History has brought us together," Nixon said, in bidding Mao
farewell. "The question is whether we, with different philosophies, but
both with feet on the ground, and having come from the people, can
make a breakthrough that will serve not just China and America, but
the whole world in the years ahead." "Your book," Mao responded, re-
ferring to Nixon's pre-presidential memoir *Six Crises*, "is not a bad
book."[78]

VIII.

IT WAS a remarkable moment—but what would Moscow make of it?
Nixon and Mao had certainly intended to unsettle the Russians. They
had little sense, however, of just how unsettled the Kremlin leadership
already was, because appearances to the contrary notwithstanding, it
too was deeply worried about maintaining its authority in a world in
which traditional forms of power seemed no longer to carry the weight
they once had. Its traumatic experience had been the one that seemed
to suggest such brutal self-confidence to everyone else: Czechoslovakia. Brezhnev had ordered the invasion out of a sense of vulnerability—the fear that the "Prague spring" reforms could spread—but the
intervention itself had appeared, from the outside at least, to have

solved the problem: why else would Brezhnev have turned it into a doctrine that was meant to apply elsewhere?

But the invasion had *not* gone well. Red Army officers almost lost control of their troops when they were jeered rather than welcomed—as they had been told they would be—in the streets of Prague. It had taken longer than expected to find Czechs who were willing to take power under Soviet occupation. The invasion sparked protests from the Yugoslavs, the Romanians, and the Chinese, as well as from communist and other left-wing parties in Western Europe that normally deferred to Moscow's decisions. There had even been a small demonstration in front of Lenin's tomb in Red Square, an unheard-of event confirming what Kremlin leaders had long suspected: that much greater discontent lay beneath the surface inside the Soviet Union itself.[79]

The Brezhnev Doctrine, then, was a brave front: Soviet leaders were well aware of the price they would pay if they ever had to put it into effect. Their chief priority during the 1970s was to ensure that they would not have to, and that required improving relations with the United States and its NATO allies. The reasons had to do with the failures of Marxism-Leninism to meet the expectations held out for it: states like Poland, Hungary, and East Germany now faced a stagnant, even declining, standard of living—all the more depressing when contrasted with the prosperity of West Germany and the rest of Western Europe. Military intervention could never solve that problem; indeed it would probably worsen it by provoking western economic sanctions. It made sense, then, to seek détente with the United States, for only that could ensure the continued stability of the Soviet sphere of influence in Eastern Europe.

The West Germans had already paved the way by suggesting that if Germany could not be unified, then perhaps East Germany, Eastern Europe, and even the Soviet Union itself could in time be changed. A carefully controlled flow of people, goods, and ideas across Cold War boundaries might lower tensions, expand relationships, and over the long term moderate the authoritarian character of communist regimes. The primary goal would be geopolitical stability, but *Ostpolitik*, as the policy came to be known, could also provide social stability by reducing the frustrations that were sure to arise within both Germanys as it became clear that they were to remain divided. Willy Brandt, *Ostpolitik*'s chief architect, became West German chancellor in 1969, by which time there was yet another reason to pursue this scheme: it could undercut the position of protesters, not just in his country but elsewhere in Europe, who had come to regard a frozen Cold War as the most oppressive of all the "establishments" they confronted.[80]

Nixon and Kissinger were initially wary of *Ostpolitik*, probably because they had not thought of it first. But they quickly came to see how it could fit within a wider strategy: economic necessity could combine with the opening to China to push the Soviet Union into negotiations with the United States on a range of issues—limiting strategic arms, negotiating an end to the Vietnam War, increasing East-West trade—that would at the same time defuse the domestic critics who had come so close, in the last years of Johnson's presidency and the first years of Nixon's, to paralyzing American foreign policy. The conditions were right, in short, for a new strategy of containment. This one, however, would be *jointly* set in motion by the major Cold War adversaries themselves. They would aim it at the threat from youthful rebels within their own societies whose actions—rather in the way the danger from nuclear weapons had also done—had put them all in the same boat.

President Nixon had come into office in January, 1969, determined to extricate the United States from the Vietnam War, to regain the initiative in the Cold War, and to restore the authority of government at home. As the November, 1972, election campaign drew to a close, he could credibly claim to have achieved the first two objectives, and to be well on the way toward accomplishing the third. A peace settlement with North Vietnam was, as Kissinger, put it, "at hand." A slow but steady withdrawal of American forces from South Vietnam, together with the elimination of the military draft, had taken the steam out of domestic anti-war protests. And with his "opening" to China, Nixon had placed the United States in the enviable position of being able to play off its Cold War adversaries against one another. He had, earlier that year, become the first American president to visit both Beijing and Moscow. He could exert "leverage"—always a good thing to have in international relations—by "tilting" as needed toward the Soviet Union or China, who were by then so hostile to one another that they competed for Washington's favor. It was a performance worthy of Metternich, Castlereagh, and Bismarck, the great grand strategists that Kissinger, in his role as a historian, had written about, and had so admired.

Vindication came on election day, November 7th, when Nixon annihilated his Democratic opponent, George McGovern, by a 61 to 37 percent majority in the popular vote. The electoral vote margin was even more impressive: 520–17, with McGovern carrying only Massachusetts and the District of Columbia. It was not the result one might have expected two and a half years earlier, when a haunted Nixon had warned of a helpless United States. As Kissinger wrote his boss, flatteringly, but not inaccurately, it had been quite an achievement to have taken "a divided nation, mired in war, losing its confidence, wracked by intellectuals without conviction, and [given] it a new purpose."[81] Power, or so it seemed, was reasserting itself.

But the nation would soon see Nixon haunted again, this time irreversibly, not by Vietnamese insurgents or radical students but by the *legal* consequences of a petty burglary that would drive him from office. The rule of law, within the United States at least, outweighed the accomplishments of grand strategy. And Watergate was just the tip of an iceberg, for over the next two decades the course of the Cold War itself would be driven by a force that went beyond state power: the recovery, within an international system that had long seemed hostile to it, of a *common* sense of equity. Morality itself, in the evolving Alice-in-Wonderland-like Cold War game, was becoming a mallet.

CHAPTER FIVE

THE RECOVERY OF EQUITY

For a man who wants to make a profession of good in all regards must come to ruin among so many who are not good. Hence it is necessary to a prince, if he wants to maintain himself, to learn to be able not to be good, and to use this and not use it according to necessity.

—Niccolò Machiavelli[1]

To the Soviet leadership such a precipitous collapse . . . came as an unpleasant surprise. . . . [T]here was perplexity in the minds of the Kremlin leaders, who were at a loss to understand the mechanics of how a powerful president could be forced into resignation by public pressure and an intricate judicial procedure based on the American Constitution—all because of what they saw as a minor breach of conduct. Soviet history knew no parallel.

—Anatoly Dobrynin[2]

THE WATERGATE CRISIS surprised Nixon, as well as the Soviet ambassador and the Kremlin leadership. How could the most powerful man in the world be brought down by what his own press spokesman described as a "third-rate burglary," detected only because the bungling thieves had taped a door lock horizontally instead of vertically, so that the end of the tape was visible to a graveyard shift security guard? The discovery of a break-in at the Democratic National Committee head-quarters in the Watergate building in Washington shortly after 1:00 AM on June 17, 1972, set in motion a series of events that would force the first resignation of an American president. The disproportion between the offense and its consequences left Nixon incredulous: "[A]ll the terrible battering we have taken," he commiserated with himself shortly before leaving office, "is really pygmy-sized when compared to what we have done, and what we can do in the future not only for peace in the world but, indirectly, to effect the well-being of people everywhere."[3] Perhaps so, but what Watergate also revealed was that Americans placed the rule of law above the wielding of power, however praiseworthy the purposes for which power was being used. Ends did not always justify means. Might alone did not make right.

"Well, when the president does it, that means it is not illegal," Nixon would later explain, in a lame attempt to justify the wiretaps and break-ins he had authorized in an effort to plug leaks within his administration regarding the conduct of the Vietnam War. "If the president, for example, approves something because of . . . national security, or in this case because of a threat to internal peace and order of significant magnitude, then the president's decision . . . enables those who carry it out to [do so] without violating a law."[4] The claim was not a new one. Every chief executive since Franklin D. Roosevelt had sanctioned acts of questionable legality in the interests of national security, and Abraham Lincoln had done so more flagrantly than any of them in order to preserve national unity. Nixon, however, made several mistakes that were distinctly his own. The first was to exaggerate the problem confronting him: the leaking of *The Pentagon Papers* to the *New York Times* was not a threat comparable to secession in 1861, or to the prospect of subversion during World War II and the early Cold War. Nixon's second mistake was to employ such clumsy agents that they got themselves caught. And his third mistake—the one that ended his presidency—was to lie about what he had done in a futile attempt to cover it up.[5]

Watergate might have remained only an episode in the domestic history of the United States except for one thing: distinctions between might and right were also beginning to affect the behavior of the Cold War superpowers. The last years of the Nixon administration marked the first point at which the United States and the Soviet Union encountered constraints that did not just come from the nuclear stalemate, or from the failure of ideologies to deliver what they had promised, or from challenges mounted by the deceptively "weak" against the apparently "strong." They came as well now from a growing insistence that the rule of law—or at least basic standards of human decency—should govern the actions of states, as well as those of the individuals who resided within them.

I.

THERE HAD long been hope that force alone would not always shape relations among nations. "The greatest problem for the human species," the philosopher Immanuel Kant wrote, as early as 1784, "is that of attaining a civil society which can administer universal justice."[6] Woodrow Wilson intended that the League of Nations impose upon states some of the same legal constraints that states—at least the more progressive ones—imposed upon their own citizens. The founders of the United Nations designed it in such a way as to repair the League's many deficiencies while preserving its purpose: the new organization's charter committed it "to the equal rights of men and women and nations large and small," and to the establishment of conditions "under which justice and respect for the obligations arising from treaties and other sources of international law can be maintained."[7] The order that came from balancing power within the international system was no longer to be an end in itself: the priority henceforth would be to secure agreement, among the states that made up that system, upon some externally derived standard of justice.

It is difficult today to evoke the optimism that existed, at the time of its founding, that the United Nations might actually accomplish this task: such is the disrepute into which the organization has fallen in the eyes of its many critics. In 1946, though, the Truman administration trusted the United Nations sufficiently that it proposed turning over its atomic weapons and the means of producing them—admittedly under conditions it would have specified—to the new international body. Four years later, the United States took the North Korean invasion of South Korea to the United Nations instantly, and for the next three years fought the war that followed under its flag. Truman's own commitment to global governance was deep and emotional: throughout his adult life he carried in his wallet the passage from Alfred Tennyson's poem *Locksley Hall* which looked forward to "the Parliament of Man, the Federation of the World."[8]

But the harsh realities of the Cold War quickly ensured that Tennyson's dream—and Truman's—remained only that. Although the United States and the Soviet Union were founding members of the United Nations, they each reserved the right of veto within the Security Council, the body charged with enforcing its resolutions. Great Britain, France, and China (still under Chiang Kai-shek's Nationalists) received the same privilege. This meant that the United Nations could act only when its most powerful members agreed on the action, an arrangement that obscured the distinction between might and right. And the veto-empowered members of the Council were unlikely to reach such agreements because they differed so widely on how to define "justice." For the Americans, that term meant political democracy, market capitalism, and—in principle if not always in practice—respect for the rights of individuals. For the British and the French, still running colonial empires, it meant something short of that; for the Chinese Nationalists, facing the prospect that the Chinese Communists might eject them from power, it meant even less. And for Stalin's Soviet Union, "justice" meant the unquestioning acceptance of authoritarian politics, command economies, and the right of the proletariat to advance, by whatever means the dictatorship that guided it chose to employ, toward a worldwide "classless" society.

It was hardly surprising, then, that the United Nations functioned more as a debating society than as an organization capable of defining principles and holding states accountable to them. As George Kennan complained early in 1948, positions taken there resembled "a contest of *tableaux morts:* there is a long period of preparation in relative obscurity; then the curtain is lifted; the lights go on for a brief moment; the posture of the group is recorded for posterity by the photography of voting; and whoever appears in the most graceful and impressive position has won." If the great powers could agree to rely on it for that purpose, Kennan added, this "parliamentary shadow-boxing . . . would indeed be a refined and superior manner of settling international differences."[9] But that was not to be. The general view in Washington—certainly Kennan's—was that, as the Joint Chiefs of Staff had put it, "faith in the ability of the United Nations as presently constituted to protect, now or hereafter, the security of the United States would mean only that the faithful have lost sight of the vital security interest of the United States."[10]

The United Nations General Assembly did manage to pass, in December of 1948, a "Universal Declaration of Human Rights." But it did so without the support of the Soviet Union and its allies as well as Saudi Arabia and South Africa—all of whom abstained—and without providing any enforcement mechanisms.[11] Far more deeply entrenched in the organization's charter and in its practices was the principle of non-intervention in the internal affairs of sovereign states—even when the most powerful of these states violated that principle. There would be, thus, no United Nations condemnation when the Soviet Union used military force to suppress dissent in East Germany in 1953, Hungary in 1956, and Czechoslovakia in 1968, or when the United States employed covert action to overthrow the governments of Iran in 1953, Guatemala in 1954, and attempted to do so in Cuba in 1961 and in Chile a decade later. Nor did the United Nations protest the human costs involved when Stalin launched his postwar purges inside the Soviet Union and Eastern Europe, or when the United States aligned itself with authoritarian regimes to keep communists from coming to power in the "third world," or when Mao Zedong allowed so many millions of Chinese to starve as a result of his Great Leap Forward.

What all of this meant, then, was that if constraints on power for the purposes of securing justice were to arise at all, they would have to come not from the United Nations but from the states that were themselves fighting the Cold War. That seemed improbable during the late 1940s and the early 1950s: why would a superpower limit its power? By the mid-1970s, though, the improbable had become irreversible. The process by which this happened was most visible in the United States, where the Cold War at first widened, but subsequently narrowed, the gap between the wielding of power in world affairs and the principles of universal justice.

II.

AMERICAN officials were, at first, reasonably confident that they could contain the Soviet Union and international communism without abandoning standards of behavior drawn from their own domestic experience.[12] They believed firmly that aggression was linked to autocracy, and that a stable international order could best be built upon such principles as freedom of speech, freedom of belief, freedom of enterprise, and freedom of political choice. "The issue of Soviet-American relations is in essence a test of the over-all worth of the United States as a nation among nations," Kennan wrote in the summer of 1947. "To avoid destruction the United States need only measure up to its own best traditions and prove itself worthy of preservation as a great nation. Surely, there was never a fairer test . . . than this."[13]

It may have been a fair test, but it was not an easy one: almost at once pressures began to build to allow actions abroad that would not have been acceptable at home. The Marshall Plan itself—at first glance a successful projection of domestic values into the Cold War—illustrated the problem. Its goal was to secure political freedom by means of economic rehabilitation in the remaining non-communist states of Europe: only hungry and demoralized people, the plan's architects assumed, would vote communists into office. But recovery and the restoration of self-confidence would take time; meanwhile balloting was already taking place. The problem was particularly acute in Italy, where a large communist party generously financed from Moscow looked likely to win the April, 1948, elections. Had it done so the effects—in the wake of the February coup in Czechoslovakia—could have been psychologically devastating. "If Italy goes Red," one State Department adviser warned, "Communism cannot be stopped in Europe."[14] And with American aid only beginning to flow, the Marshall Plan had little beyond promises to rely upon.

The newly established Central Intelligence Agency had neither the capability nor the authority at the time to conduct covert operations: such was the relative innocence of the era. But with the State Department's encouragement, it stepped into the breach. It quickly organized secret financing for the Christian Democrats and other non-communist parties in Italy, while supporting a letter-writing campaign by Italian-Americans to friends and relatives there. These improvised measures worked: the Italian communists were overwhelmed at the polls on April 18th–19th. Kennan concluded, as he later recalled, that "in the unusual circumstances prevailing . . . there was occasional need for actions by the United States Government that did not fit into its overt operations and for which it could not accept formal responsibility."[15] Shortly thereafter, the National Security Council expanded the role of the C.I.A. to include

> propaganda, economic warfare; preventive direct action, including sabotage, anti-sabotage, demolition and evacuation measures; subversion against hostile states, including assis-

tance to underground resistance movements, guerillas and refugee liberation groups, and support of indigenous anti-communist elements in threatened countries of the free world.

All of these activities were to be conducted in such a way "that if uncovered the US Government can plausibly disclaim any responsibility for them."[16] In short, American officials were to learn to lie.

So how did this square with Kennan's earlier claim that the United States need only "measure up to its own best traditions" to "prove itself worthy of preservation as a great nation"? Kennan insisted that the State Department monitor C.I.A. activities to ensure that "plausible deniability" would not mean the lifting of all restraints: he personally expected "specific knowledge of the objectives of every operation and also of the procedures and methods employed where [these] involve political decisions." He acknowledged that such initiatives would have to have "the greatest flexibility and freedom from the regulations and administrative standards governing ordinary operations."[17] They would, however, be rare: the option would be available "when and if an occasion arose when it might be needed," but "[t]here might be years when we wouldn't have to do anything like this." As Kennan later admitted: "It did not work out at all the way I had conceived it."[18]

The number of C.I.A. employees involved in covert operations grew from 302 in 1949 to 2,812 in 1952, with another 3,142 overseas "contract" personnel. They were stationed, by then, at forty-seven locations outside of the United States—up from seven in 1949—and the annual budget for secret activities had mushroomed from $4.7 million to $82 million.[19] Nor were these actions infrequent. As the Eisenhower administration took office, the C.I.A. was regularly attempting to infiltrate spies, saboteurs, and resistance leaders into the Soviet Union, Eastern Europe, and China. It was financing ostensibly independent radio stations broadcasting to those countries, as well as labor unions, academic conferences, scholarly journals, and student organizations—

some of them inside the United States. It was cooperating with the Air Force to fly reconnaissance missions that routinely violated the airspace of the U.S.S.R. and other communist states. It was experimenting with toxins and mind-control drugs. It was mounting counter-insurgency operations in the Philippines. And, working with local supporters and exile groups, it would successfully overthrow the left-leaning governments of Mohammed Mossadegh in Iran in 1953, and of Jacobo Arbenz Guzmán in Guatemala in 1954, both of whom had nationalized foreign-owned properties in their respective countries, causing Washington to suspect them of sympathy for communism.[20] The expanding scale and audacity of covert operations led Kennan to admit, years later, that recommending them had been "the greatest mistake I ever made."[21]

Few officials within the Truman and Eisenhower administrations shared that view. For them the issue was simple: the Soviet Union had been engaging in espionage, financing "front" organizations, subverting foreign governments, and seeking to control minds since the earliest days of the Bolshevik Revolution. It respected no moral or legal constraints. As NSC-68, a top-secret review of national security strategy, pointed out in 1950, "the Kremlin is able to select whatever means are expedient in seeking to carry out its fundamental design." The principal author of that document was Paul Nitze, Kennan's successor as director of the State Department's Policy Planning Staff. Confronted by such dangers, Nitze insisted, free societies would have to suspend their values if they were to defend themselves:

> The integrity of our system will not be jeopardized by any measures, overt or covert, violent or non-violent, which serve the purposes of frustrating the Kremlin design, nor does the necessity for conducting ourselves so as to affirm our values in action as well as words forbid such measures, provided only they are appropriately calculated to that end and are not so excessive or misdirected as to make us enemies of the people instead of the evil men who have enslaved them.[22]

The chief purpose of NSC-68 had been to make the case for "flexible response": a strategy of responding to aggression wherever it took place, without expanding the conflict or backing away from it. Eisenhower jettisoned that approach because of its costs, relying instead on the threat of nuclear retaliation.[23] But he and subsequent presidents through Nixon retained the view, most clearly articulated in NSC-68, that the legal and moral restraints limiting government action at home need not do so in the world at large: within that wider sphere, the United States had to be free to operate as its adversaries did.

"[W]e are facing an implacable enemy whose avowed objective is world domination," the Doolittle Report, a highly classified evaluation of C.I.A. covert operations, concluded in 1954. "There are no rules in such a game. Hitherto acceptable norms of human conduct do not apply."[24] Eisenhower agreed. "I have come to the conclusion that some of our traditional ideas of international sportsmanship are scarcely applicable in the morass in which the world now flounders," he wrote privately in 1955. "Truth, honor, justice, consideration for others, liberty for all—the problem is how to preserve them . . . when we are opposed by people who scorn . . . these values. I believe that we can do it," and here he underlined his words for emphasis, "but *we must not confuse these values with mere procedures, even though these last may have at one time held almost the status of moral concepts.*"[25]

And so the Cold War transformed American leaders into Machiavellians. Confronted with "so many who are not good," they resolved "to learn to be able not to be good" themselves, and to use this skill or not use it, as the great Italian cynic—and patriot—had put it, "according to necessity."

III.

It MIGHT become necessary, the Doolittle Report suggested, for the American people to "be made acquainted with, understand and support this fundamentally repugnant philosophy."[26] But no administration from Eisenhower's through Nixon's tried publicly to justify learning "not to be good." The reasons were obvious: covert operations could hardly remain covert if openly discussed, nor would departures from "hitherto acceptable norms of human conduct" be easy to explain in a society still resolutely committed to the rule of law. The resulting silence postponed, but did not resolve, the issue of how to reconcile Machiavellian practices with the constitutionally based principle of accountability, whether to Congress, the media, or the public at large. As a result, Americans did gradually become acquainted with the "repugnant philosophy" their leaders thought necessary to fight the Cold War, although rarely in ways those leaders had intended.

As the scope and frequency of covert operations increased, it became more difficult to maintain "plausible deniability."[27] Rumors of American involvement in the Iranian and Guatemalan coups began to circulate almost at once, and although these would not be confirmed officially for many years,[28] they were persuasive enough at the time to give the C.I.A. publicity it did not want. By the end of the 1950s, it had an almost mythic reputation throughout Latin America and the Middle East as an instrument with which the United States could depose governments it disliked, whenever it wished to do so.

The consequences, in both regions, proved costly. In the Caribbean, the overthrow of Arbenz inadvertently *encouraged* communism: outraged by what had happened in Guatemala, Fidel Castro, Che Guevara, and their supporters resolved to liberate Cuba from Washington's sphere of influence and turn it into a Marxist-Leninist state. When, after they seized power in 1959, the C.I.A. tried to overthrow *them*, it failed miserably. The unsuccessful Bay of Pigs landing in April, 1961, exposed the most ambitious covert operation the Agency had yet attempted, humiliated the newly installed Kennedy administration, strengthened relations between Moscow and Havana, and set in motion the series of events that would, within a year and a half, bring the world to the brink of nuclear war.[29]

Meanwhile, the Shah of Iran, restored to power by the Americans in 1953, was consolidating an increasingly repressive regime which Washington found impossible to disavow. Once again, a tail wagged a dog, linking the United States to an authoritarian leader whose only virtues were that he maintained order, kept oil flowing, purchased American arms, and was reliably anti-communist. Iranians were sufficiently fed up by 1979 that they overthrew the Shah, denounced the United States for supporting him, and installed in power under the Ayatollah Ruhollah Khomeini the first radically Islamist government anywhere in the world.[30]

Not all C.I.A. operations ended this badly. In April, 1956, one of the most successful of them was, quite literally, exposed when the Russians invited reporters to tour a tunnel the Agency had constructed, extending from West Berlin a third of a mile into East Berlin, by which it had intercepted Soviet and East German cable and telephone communications for more than a year. This early example of wiretapping elicited more praise than criticism in the United States, however: the general reaction was that this was exactly the sort of thing American spies should be doing.[31] Two months later, the C.I.A. arranged for the publication of excerpts from Khrushchev's secret speech denouncing Stalin at the 20th Party Congress. Obtained through Polish and Israeli sources, this purloined document provoked few qualms either, despite the fact that it fed the unrest that led to a near revolt in Poland and a real one in Hungary later that year. What did induce regrets were inadequately supervised broadcasts over the C.I.A.-financed Radio Free Europe which convinced many Hungarians that the United States would defend them from Soviet retaliation. The Agency quietly concluded that in this case it had indeed gone too far, but kept public embarrassment to a minimum.[32]

The first open debate over the ethics of espionage came in May, 1960, when the Russians shot down Francis Gary Powers's U-2 near Sverdlovsk. Eisenhower had long worried about how he might justify such flights if they should ever become public: any *Soviet* violation of *American* airspace, he once admitted, would lead him to ask Congress for an immediate declaration of war. "Plausible deniability" provided some assurance that this double standard could be maintained. Given the altitude at which the U-2 operated, Eisenhower was told, neither the plane nor the pilot would remain intact if anything went wrong. Informed that the plane was down, the president therefore authorized an official lie: a State Department press spokesman announced that a weather aircraft had simply wandered off course. Khrushchev then gleefully displayed the remnants of the U-2, the photographs it had taken, and its pilot, alive and well—forcing a furious Eisenhower to acknowledge his falsehood. "I didn't realize how high a price we were going to have to pay for that lie," he later recalled. "And if I had it to do over again, we would have kept our mouths shut."[33]

The idea that their leaders might lie was new to the American people. There were no serious consequences for Eisenhower, however: he would soon be leaving office, and most Americans admired the C.I.A.'s skill in building the U-2 and keeping it flying for so long— even if, like Eisenhower, they would never have tolerated Soviet flights over the United States. Shortly after taking office, President Kennedy had to admit that he too had lied when he denied, at a press conference just prior to the Bay of Pigs landing, that American forces would be used in any effort to overthrow Castro. To Kennedy's astonishment, his approval rating in the polls went *up:* getting rid of a Marxist regime in the Caribbean was a popular cause, and the new president got credit for attempting it, even if he had failed. "The worse you do," he concluded, "the better they like you."[34]

But what if a president should lie—and do so repeatedly—in an *unpopular* cause? Lyndon Johnson knew that an expanded war in Vietnam would be just that. "I don't think the people . . . know much about Vietnam and I think they care a hell of a lot less," he worried privately in May, 1964. But "we haven't got much choice, . . . we are treaty-bound, . . . we are there, [and if South Vietnam falls] this will be a domino that will kick off a whole list of others. . . . [W]e've just got to prepare for the worst."[35] Johnson sought to do this by denying,

throughout the presidential campaign of that year, any intention to escalate the war, deliberately allowing his opponent, Barry Goldwater, to
endorse that course of action. After his overwhelming victory, Johnson
authorized the escalation he had promised not to undertake, apparently
in the belief that he could win the war quickly before public opinion
could turn against it. "I consider it a matter of the highest importance,"
he instructed his aides in December, "that the substance of this position
should not become public except as I specifically direct."[36]

The war, though, did not end quickly: instead it escalated with no
end in sight. Johnson knew that the prospects were grim, but he could
not bring himself to explain this openly. His reasons went beyond his
own personal political fortunes. He had presided, by mid-1965, over the
greatest wave of domestic reform legislation since the New Deal, and
there was more to be done. "I was determined," he later recalled, "to
keep the war from shattering that dream, which meant that I had no
choice but to keep my foreign policy in the wings. . . . I knew the Congress as well as I know Lady Bird, and I knew that the day it exploded
into a major debate on the war, that day would be the beginning of the
end of the Great Society."[37]

The dilemma, then, was a cruel one. American interests in the Cold
War, Johnson believed, required that the United States persist in Vietnam until it prevailed. But he was also convinced that he could not reveal what it would take to win without sacrificing the Great Society:
the nation would not simultaneously support major expenditures for
both "guns" and "butter." So he sacrificed public trust instead. The
term "credibility gap" grew out of Johnson's sustained attempt to conceal the costs—together with the pessimism with which the C.I.A. and
other intelligence agencies, as well as his own war planners, evaluated
the prospects for success—of the largest American military operation
since the Korean War.[38]

It is difficult to understand how Johnson thought he could get away
with this. Part of the explanation may simply be that when all alternatives are painful, the least painful one is to make no choice: certainly

Johnson postponed choosing between the Great Society and the Vietnam War for as long as possible. Part of it may also have been Johnson's personal belief that the most affluent society in the world could afford to spend whatever was required to ensure security abroad and equity at home, whatever the public or the Congress thought.[39] But that economic argument failed to consider whether Americans could sustain their morale as the human costs of the war rose while the prospects of victory faded. By the beginning of 1968 several hundred American troops were being killed in action *per week,* and yet the Tet Offensive of late January and early February showed that *no* location within South Vietnam—not even the American embassy in Saigon—was secure. Tet turned out to be a military defeat for the North Vietnamese: the mass uprising they had hoped to provoke did not occur. But it was also a psychological defeat for the Johnson administration, and that at the time was more important. The president acknowledged this at the end of March when he refused to send still more troops to fight in the war, while announcing his own surprise decision not to seek re-election.[40]

It seems likely, though, that one other legacy of the early Cold War influenced Johnson's handling of the Vietnam War: it was that American presidents had long been free to act abroad in ways for which they need not account at home. Had not Eisenhower authorized intercepted communications, violations of airspace, and in two instances the actual overthrow of foreign governments? Had not Kennedy failed to overthrow another, and been cheered for making the effort? It was easy to conclude, as Johnson entered the White House in 1963 on a wave of grief over Kennedy's assassination and of goodwill toward himself, that the presidency was all-powerful: that he could continue to employ, as NSC-68 had put it, "any measures, overt or covert, violent or non-violent," that would advance the American cause in the Cold War, without jeopardizing "the integrity of our system." But by the time Johnson left the White House in 1969, that proposition looked much less plausible: the manner in which he had fought the Vietnam War had left the American system, both abroad and at home, in deep trouble.

The authors of NSC-68 had assumed that there could be separate standards of conduct in these two spheres: that American leaders could learn "not to be good" in waging the Cold War while remaining "good" within the framework of their own domestic democratic society. It had been hard enough to maintain that separation during the Eisenhower and Kennedy years: both presidents had been forced to admit that their "denials" in the U-2 and Bay of Pigs incidents had not been "plausible." With the Vietnam War, the line between what was allowed overseas and what was permitted at home disappeared altogether. The Johnson administration found it impossible to plan or prosecute the war without repeatedly concealing its intentions from the American people, and yet the decisions it made profoundly affected the American people. Far from measuring up to "its own best traditions" in fighting the Cold War, as Kennan had hoped it would, the United States in fighting the Vietnam War appeared to be sacrificing its own best traditions of constitutional and moral responsibility.

IV.

RICHARD NIXON inherited this situation, then made it much worse. One of the most geopolitically adept leaders of modern times, he also happened to be the American president least inclined—ever—to respect constraints on his own authority. After all that had happened during the Johnson years, he still believed that the requirements of national security, as he defined them, outweighed whatever obligations of accountability, even legality, the presidency demanded. Nixon's actions went well beyond the idea that there could be separate standards of behavior at home and abroad: instead he made the homeland itself a Cold War battleground. There, however, he encountered an adversary more powerful than either the Soviet Union or the international communist movement. It was the Constitution of the United States of America.

"I can say unequivocally," Nixon wrote after resigning the presidency, "that without secrecy there would have been no opening to China, no SALT agreement with the Soviet Union, and no peace agreement ending the Vietnam war."[41] There is little reason to doubt that claim. To have consulted the Departments of State and Defense, the C.I.A., the appropriate Congressional committees, and all allies whose interests would have been affected *prior* to Kissinger's 1971 Beijing trip would only have ensured that it not take place. To have attempted arms control negotiations with Moscow in the absence of a "back channel" that allowed testing positions before taking them would probably have guaranteed failure. And the only way Nixon saw to break the long stalemate in the Vietnamese peace talks—short of accepting Hanoi's demands for an immediate withdrawal of American forces and the removal from power of the South Vietnamese government—was to increase military and diplomatic pressure on North Vietnam while simultaneously decreasing pressures from within Congress, the antiwar movement, and even former members of the Johnson administration to accept Hanoi's terms. That too required operating both openly and invisibly.

Where Nixon went wrong was not in his use of secrecy to conduct foreign policy—diplomacy had always required that—but in failing to distinguish between actions he could have justified if exposed and those he could never have justified. Americans excused the lies Eisenhower and Kennedy told because the operations they covered up turned out to be defensible when uncovered. So too did the methods by which Nixon brought about the China opening, the SALT agreement, and the Vietnam cease-fire: the results, in those instances, made reliance on secrecy, even deception, seem reasonable.

But what about the secret bombing of a sovereign state? Or the attempted overthrow of a democratically elected government? Or the bugging of American citizens without legal authorization? Or burglaries carried out with presidential authorization? Or the organization of a conspiracy, inside the White House itself, to hide what had happened? Nixon allowed all of this during his first term; his reliance on secrecy became so compulsive that he employed that tactic in situations for which there could never be a plausible justification. So when plausible denial was no longer possible—in large part because Nixon, with his secret Oval Office taping system, had even bugged himself—a constitutional crisis became unavoidable.

The process began in the spring of 1969 when Nixon ordered the bombing of Cambodia in an effort to interdict the routes through that country and Laos along which the North Vietnamese had for years sent troops and supplies into South Vietnam. The decision was militarily justifiable, but Nixon made no effort to explain it publicly. Instead he authorized the falsification of Air Force records to cover up the bombing, while insisting for months afterward that the United States was respecting Cambodian neutrality. The bombing was no secret, obviously, to the Cambodians themselves, or the North Vietnamese, or their Chinese and Soviet allies. Only Americans were kept in the dark, and the reason, as Nixon later acknowledged, was to avoid anti-war protests. "My administration was only two months old, and I wanted to provoke as little public outcry as possible at the outset."[42]

That, however, was how Johnson's "credibility gap" had developed, and Nixon soon had one too. Exploiting well-placed sources, the *New York Times* quickly reported the bombing of Cambodia, as well as the administration's plans to begin a gradual withdrawal of American troops from Vietnam. An angry Nixon responded by ordering wiretaps on the phones of several Kissinger assistants whom the Justice Department and the Federal Bureau of Investigation suspected of having leaked the information. They remained in place, with Kissinger's approval, even after some of these aides had left the government, and they were soon extended to include journalists who could not have been involved in the original leaks.[43] The line between defensible and indefensible secrecy, already blurred in the Johnson administration, was now even less distinct.

Then in October, 1970, the democratically elected Marxist government of Salvador Allende took power in Chile. Nixon claimed, in public, to respect this outcome: "[F]or the United States to have . . . intervened in a free election . . . would have had repercussions all over Latin America that would have been far worse than what has happened in Chile."[44] But his administration *had* intervened there, and was continuing to do so even as Nixon made this statement early in 1971. Following a precedent set by Johnson, the C.I.A. had undertaken a series of undercover initiatives meant to favor Allende's opponents during the election campaign. When he won anyway, Nixon authorized the Agency "to prevent Allende from coming to power or to unseat him."[45] This led the C.I.A. to help set in motion a military coup that failed to prevent Allende's inauguration, but that did result in the kidnapping and assassination of General René Schneider, the commander-in-chief of the Chilean armed forces. Over the next three years, the Agency persisted in its efforts to destabilize Allende's regime.

Fortunately for the administration, none of this leaked at the time: instead Nixon got credit for his apparent restraint in Chile. But the gap between what *appeared* to be happening and what was *actually* happening was widening, while the prospects for defending the disparity—should it become public—were diminishing. Attempting to deny Allende the office he had won, one of Kissinger's aides commented, was "patently a violation of our own principles. . . . If these principles have any meaning, we normally depart from them only to meet the gravest threat . . . to our survival. Is Allende a mortal threat to the U.S.? It is hard to argue this."[46]

At home, even less defensible acts followed. In June, 1971, Daniel Ellsberg, a former Defense Department official, turned over to the *New York Times* what came to be called *The Pentagon Papers,* a classified history of the origins and escalation of the Vietnam War ordered by Johnson's secretary of defense, Robert McNamara. Nothing in this history compromised national security or criticized Nixon's handling of the war, but he regarded the leak as a dangerous precedent and a personal affront. Lacking confidence in the ability of the F.B.I. or the courts to

ABOVE: U.S. and Soviet troops meet at Torgau, Germany, April, 1945. BELOW: Winston Churchill, Harry S. Truman, and Joseph Stalin meet at Potsdam, July, 1945.

West Berlin children cheering the airlift, 1948.

American Marines retreating after Chinese intervention in Korea, December, 1950.

U.S. thermonuclear weapon test, Marshall Islands, 1958.

House in atomic bomb test, Nevada, 1953.

Family in bomb shelter, Garden City, New York, 1955.

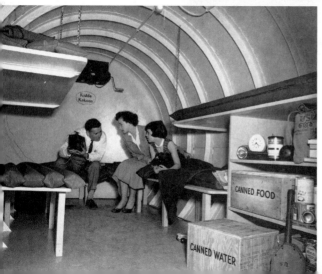

East Berliners battling Soviet tanks, 1953.

Hungarians spitting on Stalin's statue, Budapest, 1956.

Dwight D. Eisenhower and Nikita Khrushchev, Washington, D.C., September, 1959.

ABOVE: West Berlin, 1952.

LEFT: East Berlin, 1954.

BELOW: The Berlin Wall, 1961.

Fidel Castro *(center)* entering
Havana, January, 1959.

John F. Kennedy announcing
the U.S. blockade of Cuba,
October, 1962.

BELOW: Soviet freighter
removing missiles from
Cuba, November, 1962.

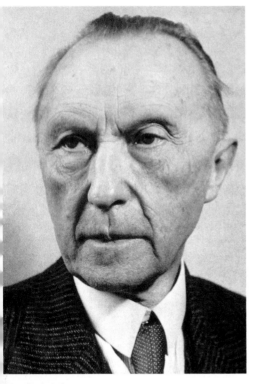

Konrad Adenauer, 1949.

Walter Ulbricht, ca. 1950.

Charles de Gaulle, 1967.

Mao Zedong, ca. 1960.

BELOW: Student protester after clash with police, Paris, 1968.

ABOVE: Washington anti-war demonstration, 1969.
BELOW: Czechs condemning Soviet troops as invaders, Prague, 1968.

Mao welcoming Richard Nixon, Beijing, February, 1972.

Leonid Brezhnev and Nixon, Moscow, May, 1972.

Anwar el-Sadat and
Henry Kissinger,
Cairo, 1973.

North Vietnamese troops
entering Saigon, 1975.

BELOW: Soviet troops
entering Kabul,
Afghanistan, 1980.

Nixon leaving the White House after resigning, with his successor, Gerald Ford, August, 1974.

Brezhnev, Andrei Gromyko, and Konstantin Chernenko at the Helsinki conference, July, 1975.

Pope John Paul II in Częstochowa, Poland, June, 1979.

Lech Wałęsa at the Gdansk shipyard, August, 1980.

LEFT: Deng Xiaoping, ca. 1970s.

LEFT: Deng Xiaoping, ca. 1970s.

RIGHT: Margaret Thatcher, ca. 1979.

BELOW: Mikhail Gorbachev and Ronald Reagan at Geneva, November, 1985.

ABOVE: "Goddess of Democracy" statue in Tiananmen Square, Beijing, May 30, 1989.
LEFT: Reagan lecturing at Moscow State University, May, 1988.
BELOW: Hungarians dismantling barbed wire along the Austrian border, May, 1989.

Gorbachev *(center)* and Erich Honecker *(right)* at a parade celebrating the fortieth anniversary of the German Democratic Republic, East Berlin, October, 1989.

The Berlin Wall, November, 1989.

ABOVE: President Václav Havel of Czechoslovakia and the Rolling Stones, Prague, 1990.

LEFT: Muscovites celebrating the defeat of the coup, August, 1991.

BELOW: Last days of the Soviet Union: Red Square, December, 1991.

deal with this and similar cases, the president demanded the formation of a team within the White House that would prevent the further unauthorized release of sensitive material. "We're up against an enemy, a conspiracy," he insisted. "*We are going to use any means.* Is that clear?"[47]

Nixon's staff quickly assembled an improbable gang of retired police detectives as well as former C.I.A. and F.B.I. agents—soon to be known, for their assignment to plug leaks, as the "Plumbers." Over the next year they undertook a series of burglaries, surveillance operations, and wiretaps that had to be kept secret because, despite their White House authorization, they were illegal. "I don't think this kind of conversation should go on in the attorney general's office," a nervous Nixon aide commented, after the Plumbers had briefed the attorney general, John Mitchell, on their operations.[48] Mitchell himself became nervous when, on the morning of June 17, 1972, several of the Plumbers found themselves under arrest inside the headquarters of the Democratic National Committee in the Watergate building—a place where, by the laws Mitchell was charged with enforcing, they were definitely not supposed to be.[49]

It would take until August 9, 1974—the date of Nixon's resignation—for all the consequences of this bungled break-in to unfold. What was set in motion on the morning of the arrests, however, was a reassertion of moral, legal, and ultimately constitutional principle over presidential authority. It proceeded through the trial and conviction of the hapless burglars, their implication of the administration officials who had supervised and financed their operations, an increasingly startling series of revelations in the media, a diminishingly credible sequence of presidential denials, the appointment of a special prosecutor, a highly public Senate investigation, the exposure of Nixon's Oval Office taping system, legal challenges to get the tapes released, the approval of impeachment resolutions by the House of Representatives, and in the end a Supreme Court ruling that the president had to turn over the single "smoking-gun" tape that proved his complicity in the cover-up.

At that point, facing conviction and removal from office, Nixon gave up his office. He thereby acknowledged that the president of the United States was *not* in fact free to use whatever means he considered necessary to protect national security interests. There was, even within that sensitive realm, a standard of behavior that he alone could not determine. Contrary to what Nixon had assumed, the president was not above the law.

V.

NOR DID the law itself remain static. The president's behavior provoked Congress into reclaiming much of the authority over the conduct of national security policy that it had abdicated during the early Cold War. This happened first with respect to Vietnam, where by the end of January, 1973, Nixon and Kissinger had forced Hanoi to accept a cease-fire on terms that the United States could accept—and could impose on its reluctant South Vietnamese ally. But they had also had to withdraw almost all American troops from the region: that had been necessary to defuse domestic anti-war sentiment, while fending off pressures on Capitol Hill to legislate an end to American involvement in the war.

Nixon had no illusions that the North Vietnamese would willingly abide by the cease-fire. But he did expect to compel compliance by threatening—and if necessary resuming—the bombing that had caused Hanoi to accept the cease-fire in the first place. The United States had, after all, reserved the right to act similarly to enforce a Korean cease-fire that had lasted for two decades. The situation in Vietnam was less promising; still the hope, Kissinger recalled, was "that Nixon's renown for ruthlessness would deter gross violations."[50]

But Watergate had severely weakened the president. Frustrated by a long and bitter war, utterly distrustful of Nixon's intentions, sensing that his authority was crumbling, Congress voted in the summer of 1973 to terminate all combat operations in Indochina. It then passed the War Powers Act, which imposed a sixty-day limit on all future military deployments without Congressional consent. Nixon's vetoes were overridden and the restrictions became law. It was left to his successor, Gerald Ford, to suffer the consequences: when North Vietnam invaded and conquered South Vietnam in the spring of 1975, he was unable to do anything about it. "Our domestic drama," Kissinger later commented, "first paralyzed and then overwhelmed us."[51]

Much the same thing happened with intelligence operations. The C.I.A. had always operated under minimal Congressional oversight: the assumption had been that the nation's representatives neither needed nor wanted to know what the Agency was doing. That attitude survived the U-2 and Bay of Pigs incidents, the onset and escalation of the Vietnam War, even the revelation, in 1967, that the C.I.A. had for years been secretly funding academic conferences, journals, and research, as well as the National Student Association.[52] But it did not survive Watergate.

The evidence that former C.I.A. employees had been part of the Plumbers unit—and that Nixon had sought the Agency's cooperation in arranging a cover-up—led to pressures from within the organization to review potentially illegal activities, and to scrutiny from without that was meant to expose them. In December, 1974, the *New York Times* revealed that the C.I.A. had run its own program of domestic surveillance against anti-war protesters during the Johnson and the Nixon administrations, involving both wiretaps and the interception of mail. The director of Central Intelligence, William Colby, promptly confirmed the story, acknowledging that the Agency had violated its own charter—which prohibited activities inside the United States—and that it had broken the law.[53]

There quickly followed the appointment of three commissions, one presidential and one each in the Senate and the House of Representatives, to investigate C.I.A. abuses. With Colby cooperating, the Agency's "skeletons"—assassination plots, surveillance operations, concealed subsidies, connections to Watergate, and the attempt to prevent a constitutionally elected government in Chile from taking power—all went on public display. As had been the case during Nixon's last years in office, the nation again faced the question of whether the United States should, or even could, maintain separate standards in fighting the Cold War from what it was prepared to accept at home.

Events in Chile posed the dilemma most clearly. A successful military coup had finally taken place in Santiago in September, 1973. It left Allende dead—probably by suicide—and a reliably anti-communist government in power headed by General Augusto Pinochet. Direct C.I.A. complicity was never established, but Nixon and Kissinger openly welcomed the outcome and sought to cooperate with the new Chilean leader. By the time the C.I.A. investigations got under way in 1975, however, Pinochet's government had imprisoned, tortured, and executed thousands of Allende supporters—some of them American citizens. Chile, for many years a democracy, now had one of the most repressive dictatorships Latin America had ever seen.[54]

What the United States did in Chile differed little from what it had done, two decades earlier, in Iran and Guatemala. But the 1970s were not the 1950s: once the information got out that the Nixon administration had tried to keep Allende from the office to which he had been elected and had sought to remove him once there, "plausible denial" became impossible. That made questions about responsibility unavoidable. Could Allende have remained in power if there had been no American campaign against him? Would he have retained democratic procedures had he done so? Should the United States have refrained, to the extent that it did, from condemning Pinochet's abuses? Had it made a greater effort, might it have stopped them? There are, even today, no clear answers: Washington's role in Chile's horrors remains a hotly contested issue among both historians of these events and participants in them.[55] What was clear at the time, though, was that the C.I.A.'s license to operate without constraints had produced actions in Chile that, by its own admission, failed the "daylight" test. They could not be justified when exposed to public view.

Congress responded by prohibiting actions that *might*, in the future, lead to similar results. It chose to make this point in Angola, a former Portuguese colony where a three-way struggle for power was under way in 1975, with the competitors looking to the United States, the Soviet Union, and China for support. There was no possibility, in the aftermath of Vietnam, of direct American military intervention: covert funding for the pro-American National Front for the Liberation of Angola seemed the only available option. But with the C.I.A. under intense scrutiny, there was no way to arrange this without the approval of Congressional leaders, and as soon as they were consulted the plan became overt and opposition to it became intense. Because abuses had taken place in Chile and other parts of the world, the Senate voted in December, 1975, to deny *any* secret use of funds in Angola, despite the likelihood that this action would leave the country, by default, under Moscow's influence. It was, Ford complained, an "abdication of responsibility" that would have "the gravest consequences for the long-term position of the United States and for international order in general."[56]

That turned out to be an exaggeration. The Soviet Union had been reluctantly dragged into Angola by its Cuban ally, and gained little from the experience.[57] What had happened in Washington, though, was significant: distrust between the executive and legislative branches of government was now so deep that the United States Congress was passing laws—always blunt instruments—to constrain the use of *United States* military and intelligence capabilities. It was as if the nation had become its own worst enemy.

VI.

IF THE White House, the Pentagon, and the C.I.A. were not above the law—indeed if legal standards could shift to guarantee this—then could the overall conduct of American foreign policy be held accountable to some comparably independent set of moral standards? Did learning "not to be good . . . according to necessity" mean abandoning all sense of what it meant to be "good" in working within the Cold War international system? And where, in all of this, did détente fit?

It would have been difficult, by any traditional moral principle, to justify the artificial division of entire countries like Germany, Korea, and Vietnam—and yet the United States and its allies had expended thousands of lives and billions of dollars to maintain those divisions. It strained democratic values to embrace right-wing dictatorships throughout much of the "third world" as a way of preventing the emergence of left-wing dictatorships, and yet every administration since Truman's had done this. And surely Mutual Assured Destruction could only be defended if one considered hostage-taking on a massive scale—deliberately placing civilian populations at risk for nuclear annihilation—to be a humane act. American strategists did just that, however, because they saw no better way to deter a much greater evil, the possibility of an all-out nuclear war. As the Cold War wore on, they went from regarding these compromises as regrettable to considering them necessary, then normal, and then even desirable.[58] A kind of moral anesthesia settled in, leaving the stability of the Soviet-American relationship to be valued over its fairness because the alternative was too frightening to contemplate. Once it became clear that everybody was in the same lifeboat, hardly anybody wanted to rock it.

This moral *ambivalence* was not moral *equivalence*. The United States never found it necessary to violate human rights on the scale that the Soviet Union, its Eastern European allies, and the Chinese under Mao Zedong had done. But Washington officials had long since convinced themselves that the only way they could prevent those violations would be to go to war, a prospect that could only make things much worse. American military action, John Foster Dulles warned publicly at the time of the 1956 Hungarian uprising, "would . . . precipitate a full-scale world war and probably the result of that would be all these people wiped out."[59] As late as the Soviet invasion of Czechoslovakia in 1968, the Johnson administration saw little it could do beyond protesting the offense, warning against repeating it elsewhere, and canceling the summit at which the outgoing president and the new Soviet leader, Leonid Brezhnev, were to have begun negotiations on limiting strategic arms. What happened in Eastern Europe, Johnson's secretary of state, Dean Rusk, later explained, had "never been an issue of war and peace between us and the Soviet Union—however ignoble this sounds."[60]

Détente had been meant to lower the risks of nuclear war, to encourage a more predictable relationship among Cold War rivals, and to help them recover from the domestic disorders that had beset them during the 1960s. It had not been intended, in any immediate sense, to secure justice: that could only emerge, most of its supporters believed, from within a balance of power that each of the great powers considered legitimate. Kissinger was the most thoughtful advocate of this position. Legitimacy, he had written in 1957 of the post-1815 European settlement, "should not be confused with justice."

> It implies the acceptance of the framework of the international order by all the major powers, at least to the extent that no state is so dissatisfied that . . . it expresses its dissatisfaction in a revolutionary foreign policy. A legitimate order does not make conflicts impossible, but it limits their scope.[61]

Kissinger was still making this point in October, 1973, after Nixon appointed him secretary of state: "The attempt to impose absolute justice by one side will be seen as absolute injustice by all others. . . . Stability depends on the relative satisfaction and therefore also the relative dissatisfaction of the various states."

Kissinger was careful to caution against "becoming obsessed with stability." An "excessively pragmatic policy" would "lack not only direction, but also roots and heart." It would provide "no criteria for other nations to assess our performance and no standards to which the

American people can rally." But an "excessively moralistic" approach to Cold War diplomacy could become "quixotic or dangerous," leading to "ineffectual posturing or adventuristic crusades." The responsible policy-maker, therefore, "must compromise with others, and this means to some extent compromising with himself."[62] The morality inherent in détente lay in its avoidance of war and revolution, no small accomplishment in a nuclear age. Kant's goal of universal justice, however, could only follow from a universal acceptance, for the foreseeable future, of the Cold War status quo.

This argument, however, left one issue unresolved: if détente was indeed diminishing the danger of nuclear war, then why would it continue to be so dangerous to apply moral standards in conducting the Cold War? If that conflict was becoming the *normal* condition of international relations, did that mean the United States would have to accept amorality as a permanent characteristic of its foreign policy? How would that square with Kissinger's acknowledgment that "America cannot be true to itself without moral purpose"?[63] This was the dilemma the new secretary of state faced in taking over the direction of foreign policy from the increasingly beleaguered Nixon: securing the status quo abroad was making support for it vulnerable at home.

The vulnerabilities appeared most clearly with respect to human rights. Soon after the 1972 Moscow summit, Kremlin leaders imposed an exit tax on emigrants leaving the U.S.S.R., supposedly to recover the costs of their state-financed education. It seemed a small brutality compared to the many larger ones that had preceded it, but it came at a time when concerns were growing within the United States about the treatment of Soviet Jews and dissidents. The exit tax provoked a backlash in Congress, where Senator Henry M. Jackson and Representative Charles Vanik proposed an amendment to the otherwise routine Trade Reform Act that would have denied "most-favored nation" treatment and Export-Import Bank credits to any "non-market economy" that restricted or taxed the right to emigrate. The United States, Jackson argued—no doubt with his own presidential aspirations in mind—

should use its economic strength, not to reward the Soviet Union for its external behavior, but to change its *internal* behavior: "When we have something we feel strongly about . . . [then] we should put that issue of principle on the table knowing that the Russians are not going to agree to it."[64]

Kissinger protested that the provisions of the Trade Reform Act had been among the carefully balanced sticks and carrots that had persuaded the Soviet Union at last to agree on the limitation of strategic arms. To add new demands after the deal had been made—especially demands that required the Russians to alter internal policies as a result of outside pressure—could only be a mandate "for an unfulfillable course that sapped our credibility abroad without giving us the tools to deal with the consequences of the resulting tension." Quiet diplomacy would do more for Soviet Jews, dissidents, and other potential emigrants than public posturing; and in the absence of an amicable Soviet-American relationship it would hardly be possible to do anything for them.[65] Moscow's objections to the Jackson-Vanik amendment had an even deeper basis. As Ambassador Dobrynin later admitted, "the Kremlin was afraid of emigration in general (irrespective of nationality or religion) lest an escape hatch from the happy land of socialism seem to offer a degree of liberalization that might destabilize the domestic situation."[66]

What this meant, though, was that in its search for geopolitical stability, the Nixon administration had begun to support domestic stability inside the U.S.S.R. It had sought to manage the Cold War international system much as Metternich and Castlereagh had managed Europe after Napoleon—by *balancing* the antagonisms within it. But that 19th-century arrangement had accepted the internal character of the states being balanced: calls for reform, in the era Kissinger had written about as a historian, could easily be brushed aside. That was less easy to do in the more transparent and democratic age within which he himself sought to direct the course of events.

Kissinger never intended that détente would secure the future of Soviet authoritarianism. "Brezhnev's gamble," he had written Nixon in the summer of 1973, "is that as these policies gather momentum and longevity, their effects will not undermine the very system from which Brezhnev draws his power and legitimacy. Our goal on the other hand is to achieve precisely such effects over the long run."[67] But with Jackson-Vanik, the long run became the present: the amendment won support from opposite ends of the ideological spectrum. Liberals, convinced that foreign policy always ought to pursue justice, condemned Kissinger's cynicism in seeking stability first. Conservatives, certain that the Soviet Union could never be trusted, denounced Kissinger's naiveté in being willing to do so. And with Nixon approaching the end of his presidency, there was little he could do to help resist these pressures.

The Jackson-Vanik amendment passed both houses of Congress early in 1975, several months after Nixon left office. The Soviet Union responded by canceling the entire trade deal. The causes of emigration, commerce, and détente itself suffered as a result: whatever "thaw" had occurred in the Cold War now seemed to be ending. But these events had advanced a different cause. Through a circuitous process involving its own constitutional checks and balances, the presidential aspirations of an ambitious senator, and the diminishing power of an ethically challenged president, the United States had wound up taking a position consistent with the 1948 United Nations Universal Declaration on Human Rights: that neither national sovereignty nor the demands of diplomacy should allow states to treat their own citizens in any way they pleased. There was after all, if not a universal standard of justice, then at least a basic standard of human decency that ought to take precedence, even over efforts to stabilize the Cold War.

VII.

THIS REALIGNMENT of American strategy with legal and moral principles would have had little effect on the course of the Cold War, however, had there not been echoes of it on the other side. These were at first difficult to detect. The Soviet leadership appeared to have become *less* tolerant of dissent at home and in Eastern Europe than it had been during the last years of the Khrushchev era. The invasion of Czechoslovakia and its subsequent justification, the Brezhnev Doctrine, set the stage for a tightening of ideological discipline, a rejection of experimentation in the media and the arts, and the increasingly harsh repression of even mild political protests.[68] However much détente might have improved relations with the West, Brezhnev and his colleagues seemed determined to control everything—even ideas—within their sphere of influence. They justified this not through an appeal to morality or law, but to ideology: to the claim that, in Marxism-Leninism, they had discovered the mechanisms by which history worked, and thus the means by which to improve the lives people lived.

But it had long been clear that history was *not* working in this way. Khrushchev revealed that Lenin and Stalin had enslaved far more people than they had liberated; and by the time of his overthrow the Soviet Union and its Eastern Europe satellites had fallen far behind the United States and most of the rest of the capitalist world in most of the economic indices that measured prosperity. It had even been necessary, in 1968, to use force to keep communism in power in Czechoslovakia, an act that shattered whatever illusions remained that anyone might voluntarily embrace that ideology. "Our tanks in Prague . . . 'fired' at ideas," one young Soviet journalist wrote at the time. "With a fist to the jaw of thinking society, they thought they had knocked out . . . its thinking processes. . . . [Instead they] 'awakened' new layers within the Party intelligentsia who would repeat the [Prague] attempt with more success."[69]

Not immediately, to be sure. It would take time for thoughts alone to ensure that tanks would never again be used. The suppression of the "Prague spring" did, however, have a powerful psychological effect: it led a growing number of people in the Soviet Union and Eastern Europe to continue to defer in public to Marxist-Leninist doctrine, while privately ceasing to believe in it. There developed what the historian Timothy Garton Ash has called a "double life": "The split between the public and the private self, official and unofficial language, outward conformity and inward dissent. . . . I applaud conduct by the state that I would never endorse in private life."[70] It was just the opposite from what was happening inside the United States, where by the mid-1970s the gap between what people believed in and what their leaders did had significantly narrowed. The credibility gap was migrating from Washington to Moscow. And Brezhnev was even less prepared to deal with it than Nixon had been.

His problem was that the Communist Party of the Soviet Union, like all other ruling communist parties, drew its authority from its claim to historical infallibility: that left it vulnerable when events failed to follow the script. Once it became clear that that was happening, there was little left—apart from a morally and legally indefensible use of force, as in Czechoslovakia—to justify the party's existence. Its legitimacy rested on an increasingly implausible ideology, and nothing more. Whatever the excesses of American leaders during the Vietnam and Watergate years, they never had to face *that* difficulty.

Brezhnev could have diminished the party's vulnerability by qualifying its claim to a monopoly on wisdom—but that would have produced challenges to its monopoly on power, and that he was not prepared to do. "This is dangerous," K.G.B. chief Yuri Andropov warned in a 1974 Politburo discussion of criticisms that had already surfaced from the Soviet Union's most distinguished writer, Aleksandr Solzhenitsyn, and its most prominent physicist, Andrei Sakharov. "[T]here are hundreds and thousands of people among whom Solzhenitsyn will find support. . . . [I]f we remain inactive on Sakharov, then how will [other] academicians . . . behave in the future?"[71] The only strengths these dissidents deployed lay in their pens, their voices, and their principles. Yet principles were contagious, and the Soviet system, shielded only by ideology, had insufficient immunity to them.

With internal reform too risky, the Kremlin leadership turned toward diplomacy: if the world acknowledged the legitimacy of its rule, then how could a few malcontents—even famous ones—get anyone else to object to it? That was one of the reasons why Brezhnev liked détente, a fundamental premise of which was that the West would not seek to alter the internal character of Marxist-Leninist regimes. The objective instead would be to encourage their responsible behavior within the international arena. That did not mean giving up the class struggle: Brezhnev insisted that it would continue where it safely could, especially in the "third world."[72] He was, however, prepared to concede the permanence of NATO and, by implication, a continuing role for the United States in Europe. In return, he expected the Americans and their NATO allies formally to ratify post–World War II boundaries in Eastern Europe.

This was not a new idea. As early as 1954, Molotov had proposed a conference at which the nations of Europe—but not the United States—would meet to confirm their existing borders. That plan went nowhere, but as Kissinger once noted, Moscow's diplomacy "makes up in persistence what it lacks in imagination."[73] The Soviet foreign ministry revived Molotov's proposal regularly over the next decade and a half, modifying it to include the Americans. Meanwhile, NATO had endorsed negotiations with the Warsaw Pact on mutual force reductions in Europe, while Brandt's *Ostpolitik* had produced a Soviet–West German treaty recognizing the long-contested boundary of postwar Poland, as well as an agreement among the four powers occupying Berlin to continue the status quo in that city. It was clear, then, that no one had an interest in changing the European political map: that made renewed Soviet pressure for a "Conference on Security and Co-operation in Europe" seem relatively harmless to the Americans and, to several of their NATO partners, a potentially positive development.[74]

For Brezhnev, however, such a conference would mean much more. It would require the United States and its allies to state publicly and in writing that they accepted the postwar division of Europe. The Kremlin leader was almost capitalist in the importance he attached to this contractual obligation, which he believed would discourage future "Prague springs," reinforce the Brezhnev Doctrine, deflate dissidents inside the U.S.S.R., and ensure his own reputation as a man of peace.[75] And he was willing to make extraordinary concessions to get this commitment. They included promising advance notice for military maneuvers, permitting the peaceful change of international borders, allowing signatory states to join or leave alliances, and, most surprisingly, recognizing "the universal significance of human rights and fundamental freedoms . . . in conformity with the purposes and principles of the Charter of the United Nations and with the Universal Declaration of Human Rights."[76]

The Russians were admittedly nervous about this last condition, but it had originated with the West Europeans and the Canadians, not the Americans, which made it difficult to oppose.[77] Moreover, the liberties it specified appeared in the largely unimplemented Soviet constitution: that too would have made rejection awkward. Nor would it be easy, solely on these grounds, to back out of a conference for which the U.S.S.R. had pressed for so long. So the Politburo agreed, with misgivings, to the inclusion of human rights provisions in the conference's "Final Act." "We are masters in our own house," Foreign Minister Andrei Gromyko assured Brezhnev. The Soviet government and no one else would decide what the recognition of "human rights and fundamental freedoms" actually meant.[78]

The Conference on Security and Cooperation in Europe opened in Helsinki on July 30, 1975. Brezhnev dozed through its many speeches, and two days later he, Ford, and the leaders of thirty-three other states signed the long and complex document that had brought them together. The consequences, on all sides, were unexpected. As Kissinger later put it: "Rarely has a diplomatic process so illuminated the limitations of human foresight."[79]

VIII.

WITHIN THE UNITED STATES, liberals and conservatives alike denounced Ford and Kissinger for having *abandoned* the cause of human rights. Brezhnev's motives in wanting the Helsinki agreement, they argued, were all too transparent: pursuing détente was hardly worth it if it meant perpetuating injustice by recognizing Soviet control in Eastern Europe. A series of administration missteps inadvertently advanced this argument. Just prior to the Helsinki conference, Kissinger had advised Ford not to receive Solzhenitsyn—by then an involuntary exile from the Soviet Union and a bitter critic of détente—at the White House: this came across as excessive deference to Moscow. Then, in December, 1975, a Kissinger aide, Helmut Sonnenfeldt, told what he thought was an off-the-record meeting with American diplomats that the administration hoped to end the "inorganic, unnatural relationship" between the Soviet Union and the Eastern Europeans. When the comment leaked, it was taken as acknowledging that the Russians were in that part of the world to stay.[80]

These episodes made Helsinki a liability to Ford during the 1976 presidential campaign, as both Ronald Reagan, his challenger from within the Republican Party, and Jimmy Carter, the nominee of the Democratic Party, condemned the agreement. Ford found it necessary to prohibit subordinates from even using the word "détente"; he also disassociated himself from Kissinger as the election approached. And then on October 6th, while debating Carter, the president committed one final, fatal gaffe: briefed to deny the existence of the "Sonnenfeldt Doctrine," he instead denied that the Soviet Union dominated Eastern Europe.[81] That ensured Carter's election, and so after January 20, 1977, neither Ford nor Kissinger retained any further responsibility for the conduct of American foreign policy. The Helsinki conference was one of the reasons.

Helsinki's effects inside the Soviet Union and Eastern Europe, however, were equally unexpected, and far more significant. Brezhnev had looked forward, Dobrynin recalls, to the "publicity he would gain . . . when the Soviet public learned of the final settlement of the postwar boundaries for which they had sacrificed so much."

> As to the humanitarian issues, these could be mentioned at home just vaguely, without much publicity. He thought this would not bring much trouble inside our country. But he was wrong. The condition of Soviet dissidents certainly did not change overnight, but they were definitely encouraged by this historic document. Its very publication in *Pravda* gave it the weight of an official document. It gradually became a manifesto of the dissident and liberal movement, a development totally beyond the imagination of the Soviet leadership.[82]

Helsinki became, in short, a legal and moral trap.[83] Having pressed the United States and its allies to commit themselves in writing to recognizing existing boundaries in Eastern Europe, Brezhnev could hardly repudiate what *he* had agreed to in the same document—also in writing—with respect to human rights. Without realizing the implications, he thereby handed his critics a standard, based on universal principles of justice, rooted in international law, independent of Marxist-Leninist ideology, against which they could evaluate the behavior of his and other communist regimes.

What this meant was that the people who lived under these systems—at least the more courageous—could claim official permission to say what they thought: perhaps it might *not* be necessary to live a "double life" for all time to come. Andropov's 1974 nightmare became a reality as thousands of individuals who lacked the prominence of Solzhenitsyn and Sakharov began to stand with them in holding the U.S.S.R. and its satellites accountable for human rights abuses. By the summer of 1976 a Public Group to Promote Observance of the

Helsinki Accords was operating in Moscow with Sakharov's endorsement, and similar "Helsinki Groups" were sprouting throughout Eastern Europe.[84] Begun by the Kremlin in an effort to legitimize Soviet control in that part of the world, the Helsinki process became instead the basis for legitimizing *opposition* to Soviet rule.

The effects, to put it mildly, were unpredictable. It is unlikely, for example, that the aging leaders in Moscow followed the fortunes of a scruffy, anti-establishment Czechoslovak rock band, the "Plastic People of the Universe," formed in the aftermath of the invasion of that country in 1968. Given to performing in secret while dodging the police, the band ran out of luck in 1976, when its members were arrested. Their trial provoked several hundred intellectuals into signing, on January 1, 1977, a manifesto called Charter 77, which politely but pointedly called upon the Czech government to respect the free expression provisions of the Helsinki Final Act, which with Brezhnev's approval it had signed. Several of the "Chartists" themselves were then arrested. One of them, the playwright—and lover of rock music—Václav Havel, spent four years in prison, followed by many more years of close surveillance after his release.[85]

That gave Havel the motive and the time, through his essays and plays, to become the most influential chronicler of his generation's disillusionment with communism. He was, it has been said, "a Lennonist rather than a Leninist."[86] Havel did not call for outright resistance: given the state's police powers, there would have been little point in that. Instead he encouraged something more subtle, developing standards for *individual* behavior *apart* from those of the state. People who failed to do this, he wrote, "confirm the system, fulfill the system, make the system, *are* the system." But people who were true to what they themselves believed—even in so small a matter as a brewer deciding to brew better beer than the official regulations called for—could ultimately subvert the system. "[W]hen one person cries out, 'The emperor is naked!'—when a single person breaks the rules of the game, thus exposing it as a game—everything suddenly appears in another light, and the whole crust seems then to be made of a tissue on the point of tearing, and disintegrating uncontrollably."[87]

Havel gave voice—just as Brezhnev inadvertently gave legitimacy—to the pressures that had been building throughout the Soviet Union and Eastern Europe to end the double life that Marxism-Leninism had seemed to require: all at once a vision beckoned of a society in which universal morality, state morality, and individual morality might all be the same thing. At which point God, or at least His agents, intervened to make that vision an unexpected—and to the Kremlin a profoundly alarming—reality.

Karol Wojtyła, an accomplished actor, poet, playwright, and athlete, had entered the priesthood in 1946, and had been appointed archbishop of Kraków in 1964 with the full approval of the Polish Communist Party, which vetoed seven other candidates. It would be hard to find a clearer example of historical fallibility, for Pope Paul VI made Wojtyła a cardinal in 1967, and then on October 16, 1978, his fellow cardinals elected him, at fifty-eight, the youngest pope in 132 years, the first non-Italian pope in 455 years, and the first Slavic pope ever. "How could you possibly allow the election of a citizen of a socialist country as pope?" Andropov demanded of his unfortunate bureau chief in Warsaw. There was no good answer to this, for not even the K.G.B. controlled papal conclaves.

Nor, as it soon became clear, did it control the spiritual life of the Polish people. "The Pope is our enemy," a desperate party directive warned, shortly before John Paul II made his first visit, as supreme pontiff, to his native country:

> He is dangerous, because he will make St. Stanisław [the patron saint of Poland] . . . a defender of human rights. . . .
> [O]ur activities designed to atheize the youth not only cannot diminish but must intensely develop. . . . In this respect all means are allowed and we cannot allow any sentiments.

"Take my advice," Brezhnev told Polish party leader Edward Gierek, "don't give him any reception. It will only cause trouble." When Gierek protested that he could hardly turn away the first Polish pope, the old man in the Kremlin relented: "Well, do as you wish. But be careful you don't regret it."[88]

It was, for once from Brezhnev, an accurate prediction of things to come. But it was too late to prevent them, because Wojtyła had been working quietly for years—as priest, archbishop, and cardinal—to preserve, strengthen, and expand the ties between the individual morality of Poles and the universal morality of the Roman Catholic Church. Now, as pope, he witnessed his success.

When John Paul II kissed the ground at the Warsaw airport on June 2, 1979, he began the process by which communism in Poland— and ultimately everywhere else in Europe—would come to an end. Hundreds of thousands of his countrymen cheered his entry into the city, shouting, "We want God, we want God!" A million greeted him the next day in Gniezno. At Częstochowa on the following day the crowds were even larger: here the pope slyly reminded the authorities that the church's teaching on religious freedom "directly tallies with the principles promulgated in fundamental state and international documents, including the Constitution of the Polish People's Republic."

By the time the pope reached his home city of Kraków, between 2 and 3 million people were there to welcome him, many of them the young people the party had hoped to "atheize." "Who's making all this noise?" the pope joked. "Stay with us!" they chanted in response. "Stay with us!" As he left the city in which, as he put it, "every stone and every brick is dear to me," John Paul reiterated the great theme of his papacy: "Be not afraid."

> You must be strong, dear brothers and sisters . . . with the
> strength of *faith*. . . . You must be strong with the strength of
> *hope*. . . . You must be strong with *love*, which is stronger than

death. . . . When we are strong with the Spirit of God, we are also strong with faith in man. . . . There is therefore no need to fear.[89]

"The Pope!" Josef Stalin was reputedly fond of asking. "How many divisions has *he* got?"[90] John Paul II, during the nine days he spent in Poland in 1979, provided the answer. This too was a development, as Dobrynin might have put it, "totally beyond the imagination of the Soviet leadership."

CHAPTER SIX
ACTORS

Be not afraid!

—John Paul II[1]

Seek truth from facts.

—Deng Xiaoping[2]

We can't go on living like this.

—Mikhail Gorbachev[3]

THE POPE HAD BEEN an actor before he became a priest, and his triumphant return to Poland in 1979 revealed that he had lost none of his theatrical skills. Few leaders of his era could match him in his ability to use words, gestures, exhortations, rebukes—even jokes—to move the hearts and minds of the millions who saw and heard him. All at once a single individual, through a series of dramatic performances, was changing the course of history. That was in a way appropriate, because the Cold War itself was a kind of theater in which distinctions between illusions and reality were not always obvious. It presented great opportunities for great actors to play great roles.

These opportunities did not become fully apparent, however, until the early 1980s, for it was only then that the *material* forms of power upon which the United States, the Soviet Union, and their allies had lavished so much attention for so long—the nuclear weapons and missiles, the conventional military forces, the intelligence establishments, the military-industrial complexes, the propaganda machines—began to lose their potency. Real power rested, during the final decade of the Cold War, with leaders like John Paul II, whose mastery of *intangibles*—of such qualities as courage, eloquence, imagination, determination, and faith—allowed them to expose disparities between what people believed and the systems under which the Cold War had obliged them to live. The gaps were most glaring in the Marxist-Leninist world: so much so that when fully revealed there was no way to close them other than to dismantle communism itself, and thereby end the Cold War.

Accomplishing this required actors. Only their dramatizations could remove the mental blinders, themselves the products of material capabilities, that had led so many people to conclude that the Cold War would last indefinitely. An entire generation had grown up regarding the absurdities of a superpower stalemate—a divided Berlin in the middle of a divided Germany in the midst of a divided Europe, for example—as the natural order of things. Strategists of deterrence had convinced themselves that the best way to defend their countries was to have no defenses at all, but rather tens of thousands of missiles poised for launch on a moment's notice. Theorists of international relations insisted that bipolar systems were more stable than multipolar systems, and that Soviet-American bipolarity would therefore last for as far into the future as anyone could see.[4] Diplomatic historians maintained that the Cold War had evolved into a "long peace," an era of stability comparable to those Metternich and Bismarck had presided over in the 19th century.[5] It took visionaries—saboteurs of the status quo—to widen the range of historical possibility.

John Paul II set the pattern by rattling the authorities throughout Poland, the rest of Eastern Europe, and even the Soviet Union. Others quickly followed his example. There was Lech Wałęsa, the young Pol-

ish electrician who stood outside the locked gate of the Lenin shipyard in Gdansk one day in August, 1980—with the pope's picture
nearby—to announce the formation of *Solidarność*, the first independent trade union ever in a Marxist-Leninist country. There was Margaret Thatcher, the first woman to become prime minister of Great
Britain, who relished being tougher than any man and revived the reputation of capitalism in Western Europe. There was Deng Xiaoping,
the diminutive, frequently purged, but relentlessly pragmatic successor
to Mao Zedong, who brushed aside communism's prohibitions on free
enterprise while encouraging the Chinese people to "get rich."

There was Ronald Reagan, the first professional actor to become
president of the United States, who used his theatrical skills to rebuild
confidence at home, to spook senescent Kremlin leaders, and after a
young and vigorous one had replaced them, to win his trust and enlist
his cooperation in the task of changing the Soviet Union. The new
leader in Moscow was, of course, Mikhail Gorbachev, who himself
sought to dramatize what distinguished him from his predecessors: in
doing so, he swept away communism's emphasis on the class struggle,
its insistence on the inevitability of a world proletarian revolution, and
hence its claims of historical infallibility.

It was an age, then, of leaders who through their challenges to the
way things were and their ability to inspire audiences to follow them—
through their successes in the *theater* that was the Cold War—
confronted, neutralized, and overcame the forces that had for so long
perpetuated the Cold War. Like all good actors, they brought the play
at last to an end.

I.

THEY COULD hardly have done this had the stage not been set by the
collapse of détente. When first worked out in Washington, Moscow,
and other Cold War capitals, that strategy had looked like a hopeful

development. It did not free the world from crises, but the new spirit of cooperation did seem to limit their frequency and severity: Soviet-American relations in the late 1960s and the early 1970s were much less volatile than during the first two decades of the Cold War, when confrontations erupted almost annually. This was a major accomplishment, because with the superpowers now commanding roughly the same capacity to destroy one another, the risks of escalation were even greater than they once had been. Détente was turning a dangerous situation into a predictable *system*, with a view to ensuring survivability for the post-1945 geopolitical settlement, as well as for humanity at large.

Humanity, however, was not particularly grateful. For just as the Cold War had frozen the results of World War II in place, so détente sought to freeze the Cold War in place. Its purpose was not to end that conflict—the differences dividing its antagonists were still too deep for that—but rather to establish rules by which it would be conducted. These included avoiding direct military clashes, respecting existing spheres of influence, tolerating physical anomalies like the Berlin Wall and mental anomalies like the doctrine of Mutual Assured Destruction, refraining from efforts to discredit or undermine leaders on each side, and even a mutual willingness, through the new technology of reconnaissance satellites, to allow spying as long as it took place hundreds of miles above the earth.[6] The architects of détente looked forward to the possibility, as Kissinger put it in 1976, of "transform[ing] ideological conflict into constructive participation in building a better world."[7] But because change still seemed dangerous, they agreed to accept, for the foreseeable future, the world as it was.

What that meant was that certain nations would continue to live under authoritarian rule while others could elect and remove governments by constitutional means. Certain economies would continue to benefit from the efficiencies of open markets; others would stagnate under central planning. Certain societies would continue to enjoy the right of free expression; others could stay safe only by staying silent.

And everyone would still face the possibility of nuclear incineration if the delicate mechanisms of deterrence should ever fail. Détente denied equal opportunity, except in annihilation.

It might have lasted if elites still ran the world, but deference to authority was not what it once had been. There were now more freely elected governments than ever before, which meant that more people could depose their leaders than ever before.[8] Democracy still seemed a distant prospect in Marxist-Leninist countries; even there, though, officially sanctioned higher education was making it difficult for governments to prevent people from thinking for themselves, despite the fact that they generally had to keep their thoughts to themselves.[9] And where democracy and education had not spread, as in most of the "third world," another global trend—the advent of mass communications— was making it possible to mobilize movements in ways that leaders did not always anticipate, and could not always control.[10]

So as it became clear that the nuclear danger was diminishing, that the credibility of command economies was wearing thin, and that there were still universal standards of justice, it became harder to defend the idea that a few powerful leaders at the top, however praiseworthy their intentions, still had the right to determine how everyone else lived. Despite its elite origins, détente required support from below, and this proved difficult to obtain. It was like a building constructed on quicksand: the foundations were beginning to crack, even as the builders were finishing off the façade.

II.

THE CENTERPIECE of détente was the Soviet-American effort to limit the nuclear arms race. The Strategic Arms Limitation Talks, which got under way late in 1969, had by 1972 produced a Soviet-American agreement capping the number of intercontinental and submarine-launched ballistic missiles each side could deploy, as well as a treaty banning anything other than symbolic defenses against such missiles. Signed by Nixon and Brezhnev at the Moscow summit, the SALT I accords, as they came to be called, were significant for several reasons. They reflected recognition on the part of both superpowers that a continuing arms race could only make them less secure. They represented an acknowledgment on the part of the United States that the Soviet Union was now its equal in nuclear capabilities, and in some categories of weaponry its superior. They legitimized the logic of Mutual Assured Destruction: that remaining defenseless against a nuclear attack was the best way to keep one from happening. And they accepted satellite reconnaissance as a method of verifying compliance with these agreements.[11]

But the SALT process, like détente itself, also evaded issues. One was nuclear arms reduction: the Moscow agreements froze existing ICBM and SLBM deployments, but did nothing to cut them back, or even to restrict the number of warheads each missile could carry. Imbalances were also a problem: SALT I left the Soviet Union well ahead of the United States in ICBMs, and with a smaller lead in SLBMs. The Nixon administration justified this asymmetry on the grounds that American missiles were more accurate than their Soviet counterparts and in large part equipped with multiple warheads. It also pointed out that SALT I placed no restrictions on long-range bombers, where the Americans had long enjoyed superiority, or on the shorter-range bombers and missiles they had placed on aircraft carriers and with NATO allies, or on the nuclear capabilities of Great Britain and France.[12]

The complexity of that argument made it difficult to sell to the United States Congress, however, which found it hard to understand why it should approve Soviet superiority in *any* category of strategic weaponry. That left an opening for Senator Henry Jackson—whose Jackson-Vanik amendment would soon strain Soviet-American relations in another way—to secure passage of a resolution requiring that all subsequent arms control agreements provide for numerical equality in all weapons systems covered. Jackson's resolution complicated the next round of negotiations—SALT II—because Soviet and American military planners had deliberately chosen not to duplicate each other's strategic arsenals. Now the negotiators would have to find a way, nonetheless, to impose equivalent limits on weapons systems that were not themselves equivalent. "How to accomplish it," Kissinger recalled, "was generously left to my discretion."[13]

It had taken two and a half years to negotiate the 1972 SALT I agreements, which tolerated asymmetries. The SALT II negotiations, which could not, were still dragging on when the Ford administration left office five years later. The Congress—and, increasingly, the Defense Department and the strategic studies community—was no longer willing to trust Kissinger to continue making the kinds of trade-offs among weapons systems that had produced SALT I: his methods, critics charged, had been too secret, too prone to miscalculation, too trusting that the Russians would keep their promises. SALT II was a more open process, but it was also for just this reason a less successful one.[14]

Jimmy Carter hoped, by dramatic means, to fix it. He had pledged during the 1976 campaign not simply to freeze strategic arsenals but to seek deep cuts in them—he even promised in his inaugural address to move toward the elimination of nuclear weapons altogether. But Carter had taken a still stronger position on human rights: having criticized Ford and Kissinger for failing to press the Russians sufficiently on this issue, he could hardly avoid doing so himself. So Carter did both things at once. He startled Kremlin leaders by calling for significantly greater reductions in strategic arms than the Ford administration had proposed, but he simultaneously irritated them by initiating a direct correspondence with Sakharov and by receiving Soviet dissidents at the White House. Carter himself was surprised, in turn, when Brezhnev harshly rejected his "deep cuts" proposal. SALT II was put on hold yet again.[15]

If Carter's decisions were shortsighted, Brezhnev's more than matched them. By the time the new American administration took office, the Soviet leader had developed serious health problems, brought on in part by excessive drug use.[16] This made it difficult for him to focus on the intricacies of arms control, which even healthy leaders found hard to master. As a result, Brezhnev largely relinquished responsibility for these matters to the Soviet military, which undertook a series of initiatives that seemed to stretch the spirit of SALT I. They included ambitious programs for missile modernization and civil defense, together with a continuing emphasis, in strategic doctrine, on offensive operations.[17] This made it easier for American critics of arms control to substantiate their own skepticism about SALT II.

Then, in 1977, the Soviet Union began deploying a new and highly accurate intermediate-range missile—the SS-20—against targets in Western Europe. Both sides had positioned such missiles in the past, but the SS-20 was a significant upgrade and the United States and its NATO allies were given no warning. Remarkably, neither was the Soviet foreign ministry: the Politburo approved the deployment solely on military grounds. The Kremlin's top American specialist, Georgi Arbatov, later admitted that "[m]ost of our experts and diplomats found out about it through the Western press." It was, Anatoly Dobrynin acknowledged, a "particularly disastrous" decision, because it provoked demands within NATO—completely unexpected in Moscow—for an American counter-deployment.[18] By 1979 the Carter administration was ready with a proposal to install Pershing II and cruise missiles at selected sites in Western Europe. The Pershings were reputed to be fifteen times more accurate than the SS-20s. Flying time to Moscow would be about ten minutes.[19]

Despite these setbacks, the SALT II negotiators finally produced a complex treaty, which Carter and an obviously unhealthy Brezhnev signed at Vienna in June, 1979. But by that time the whole arms control process was under fire from critics within both the Democratic and Republican parties who claimed that it had accomplished nothing toward reducing the nuclear danger, that it had endangered western security by allowing improvements in Soviet capabilities, and that it was unverifiable. Carter submitted the treaty to the Senate nonetheless, but then in a misguided effort to demonstrate his own toughness, he challenged Moscow on what he claimed was the recent deployment of a Soviet "combat brigade" in Cuba. Further research produced the embarrassing fact that the unit had been there since 1962, and that its presence had been part of the deal by which Kennedy and Khrushchev had resolved the Cuban missile crisis. The controversy caused the Senate to delay consideration of the SALT II treaty, and it was still languishing in that body in December, 1979, when NATO agreed to the Pershing II and cruise missile deployments—only to have the Soviet Union respond by invading Afghanistan.[20]

III.

THE SEQUENCE of events that led it to do so can be traced back to another agreement—even more problematic than SALT I—reached at the 1972 Moscow summit. In a joint statement of "Basic Principles," Nixon and Brezhnev promised that their countries would seek to avoid "efforts to obtain unilateral advantage at the expense of the other."[21] Taken literally, this seemed to imply that the stability that had come to characterize superpower relations in Europe and Northeast Asia would now extend throughout the rest of Asia, the Middle East, Africa, and Latin America: that Washington and Moscow would reject whatever opportunities might arise to shift the status quo in those parts of the world. It soon became clear, though, that the "Basic Principles" were not to be taken literally. Like SALT, they papered over cracks.

The Russians welcomed the "Basic Principles" as yet another acknowledgment of parity with the Americans. Brezhnev was careful to insist, however, that the class struggle would continue: "That is to be expected since the world outlook and the class aims of socialism and capitalism are opposite and irreconcilable."[22] The Americans saw the "Basic Principles" as a way to constrain the Russians. "Of course [they] were not a legal contract," Kissinger explained. They "established a standard of conduct by which to judge whether real progress was being made. . . . [E]fforts to reduce the danger of nuclear war . . . had to be linked to an end of the constant Soviet pressure against the global balance of power."[23] Despite appearances, then, there was no meeting of minds at Moscow on managing spheres of influence in the "third world." If anything, the years that followed saw an intensified search for unilateral advantages there.

The first opportunity fell to the Americans. The Moscow summit had come as a shock to Anwar el-Sadat, Nasser's successor as president of Egypt. The Soviet Union had done nothing to prevent Israel from taking the Sinai Peninsula and the Gaza Strip during the 1967 Six-Day War, and now Brezhnev seemed to be ruling out future efforts to help Egypt get these territories back.[24] Sadat decided, accordingly, to end his country's long-time relationship with the U.S.S.R. and to seek a new one with the United States—which, as Israel's ally, might be in a better position to deliver Israeli concessions. When Nixon and Kissinger ignored him, even after Sadat expelled some 15,000 Soviet military advisers from Egypt, he found a way to get their attention by launching a surprise attack across the Suez Canal in October, 1973. It was a war Sadat expected to lose, fought for a political objective he shrewdly calculated he would win. For would the Americans let Israel humiliate a leader who had already diminished Soviet influence in the Middle East?

They would not. After the Israelis repelled the Egyptian attack with the help of massive American arms shipments, Kissinger rebuffed a demand by Brezhnev for a jointly enforced cease-fire, even ordering a brief nuclear alert to reinforce the rejection. He then personally negotiated an end to hostilities, earning gratitude in both Cairo and Tel Aviv while the Russians gained nothing at all. Five years later, after negotiations with the Israelis mediated by President Carter, Sadat got the Sinai back, along with the Nobel Peace Prize he shared with Israeli Prime Minister Menachem Begin. The Egyptian leader, Kissinger

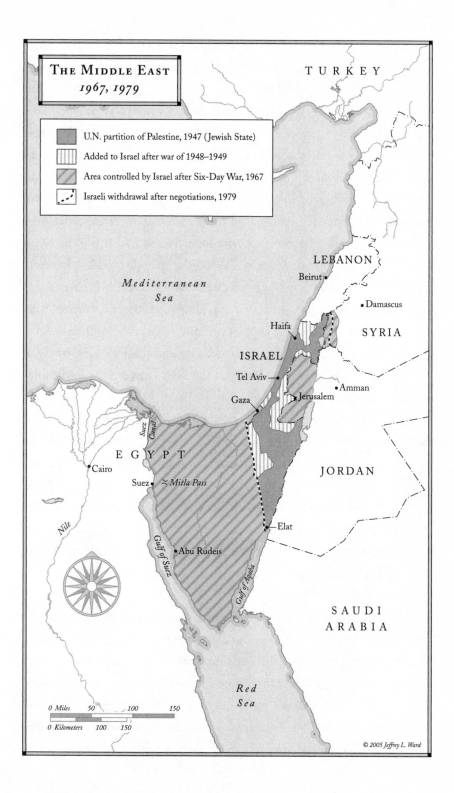

THE MIDDLE EAST
1967, 1979

U.N. partition of Palestine, 1947 (Jewish State)

Added to Israel after war of 1948–1949

Area controlled by Israel after Six-Day War, 1967

Israeli withdrawal after negotiations, 1979

TURKEY

LEBANON
Beirut

Damascus

Mediterranean
Sea

Haifa

ISRAEL

SYRIA

Tel Aviv

Jerusalem
Amman

Gaza

JORDAN

Suez Canal

EGYPT

Cairo

Suez · ⁓ Mitla Pass

Nile

Gulf of Suez

Abu Rudeis

Elat

Gulf of Aqaba

SAUDI
ARABIA

0 Miles   50   100   150
0 Kilometers   100   150

Red
Sea

© 2005 Jeffrey L. Ward

concluded, had been "a remarkable man." He seemed "free of the obsession with detail by which mediocre leaders think they are mastering events, only to be engulfed by them."[25]

This may have been subtle self-criticism, for it was Sadat who masterfully dangled the opportunity to eject the Soviet Union from the Middle East—and it was Nixon and Kissinger who took the bait. Détente, Kissinger later claimed, had been "partly a tranquilizer for Moscow as we sought to draw the Middle East into closer relations with us at the Soviets' expense."[26] But this smacks of retrospective justification: there is little evidence that he or Nixon had this purpose in mind before Sadat made his move. What the episode revealed, instead, was the shakiness of détente: if a regional power could maneuver a superpower into seeking unilateral advantage at the expense of the other—thereby violating its explicit promise to the other—then as Dobrynin observed, détente "was very delicate and fragile." The 1973 war and its aftermath "definitely damaged the trust between the leadership of both countries."[27]

Dobrynin's superiors were no better at resisting temptations when they arose. In the years that followed, the Soviet Union's commitment to the class struggle pulled it into parts of the world that, by any realistic calculation of interests, could hardly have been considered vital. At least the Middle East, from which Kissinger sought to exclude the Russians, was strategically significant to the United States. But what was the importance, for the Soviet Union, of Vietnam, Angola, Somalia, and Ethiopia, all countries in which Moscow expanded its influence during the mid-1970s?

The only thing that linked these involvements, Dobrynin recalled, was "a simple but primitive idea of international solidarity, which meant doing our duty in the anti-imperialist struggle." That pattern had first appeared in Vietnam, where Hanoi's appeals to "fraternal solidarity" had regularly deflected Soviet pressure to end the war with the Americans, about which Kremlin leaders had never been enthusiastic. But North Vietnam's victory in 1975—together with the Congressional prohibition on intervention in Angola—shifted the calculations: if the United States could be defeated in Southeast Asia and deterred in southern Africa, then how credible could American strength be elsewhere? Perhaps the class struggle in the "third world" really was taking hold. Such views were strongest, Dobrynin has argued, in the International Department of the Soviet Communist Party: "[C]onvinced that all struggle in the Third World had an ideological basis," party leaders "managed to involve the Politburo in many Third World adventures." The military establishment went along: "[S]ome of our top generals . . . were emotionally pleased by the defiance of America implied by our showing the flag in remote areas."[28]

It was an unwise strategy, however, because it led the Politburo to relinquish control over where, when, and how it deployed resources: it felt obliged to respond whenever Marxists competing for power called upon it to do so. The policy went well beyond support for "genuine national liberation movements," Dobrynin noted; instead it amounted "to interference on an ideological basis in the internal affairs of countries where domestic factions were struggling for power." It was a kind of "ideological bondage."[29] And it quickly became the victim of victories in Vietnam and Angola. "As often happens in politics," Arbatov has pointed out, "if you get away with something and it looks as if you've been successful, you are practically doomed to repeat the policy. You do this until you blunder into a really serious mess."[30]

The blunders began in 1977 when Somalia, a Soviet client, attacked a recently installed Marxist regime in neighboring Ethiopia. Under pressure as in Angola from the militant Cubans, the Russians switched sides, leaving the Carter administration to align itself with the Somalis and gain useful naval facilities on the Red Sea. It was not at all clear what Moscow gained by supporting the Ethiopians, apart from the thanks of a brutal dictatorship in an impoverished landlocked country and solidarity with Fidel Castro. These events did, however, further poison relations with the United States. As Dobrynin later acknowledged:

We made a serious mistake in involving ourselves in the conflict between Somalia and Ethiopia and in the war in Angola.
Our supply of military equipment to these areas, the activities
there of Cuban troops, and especially our airlift to get them
there, persuaded Americans that Moscow had undertaken a
broad offensive against them for control over Africa. Although that was not really the case, these events strongly affected détente.

They did little, however, to alter the course of the Cold War. The efforts the superpowers expended on Africa during the 1970s, Dobrynin
concluded in the 1990s, were "almost entirely in vain. . . . Twenty years
later no one (except historians) could as much as remember them."[31]

That was certainly not true of what came next. In April, 1978, to the
surprise of Moscow, a Marxist coup took place in Afghanistan, resulting in the overthrow of that country's pro-American government. The
temptation to exploit this opportunity was too great to resist, and soon
the Soviet Union was sending aid to the new regime in Kabul, which
undertook an ambitious program to support land reform, women's
rights, and secular education. It did so, however, just as the revolution
was brewing in neighboring Iran, which in January, 1979—in a severe
setback for the United States—forced its long-time ally Shah Reza
Khan Pahlavi into exile, replacing him with the Ayatollah Khomeini.
The Russians and their new Afghan clients were no more prepared for
this development than the Americans had been, and in mid-March a
violent rebellion broke out in Herat, close to the Iranian border, which
resulted in the deaths of some 5,000 people including fifty Soviet advisers and their families. The Afghans blamed Khomeini, but from
Moscow's perspective the unpopularity of the Kabul regime was also
responsible.[32]

"Do you have support among the workers, city dwellers, [and] the
petty bourgeoisie?" Soviet Premier Alexei Kosygin demanded of

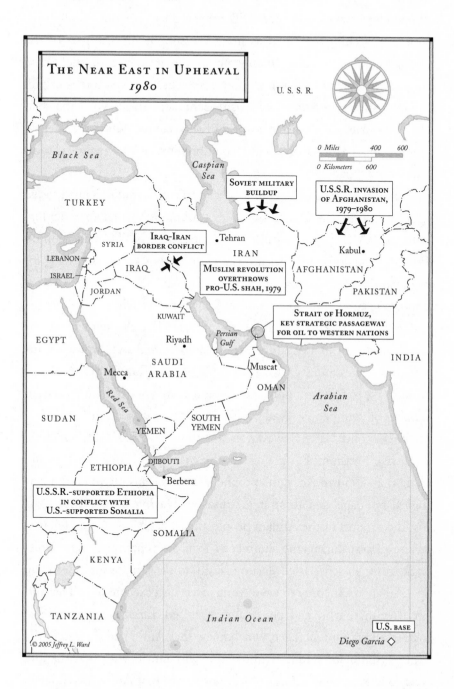

THE NEAR EAST IN UPHEAVAL
1980

U. S. S. R.

0 Miles   400   600

0 Kilometers   600

Black Sea

Caspian Sea

TURKEY

SOVIET MILITARY BUILDUP

U.S.S.R. INVASION OF AFGHANISTAN, 1979–1980

SYRIA

IRAQ-IRAN BORDER CONFLICT

•Tehran

IRAN

Kabul•

LEBANON—

ISRAEL—

IRAQ

MUSLIM REVOLUTION OVERTHROWS PRO-U.S. SHAH, 1979

AFGHANISTAN

JORDAN

PAKISTAN

KUWAIT

STRAIT OF HORMUZ, KEY STRATEGIC PASSAGEWAY FOR OIL TO WESTERN NATIONS

EGYPT

Persian Gulf

Riyadh•

•Muscat

INDIA

Mecca•

SAUDI ARABIA

OMAN

Arabian Sea

Red Sea

SUDAN

SOUTH YEMEN

YEMEN

ETHIOPIA

DJIBOUTI

•Berbera

U.S.S.R.-SUPPORTED ETHIOPIA IN CONFLICT WITH U.S.-SUPPORTED SOMALIA

SOMALIA

KENYA

TANZANIA

Indian Ocean

U.S. BASE

Diego Garcia ◇

© 2005 Jeffrey L. Ward

Afghan Prime Minister Nur Mohammed Taraki in a top-secret telephone conversation. "Is there still anyone on your side?" Taraki's response was chilling: "There is no active support on the part of the
population. It is almost wholly under the influence of the Shiite
slogans—follow not the infidels, but follow us."[33] It was a meaningful
moment in the history of Marxism-Leninism: an ideology that had
claimed to know the path to a world proletarian revolution found itself
confronting a regional religious revolution for which its analytical tools
were wholly inadequate.

Soviet leaders considered military intervention, but quickly decided
against it. With the Carter-Brezhnev summit at Vienna approaching,
with the SALT II treaty still to be signed, with NATO's decision on
Pershing and cruise missiles not yet made, with Moscow preparing for
the 1980 Olympic games, and with détente still alive, it seemed an in-
opportune time to invade a country known for its skill in repelling invaders as far back as Alexander the Great. "The deployment of our
forces in the territory of Afghanistan would immediately arouse the international community," Kosygin explained to Taraki. "[O]ur troops
would have to fight not only with foreign aggressors, but with a certain
number of your people. And people do not forgive such things."[34]

Nine months later, however, the Politburo reversed itself, launching
a massive invasion of Afghanistan, the consequences of which would
more than confirm Kosygin's prophecy. The reasons reveal how "ideological bondage" led to strategic disaster. Having for the most part
lost the support of the Afghan people, the leadership in Kabul fell into
near civil war during the summer of 1979. In September, Taraki, just
back from Moscow, tried unsuccessfully to assassinate his chief rival,
Hafizullah Amin, only to have Amin arrest and execute him. That upset Brezhnev, who had personally promised Taraki support; it also
alarmed Soviet intelligence, which knew that Amin had studied in the
United States and had now initiated quiet contacts with Washington.
The concern, as one K.G.B. officer put it, was that Amin was "doing a
Sadat on us"—that if left in power, he would kick the Russians out, al-

low the Americans in, and invite them to place "their control and intelligence centers close to our most sensitive borders."[35] There seemed to be no alternative to replacing the new Afghan leader, but the only way to do that, the Soviet defense ministry insisted, was to send in some 75,000 troops to crush whatever internal resistance or foreign intervention might follow.

And what of the international reaction to such a move? The Vienna summit had now been held, the SALT II treaty was stalled in the United States Senate, and early in December the NATO allies had voted to go ahead with the deployment of Pershing II and cruise missiles. With all of this in mind, the top Politburo leaders—proceeding with minimal consultation as they had in authorizing the SS-20 deployment—ordered a full-scale invasion of Afghanistan. Military operations were to begin, with tactless timing, on Christmas Day. No one in the Soviet embassy in Washington was asked to predict the American reaction: whatever it might be, Foreign Minister Gromyko assured Dobrynin, it need not be taken into account. The whole thing would all be over, Brezhnev himself promised, "in three or four weeks."[36]

IV.

DÉTENTE had failed, then, to halt the nuclear arms race, or to end superpower rivalries in the "third world," or even to prevent the Soviet Union from using military force again to save "socialism," as it had in Czechoslovakia twelve years earlier. That much was clear in January, 1980, a month in which President Carter withdrew the SALT II treaty from the Senate, imposed embargoes on grain and technology shipments to the U.S.S.R., asked for a significant increase in defense spending, announced that the United States would boycott the Moscow Olympics, and denounced the invasion of Afghanistan as "the most serious threat to the peace since the Second World War." It was a striking shift for a president who, on taking office three years earlier, had hoped to bring the Cold War to an end. Even Gromyko had to admit that "[t]he international situation . . . has taken a turn for the worse."[37]

What was not so clear at the time, though, was what all this meant for the global balance of power. Most experts would probably have agreed that it had been tilting in Moscow's favor through most of the 1970s. The United States had acknowledged strategic parity with the Soviet Union in SALT I, while that country had claimed the right, through the Brezhnev Doctrine, to resist all challenges to Marxism-Leninism wherever they might occur. Despite Kissinger's success in excluding the Russians from the Egyptian-Israeli peace negotiations, the 1973 war had triggered an Arab oil embargo, followed by price increases that would stagger western economies for the rest of the decade. Meanwhile the U.S.S.R., a major oil exporter, was raking in huge profits. That made it possible to hold military spending steady as a percentage of gross national product during the 1970s, perhaps even to increase it—at a time when the equivalent United States budget, for reasons relating to both economics and politics, was being cut in half.[38]

Americans seemed mired in endless arguments with themselves, first over the Vietnam War, then Watergate, then, during Carter's presidency, over charges that he had failed to protect important allies like the Shah of Iran or Anastasio Somoza, the Nicaraguan dictator whose government fell to the Marxist Sandinistas in the summer of 1979. The low point came in November of that year when Iranians invaded the United States embassy in Teheran, taking several dozen diplomats and military guards hostage. This humiliation, closely followed by the Soviet invasion of Afghanistan a few weeks later, made it seem as though Washington was on the defensive everywhere, and Moscow was on a roll. Kissinger captured the prevailing pessimism when he acknowledged in the first volume of his memoirs, published that year, that "our *relative* position was bound to decline as the USSR recovered from World War II. Our military and diplomatic position was never more favorable than at the *very beginning* of the containment policy in the late 1940s."[39]

In this instance, though, Kissinger's shrewdness as a historian deserted him. For it has long since been clear—and should have been clearer at the time—that the Soviet Union and its Warsaw Pact allies were on the path to decline, and that détente was concealing their difficulties. One hint of this came as early as March, 1970, when in the spirit of *Ostpolitik* the East German authorities invited West German Chancellor Brandt to visit Erfurt, unwisely giving him a hotel room with a window overlooking a public square. To their intense embarrassment, hundreds of East Germans gathered under it to cheer their visitor: "[T]he preparation for the Erfurt meeting," party officials admitted, "was not fully recognized as a key component in the class conflict between socialism and imperialism."[40]

More serious signs of discontent arose in Poland the following December, when protests over food prices led the army to fire on and kill dozens of striking workers in Gdansk and Gdynia. Significantly, this crisis did not lead Moscow to invoke the Brezhnev Doctrine: instead Soviet leaders ordered an increase in the production of consumer goods—and they approved imports of food and technology from Western Europe and the United States. This made stability in the region contingent not on the use of military force, but rather on the willingness of capitalists to extend credit, a striking vulnerability for Marxist-Leninist regimes.[41]

Nor was the oil windfall without its downside. The Soviet Union chose to pass along price increases to the Eastern Europeans: this led to a doubling of their oil costs within a year. While not as dramatic as the increases the West faced, the unanticipated expenses undercut the improvements in living standards Moscow had hoped to achieve.[42] Meanwhile, swelling oil revenues were diminishing incentives for Soviet planners to make their own economy more productive. It was no source of strength for the U.S.S.R. to be sustaining a defense burden that may well have been *three times* that of the United States by the end of the 1970s, when its gross domestic product was only about *one-sixth* the size of its American counterpart.[43] "[W]e were arming ourselves like addicts," Arbatov recalled, "without any apparent political need."[44] And oil fueled the addiction.

From this perspective, then, the Soviet Union's support for Marxist revolutionaries in Africa, its SS-20 deployment, and its invasion of Afghanistan look less like a coordinated strategy to shift the global balance of power and more like the absence of any strategy at all. For what kind of logic assumes the permanence of unexpected windfalls? What kind of regime provokes those upon whom it has become economically dependent? What kind of leadership, for that matter, commits itself to the defense of human rights—as at Helsinki in 1975—but then is surprised when its own citizens claim such rights? The U.S.S.R. under Brezhnev's faltering rule had become incapable of performing the most fundamental task of any effective strategy: the efficient use of available means to accomplish chosen ends. That left the field open for leaders elsewhere who were capable of such things.

V.

THEY CAME, like John Paul II, from unexpected origins: perhaps that is what led them to question the conventional wisdom of the 1970s—indeed of the entire Cold War—from unexpected points of view. They took advantage of the fact that détente, despite the hopes held for it, had changed so little. They used to the utmost their strengths as *individuals:* their personal character, their perseverance in the face of adversity, their fearlessness and frankness, but above all their dramatic skill, not only in conveying these qualities to millions of other people, but also in persuading those millions themselves to embrace those qualities. They made the 1980s astonishingly different from the 1970s. And they began the process of ending the Cold War.

It could hardly have been anticipated, for example, that a long-time follower of Mao Zedong, at five feet in height barely visible beside him, would use the power of the Chinese Communist Party to give his country a market economy: "It doesn't matter if the cat is white or black," Deng Xiaoping liked to say, "so long as it catches mice." Deng's views on cats—by which he meant ideologies—got him into trouble with Mao during the Cultural Revolution, and at the time of Nixon's 1972 visit to Beijing, Deng was in exile with his family growing vegetables, chopping wood, working in a tractor repair plant, and nursing his son, whom Red Guards had thrown from the roof of a building, permanently paralyzing him. Mao called Deng back to Beijing the following year, acknowledging that he had "done good deeds seventy percent of the time and bad deeds thirty percent"—only to purge him again in 1976. Always resilient, Deng fled to southern China, hid out, and patiently awaited yet another rehabilitation. It came shortly after Mao's death in September of that year, and by the end of 1978 Deng had outmaneuvered all of his rivals to become China's "paramount" leader.[45]

He had already by then turned the tables on his predecessor by claiming that *Mao* had been right seventy percent of the time and wrong thirty percent: this now became party doctrine.[46] Among the "right" things Mao had done were reviving China as a great power, maintaining the Communist Party's political monopoly, and opening relations with the United States as a way of countering the Soviet Union. Among the "wrong" things was Mao's embrace of a disastrously administered command economy. With this pronouncement on percentages, Deng won himself room to pursue a very different path.

It involved experimenting with markets at local and regional levels, after which Deng would declare whatever worked to be consistent with Marxist-Leninist principles. Through this bottom-up approach, he showed that a communist party could significantly, even radically, improve the lives of the people it ruled—but only by embracing capitalism. Per capita income tripled in China between 1978 and 1994. Gross domestic product quadrupled. Exports expanded by a factor of ten. And by the time of Deng's death in 1997, the Chinese economy had become one of the largest in the world.[47] The contrast with the moribund

Soviet economy, which despite high oil prices showed no growth at all in the 1970s and actually contracted during the early 1980s, was an indictment from which Soviet leaders never recovered. "After all," the recently deposed Mikhail Gorbachev commented ruefully in 1993, "China today is capable of feeding its people who number more than one billion."[48]

Nor could it have been expected that the first woman to become prime minister of Great Britain would challenge the social welfare state in Western Europe. Margaret Thatcher's path to power, like Deng's, had not been easy. Born without wealth or status, disadvantaged by gender in a male-dominated political establishment, she rose to the top through hard work, undisguised ambition, and an utter unwillingness to mince words. Her principal targets were high taxes, nationalized industries, deference to labor unions, and intrusive government regulation. "No theory of government was ever given a fairer test . . . than democratic socialism received in Britain," she later argued. "Yet it was a miserable failure in every respect." The results she produced after eleven years in power were not as impressive as Deng's, but they did show that privatization, deregulation, and the encouragement of entrepreneurs—even, critics said, of greed—could command wide popular support.[49] That too was a blow to Marxism, for if capitalism really did exploit "the masses," why did so many among them cheer the "iron lady"?

Thatcher minced no words either about détente. "[W]e can argue about Soviet motives," she told an American audience soon after taking office, "but the fact is that the Russians have the weapons and are getting more of them. It is simple prudence for the West to respond." The invasion of Afghanistan did not surprise her: "I had long understood that *détente* had been ruthlessly used by the Soviets to exploit western weakness and disarray. I knew the beast."[50] Not since Churchill had a British leader used language in this way: suddenly *words,* not euphemisms, were being used again to speak *truths,* not platitudes. From California a former movie actor turned politician turned broadcaster gave the new prime minister a rave review. "I couldn't be happier," Ronald Reagan told his radio audience. "I've been rooting for her . . . since our first meeting. If anyone can remind England of the greatness she knew . . . when alone and *unafraid* her people fought the Battle of Britain it will be the Prime Minister the Eng[lish] press has already nicknamed 'Maggie.'"[51]

Soon to declare his own candidacy for the presidency of the United States, Reagan had already made it clear what *he* thought of détente: "[I]sn't that what a farmer has with his turkey—until thanksgiving day?"[52] His rise to power, like that of Deng, Thatcher, and John Paul II, would also have been difficult to anticipate, but at least his acting skills were professionally acquired. His fame as a film star predated the Cold War, even World War II, and gave him a head start when he went into politics. It also caused his opponents—sometimes even his friends—to underestimate him, a serious mistake, for Reagan was as skillful a politician as the nation had seen for many years, and one of its sharpest grand strategists ever.[53] His strength lay in his ability to see beyond complexity to simplicity. And what he saw was simply this: that because détente perpetuated—and had been meant to perpetuate—the Cold War, only killing détente could end the Cold War.

Reagan came to this position through faith, fear, and self-confidence. His faith was that democracy and capitalism would triumph over communism, a "temporary aberration which will one day," he predicted in 1975, "disappear from the earth because it is contrary to human nature."[54] His fear was that before that happened human beings would disappear as the result of a nuclear war. "[W]e live in a world," he warned in 1976, "in which the great powers have aimed . . . at each other horrible missiles of destruction . . . that can in minutes arrive at each other's country and destroy virtually the civilized world we live in."[55] It followed that neither communism nor nuclear weapons should continue to exist, and yet détente was ensuring that both did. "I don't know about you," he told a radio audience in 1977, "but I [don't] exactly tear my hair and go into a panic at the possibility of losing détente."[56] It was that jaunty self-confidence—Reagan's ability to threaten détente without seeming threatening himself—that propelled him to a landslide victory over Carter in November, 1980, thereby bringing him to power alongside the other great contemporaries, and the other great actors, of his age.

There was one more—as it happened, another Pole—whose name few people would have known only a few months earlier. A short, squat man with a drooping mustache and jerky Charlie Chaplin–like movements, he had seen the shootings at the Gdansk shipyard in 1970, and had been sacked from his job there in 1976 for trying to organize the workers. Now, on August 14, 1980, with protests mounting once again, the shipyard director was trying to calm an angry crowd. Lech Wałęsa scrambled up on an excavator behind him, tapped him on the shoulder, and said: "Remember me?" Two weeks later—after lots of scrambling to rally his supporters from atop excavators, trucks, and the shipyard gate—Wałęsa announced the formation of the first independent and self-governing trade union ever in the Marxist-Leninist world. The pen with which he co-signed the charter for *Solidarność* (Solidarity) bore the image of John Paul II. And from Rome the pontiff let it be known, quietly but unmistakably, that he approved.[57]

It was a moment at which several trends converged: the survival of a distinctive Polish identity despite the attempts of powerful neighbors, over several centuries, to try to smother it; the church's success in maintaining its autonomy through decades of war, revolution, and occupation; the state's incompetence in managing the post–World War II economy, which in turn discredited the ruling party's ideology. But trends hardly ever converge automatically. It takes leaders to make them do so, and here the actor-priest from Kraków and the actor-electrician from Gdansk played to each other's strengths—so much so that plans began to be made to remove them both from the stage.

The agent was Mehmet Ali Ağca, a young Turk who may have plotted to kill Wałęsa on a January, 1981, visit to Rome, and who did shoot and almost kill the pope in St. Peter's Square on May 13, 1981. Ağca's ties to Bulgarian intelligence quickly became clear. Soviet complicity was more difficult to establish, but it strains credulity to suggest that the Bulgarians would have undertaken an operation of this importance without Moscow's approval. The Italian state prosecutor's official report hinted strongly at this: "In some secret place, where every secret is wrapped in another secret, some political figure of great power . . . mindful of the needs of the Eastern bloc, decided that it was necessary to kill Pope Wojtyla." The pope's biographer put it more bluntly: "The simplest and most compelling answer . . . [is that] the Soviet Union was not an innocent in this business."[58]

John Paul II recovered, attributing his survival to divine intervention. But Solidarity found its survival increasingly at risk as Kremlin leaders, alarmed that any communist government would share power with anybody, pressed the Polish authorities to suppress it. "Our friends listen, agree with our recommendations, but do practically nothing," Brezhnev fumed, "[a]nd the counterrevolution is advancing on every front." It could even take hold within the U.S.S.R. itself: what was happening in Poland was "having an influence . . . in the western oblasts of our country," K.G.B. chief Yuri Andropov warned. "Additionally, . . . spontaneous demonstrations have flared up in parts of Georgia, [with] groups of people shouting anti-Soviet slogans. . . . So we have to take strict measures here as well."[59]

Apart from warning the Poles and cracking down on its own dissidents, however, it was not at all clear what the Soviet Union could do about the challenge Solidarity posed. Reagan's election ensured that any occupation of Poland would provoke an even harsher response than Carter's to the invasion of Afghanistan; meanwhile the Red Army was bogged down in that latter country with costs and casualties mounting and no exit strategy in sight. The Soviet economy could hardly stand the strain of supporting Eastern Europe, something it would have to do if, as seemed certain in the event of military action

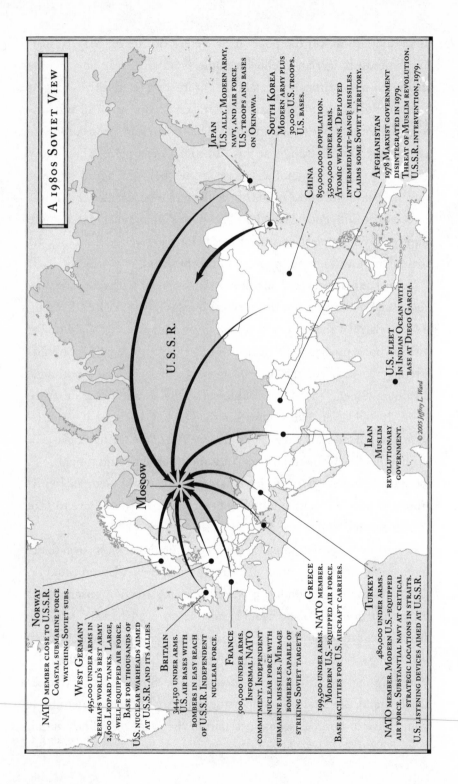

A 1980s SOVIET VIEW

NORWAY
NATO member close to U.S.S.R. Coastal submarine force watching Soviet subs.

WEST GERMANY
495,000 under arms in perhaps world's best army. 2,600 Leopard tanks. Large, well-equipped air force. Base for thousands of U.S. nuclear warheads aimed at U.S.S.R. and its allies.

BRITAIN
344,150 under arms. U.S. air bases with bombers in easy reach of U.S.S.R. Independent nuclear force.

FRANCE
500,000 under arms. Informal NATO commitment. Independent nuclear force with submarine missiles. Mirage bombers capable of striking Soviet targets.

GREECE
199,500 under arms. NATO member. Modern U.S.-equipped air force. Base facilities for U.S. aircraft carriers.

TURKEY
480,000 under arms. NATO member. Modern U.S.-equipped air force. Substantial navy at critical strategic locations in straits. U.S. listening devices aimed at U.S.S.R.

JAPAN
U.S. ally. Modern army, navy, and air force. U.S. troops and bases on Okinawa.

SOUTH KOREA
Modern army plus 30,000 U.S. troops. U.S. bases.

CHINA
850,000,000 population. 3,500,000 under arms. Atomic weapons. Deployed intermediate-range missiles. Claims some Soviet territory.

AFGHANISTAN
1978 Marxist government disintegrated in 1979. Threat of Muslim revolution. U.S.S.R. intervention, 1979.

IRAN
Muslim revolutionary government.

U.S. FLEET
In Indian Ocean with base at Diego Garcia.

U.S.S.R.

Moscow

© 2005 Jeffry L. Ward

against Poland, the West imposed still further sanctions. Moreover, the Polish situation was not like the one in Czechoslovakia in 1968. General Anatoly Gribkov recalls warning his superiors:

> In Czechoslovakia, events developed beginning with the highest echelons of power. In Poland, on the other hand, it is the people rising up who have all stopped believing in the government of the country and the leadership of the Polish United Workers Party. . . . The Polish armed forces are battle-ready and patriotic. They will not fire on their own people.[60]

By December, 1981, the Politburo had decided *not* to intervene: "[E]ven if Poland falls under the control of 'Solidarity,' that is the way it will be," Andropov told his colleagues. "If the capitalist countries pounce on the Soviet Union, . . . that will be very burdensome for us. We must be concerned above all with our own country." The Kremlin's top ideologist, Mikhail Suslov, agreed: "If troops are introduced, that will mean a catastrophe. I think we have reached a unanimous view here on this matter, and there can be no consideration at all of introducing troops."[61]

This was a remarkable decision in two respects. It meant, first, the end of the Brezhnev Doctrine, and hence of the Soviet Union's willingness—extending all the way back through Hungary in 1956 and East Germany in 1953—to use force to preserve its sphere of influence in Eastern Europe. But it also acknowledged that the world's most powerful Marxist-Leninist state no longer represented proletarians beyond its borders, for in Poland at least the workers themselves had rejected that ideology. Had these conclusions become known at the time, the unraveling of Soviet authority that took place in 1989 might well have occurred eight years earlier.

But they did not become known: in a rare instance of successful dramatization, the Politburo convinced the new Polish leader, General Wojciech Jaruzelski, that the U.S.S.R. was *about* to intervene. Desperate to avoid that outcome, he reluctantly imposed martial law on the morning of December 13, 1981, imprisoned the organizers of Solidarity, and abruptly ended the experiment of granting workers autonomy within a workers' state. Ever the actor, Lech Wałęsa had his line ready for the occasion. "This is the moment of your defeat," he told the men who came to arrest him. "These are the last nails in the coffin of Communism."[62]

VI.

ON MARCH 30, 1981, six weeks before the attempt on the pope's life, another would-be assassin shot and almost killed Reagan. The Soviet Union had nothing to do with this attack: it was the effort, rather, of a demented young man, John W. Hinckley, to impress his own movie star idol, the actress Jodie Foster. The improbable motive behind this near-fatal act suggests the importance and vulnerability of individuals in history, for had Reagan's vice president, George H. W. Bush, succeeded him at that point, the Reagan presidency would have been a historical footnote and there probably would not have been an American challenge to the Cold War status quo. Bush, like most foreign policy experts of his generation, saw that conflict as a permanent feature of the international landscape. Reagan, like Wałęsa, Thatcher, Deng, and John Paul II, definitely did not.[63]

He shared their belief in the power of words, in the potency of ideas, and in the uses of *drama* to shatter the constraints of conventional wisdom. He saw that the Cold War itself had become a convention: that too many minds in too many places had resigned themselves to its perpetuation. He sought to break the stalemate—which was, he believed, largely psychological—by exploiting Soviet weaknesses and asserting western strengths. His preferred weapon was public oratory.

The first example came at Notre Dame University on May 17, 1981, only a month and a half after Reagan's brush with death. The pope himself had been shot five days earlier, so this could have been an occasion for somber reflections on the precariousness of human existence. Instead, in the spirit of John Paul II's "be not afraid," a remarkably recovered president assured his audience "[t]hat the years ahead are great ones for this country, for the cause of freedom and the spread of civilization." And then he made a bold prediction, all the more striking for the casualness with which he delivered it:

> The West won't contain communism, it will transcend communism. It won't bother to . . . denounce it, it will dismiss it as some bizarre chapter in human history whose last pages are even now being written.

This was a wholly new tone after years of high-level pronouncements about the need to learn to live with the U.S.S.R. as a competitive superpower. Now Reagan was focusing on the *transitory* character of Soviet power, and on the certainty with which the West could look forward to its demise.[64]

The president developed this theme in an even more dramatic setting on June 8, 1982. The occasion was a speech to the British Parliament, delivered at Westminster with Prime Minister Thatcher in attendance. Reagan began by talking about Poland, a country which had "contributed mightily to [European] civilization" and was continuing to do so "by being magnificently unreconciled to oppression." He then echoed Churchill's 1946 "Iron Curtain" speech by reminding his audience:

> From Stettin in the Baltic to Varna on the Black Sea, the regimes planted by totalitarianism have had more than 30 years to establish their legitimacy. But none—not one regime—has yet been able to risk free elections. Regimes planted by bayonets do not take root.

Karl Marx, Reagan acknowledged, had been right: "We are witnessing today a great revolutionary crisis, . . . where the demands of the economic order are conflicting directly with those of the political order." That crisis was happening, though, not in the capitalist West, but in the Soviet Union, a country "that runs against the tides of history by denying human freedom and human dignity," while "unable to feed its own people." Moscow's nuclear capabilities could not shield it from these facts: "Any system is inherently unstable that has no peaceful means to legitimize its leaders." It followed then, Reagan concluded—pointedly paraphrasing Leon Trotsky—that "the march of freedom and democracy . . . will leave Marxism-Leninism on the ash-heap of history."[65]

The speech could not have been better calculated to feed the anxieties the Soviet leadership already felt. Martial law had clamped a lid on reform in Poland, but that only fueled resentment there and elsewhere in Eastern Europe. Afghanistan had become a bloody stalemate. Oil prices had plummeted, leaving the Soviet economy in shambles. And the men who ran the U.S.S.R. seemed literally to exemplify its condition: Brezhnev finally succumbed to his many ailments in November, 1982, but Andropov, who succeeded him, was already suffering from the kidney disease that would take his life a year and a half later. The contrast with the vigorous Reagan, five years younger than Brezhnev but three years older than Andropov, was too conspicuous to miss.

Then Reagan deployed religion. "There is sin and evil in the world," he reminded the National Association of Evangelicals on March 8, 1983, in words the pope might have used, "and we're enjoined by Scripture and the Lord Jesus to oppose it with all our might." As long as communists "preach the supremacy of the state, declare its omnipotence over individual man, and predict its eventual domination of all peoples on Earth, they are the focus of evil in the modern world." Therefore:

I urge you to speak out against those who would place the
United States in a position of military and moral inferior-

ity. . . . I urge you to beware the temptation of pride—the
temptation of blithely declaring yourselves above it all and la-
bel[ing] both sides equally at fault, [of ignoring] the facts of
history and the aggressive impulses of an evil empire.

Reagan chose the phrase, he later admitted, "with malice afore-
thought. . . . I think it worked."[66] The "evil empire" speech completed
a rhetorical offensive designed to expose what Reagan saw as the central error of détente: the idea that the Soviet Union had earned geopolitical, ideological, economic, and moral legitimacy as an equal to the
United States and the other western democracies in the post–World
War II international system.

The onslaught, however, was not limited to words. Reagan accelerated Carter's increase in American military spending: by 1985 the Pentagon's budget was almost twice what it had been in 1980.[67] He did
nothing to revive the SALT II treaty, proposing instead START—
Strategic Arms *Reduction* Talks—which both his domestic critics and
the Russians derided as an effort to kill the whole arms control process.
The reaction was similar when Reagan suggested *not* deploying Pershing II and cruise missiles if the Soviet Union would dismantle *all* of its
SS-20s. After Moscow contemptuously rejected this "zero-option," the
installation of the new NATO missiles went ahead, despite a widespread nuclear freeze movement in the United States and vociferous
anti-nuclear protests in western Europe.

But Reagan's most significant deed came on March 23, 1983, when
he surprised the Kremlin, most American arms control experts, and
many of his own advisers by repudiating the concept of Mutual Assured Destruction. He had never thought that it made much sense: it
was like two Old West gunslingers "standing in a saloon aiming their
guns to each other's head—permanently." He had been shocked to
learn that there were no defenses against incoming missiles, and that in
the curious logic of deterrence this was supposed to be a good thing.[68]
And so he asked, in a nationally televised speech: "What if . . . we

could intercept and destroy strategic ballistic missiles before they reached our own soil or that of our allies?" It was an "emperor's new clothes" question, which no one else in a position of responsibility in Washington over the past two decades had dared to ask.

The reason was that *stability* in Soviet-American relations had come to be prized above all else. To attempt to build defenses against offensive weapons, the argument ran, could upset the delicate equilibrium upon which deterrence was supposed to depend. That made sense if one thought in static terms—if one assumed that the nuclear balance defined the Cold War and would continue to do so indefinitely. Reagan, however, thought in evolutionary terms. He saw that the Soviet Union had lost its ideological appeal, that it was losing whatever economic strength it once had, and that its survival as a superpower could no longer be taken for granted. That made stability, in his view, an outmoded, even immoral, priority. If the U.S.S.R. was crumbling, what could justify continuing to hold East Europeans hostage to the Brezhnev Doctrine—or, for that matter, continuing to hold Americans hostage to the equally odious concept of Mutual Assured Destruction? Why not hasten the disintegration?

That is what the Strategic Defense Initiative was intended to do. It challenged the argument that vulnerability could provide security. It called into question the 1972 Anti-Ballistic Missile Treaty, a centerpiece of SALT I. It exploited the Soviet Union's backwardness in computer technology, a field in which the Russians knew that they could not keep up. And it undercut the peace movement by framing the entire project in terms of *lowering* the risk of nuclear war: the ultimate purpose of SDI, Reagan insisted, was not to freeze nuclear weapons, but rather to render them "impotent and obsolete."[69]

This last theme reflected something else about Reagan that almost everybody at the time missed: he was the only nuclear abolitionist ever to have been president of the United States. He made no secret of this, but the possibility that a right-wing Republican anti-communist promilitary chief executive could also be an anti-nuclear activist defied so

many stereotypes that hardly anyone noticed Reagan's repeated promises, as he had put it in the "evil empire" speech, "to keep America
strong and free, while we negotiate real and verifiable reductions in the
world's nuclear arsenals and one day, with God's help, their total elimination."[70]

Reagan was deeply committed to SDI: it was not a bargaining chip
to give up in future negotiations. That did not preclude, though, using
it as a bluff: the United States was years, even decades, away from developing a missile defense capability, but Reagan's speech persuaded
the increasingly frightened Soviet leaders that this was about to happen. They were convinced, Dobrynin recalled, "that the great technological potential of the United States had scored again and treated
Reagan's statement as a real threat."[71] Having exhausted their country
by catching up in offensive missiles, they suddenly faced a new round
of competition demanding skills they had no hope of mastering. And
the Americans seemed not even to have broken into a sweat.

The reaction, in the Kremlin, approached panic. Andropov had
concluded, while still head of the K.G.B., that the new administration
in Washington might be planning a surprise attack on the Soviet
Union. "Reagan is unpredictable," he warned. "You should expect anything from him."[72] There followed a two-year intelligence alert, with
agents throughout the world ordered to look for evidence that such
preparations were under way.[73] The tension became so great that when
a South Korean airliner accidentally strayed into Soviet airspace over
Sakhalin on September 1, 1983, the military authorities in Moscow assumed the worst and ordered it shot down, killing 269 civilians, 63 of
them Americans. Unwilling to admit the mistake, Andropov maintained that the incident had been a "sophisticated provocation organized by the U.S. special services."[74]

Then something even scarier happened that attracted no public
notice. The United States and its NATO allies had for years carried out
fall military exercises, but the ones that took place in November—
designated "Able Archer 83"—involved a higher level of leadership

participation than was usual. The Soviet intelligence agencies kept a close watch on these maneuvers, and their reports caused Andropov and his top aides to conclude—briefly—that a nuclear attack was imminent. It was probably the most dangerous moment since the Cuban missile crisis, and yet no one in Washington knew of it until a well-placed spy in the K.G.B.'s London headquarters alerted British intelligence, which passed the information along to the Americans.[75]

That definitely got Reagan's attention. Long worried about the danger of a nuclear war, the president had already initiated a series of quiet contacts with Soviet officials—mostly unreciprocated—aimed at defusing tensions. The Able Archer crisis convinced him that he had pushed the Russians far enough, that it was time for another speech. It came at the beginning of Orwell's fateful year, on January 16, 1984, but Big Brother was nowhere to be seen. Instead, in lines only he could have composed, Reagan suggested placing the Soviet-American relationship in the capably reassuring hands of Jim and Sally and Ivan and Anya. One White House staffer, puzzled by the hand-written addendum to the prepared text, exclaimed a bit too loudly: "Who wrote this shit?"[76]

Once again, the old actor's timing was excellent. Andropov died the following month, to be succeeded by Konstantin Chernenko, an enfeebled geriatric so zombie-like as to be beyond assessing intelligence reports, alarming or not. Having failed to prevent the NATO missile deployments, Foreign Minister Gromyko soon grudgingly agreed to resume arms control negotiations. Meanwhile Reagan was running for re-election as both a hawk and a dove: in November he trounced his Democratic opponent, Walter Mondale. And when Chernenko died in March, 1985, at the age of seventy-four, it seemed an all-too-literal validation of Reagan's predictions about "last pages" and historical "ash-heaps." Seventy-four himself at the time, the president had another line ready: "How am I supposed to get anyplace with the Russians, if they keep dying on me?"[77]

VII.

"WE CAN'T go on living like this," Mikhail Gorbachev recalls saying to his wife, Raisa, on the night before the Politburo appointed him, at the age of fifty-four, to succeed Chernenko as general secretary of the Communist Party of the U.S.S.R.[78] That much was obvious not just to Gorbachev but even to the surviving elders who selected him: the Kremlin could not continue to be run as a home for the aged. Not since Stalin had so young a man reached the top of the Soviet hierarchy. Not since Lenin had there been a university-educated Soviet leader. And never had there been one so open about his country's shortcomings, or so candid in acknowledging the failures of Marxist-Leninist ideology.

Gorbachev had been trained as a lawyer, not an actor, but he understood the uses of personality at least as well as Reagan did. Vice President Bush, who represented the United States at Chernenko's funeral, reported back that Gorbachev "has a disarming smile, warm eyes, and an engaging way of making an unpleasant point and then bouncing back to establish real communication with his interlocutors." Secretary of State George Shultz, who was also there, described him as "totally different from any Soviet leader I've ever met." Reagan himself, on meeting Gorbachev at the November, 1985, Geneva summit, found "warmth in his face and style, not the coldness bordering on hatred I'd seen in most other senior Soviet leaders I'd met until then."[79]

For the first time since the Cold War began the U.S.S.R. had a ruler who did not seem sinister, boorish, unresponsive, senile—or dangerous. Gorbachev was "intelligent, well-educated, dynamic, honest, with ideas and imagination," one of his closest advisers, Anatoly Chernyaev, noted in his private diary. "Myths and taboos (including ideological ones) are nothing for him. He could flatten any of them." When a Soviet citizen congratulated him early in 1987 for having replaced a regime of "stone-faced sphinxes," Gorbachev proudly published the letter.[80]

What would replace the myths, taboos, and sphinxes, however, was less clear. Gorbachev knew that the Soviet Union could not continue on its existing path, but unlike John Paul II, Deng, Thatcher, Reagan, and Wałęsa, he did not know what the new path should be. He was at once vigorous, decisive, and adrift: he poured enormous energy into shattering the status quo without specifying how to reassemble the pieces. As a consequence, he allowed circumstances—and often the firmer views of more far-sighted contemporaries—to determine his own priorities. He resembled, in this sense, the eponymous hero of Woody Allen's movie *Zelig*, who managed to be present at all the great events of his time, but only by taking on the character, even the appearance, of the stronger personalities who surrounded him.[81]

Gorbachev's malleability was most evident in his dealings with Reagan, who had long insisted that he could get through to a Soviet leader if he could ever meet one face-to-face. That had not been possible with Brezhnev, Andropov, or Chernenko, which made Reagan all the keener to try with Gorbachev. The new Kremlin boss came to Geneva bristling with distrust: the president, he claimed, was seeking "to use the arms race . . . to weaken the Soviet Union. . . . But we can match any challenge, though you might not think so." Reagan responded that "we would prefer to sit down and get rid of nuclear weapons, and with them, the threat of war." SDI would make that possible: the United States would even share the technology with the Soviet Union. Reagan was being emotional, Gorbachev protested: SDI was only "one man's dream." Reagan countered by asking why "it was so horrifying to seek to develop a defense against this awful threat."[82] The summit broke up inconclusively.

Two months later, though, Gorbachev proposed publicly that the United States and the Soviet Union commit themselves to ridding the world of nuclear weapons by the year 2000. Cynics saw this as an effort to test Reagan's sincerity, but Chernyaev detected a deeper motive.

Gorbachev, he concluded, had "really decided to end the arms race no matter what. He is taking this 'risk' because, as he understands, it's no risk at all—because nobody would attack us even if we disarmed completely."[83] Just two years earlier Andropov had thought Reagan capable of launching a surprise attack. Now Gorbachev felt confident that the United States would never do this. Reagan's position had not changed: he had always asked Soviet leaders to "trust me."[84] After meeting Reagan, Gorbachev began to do so.

A nuclear disaster did, nevertheless, occur—not because of war but as the result of an explosion at the Chernobyl nuclear power plant on April 26, 1986. This event also changed Gorbachev. It revealed "the sicknesses of our system . . . the concealing or hushing up of accidents and other bad news, irresponsibility and carelessness, slipshod work, wholesale drunkenness." For decades, he admonished the Politburo, "scientists, specialists, and ministers have been telling us that everything was safe. . . . [Y]ou think that we will look on you as gods. But now we have ended up with a fiasco." Henceforth there would have to be *glasnost'* (publicity) and *perestroika* (restructuring) within the Soviet Union itself. "Chernobyl," Gorbachev acknowledged, "made me and my colleagues rethink a great many things."[85]

The next Reagan-Gorbachev summit, held the following October in Reykjavik, Iceland, showed how far the rethinking had gone. Gorbachev dismissed earlier Soviet objections and accepted Reagan's "zero option," which would eliminate all intermediate-range nuclear missiles in Europe. He went on to propose a 50 percent cut in Soviet and American strategic weapons, in return for which the United States would agree to honor the Anti-Ballistic Missile Treaty for the next decade while confining SDI to laboratory testing. Not to be outdone, Reagan suggested phasing out all intercontinental ballistic missiles within that period and reiterated his offer to share SDI. Gorbachev was skeptical, leading Reagan to wonder how anyone could object to "defenses against non-existent weapons." The president then proposed a return to Reykjavik in 1996:

He and Gorbachev would come to Iceland, and each of them would bring the last nuclear missile from each country with them. Then they would give a tremendous party for the whole world. . . . The President . . . would be very old by then and Gorbachev would not recognize him. The President would say "Hello, Mikhail." And Gorbachev would say, "Ron, is it you?" And then they would destroy the last missile.

It was one of Reagan's finest performances, but Gorbachev for the moment remained unmoved: the United States would have to give up the right to deploy SDI. That was unacceptable to Reagan, who angrily ended the summit.[86]

Both men quickly recognized, though, the significance of what had happened: to the astonishment of their aides and allies, the leaders of the United States and the Soviet Union had found that they shared an interest, if not in SDI technology, then at least in the principle of nuclear abolition. The logic was Reagan's, but Gorbachev had come to accept it. Reykjavik, he told a press conference, had not been a failure: "[I]t is a breakthrough, which allowed us for the first time to look over the horizon."[87]

The two men never agreed formally to abolish nuclear weapons, nor did missile defense come anywhere close to feasibility during their years in office. But at their third summit in Washington in December, 1987, they did sign a treaty providing for the dismantling of all intermediate-range nuclear missiles in Europe. *"Dovorey no provorey,"* Reagan insisted at the signing ceremony, exhausting his knowledge of the Russian language: "Trust but verify." "You repeat that at every meeting," Gorbachev laughed. "I like it," Reagan admitted.[88] Soon Soviet and American observers were witnessing the actual destruction of the SS-20, Pershing II, and cruise missiles that had revived Cold War tensions only a few years before—and pocketing the pieces as souvenirs.[89] If by no means "impotent," certain categories of nuclear weapons had surely become "obsolete." It was Reagan, more than any-one else, who made that happen.

Gorbachev's impressionability also showed up in economics. He had been aware, from his travels outside the Soviet Union before as-suming the leadership, that "people there . . . were better off than in our country." It seemed that "our aged leaders were not especially wor-ried about our undeniably lower living standards, our unsatisfactory way of life, and our falling behind in the field of advanced technolo-gies."[90] But he had no clear sense of what to do about this. So Secre-tary of State Shultz, a former economics professor at Stanford, took it upon himself to educate the new Soviet leader.

Shultz began by lecturing Gorbachev, as early as 1985, on the im-possibility of a closed society being a prosperous society: "People must be free to express themselves, move around, emigrate and travel if they want to. . . . Otherwise they can't take advantage of the opportunities available. The Soviet economy will have to be radically changed to adapt to the new era." "You should take over the planning office here in Moscow," Gorbachev joked, "because you have more ideas than they have." In a way, this is what Shultz did. Over the next several years, he used his trips to that city to run tutorials for Gorbachev and his advis-ers, even bringing pie charts to the Kremlin to illustrate his argument that as long as it retained a command economy, the Soviet Union would fall further and further behind the rest of the developed world.[91]

Gorbachev was surprisingly receptive. He echoed some of Shultz's thinking in his 1987 book, *Perestroika:* "How can the economy ad-vance," he asked, "if it creates preferential conditions for backward en-terprises and penalizes the foremost ones?"[92] When Reagan visited the Soviet Union in May, 1988, Gorbachev arranged for him to lecture at Moscow State University on the virtues of market capitalism. From beneath a huge bust of Lenin, the president evoked computer chips, rock stars, movies, and the "irresistible power of unarmed truth." The students gave him a standing ovation.[93] Soon Gorbachev was repeating what he had learned to Reagan's successor, George H. W. Bush: "Whether we like it or not, we will have to deal with a united, integrated, European economy. . . . Whether we want it or not, Japan is one more center of world politics. . . . China . . . is [another] huge reality. . . . All these, I repeat, are huge events typical of a regrouping of forces in the world."[94]

Most of this, however, was rhetoric: Gorbachev was never willing to leap directly to a market economy in the way that Deng Xiaoping had done. He reminded the Politburo late in 1988 that Franklin D. Roosevelt had saved American capitalism by "borrow[ing] socialist ideas of planning, state regulation, [and] . . . the principle of more social fairness." The implication was that Gorbachev could save socialism by borrowing from capitalism, but just how remained uncertain. "[R]epeated incantations about 'socialist values' and 'purified ideas of October,'" Chernyaev observed several months later, "provoke an ironic response in knowing listeners. . . . [T]hey sense that there's nothing behind them."[95] After the Soviet Union collapsed, Gorbachev acknowledged his failure. "The Achilles heel of socialism was the inability to link the socialist goal with the provision of incentives for efficient labor and the encouragement of initiative on the part of individuals. It became clear in practice that a market provides such incentives best of all."[96]

There was, however, one lesson Reagan and his advisers tried to teach Gorbachev that he did not need to learn: it had to do with the difficulty of sustaining an unpopular, overextended, and antiquated empire. The United States had, since Carter's final year in office, provided covert and sometimes overt support to forces resisting Soviet influence in Eastern Europe, Afghanistan, Central America, and elsewhere. By 1985 there was talk in Washington of a "Reagan Doctrine": a campaign to turn the forces of nationalism against the Soviet Union by making the case that, with the Brezhnev Doctrine, it had become the last great imperialist power. Gorbachev's emergence raised the possibility of convincing a Kremlin leader himself that the "evil empire" was a lost cause, and over the next several years Reagan tried to do this. His methods included quiet persuasion, continued assistance to anti-Soviet resistance movements, and as always dramatic speeches: the most sensational one came at the Brandenburg Gate in West Berlin on June 12, 1987, when—against the advice of the State Department—the president demanded: "Mr. Gorbachev, tear down this wall!"[97]

For once, a Reagan performance fell flat: the reaction in Moscow was unexpectedly restrained. Despite this challenge to the most visible symbol of Soviet authority in Europe, planning went ahead for the Intermediate-Range Nuclear Forces Treaty and the Washington summit later that year. The reason, it is now clear, is that the Brezhnev Doctrine had died when the Politburo decided, six years earlier, against invading Poland. From that moment on Kremlin leaders depended upon *threats* to use force to maintain their control over Eastern Europe—but they knew that they could not actually use force. Gorbachev was aware of this, and had even tried to signal his Warsaw Pact allies, in 1985, that they were on their own: "I had the feeling that they were not taking it altogether seriously."[98] So he began making the point openly.

One could always "suppress, compel, bribe, break or blast," he wrote in his book *Perestroika*, "but only for a certain period. From the point of view of long-term, big-time politics, no one will be able to subordinate others. . . . Let everyone make his own choice, and let us all respect that choice."[99] Decisions soon followed to begin withdrawing Soviet troops from Afghanistan and to reduce support for Marxist regimes elsewhere in the "third world." Eastern Europe, though, was another matter: the prevailing view in Washington as well as in European capitals on both sides of the Cold War divide was that the U.S.S.R. would never voluntarily relinquish its sphere of influence there. "Any Soviet yielding of the area," one western analyst commented in 1987, "not only would undermine the ideological claims of Communism . . . and degrade the Soviet Union's credentials as a confident global power, but also would gravely jeopardize a basic internal Soviet consensus and erode the domestic security of the system itself."[100]

For Gorbachev, though, any attempt to *maintain* control over unwilling peoples through the use of force would degrade the Soviet system by overstretching its resources, discrediting its ideology, and resisting the irresistible forces of democratization that, for both moral and practical reasons, were sweeping the world. And so he borrowed a trick from Reagan by making a dramatic speech of his own: he announced to the United Nations General Assembly, on December 7, 1988, that the Soviet Union would *unilaterally* cut its ground force commitment to the Warsaw Pact by half a million men. "It is obvious," he argued, "that force and the threat of force cannot be and should not be an instrument of foreign policy. . . . Freedom of choice is . . . a universal principle, and it should know no exceptions."[101]

The speech "left a huge impression," Gorbachev boasted to the Politburo upon his return to Moscow, and "created an entirely different background for perceptions of our policies and the Soviet Union as a whole."[102] He was right about that. It suddenly became apparent, just as Reagan was leaving office, that the Reagan Doctrine had been pushing against an open door. But Gorbachev had also made it clear, to the peoples and the governments of Eastern Europe, that the door was now open.

CHAPTER SEVEN
THE TRIUMPH OF HOPE

*The French Revolution was a Utopian attempt to overthrow a
traditional order—one with many imperfections, certainly—
in the name of abstract ideas, formulated by vain intellectuals,
which lapsed, not by chance but through weakness and wicked-
ness, into purges, mass murder and war. In so many ways it
anticipated the still more terrible Bolshevik Revolution of 1917.*

—MARGARET THATCHER[1]

*[P]erhaps the ultimately decisive factor . . . is that characteristic
of revolutionary situations described by Alexis de Tocqueville
more than a century ago: the ruling elite's loss of belief in its own
right to rule. A few kids went on the streets and threw a few
words. The police beat them. The kids said: You have no right to
beat us! And the rulers, the high and mighty, replied, in effect:
Yes, we have no right to beat you. We have no right to preserve
our rule by force. The end no longer justifies the means.*

—TIMOTHY GARTON ASH[2]

THE YEAR 1989 marked the 200th anniversary of the great revolution
in France that swept away the *ancien régime,* and with it the old idea
that governments could base their authority on a claim of inherited legitimacy. Even as the celebrations were taking place, another revolu-

tion in Eastern Europe was sweeping away a somewhat newer idea: that governments could base their legitimacy on an ideology that claimed to know the direction of history. There was a certain delayed justice in this, for what happened in 1989 was what was supposed to have happened in Russia in 1917: a spontaneous uprising of workers and intellectuals of the kind Marx and Lenin had promised would produce a classless society throughout the world. But the Bolshevik Revolution had hardly been spontaneous, and over the next seven decades the ideology it empowered produced only dictatorships which called themselves people's democracies. It seemed appropriate, then, that the revolutions of 1989 rejected Marxism-Leninism even more decisively than the French Revolution two centuries earlier had overthrown the divine right of kings.

Nevertheless, the upheavals of 1989, like those of 1789, caught everyone by surprise. Historians could of course look back, after the fact, and specify causes: frustration that the temporary divisions of the World War II settlement had become the permanent divisions of the postwar era; fear of the nuclear weapons that had produced that stalemate; resentment over the failure of command economies to raise living standards; a slow shift in power from the supposedly powerful to the seemingly powerless; the unexpected emergence of *independent* standards for making moral judgments. Sensing these trends, the great actor-leaders of the 1980s had found ways to dramatize them to make the point that the Cold War need not last forever. Not even they, however, foresaw how soon and how decisively it would end.

What no one understood, at the beginning of 1989, was that the Soviet Union, its empire, its ideology—and therefore the Cold War itself—was a sandpile ready to slide. All it took to make that happen were a few more grains of sand.[3] The people who dropped them were not in charge of superpowers or movements or religions: they were ordinary people with simple priorities who saw, seized, and sometimes stumbled into opportunities. In doing so, they caused a collapse no one could stop. Their "leaders" had little choice but to follow.

One particular leader, however, did so in a distinctive way. He ensured that the great 1989 revolution was the first one ever in which almost no blood was shed. There were no guillotines, no heads on pikes, no officially sanctioned mass murders. People did die, but in remarkably small numbers for the size and significance of what was happening. In both its ends *and* its means, then, this revolution became a triumph of hope. It did so chiefly because Mikhail Gorbachev chose not to act, but rather to be acted upon.

I.

THE YEAR began quietly enough with the inauguration, on January 20, 1989, of George H. W. Bush as president of the United States. As Reagan's vice president, Bush had witnessed Gorbachev's emergence and the events that followed, but he was less convinced than his predecessor of their revolutionary character: "Did we see what was coming when we took office? No, we did not, nor could we have planned it."[4] The new chief executive wanted a pause for reassessment, and so ordered a review of Soviet-American relations that took months to complete. Brent Scowcroft, Bush's national security adviser, was even more doubtful:

> I was suspicious of Gorbachev's motives and skeptical about his prospects. . . . He was attempting to kill us with kindness. . . . My fear was that Gorbachev could talk us into disarming without the Soviet Union having to do anything fundamental to its own military structure and that, in a decade or so, we could face a more serious threat than ever before.[5]

Gorbachev, for his part, was wary of the Bush administration. "These people were brought up in the years of the Cold War and still do not have any foreign policy alternative," he told the Politburo shortly before

Bush took office. "I think that they are still concerned that they might be on the losing side. Big breakthroughs can hardly be expected."[6]

That Bush and Gorbachev anticipated so little suggests how little control they had over what was about to happen. Calculated challenges to the status quo, of the kind John Paul II, Deng, Thatcher, Reagan, and Gorbachev himself had mounted over the past decade, had so softened the status quo that it now lay vulnerable to less predictable assaults from little-known leaders, even from unknown individuals. Scientists know this condition as "criticality": a minute perturbation in one part of a system can shift—or even crash—the entire system.[7] They also know the impossibility of anticipating when, where, and how such disruptions will occur, or what their effects will be. Gorbachev was no scientist, but he came to see this. "[L]ife was developing with its own dynamism," he commented in November. "[E]vents were moving very fast . . . and one should not fall behind. . . . There was no other way for a leading party to act."[8]

This pattern of leading parties scrambling not to fall behind showed up first in Hungary, where since Khrushchev's suppression of the 1956 uprising János Kádár's regime had slowly, steadily, and discreetly regained a degree of autonomy within the Soviet bloc. By the time Gorbachev came to power in 1985, Hungary had the most advanced economy in Eastern Europe, and was beginning to experiment with political liberalization. Younger reformers forced Kádár to retire in 1988, and early in 1989 the new Hungarian prime minister, Miklós Németh, visited Gorbachev in Moscow. "Every socialist country is developing in its idiosyncratic way," Németh reminded his host, "and their leaders are above all accountable to their own people." Gorbachev did not disagree. The 1956 protests, he admitted, had begun "with the dissatisfaction of the people." They had only then "escalated into a counterrevolution and bloodshed. This cannot be overlooked."[9]

The Hungarians certainly did not overlook what Gorbachev had said. They had already established an official commission to reassess the events of 1956. The rebellion, it concluded, had been a "popular uprising against an oligarchic system of power which had humiliated the nation." When it became clear that Gorbachev would not object to this finding, the authorities in Budapest approved a ceremonial acknowledgment of it: the reburial of Imre Nagy, the Hungarian premier who had led the rebellion, and whom Khrushchev had ordered executed. Two hundred thousand Hungarians attended the state funeral, an emotional event held on June 16, 1989. Meanwhile Németh, on his own authority, had taken a more significant step. He refused to approve funds for the continued maintenance of the barbed wire along the border between Hungary and Austria, across which the refugees of 1956 had tried to flee. Then, on the grounds that the barrier was obsolete and hence a health hazard, he ordered the guards to begin dismantling it. The East Germans, alarmed, protested to Moscow, but the surprising word came back: "We can't do anything about it."[10]

Equally unexpected developments were taking place in Poland, where Jaruzelski had long since released Wałęsa from prison and lifted martial law. During the late 1980s the government had performed a delicate dance with Solidarity—still officially banned—as each sought legitimacy while discovering a mutual dependency. By the spring of 1989 the economy was in crisis yet again. Jaruzelski tried to solve the problem by re-recognizing Solidarity and allowing its representatives to compete in a "non-confrontational" election for a new bicameral legislature. Wałęsa went along reluctantly, expecting the elections to be rigged. But to everyone's astonishment, Solidarity's candidates swept all the seats they had contested in the lower house, and all but one in the upper house.

The June 4th results had been "a huge, startling success," one Solidarity organizer commented, and Wałęsa found himself scrambling once more, this time to help *Jaruzelski* save face. "Too much grain has ripened for me," he joked, "and I can't store it all in my granary." Moscow's reaction was not what it had been to Solidarity's rise a decade earlier. "This is entirely a matter to be decided by Poland," one of Gorbachev's top aides commented. And so on August 24, 1989, the first non-communist government in postwar Eastern Europe formally took power. The new prime minister, Tadeusz Mazowiecki, was sufficiently shaken by what had happened that he fainted during his own installation ceremony.[11]

Gorbachev by this time had already allowed elections in the Soviet Union for a new Congress of People's Deputies: he had "not give[n] a thought," he told Jaruzelski, "to hampering changes."[12] The Congress convened in Moscow on May 25th, and for several days television viewers throughout the U.S.S.R. relished the unprecedented sight of a vociferous opposition haranguing the government. "[E]veryone was so sick of singing the praises of Brezhnev that it now became a must to chide the leader," Gorbachev recalled. "Being disciplined people, my Politburo colleagues did not show that they were unhappy. Nevertheless, I sensed their bad mood. How could it be otherwise when it was already clear to everybody that the days of Party dictatorship were over?"[13]

However true that might be in Hungary, Poland, and the Soviet Union, it was not the case in China. There Deng Xiaoping's economic reforms had brought pressures for political change, a course he was not prepared to take. When former general secretary Hu Yaobang, whom Deng had deposed for having advocated openness, suddenly died in mid-April, student protesters began a series of demonstrations that filled Tiananmen Square, in central Beijing. Gorbachev, on his first trip to China, arrived in the midst of these. "Our hosts," he observed, "were extremely concerned about the situation," and with good reason, for the dissidents cheered the Kremlin leader. "In the Soviet Union they have Gorbachev," one banner read. "In China, we have whom?" Shortly after his departure, the students unveiled a plaster "Goddess of Democracy," modeled on the Statue of Liberty, directly across from Mao's portrait over the entrance to the Forbidden City and just in front of his mausoleum.[14]

Whatever Mao might have thought of this, it was too much for Deng, and on the night of June 3–4, 1989, he ordered a brutal crackdown. How many people died as the army took back the square and the streets surrounding it is still not clear, but the toll was several times greater than that for the entire year of revolutionary upheavals in Europe.[15] Nor is there a consensus, even now, as to how the Chinese Communist Party retained power when its European counterparts were losing power: perhaps it was the willingness to use force; perhaps the fear of chaos if the party was overthrown; perhaps the fact that Deng's version of capitalism in the guise of communism had genuinely improved the lives of the Chinese people, however stunted their opportunities for political expression might be. What was clear was that Gorbachev's example had shaken Deng's authority. Whether Deng's example would now shake Gorbachev's authority remained to be seen.

One European communist who hoped it might was Erich Honecker, the long-time hard-line ruler of East Germany. His most recent election, held in May, 1989, had produced an implausible 98.95 percent vote in favor of his government. After the Tiananmen massacre Honecker's secret police chief, Erich Mielke, commended the Chinese action to his subordinates as "resolute measures in suppression of . . . counterrevolutionary unrest." East German television repeatedly ran a Beijing-produced documentary praising "the heroic response of the Chinese army and police to the perfidious inhumanity of the student demonstrators."[16] All of this seemed to suggest that Honecker had the German Democratic Republic under control—until the regime noticed that an unusually large number of its citizens were taking their summer vacations in Hungary.

When the Hungarian authorities took down the barbed wire along the Austrian border, they had intended only to make it easier for their own citizens to get through. But the word spread, and soon thousands of East Germans were driving their tiny wheezing polluting Trabants through Czechoslovakia and Hungary to the border, abandoning them there, and walking across. Others crowded into the West German embassy in Budapest, demanding asylum. By September, there were 130,000 East Germans in Hungary and the government announced that, for "humanitarian" reasons, it would not try to stop their emigration to the West. Honecker and his associates were furious: "Hungary is betraying socialism," Mielke fumed. "We have to guard against being discouraged," another party official warned. "[B]ecause of developments in the Soviet Union, Poland, and Hungary . . . [m]ore and more people are asking how is socialism going to survive at all?"[17]

That was an excellent question, for soon some 3,000 East German asylum-seekers had climbed the fence surrounding West Germany's embassy in Prague and crammed themselves inside, with full television coverage. The Czech government, unhappy about the publicity but unwilling to open its own borders, pressed Honecker to resolve the situation. With the G.D.R.'s fortieth anniversary coming up the following month, he too was eager to end the embarrassment. He finally agreed that the East Germans in Prague could go to West Germany, but only in sealed trains traveling through the territory of the G.D.R., which would allow him to claim that he had expelled them. The trains were cheered along the way, though, and additional East Germans tried to board them. When the police asked to see identity cards one last time, some passengers threw them at their feet. "The feeling was," one remembered, "'There's your card—you can't threaten me anymore.' It was very satisfying."[18]

Meanwhile guests—including Gorbachev himself—were arriving in East Berlin for the official commemorations on October 7–8, 1989. To the horror of his hosts, the Soviet leader turned out to be even more popular than he had been in Beijing. During the parade down the Unter den Linden the marchers abandoned the approved slogans and began shouting, "Gorby, help us! Gorby, stay here!" Watching from the reviewing platform next to an ashen Honecker, Gorbachev could see that

> [t]hese were specially chosen young people, strong and good-looking. . . . [Jaruzelski], the Polish leader, came up to us and said, "Do you understand German?" I said, "I do, a little bit."

"Can you hear?" I said, "I can." He said, "This is the end." And that was the end: The regime was doomed.

Gorbachev tried to warn the East Germans of the need for drastic changes: "[O]ne cannot be late, otherwise one will be punished by life." But as he later recalled, "Comrade Erich Honecker obviously considered himself No. 1 in socialism, if not in the world. He did not really perceive any more what was actually going on." Trying to get through to him was "like throwing peas against a wall."[19]

Anti-government protests had been building for weeks in Leipzig, and they resumed on October 9th, the day after Gorbachev returned to Moscow. With the Soviet guest gone, the possibility of a Deng Xiaoping solution was still there: Honecker may even have authorized one. But at this point an unexpected actor—Kurt Masur, the widely respected conductor of the Gewandhaus Orchestra—intervened to negotiate an end to the confrontation, and the security forces withdrew. There was no Tiananmen-like massacre, but that meant that there was no authority left for Honecker, who was forced to resign on October 18th. His successor, Egon Krenz, had attended the fortieth anniversary celebration of Mao's revolution in Beijing a few weeks earlier, but he did not think that firing on demonstrators would work in East Germany. It would not happen, he assured Gorbachev on November 1st, even if the unrest spread to East Berlin. There might be an attempt "to break through the Wall," Krenz added, "[b]ut such a development was not very likely."[20]

What Krenz did not expect was that one of his own subordinates, by botching a press conference, would breach the wall. After returning from Moscow Krenz consulted his colleagues, and on November 9th they decided to try to relieve the mounting tension in East Germany by relaxing—not eliminating—the rules restricting travel to the West. The hastily drafted decree was handed to Günter Schabowski, a Politburo member who had not been at the meeting but was about to brief the press. Schabowski glanced at it, also hastily, and then announced that citizens of the G.D.R. were free to leave "through any of the border crossings." The surprised reporters asked when the new rules went into effect. Shuffling through his papers, Schabowski replied: "[A]ccording to my information, immediately." Were the rules valid for travel to West Berlin? Schabowski frowned, shrugged his shoulders, shuffled some more papers, and then replied: "Permanent exit can take place via all border crossings from the G.D.R. to [West Germany] and West Berlin, respectively." The next question was: "What is going to happen to the Berlin Wall now?" Schabowski mumbled an incoherent response, and closed the press conference.[21]

Within minutes, the word went out that the wall was open. It was not, but crowds began gathering at the crossing points and the guards had no instructions. Krenz, stuck in a Central Committee meeting, had no idea what was happening, and by the time he found out the crush of people was too large to control. At last the border guards at Bornholmer Strasse took it upon themselves to open the gates, and the ecstatic East Berliners flooded into West Berlin. Soon Germans from both sides were sitting, standing, and even dancing on top of the wall; many brought hammers and chisels to begin knocking it down. Gorbachev, in Moscow, slept through the whole thing and heard about it only the next morning. All he could do was pass the word to the East German authorities: "[Y]ou made the right decision."[22]

With the wall breached, everything was possible. On November 10th, Todor Zhivkov, Bulgaria's ruler since 1954, announced that he was stepping down; soon the Bulgarian Communist Party was negotiating with the opposition and promising free elections. On November 17th, demonstrations broke out in Prague and quickly spread throughout Czechoslovakia. Within weeks, a coalition government had ousted the communists, and by the end of the year Alexander Dubček, who had presided over the 1968 "Prague spring," was installed as chairman of the national assembly, reporting to the new president of Czechoslovakia— Václav Havel.

And on December 17th the Romanian dictator Nicolai Ceauşescu, desperate to preserve his own regime, ordered his army to follow the Chinese example and shoot down demonstrators in Timişoara. Ninety-seven were killed, but that only fueled the unrest, leading Ceauşescu to call a mass rally of what he thought would be loyal supporters in Bucharest on December 21st. They turned out not to be, began jeering him, and before it could be cut off the official television transmission caught his deer-in-the-headlights astonishment as he failed to calm the crowd. Ceauşescu and his wife, Elena, fled the city by helicopter but were quickly captured, put on trial, and executed by firing squad on Christmas Day.[23]

Twenty-one days earlier, Ceauşescu had met with Gorbachev in the Kremlin. Recent events in Eastern Europe, he warned, had placed "in grave danger not just socialism in the respective countries but also the very existence of the communist parties there." "You seem concerned about this," Gorbachev responded, sounding more like a therapist than a Kremlin boss. "[T]ell me, what can we do?" Ceauşescu suggested vaguely: "[W]e could have a meeting and discuss possible solutions." That would not be enough, Gorbachev replied: change was necessary; otherwise one might wind up having to solve problems "under the marching of boots." But the East European prime ministers would be meeting on January 9th. And then Gorbachev unwisely assured his anxious guest: "You shall be alive on the 9[th of] January."[24]

It had been a good year for anniversaries, but a bad year for predictions. At the beginning of 1989, the Soviet sphere of influence in Eastern Europe seemed as solid as it had been for the past four and a half decades. But in May, Gorbachev's aide Chernyaev was noting gloomily in his diary: "[S]ocialism in Eastern Europe is disappearing. . . . Everywhere things are turning out different from what had been imagined and proposed." By October, Gennadi Gerasimov, the Soviet foreign ministry press spokesman, could even joke about it. "You know the Frank Sinatra song 'My Way'?" he replied, when asked what was left of the Brezhnev Doctrine. "Hungary and Poland are doing it their way. We now have the Sinatra doctrine."[25] At the end of the year, nothing was left: what the Red Army had won in World War II, what Stalin had consolidated, what Khrushchev, Brezhnev, Andropov, and even Chernenko had sought to preserve, was all lost. Gorbachev was determined to make the best of it.

"By no means should everything that has happened be considered in a negative light," he told Bush at their first summit meeting, held at Malta in December, 1989:

> We have managed to avoid a large-scale war for 45 years. . . . [C]onfrontation arising from ideological convictions has not justified itself either. . . . [R]eliance on unequal exchange between developed and underdeveloped countries has also been a failure. . . . Cold War methods . . . have suffered defeat in strategic terms. We have recognized this. And ordinary people have possibly understood this even better.

The Soviet leadership, the Soviet leader informed the American president, "have been reflecting about this for a long time and have come to the conclusion that the US and the USSR are simply 'doomed' to dialogue, coordination, and cooperation. There is no other choice."[26]

II.

BUSH ADMITTED to Gorbachev at the Malta summit that the United States had been "shaken by the rapidity of the unfolding changes" in Eastern Europe. He had changed his own position "by 180 degrees." He was trying "to do nothing which would lead to undermining your position." Perhaps with Reagan in mind, he promised that he would not "climb the Berlin Wall and make high-sounding pronouncements." But Bush went on to say: "I hope you understand that it is impossible to demand of us that we disapprove of German reunification." Gorbachev responded only by noting that "[b]oth the USSR and the US are integrated into European problems to different degrees. We understand your involvement in Europe very well. To look otherwise at the role of the US in the Old World is unrealistic, mistaken, and finally not constructive."[27]

A lot was implied in these exchanges. Bush was confirming that his administration had been caught off guard—as had everyone else—by what had happened. He was acknowledging Gorbachev's importance in these events: the United States did not wish to weaken him. But Bush was also signaling that the Americans and the West Germans intended now to push for German reunification, something that would have seemed wildly impractical only a few weeks earlier. Gorbachev's response was equally significant, both for what he did and did not say. He welcomed the United States as a European power, something no Soviet leader had explicitly done before. And his silence on Germany suggested ambivalence: that too was an unprecedented position for a regime that had sought reunification after World War II only if all of Germany could be Marxist, and when that proved impossible had committed itself to keeping Germany permanently divided.

There had been hints that Gorbachev might modify this position. He had told West German President Richard von Weizsäcker in 1987 that although the two German states were a current reality, "[w]here they'll be a hundred years from now, only history can decide." He had been flattered, on a trip to Bonn in June, 1989, to be greeted by crowds shouting: "Gorbi! Make love, not walls."[28] He had made a point, during the East German celebrations in October, of reciting a poem at the tomb of the unknown Red Army "liberator" which his audience had not expected to hear:

> *The oracle of our times has proclaimed unity,*
> *Which can be forged only with iron and blood,*
> *But we try to forge it with love,*
> *Then we shall see which is more lasting.*[29]

He had reassured Krenz, just before the Berlin Wall came down, that "[n]obody could ignore . . . that manifold human contracts existed between the two German states." And on the morning after the night the gates were opened in Berlin, he recalls wondering "how could you shoot at Germans who walk across the border to meet other Germans on the other side? So the policy had to change."[30]

But German reunification was, nonetheless, an unsettling prospect, not just for the Soviet Union but for all Europeans who remembered the record of the last unified German state. This anxiety transcended Cold War divisions: Gorbachev shared it with Jaruzelski, French President François Mitterrand, and even Margaret Thatcher, who warned Bush that "[i]f we are not careful, the Germans will get in peace what Hitler couldn't get in the war."[31] The one prominent European who disagreed was West German Chancellor Helmut Kohl, who surprised everyone by coming out in favor of reunification a few days before the Malta summit. Bush thought he had done so because "he wanted to be sure that Gorbachev and I did not come to our own agreement on Germany's future, as had Stalin and Roosevelt in the closing months of World War II."[32]

Kohl, then, was leading, but only barely because the East Germans themselves—having broken through the wall—quickly made it clear that they would accept nothing less than reunification. Hans Modrow, who had replaced Krenz as prime minister, informed Gorbachev at the end of January, 1990, that "[t]he majority of the people in the German Democratic Republic no longer support the idea of two German states." The government and party itself, K.G.B. chief Vladimir Kryuchkov confirmed, were falling apart. Confronted with this information, Gorbachev saw no choice: "German reunification should be regarded as inevitable."[33]

The critical question was on what terms. East Germany was still a member of the Warsaw Pact, and over 300,000 Soviet troops were stationed there. West Germany was still part of NATO, with about 250,000 American troops on its territory.[34] The Soviet government insisted that it would not allow a reunified Germany to remain within the NATO alliance: it proposed instead neutralization. The Americans and West Germans were equally insistent that the NATO affiliation remain. All kinds of suggestions surfaced for resolving this dispute, even—briefly—the thought that a unified Germany might have dual membership in both NATO and the Warsaw Pact. Thatcher, no friend of unification, nevertheless dismissed this as "the stupidest idea I've ever heard of." "[W]e were," Gorbachev recalled wistfully, "the lone advocates of such a view."[35]

In the end, Bush and Kohl persuaded Gorbachev that he had no choice but to accept a reunified Germany within the NATO alliance. He could hardly respect the East Germans' determination to dismantle their own state without also respecting the West Germans' demands to remain a part of NATO. Nor could he deny that there was less to fear from a unified Germany linked to NATO than from one operating on its own. The Americans, in the end, made only one concession to Gorbachev: they promised, in the words of Secretary of State James Baker, that "there would be no extension of NATO's jurisdiction one inch to the east"—a commitment later repudiated by Bill Clinton's administration, but only after the Soviet Union had ceased to exist.[36] Gorbachev, for his part, believed that the United States was holding out for NATO membership because it feared, otherwise, that a unified Germany might seek to expel *American* troops: "I made several attempts to convince the American President that an American 'withdrawal' from Europe was not in the interest of the Soviet Union."[37]

What this meant, then, was that Soviet and American interests were converging in support of a settlement that, only months earlier, would have been considered unthinkable: that Germany would reunify, that it would remain within NATO, and that Soviet forces stationed on German territory would withdraw while American forces stationed on German territory would remain. The critical agreement came in a meeting between Gorbachev and Kohl in July, 1990. "We cannot forget the past," the Soviet leader told his German counterpart. "Every family in our country suffered in those years. But we have to look towards Europe and take the road of co-operation with the great German nation. This is our contribution toward strengthening stability in Europe and the world."[38] And so it happened that on October 3, 1990—less than a year after the guards at the Bornholmer Strasse crossing point decided, without consulting anyone, to open the gates—the division of Germany that had begun with defeat in World War II finally came to an end.

III.

GORBACHEV by then had been cheered in East Berlin, Bonn, and Beijing, something no previous occupant of the Kremlin had ever managed. But he had also gained a less auspicious distinction: on May 1, 1990, he became the first Soviet leader to be jeered, even laughed at, while reviewing the annual May Day parade from atop Lenin's tomb in Red Square. The banners read: "Down with Gorbachev! Down with socialism and the fascist Red Empire. Down with Lenin's party." And it was all on national television. They were "political hooligans," Gorbachev sputtered, ordering an investigation. "To have set such a country in motion!" he later complained to his aides. "And now they're screaming: 'Chaos!' 'The shelves are empty!' 'The Party's falling apart!' 'There's no order!'" It was "colossal" to have achieved all that had been accomplished without "major bloodshed." But "[t]hey swear at me, curse me. . . . I have no regrets. I'm not afraid. And I won't repent or apologize for anything."[39]

Was it better, Machiavelli once asked, for a prince to be loved or feared?[40] Unlike any of his predecessors, Gorbachev chose love and mostly attained it—but only outside his own country. Within he was eliciting neither love nor fear but contempt. There were multiple reasons for this: political freedom was beginning to look like public anarchy; the economy remained as stagnant as it had been under Brezhnev;

the nation's strength beyond its borders seemed to have shrunken to that of a doormat. And now another issue was looming on the horizon: could the Soviet Union itself survive?

Lenin had organized the Union of Soviet Socialist Republics as a federation within which the Russian republic, stretching from the Gulf of Finland and the Black Sea to the Pacific Ocean, was by far the largest. The others included the Ukraine, Byelorussia, Moldavia, the Transcaucasian republics of Azerbaijan, Armenia, and Georgia, as well as the central Asian republics of Kazakhstan, Uzbekistan, Turkmenistan, Kirghizia, and Tadzhikistan. After their absorption into the Soviet Union in 1940, the Baltic States of Estonia, Latvia, and Lithuania were added to the list. By the time Gorbachev took power, there were about as many non-Russians as Russians within the U.S.S.R., and the non-Russian republics had achieved considerable cultural and linguistic autonomy—even some capacity to resist political control from Moscow.[41] Still, no one, Russian or non-Russian, saw any serious possibility of the country breaking up.

It is difficult, though, to compartmentalize reform. Gorbachev could hardly call for *perestroika* and *glasnost'* within the Soviet Union, or for letting the East Europeans and the Germans do it "their way," without encouraging non-Russian nationalities who had never fully accepted their incorporation into the U.S.S.R. These included chiefly the Baltic and Transcaucasian republics, where pressures quickly began to build for still greater autonomy, even independence. A Lithuanian professor stated the logic in a meeting with Gorbachev early in 1990:

> [T]he national revival [is] engendered by perestroika. Both are intertwined ... After the [Communist Party of the Soviet Union] resolved to base our political life on democracy, we in the Republic have considered it, first and foremost, as a proclamation of the right to self-determination. ... [W]e are convinced that you are sincere in wishing all people well and understand that you cannot make a people happy against its will.

Gorbachev found this "an indisputable argument." But "while admitting the possibility of secession in principle, I had hoped that the development of economic and political reform would outpace the secession process."[42] That, too, was a faulty prediction.

For as politics opened up while prosperity lagged behind, it became hard to see what benefits a state like Lithuania got from being part of the Soviet Union. The Lithuanians resented how that had come about—Hitler and Stalin had arranged their annexation in the 1939 Nazi-Soviet Pact. They followed closely what was happening now in Germany and Eastern Europe. Whatever lingering doubts there were disappeared in January, 1991, when Soviet troops in Vilnius fired on a crowd of demonstrators, and on February 19th, the Lithuanians decisively voted for independence. Much the same sequence of events occurred in Latvia and Estonia. Gorbachev, still hoping for love, was not inclined to resist.[43]

But if the Baltics seceded, why could the Transcaucasian republics not do the same? Or the Moldavians? Or even the Ukrainians? These were the questions confronting Gorbachev in the spring of 1991, and he had no answer for them. "[A]lthough we were slaying the totalitarian monster," Chernyaev recalled, "no consensus emerged on what would replace it; and so, as perestroika was losing its orientation, the forces it had unleashed were slipping out of control."[44] In June, the biggest republic of them all, the Russian, elected its own president. He was Boris Yeltsin, a former Moscow party boss and now Gorbachev's chief rival. The contrast could not be missed, because for all of his talk of democracy Gorbachev had never subjected himself to a popular vote. Another contrast, less evident at the time, would soon become clear: Yeltsin, unlike Gorbachev, had a grand strategic objective. It was to abolish the Communist Party, dismantle the Soviet Union, and make Russia an independent democratic capitalist state.

Yeltsin was not a popular figure in Washington. He had a reputation for heavy drinking, publicity seeking, and gratuitous attacks on Gorbachev at a time when Bush was trying to support him. He had even once picked a fight over protocol in the White House driveway with Condoleezza Rice, the president's young but formidable Soviet adviser—which he lost.[45] By 1991, though, there was no denying Yeltsin's importance: in "reassert[ing] Russian political and economic control over the republic's own affairs," Scowcroft recalled, "he was attacking the very basis of the Soviet state." It was one thing for the Bush administration to watch Soviet influence in Eastern Europe disintegrate, and then to push German reunification. It was quite another to contemplate the complete breakup of the U.S.S.R. "My view is, you dance with who is on the dance floor," Bush noted in his diary. "[Y]ou especially don't . . . [encourage] destabilization. . . . I'm wondering, where do we go and how do we get there?"[46]

Bush arrived in Moscow on July 30th to sign the START I arms control treaty, now almost wholly overshadowed by the course of events. He and Gorbachev spent a relaxed day at the Soviet leader's *dacha.* "I had the impression," Chernyaev recalled, "that I was present at the culmination of a great effort that had been made along the lines of the new thinking. . . . [I]t never resembled the 'tug of war' of the past." Bush shared the sense, but by the end of the summit had noticed that Gorbachev's "ebullient spirit was gone."[47] On the way home, the president stopped in Kiev to address the Ukrainian parliament. He tried to help Gorbachev by praising him and then reminding his audience:

> Freedom is not the same as independence. Americans will not
> support those who seek independence in order to replace a
> far-off tyranny with a local despotism. They will not aid those
> who promote a suicidal nationalism based upon ethnic hatred.

With that, though, he lost his audience. "Bush came here as a messenger for Gorbachev," one Ukrainian grumbled. "[H]e sounded less radical than our own Communist politicians. After all, they have to run for office here . . . and he doesn't." The crowning blow came when

New York Times columnist William Safire denounced Bush's "chicken Kiev" speech. It was also, arguably, a low blow, but one that captured the administration's ambivalence as it contemplated the possibility of life without the U.S.S.R.[48]

"Oh Tolya, everything has become so petty, vulgar, and provincial," Gorbachev sighed to Chernyaev on August 4th, just before leaving for his summer vacation in the Crimea. "You look at it and think, to hell with it all! But who would I leave it to? I'm so tired."[49] It was, for once, a prescient observation, for on August 18th all of Gorbachev's communication links were severed and a delegation of would-be successors arrived to tell him that he was under house arrest. His own colleagues, convinced that his policies could only result in the disintegration of the Soviet Union, had decided to replace him.

Three chaotic days followed, at the end of which three things had become clear: first, that the United States and most of the rest of the world regarded the coup as illegitimate and refused to deal with the plotters who had carried it out; second, that the plotters themselves had neglected to secure military and police support; and finally, that Boris Yeltsin, by standing on a tank outside the Russian parliament building and announcing that the coup would not succeed, had ensured its failure. Gorbachev could take little comfort in this, though, because Yeltsin had now replaced him as the dominant leader in Moscow.[50]

Yeltsin quickly abolished the Communist Party of the Soviet Union and confiscated all its property. He also disbanded the Congress of People's Deputies, the legislative body Gorbachev had created, and installed in its place a council composed of representatives from the remaining republics of the U.S.S.R. It in turn recognized the independence of the Baltic States, which led the Ukraine, Armenia, and Kazakhstan to proclaim their own. Gorbachev's authority evaporated as Yeltsin repeatedly humiliated him on national television. And on December 8th, Yeltsin signed an agreement with the leaders of the Ukraine and Byelorussia to form a "Commonwealth of Independent

States." He immediately called Bush: "Today, a very important event took place in our country. . . . Gorbachev does not know these results." The president saw the significance immediately: "Yeltsin had just told me that he . . . had decided to dissolve the Soviet Union."[51]

"What you have done behind my back . . . is . . . a disgrace!" Gorbachev protested, but there was nothing he could do: he was without a country. And so on December 25, 1991—two years to the day after the Ceaușescus' execution, twelve years to the day after the invasion of Afghanistan, and just over seventy-four years after the Bolshevik Revolution—the last leader of the Soviet Union called the president of the United States to wish him a merry Christmas, transferred to Yeltsin the codes needed to launch a nuclear attack, and reached for the pen with which he would sign the decree that officially terminated the existence of the U.S.S.R. It contained no ink, and so he had to borrow one from the Cable News Network television crew that was covering the event.[52] Determined, despite all, to put the best possible face on what had happened, he then wearily announced, in his farewell address, that: "An end has been put to the 'Cold War,' the arms race, and the insane militarization of our country, which crippled our economy, distorted our thinking and undermined our morals. The threat of a world war is no more."[53]

Gorbachev was never a leader in the manner of Václav Havel, John Paul II, Deng Xiaoping, Margaret Thatcher, Ronald Reagan, Lech Wałęsa—even Boris Yeltsin. They all had *destinations* in mind and maps for reaching them. Gorbachev dithered in contradictions without resolving them. The largest was this: he wanted to save socialism, but he would not use force to do so. It was his particular misfortune that these goals were incompatible—he could not achieve one without abandoning the other. And so, in the end, he gave up an ideology, an empire, and his own country, in preference to using force. He chose love over fear, violating Machiavelli's advice for princes and thereby ensuring that he ceased to be one. It made little sense in traditional geopolitical terms. But it did make him the most deserving recipient ever of the Nobel Peace Prize.

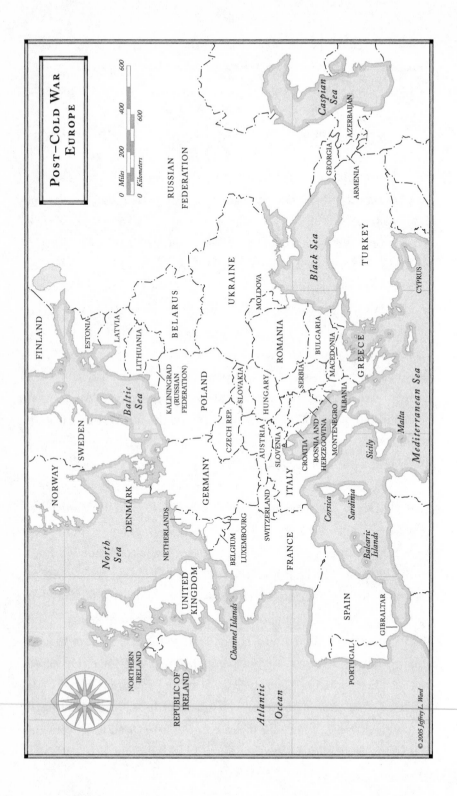

POST–COLD WAR
EUROPE

0 Miles 200 400 600

0 Kilometers 600

RUSSIAN
FEDERATION

FINLAND

NORWAY

SWEDEN

Baltic
Sea

North
Sea

DENMARK

NETHERLANDS

UNITED
KINGDOM

NORTHERN
IRELAND

REPUBLIC OF
IRELAND

Channel Islands

Atlantic
Ocean

ESTONIA

LATVIA

LITHUANIA

KALININGRAD
(RUSSIAN
FEDERATION)

BELARUS

POLAND

GERMANY

BELGIUM

LUXEMBOURG

SWITZERLAND

CZECH REP.

SLOVAKIA

AUSTRIA

SLOVENIA

HUNGARY

CROATIA

BOSNIA AND
HERZEGOVINA

MONTENEGRO

ITALY

FRANCE

Corsica

Sardinia

Balearic
Islands

SPAIN

PORTUGAL

GIBRALTAR

Sicily

Malta

UKRAINE

MOLDOVA

ROMANIA

SERBIA

BULGARIA

MACEDONIA

ALBANIA

GREECE

Black Sea

GEORGIA

ARMENIA

AZERBAIJAN

Caspian
Sea

TURKEY

CYPRUS

Mediterranean Sea

© 2005 Jeffrey L. Ward

EPILOGUE
THE VIEW BACK

AND SO THE COLD WAR ENDED, much more abruptly than it began. As Gorbachev had told Bush at Malta, it was "ordinary people" who made that happen: the Hungarians who declared their barbed wire obsolete and then flocked to a funeral for a man who had been dead thirty-one years; the Poles who surprised Solidarity by sweeping it into office; the East Germans who vacationed in Hungary, climbed embassy fences in Prague, humiliated Honecker at his own parade, persuaded the police not to fire in Leipzig, and ultimately opened a gate that took down a wall and reunited a country. Leaders—astonished, horrified, exhilarated, emboldened, at a loss, without a clue—struggled to regain the initiative, but found that they could do so only by acknowledging that what once would have seemed incredible was now inevitable. Those who could not wound up deposed, like Honecker, or reviled, like Deng, or dead, like the Ceauşescus. Gorbachev, repudiated at home but revered abroad, consoled himself by founding a think tank.[1]

One of the questions the Gorbachev Foundation wrestled with, but never resolved, was: what did it all mean? The failure to find an answer was hardly surprising, for people who live through great events are rarely the best judges of their lasting significance. Consider Christopher Columbus, who might well have looked forward at some point during his life to the 500th anniversary of his great voyages, envisaging it as a celebration of himself, his men, and the ships they sailed, as well as the monarchs who sent them on their way. Columbus could hardly have anticipated that what historians would choose to remember, when the anniversary finally did roll around in 1992, was the near genocide he had set in motion by unleashing the forces of imperialism, capitalism, technology, religion, and especially disease upon civilizations that had few defenses against them.

Columbus's reputation, in turn, would hardly have been what it was had it not been for the decision of the Hongxi emperor, in 1424, to suspend China's far more costly and ambitious program of maritime exploration, thus leaving the great discoveries to the Europeans.[2] A strange decision, one might think, until one recalls the costly and ambitious American effort to outdo the Soviet Union by placing a man on the moon, completed triumphantly on July 20, 1969. It had been, President Nixon extravagantly boasted, "the greatest week in the history of the world since the Creation."[3] But then, after only five more moon landings over the next three and a half years, Nixon suspended the manned exploration of space altogether, leaving future discoveries to be postponed indefinitely. Which emperor's behavior will seem stranger 500 years hence? It is difficult to say.

Humility is in order, therefore, when trying to assess the Cold War's significance: the recent past is bound to look different when viewed through the binoculars of a distant future. What seemed to contemporaries to be momentous issues may come to seem as trivial—and as incomprehensible—as Antarctic tourists might regard squabbles among indistinguishable penguins on drifting ice-floes. But the currents that cause historical drift will carry a certain meaning, since they will partly shape what is to come. So will drifters who hoist sails, rig rudders, and thereby devise the means of getting themselves from where they are to where they hope to go.

Karl Marx knew little about penguins, but he did acknowledge, in the sexist terminology of 1852, that "Men make their own history." Ever the determinist, he hastily qualified the claim by adding that "they do not make it just as they please; they do not make it under circumstances chosen by themselves, but under circumstances directly found, given and transmitted from the past."[4] That was as far as the greatest theorist of inevitability was willing to allow departures from it: it could never be said of Marx that he relished spontaneity. His argument suggests a method, however, for distinguishing what is likely to be remembered about the Cold War from what future generations will dismiss as the incomprehensible squabbling of indistinguishable states, ideologies, and individuals. For events involving escapes from determinism—the hoisting of sails, the rigging of rudders, and the steering of courses never before set—depart from the "normal" in ways the future will not forget, even five centuries hence.

The most important departure from determinism during the Cold War had to do, obviously, with hot wars. Prior to 1945, great powers fought great wars so frequently that they seemed to be permanent features of the international landscape: Lenin even relied on them to provide the mechanism by which capitalism would self-destruct. After 1945, however, wars were limited to those between superpowers and smaller powers, as in Korea, Vietnam, and Afghanistan, or to wars among smaller powers like the four Israel and its Arab neighbors fought between 1948 and 1973, or the three India-Pakistan wars of 1947–48, 1965, and 1971, or the long, bloody, and indecisive struggle that consumed Iran and Iraq throughout the 1980s. What never happened, despite universal fears that it might, was a full-scale war involving the United States, the Soviet Union, and their respective allies. The leaders of these countries were probably no less belligerent than those who had resorted to war in the past, but their bellicosity lacked optimism:

for the first time in history *no one* could be sure of winning, or even surviving, a great war. Like the barbed wire along the Hungarian border, *war itself—at least major wars fought between major states—had become a health hazard, and therefore an anachronism.*[5]

The historical currents that produced this outcome are not difficult to discern. They included memories of casualties and costs in World War II, but these alone would not have ruled out future wars: comparable memories of World War I had failed to do so. J. Robert Oppenheimer hinted at a better explanation when he predicted in 1946 that "if there is another major war, atomic weapons will be used."[6] The man who ran the program that built the bomb had the logic right, but the Cold War inverted it: what happened instead was that because nuclear weapons *could* be used in any new great power war, no such war took place.[7] By the mid-1950s these lethal devices, together with the means of delivering them almost instantly anywhere, had placed all states at risk. As a consequence, one of the principal reasons for engaging in war in the past—the protection of one's own territory—no longer made sense. At the same time competition for territory, another traditional cause of war, was becoming less profitable than it once had been. What good did it do, in an age of total vulnerability, to acquire spheres of influence, fortified defense lines, and strategic choke-points? It says a lot about the diminishing value of such assets that the Soviet Union, even before it broke up, peacefully relinquished so many of them.

Satellite reconnaissance and other intelligence breakthroughs also contributed to the obsolescence of major wars by diminishing the possibility of surprise in starting them, and by eliminating opportunities for concealment in waging them. Surprises could still happen, like Iraq's invasion of Kuwait in August, 1990, but only because the *interpretation* of intelligence failed, not its collection. Once the liberation of that country began early in 1991, Saddam Hussein found his military deployments so visible, and therefore so exposed to attack, that he had no choice but to withdraw. Transparency—a by-product of the Cold

War strategic arms race—created a wholly new environment that rewarded those who sought to prevent wars and discouraged those who tried to begin them.

The Cold War may well be remembered, then, as the point at which military strength, a defining characteristic of "power" itself for the past five centuries, ceased to be that.[8] The Soviet Union collapsed, after all, with its military forces, even its nuclear capabilities, fully intact. The advance of technology, together with a culture of caution that transcended ideology, caused the nature of power itself to shift between 1945 and 1991: by the time the Cold War ended, the capacity to fight wars no longer guaranteed the influence of states, or even their continued existence, within the international system.

A second escape from determinism involved *the discrediting of dictatorships.* Tyrants had been around for thousands of years; but George Orwell's great fear, while writing *1984* on his lonely island in 1948, was that the progress made in restraining them in the 18th and 19th centuries had been reversed. Despite the defeats of Nazi Germany and Imperial Japan, it would have been hard to explain the first half of the 20th century without concluding that the currents of history had come to favor authoritarian politics and collectivist economics. Like Irish monks at the edge of their medieval world, Orwell at the edge of his was seeking to preserve what little was left of civilization by showing what a victory of the barbarians would mean.[9] Big Brothers controlled the Soviet Union, China, and half of Europe by the time *1984* came out. It would have been utopian to expect that they would stop there.

But they did: the historical currents during the second half of the 20th century turned decisively against communism. Orwell himself had something to do with this: his anguished writings, together with the later and increasingly self-confident ones of Solzhenitsyn, Sakharov, Havel, and the future pope Karol Wojtyła, advanced a moral and spiritual critique of Marxism-Leninism for which it had no answer. It took time for these sails to catch wind and for these rudders to take hold, but by the late 1970s they had begun to do so. John Paul II and the other actor-leaders of the 1980s then set the course. The most inspirational alternatives the Soviet Union could muster were Leonid Brezhnev, Yuri Andropov, and Konstantin Chernenko, a clear sign that dictatorships were not what they once had been.

Meanwhile, communism had promised a better life but failed to deliver. Marx insisted that the shifts in the means of production would increase inequality, provoke anger, and thereby fuel revolutionary consciousness within the "working class." He failed, though, to anticipate the *kinds* of shifts that would take place, for as post-industrial economies evolved they began to reward lateral over hierarchical forms of organization. Complexity made planning *less* feasible than under the earlier, simpler stages of industrialization: only decentralized, largely spontaneous markets could make the millions of decisions that had to be made each day in a modern economy if supplies of goods and services were to match demands for them. As a result, dissatisfaction with capitalism never reached the point at which "proletarians of all countries" felt it necessary to unite to throw off their "chains."

That became clear during the Cold War, and it did so largely because western leaders disproved Marx's indictment of capitalism as elevating greed above all else. When set against the perversions of Marxism inflicted by Lenin and Stalin on the Soviet Union and by Mao on China—placing a ruling party and an authoritarian state in control of what was supposed to have been an automatic process of historical evolution—the effect was to discredit communism not just on economic grounds, but also because of its failure to bring about political and social justice. Just as a new world war did not come, so the anticipated world revolution did not arrive. The Cold War had produced yet another historical anachronism.

A third innovation followed: *the globalization of democratization.* By one count, the number of democracies *quintupled* during the last half of the 20th century, something that would not have been expected at the end of the first half.[10] The circumstances that made the Cold War a democratic age remain difficult to sort out, even now. The absence of great depressions and great wars had something to do with it: the 1930s and early 1940s showed how fragile democracies could be when they were present. Policy choices also helped: promoting democracy became the most visible way that the Americans and their Western European allies could differentiate themselves from their Marxist-Leninist rivals. Education too played a role: levels of literacy and years spent in school increased almost everywhere during the Cold War, and although educated societies are not always democratic societies—Hitler's Germany revealed that—it does appear that as people become more knowledgeable about themselves and the world around them, they also become less willing to have others tell them how to run their lives.

The information revolution reinforced the spread of democracy because it permitted people to inform themselves and react to what they learned more quickly than in the past. It became more difficult during the Cold War to withhold news about what was going on in the rest of the world, as well as to conceal what was happening within one's own country. This kind of "transparency" provided new kinds of leverage against authoritarian regimes, as the Helsinki process dramatically illustrated. It also brought assurance, where dictatorships had been overthrown, that they would not return.

But democracies also took root because they generally outperformed autocracies in raising living standards. Markets do not always require democracy in order to function: South Korea, Taiwan, Singapore, and China all developed successful economies under less than democratic conditions. The Cold War experience showed, though, that it is not easy to keep markets open and ideas constrained at the same time. And since markets proved more efficient than command economies in allocating resources and enhancing productivity, the resulting improvement in people's lives, in turn, strengthened democracies.

For all of these reasons, then, the world came closer than ever before to reaching a consensus, during the Cold War, that only democracy confers legitimacy. That too was a break from the determinisms of empires, imposed ideologies, and the arbitrary use of force to sustain authoritarian rule.

There was, to be sure, a great deal to regret about the Cold War: the running of risks with everyone's future; the resources expended for useless armaments; the environmental and health consequences of massive military-industrial complexes; the repression that blighted the lives of entire generations; the loss of life that all too often accompanied it. No tyrant anywhere had ever executed a *fifth* of his own people, and yet the Khmer Rouge leader Pol Pot did precisely this in the aftermath of the Vietnam War. The future will surely remember that atrocity when it has forgotten much else about the Cold War, and yet hardly anyone outside of Cambodia noticed at the time. There was no trial for crimes against humanity: Pol Pot died in a simple shack along the Thai border in 1998, and was unceremoniously cremated on a heap of junk and old tires.[11] At least there was no mausoleum.

Still, for all of this and a great deal more, the Cold War could have been worse—much worse. It began with a return of fear and ended in a triumph of hope, an unusual trajectory for great historical upheavals. It could easily have been otherwise: the world spent the last half of the 20th century having its deepest anxieties not confirmed. The binoculars of a distant future will confirm this, for had the Cold War taken a different course there might have been no one left to look back through them. That is something. To echo the Abbé Sieyès when asked what he did during the French Revolution, most of us survived.

NOTES

PROLOGUE: THE VIEW FORWARD

1. Michael Shelden, *Orwell: The Authorized Biography* (New York: Harper-Collins, 1991), p. 430. My account of Orwell's last years comes from the final chapters of this book.
2. George Orwell, *1984* (New York: Harcourt Brace, 1949), p. 267.
3. Radio-television address, January 16, 1984, *Public Papers of the Presidents of the United States: Ronald Reagan, 1984* (Washington: Government Printing Office, 1985), p. 45.

CHAPTER ONE: THE RETURN OF FEAR

1. Interviews, CNN *Cold War*, Episode 1, "Comrades, 1917–1945."
2. Alexander Werth, *Russia at War: 1941–1945* (New York: E. P. Dutton, 1964), p. 1045. British and American casualty figures are from *Britannica Online*. The Soviet figure is from Vladimir O. Pechatnov and C. Earl Edmondson, "The Russian Perspective," in Ralph B. Levering, Vladimir O. Pechatnov, Verena Botzenhart-Viehe, and C. Earl Edmondson, *Debating the Origins of the Cold War: American and Russian Perspectives* (New York: Rowman & Littlefield, 2002), p. 86.
3. Warren F. Kimball, *The Juggler: Franklin Roosevelt as Wartime Statesman* (Princeton: Princeton University Press, 1991), pp. 97–99.
4. George F. Kennan, *Memoirs: 1925–1950* (Boston: Atlantic-Little, Brown, 1967), p. 279.
5. See, on this point, Alan Bullock, *Hitler and Stalin: Parallel Lives* (New York: Knopf, 1992), p. 464.

6. Pechatnov and Edmondson, "The Russian Perspective," p. 92.

7. Geoffrey Roberts, "Stalin and Soviet Foreign Policy," in Melvyn P. Leffler and David S. Painter, eds., *Origins of the Cold War: An International History*, second edition (New York: Routledge, 2005), pp. 42–57.

8. *Ibid.*, p. 51.

9. John Lewis Gaddis, *The United States and the Origins of the Cold War, 1941–1947* (New York: Columbia University Press, 1972), p. 190.

10. Joseph Stalin, *Economic Problems of Socialism in the USSR* (Moscow: Foreign Languages Publishing House, 1952), excerpted in Robert V. Daniels, ed., *A Documentary History of Communism*, revised edition (Hanover, New Hampshire: University Press of New England, 1984), II, 172.

11. Record of Stalin-Thorez conversation, November 18, 1947, in Levering, *et al., Debating the Origins of the Cold War*, p. 174.

12. Paine's comment is from his 1776 pamphlet, *Common Sense*, excerpted in Dennis Merrill and Thomas G. Paterson, eds., *Major Problems in American Foreign Policy*, sixth edition (New York: Houghton Mifflin, 2005), I, 34.

13. John Quincy Adams speech, July 4, 1821, in *ibid.*, I, 132.

14. Address to Congress, April 2, 1917, in *ibid.*, I, 431.

15. Robert Dallek, *Franklin D. Roosevelt and American Foreign Policy, 1932–1945* (New York: Oxford University Press, 1979), p. 70.

16. Speech to the International Student Assembly, September 3, 1942, in Samuel I. Rosenman, ed., *The Public Papers and Addresses of Franklin D. Roosevelt* (New York: Random House, 1941–50), XI, 353.

17. Roy Jenkins, *Churchill: A Biography* (New York: Farrar, Straus and Giroux, 2001), pp. 350–51.

18. Vojtech Mastny, *Russia's Road to the Cold War: Diplomacy, Warfare, and the Politics of Communism, 1941–1945* (New York: Columbia University Press, 1979), pp. 156–62.

19. Nikolai Novikov to Soviet foreign ministry, September 27, 1946, in Kenneth M. Jensen, ed., *Origins of the Cold War: The Novikov, Kennan, and Roberts "Long Telegrams" of 1946*, revised edition (Washington: United States Institute of Peace, 1993), pp. 3–4.

20. Mastny, *Russia's Road to the Cold War*, p. 270. For the Stalin-Churchill agreement, see Kimball, *The Juggler*, pp. 160–64.

21. Pechatnov and Edmondson, "The Russian Perspective," p. 98.

22. W. Averell Harriman and Elie Abel, *Special Envoy to Churchill and Stalin, 1941–1946* (New York: Random House, 1975), p. 444.

23. Pechatnov and Edmondson, "The Russian Perspective," p. 109.

24. Norman M. Naimark, *The Russians in Germany: A History of the Soviet Zone of Occupation, 1945–1949* (Cambridge, Massachusetts: Harvard University Press, 1995), pp. 69–140.

25. Tsuyoshi Hasegawa, *Racing the Enemy: Stalin, Truman, and the Surrender of Japan* (Cambridge, Massachusetts: Harvard University Press, 2005), provides the most recent account.

26. For a detailed account of the David Greenglass–Julius Rosenberg and Klaus Fuchs operations, see Richard Rhodes, *Dark Sun: The Making of the Hydrogen Bomb* (New York: Simon and Schuster, 1995), pp. 27–198. A third effort, that of Ted Hall, is briefly discussed in Kai Bird and Martin J. Sherwin, *American Prometheus: The Triumph and Tragedy of J. Robert Oppenheimer* (New York: Knopf, 2005), pp. 286–87, and in an interview with Hall in CNN *Cold War,* Episode 21, "Spies."

27. Simon Sebag Montefiore, *Stalin: The Court of the Red Tsar* (New York: Knopf, 2004), p. 502.

28. *Ibid.*

29. Stalin to Molotov, Beria, Mikoyan, and Malenkov, December 9, 1945, in Levering, *et al., Debating the Origins of the Cold War,* p. 155.

30. For more on this, see Robert Jervis, *Perception and Misperception in International Politics* (Princeton: Princeton University Press, 1976), pp. 62–67.

31. Albert Resis, ed., *Molotov Remembers: Inside Kremlin Politics: Conversations with Felix Chuev* (Chicago: Ivan R. Dee, 1993), p. 8.

32. *Ibid.,* p. 73.

33. For more on these crises, see Fernande Scheid Raine, "The Iranian Crisis of 1946 and the Origins of the Cold War," in Leffler and Painter, eds., *Origins of the Cold War,* pp. 93–111; and Eduard Mark, "The Turkish War Scare of 1946," in *ibid.,* pp. 112–33.

34. Kennan, *Memoirs: 1925–1950,* pp. 292–95.

35. Kennan to State Department, February 22, 1946, U.S. Department of State, *Foreign Relations of the United States* [hereafter *FRUS*]: *1946,* VI, 699–700; "X" [George F. Kennan], "The Sources of Soviet Conduct," *Foreign Affairs,* 25 (July, 1947), 575, emphasis added.

36. Pechatnov and Edmondson, "The Russian Perspective," p. 116.

37. Novikov to Soviet Foreign Ministry, September 27, 1946, in Jensen, ed., *Origins of the Cold War: The Novikov, Kennan, and Roberts "Long Telegrams" of 1946,* pp. 3–16.

38. Viktor L. Mal'kov, "Commentary," in *ibid.,* p. 75.

39. Charles E. Bohlen, *Witness to History: 1929–1969* (New York: Norton, 1973), p. 263.

40. *Public Papers of the Presidents of the United States: Harry S. Truman, 1947* (Washington: Government Printing Office, 1963), pp. 178–79.

41. Yoram Gorlizki and Oleg Khlevniuk, *Cold Peace: Stalin and the Soviet Ruling Circle, 1945–1953* (New York: Oxford University Press, 2004), pp. 35–36.

42. Kennan, *Memoirs: 1925–1950*, p. 326.

43. John Lewis Gaddis, *We Now Know: Rethinking Cold War History* (New York: Oxford University Press, 1997), pp. 41–42.

44. Montefiore, *Stalin*, p. 569.

45. John A. Armitage, "The View from Czechoslovakia," in Thomas T. Hammond, ed., *Witnesses to the Origins of the Cold War* (Seattle: University of Washington Press, 1982), pp. 225–26.

46. Nikita S. Khrushchev, *Khrushchev Remembers,* translated and edited by Strobe Talbott (New York: Little, Brown, 1970), p. 411n.

47. John Lewis Gaddis, *The Long Peace: Inquiries into the History of the Cold War* (New York: Oxford University Press, 1987), pp. 158–59.

48. Pechatnov and Edmondson, "The Russian Perspective," p. 139.

49. James V. Forrestal to Chan Gurney, December 8, 1947, in Walter Millis, ed., *The Forrestal Diaries* (New York: Viking, 1951), pp. 350–51.

50. Gaddis, *The Long Peace,* pp. 111–12.

51. PPS/39, "United States Policy Toward China," September 7, 1948, *FRUS: 1948,* VIII, 148.

52. James Chace, *Acheson: The Secretary of State Who Created the Modern World* (New York: Simon & Schuster, 1998), p. 217.

53. Chen Jian, *Mao's China and the Cold War* (Chapel Hill: University of North Carolina Press, 2001), p. 50.

54. Gaddis, *We Now Know,* pp. 58–66.

55. Marc Selverstone, "'All Roads Lead to Moscow': The United States, Great Britain, and the Communist Monolith," Ph.D. Dissertation, Ohio University History Department, 2000, p. 380.

56. Gaddis, *We Now Know,* pp. 66–67.

57. *Ibid.,* p. 94.

58. David M. Oshinsky, *A Conspiracy So Immense: The World of Joe McCarthy* (New York: Free Press, 1983), pp. 108–9.

59. Gaddis, *The Long Peace,* p. 96.

60. Kathryn Weathersby, "Stalin and the Korean War," in Leffler and Painter, eds., *Origins of the Cold War,* pp. 274–75.

61. Gaddis, *We Now Know,* pp. 66–70, 158–61.

62. Gaddis, *The Long Peace,* p. 97.

63. Montefiore, *Stalin,* p. 608.

64. Chen Jian, *China's Road to the Korean War: The Making of the Sino-American Confrontation* (New York: Columbia University Press, 1994), p. 143. See also Shu Guang Zhang, *Mao's Military Romanticism: China and the Korean War, 1950–1953* (Lawrence: University Press of Kansas, 1995), pp. 55–86.

65. Gaddis, *We Now Know*, pp. 79–80.

66. Interview with Lt. Col. Charles Bussey, U.S. Army 24th Infantry Regiment, CNN *Cold War*, Episode 5, "Korea."

67. Zhang, *Mao's Military Romanticism*, p. 78.

68. D. Clayton James, *The Years of MacArthur: Triumph and Disaster, 1945–1964* (Boston: Houghton Mifflin, 1985), p. 536.

69. Kennan, *Memoirs: 1925–1950*, p. 319.

70. Michael Shelden, *Orwell: The Authorized Biography* (New York: Harper-Collins, 1991), p. 430.

71. "International Control of Atomic Energy," January 20, 1950, in Thomas H. Etzold and John Lewis Gaddis, eds., *Containment: Documents on American Policy and Strategy, 1945–1950* (New York: Columbia University Press, 1978), p. 380. The passage is from *Troilus and Cressida*.

CHAPTER TWO: DEATHBOATS AND LIFEBOATS

1. *Public Papers of the Presidents of the United States: Harry S. Truman, 1950* (Washington: Government Printing Office, 1965), p. 727.

2. See his classic novel about the bombing of Dresden, *Slaughterhouse-Five* (New York: Delacorte Press, 1969).

3. These figures come from the *Britannica Online* entry on the Korean War.

4. Bernard Brodie, "War in the Atomic Age," in Brodie, ed., *The Absolute Weapon: Atomic Power and World Order* (New York: Harcourt, 1946), pp. 33–34.

5. Thucydides, *History of the Peloponnesian War*, translated by Rex Warner (New York: Penguin, 1972), p. 48. No one knows how many people died in the Peloponnesian War, but this estimate comes from its most distinguished modern historian, my Yale colleague Donald Kagan. Figures on World War I and II casualties are from *Britannica Online*.

6. Carl von Clausewitz, *On War*, edited and translated by Michael Howard and Peter Paret (Princeton: Princeton University Press, 1976), p. 87.

7. See Kai Bird and Martin J. Sherwin, *American Prometheus: The Triumph and Tragedy of J. Robert Oppenheimer* (New York: Knopf, 2005), pp. 221–22.

8. Diary entries, July 16, 1945, and September 26, 1946, in Robert H. Ferrell,

ed., *Off the Record: The Private Papers of Harry S. Truman* (New York: Harper & Row, 1980), pp. 52, 99. In tracing Truman's thinking on atomic weapons I have particularly followed S. David Broscious, "Longing for International Control, Banking on American Superiority: Harry S. Truman's Approach to Nuclear Weapons," in John Lewis Gaddis, Philip H. Gordon, Ernest R. May, and Jonathan Rosenberg, eds., *Cold War Statesmen Confront the Bomb: Nuclear Diplomacy since 1945* (New York: Oxford University Press, 1999), pp. 15–38.

9. David E. Lilienthal journal, July 21, 1948, in *The Journals of David E. Lilienthal: The Atomic Energy Years, 1945–1950* (New York: Harper & Row, 1964), p. 391.

10. Civil War casualties are from *Britannica Online.* For the Somme, see John Keegan, *The Face of Battle: A Study of Agincourt, Waterloo, and the Somme* (New York: Viking, 1976), p. 260. For World War II strategic bombing, see Richard Overy, *Why the Allies Won* (New York: Norton, 1996), pp. 101–33.

11. James V. Forrestal diary, July 15, 1948, in Walter Millis, ed., *The Forrestal Diaries* (New York: Viking, 1951), p. 458.

12. Vladislav M. Zubok, "Stalin and the Nuclear Age," in Gaddis, *et al.*, eds., *Cold War Statesmen Confront the Bomb*, p. 54.

13. Lilienthal journal, February 9, 1949, in *The Journals of David E. Lilienthal: The Atomic Energy Years*, p. 464.

14. Lilienthal journal, May 18, 1948, in *ibid.*, p. 342. See also Zubok, "Stalin and the Nuclear Age," p. 52.

15. Milovan Djilas, *Conversations with Stalin,* translated by Michael B. Petrovich (New York: Harcourt, Brace & World, 1962), p. 153.

16. Zubok, "Stalin and the Nuclear Age," p. 55; John Lewis Gaddis, *The Long Peace: Inquiries into the History of the Cold War* (New York: Oxford University Press, 1987), pp. 111–12. For the costs of the Soviet atomic bomb project, see David Holloway, *Stalin and the Bomb: The Soviet Union and Atomic Energy, 1939–1956* (New Haven: Yale University Press, 1994), pp. 172–95.

17. John Lewis Gaddis, *We Now Know: Rethinking Cold War History* (New York: Oxford University Press, 1997), p. 91; Zubok, "Stalin and the Nuclear Age," p. 58.

18. Sergei N. Goncharov, John W. Lewis, and Xue Litai, *Uncertain Partners: Stalin, Mao, and the Korean War* (Stanford: Stanford University Press, 1993), p. 69.

19. The interview, with Alexander Werth, appeared in *Pravda* on September 25, 1946.

20. Holloway, *Stalin and the Bomb*, p. 264.

21. These quotes come, respectively, from Zubok, "Stalin and the Nuclear Age," p. 56, and Simon Sebag Montefiore, *Stalin: The Court of the Red Tsar* (New York: Knopf, 2004), p. 601.

22. "NRDC Nuclear Notebook: Global Nuclear Stockpiles 1945–2002," *Bulletin of the Atomic Scientists*, 58 (November/December, 2002), 102–3, also available at: http://www.thebulletin.org/issues/nukenotes/nd02nukenote.html.

23. For more on this, see Gaddis, *The Long Peace*, p. 116.

24. William Stueck, *Rethinking the Korean War: A New Diplomatic and Military History* (Princeton: Princeton University Press, 2002), p. 124. See also Roger Dingman, "Atomic Diplomacy During the Korean War," *International Security*, 13 (Winter, 1988/89), 50–91.

25. See above, p. 45.

26. Stalin to Mao, June 5, 1951, Cold War International History Project [hereafter CWIHP] *Bulletin*, #6–7 (Winter, 1995/96), 59. For the overall sequence of events, see Gaddis, *We Now Know*, pp. 103–10.

27. There is extensive information on Soviet military involvement in the Korean War at: http://www.korean-war.com/ussr.html.

28. Bird and Sherwin, *American Prometheus*, pp. 416–30; George F. Kennan, *Memoirs: 1925–1950* (Boston: Atlantic-Little Brown, 1967), pp. 471–76.

29. Gaddis, *The Long Peace*, p. 113. See also Gaddis, *We Now Know*, pp. 230–32.

30. George Cowan and N. A. Vlasov, quoted in *ibid.*, p. 224.

31. Andrew P. N. Erdmann, "'War No Longer Has Any Logic Whatever': Dwight D. Eisenhower and the Thermonuclear Revolution," in Gaddis, *et al.*, eds., *Cold War Statesmen Confront the Bomb*, p. 101.

32. *Ibid.*

33. Holloway, *Stalin and the Bomb*, pp. 336–37.

34. Gaddis, *The Long Peace*, p. 109.

35. Jonathan Rosenberg, "Before the Bomb and After: Winston Churchill and the Use of Force," in Gaddis, *et al.*, eds., *Cold War Statesmen Confront the Bomb*, p. 191.

36. James C. Hagerty diary, July 27, 1954, in *FRUS: 1952–54*, XV, 1844–45.

37. Erdmann, "Eisenhower and the Thermonuclear Revolution," pp. 106–7, 113.

38. *Ibid.*, p. 109.

39. My argument here has been strongly influenced by reading Campbell Craig, *Destroying the Village: Eisenhower and Thermonuclear War* (New York: Columbia University Press, 1999), especially pp. 67–70.

40. William Taubman, *Khrushchev: The Man and His Era* (New York: Norton, 2003), pp. 147–78.

41. Nikita S. Khrushchev, *Khrushchev Remembers: The Last Testament*, translated and edited by Strobe Talbott (Boston: Little, Brown, 1974), p. 47; James G. Blight, Bruce J. Allyn, and David A. Welch, *Cuba on the Brink: Castro, the Missile Crisis, and the Soviet Collapse* (New York: Pantheon, 1993), p. 130. For Soviet bomber and missile capabilities during this period, see Stephen J. Zaloga, *The Kremlin's Nuclear Sword: The Rise and Fall of Russia's Strategic Nuclear Forces, 1945–2000* (Washington: Smithsonian Institution, 2002), pp. 22–59.

42. For more on this, see Gaddis, *We Now Know*, pp. 234–39; also Sergei Khrushchev, *Khrushchev on Khrushchev: An Inside Account of the Man and His Era*, edited and translated by William Taubman (Boston: Little, Brown, 1990), p. 56.

43. Taubman, *Khrushchev*, p. 407.

44. McGeorge Bundy, *Danger and Survival: Choices About the Bomb in the First Fifty Years* (New York: Random House, 1988), p. 331.

45. Hope M. Harrison, *Driving the Soviets Up the Wall: Soviet–East German Relations, 1953–1961* (Princeton: Princeton University Press, 2003), pp. 111–12; Khrushchev, *Khrushchev Remembers: The Last Testament*, p. 501; Taubman, *Khrushchev*, p. 407; Dean Rusk, as told to Richard Rusk, *As I Saw It* (New York: Norton, 1990), p. 227.

46. Sergei Khrushchev, *Khrushchev on Khrushchev*, p. 356. Emphasis in original.

47. The best account of Khrushchev's American trip is in Taubman, *Khrushchev*, pp. 419–41.

48. John Ranelagh, *The Agency: The Rise and Decline of the CIA* (New York: Simon and Schuster, 1986), pp. 149–59.

49. Andrew Goodpaster interview, CNN *Cold War*, Episode 8, "Sputnik, 1949–61."

50. Michael R. Beschloss, *Mayday: Eisenhower, Khrushchev and the U-2 Affair* (New York: Harper & Row, 1986), pp. 121–22.

51. Zaloga, *The Kremlin's Nuclear Sword*, pp. 49–50.

52. Taubman, *Khrushchev*, p. 444.

53. *Ibid.*, p. 460.

54. Deputy Secretary of Defense Roswell Gilpatric, quoted in Gaddis, *We Now Know*, p. 256.

55. Taubman, *Khrushchev*, p. 536.

56. Aleksandr Fursenko and Timothy Naftali, *"One Hell of a Gamble": Khrushchev, Castro, and Kennedy, 1958–1964* (New York: Norton, 1997), p. 171. See also Taubman, *Khrushchev*, pp. 536–37.

57. Fursenko and Naftali, *"One Hell of a Gamble,"* p. 39.

58. Nikita S. Khrushchev, *Khrushchev Remembers,* translated and edited by Strobe Talbott (New York: Bantam, 1971), p. 546.

59. Taubman, *Khrushchev,* p. 537.

60. See the transcripts of conversations between American and Soviet veterans of the crisis in Blight, Allyn, and Welch, *Cuba on the Brink;* and in James G. Blight and David A. Welch, *On the Brink: Americans and Soviets Reexamine the Cuban Missile Crisis* (New York: Hill and Wang, 1989).

61. Kennedy meeting with advisers, October 22, 1962, in Ernest R. May and Philip D. Zelikow, eds., *The Kennedy Tapes: Inside the White House during the Cuban Missile Crisis* (Cambridge, Massachusetts: Harvard University Press, 1997), p. 235.

62. Taubman, *Khrushchev,* p. 552.

63. Blight, Allyn, and Welch, *Cuba on the Brink,* p. 259.

64. *Ibid.,* p. 203.

65. Gaddis, *We Now Know,* p. 262; "NRDC Nuclear Notebook: Global Nuclear Stockpiles, 1945–2002," p. 104.

66. Blight, Allyn, and Welch, *Cuba on the Brink,* p. 360.

67. Lawrence Freedman, *The Evolution of Nuclear Strategy* (New York: St. Martin's Press, 1983), p. 235.

68. *Ibid.,* p. 238.

69. CNN *Cold War,* Episode 10, "Cuba: 1959–1962."

70. Bundy, *Danger and Survival,* pp. 543–48.

71. For more on this, see Gaddis, *The Long Peace,* pp. 195–214.

72. Yann Martel, *Life of Pi* (New York: Harcourt, 2002).

CHAPTER THREE: COMMAND VERSUS SPONTANEITY

1. Benjamin Disraeli, *Sybil; or, The Two Nations* (New York: Oxford University Press, 1991; first published in 1845), pp. 65–66.

2. Bohlen memorandum, August 30, 1947, *FRUS: 1947,* I, 763–64.

3. William Taubman, *Khrushchev: The Man and His Era* (New York: Norton, 2003), pp. 427, 511.

4. Michael R. Beschloss, *The Crisis Years: Kennedy and Khrushchev, 1960–1963* (New York: HarperCollins, 1991), pp. 224–25, 227.

5. Disraeli, *Sybil,* p. 115.

6. Both quotes are in Tony Smith, *Thinking Like a Communist: State and Legitimacy in the Soviet Union, China, and Cuba* (New York: Norton, 1987), pp. 23, 48.

7. I am following here and in the next several paragraphs an argument first put forward by Arno J. Mayer in his book *Wilson vs. Lenin: Political*

Origins of the New Diplomacy, 1917–1918 (New Haven: Yale University Press, 1959).

8. The latest and best account of this process is Margaret Macmillan, *Paris 1919: Six Months That Changed the World* (New York: Random House, 2001).

9. Edward Hallett Carr, *The Twenty Years' Crisis, 1919–1939: An Introduction to the Study of International Relations* (London: Macmillan, 1940), pp. 37–38. For the context of this quotation, see Jonathan Haslam, *No Virtue Like Necessity: Realist Thought in International Relations since Machiavelli* (New Haven: Yale University Press, 2002), pp. 187–88.

10. Krystyna Kersten, *The Establishment of Communist Rule in Poland, 1943–1948*, translated by John Micgiel and Michael H. Barnhart (Berkeley: University of California Press, 1991), documents this point.

11. Reinhold Niebuhr, "Russia and the West," *The Nation*, 156 (January 16, 1943), 83. See also Richard Wightman Fox, *Reinhold Niebuhr: A Biography* (New York: Pantheon, 1985), p. 227.

12. *The Memoirs of Cordell Hull* (New York: Macmillan, 1948), II, 1681.

13. John Lewis Gaddis, *Strategies of Containment: A Critical Appraisal of American National Security Policy During the Cold War*, revised and updated edition (New York: Oxford University Press, 2005), p. 3.

14. See Harold James and Marzenna James, "The Origins of the Cold War: Some New Documents," *Historical Journal*, 37 (September, 1994), 615–22.

15. For Stalin's "election" speech of February 9, 1946, see *Vital Speeches*, 12 (March 1, 1946), 300–304.

16. Jussi M. Hanhimäki and Odd Arne Westad, eds., *The Cold War: A History in Documents and Eyewitness Accounts* (New York: Oxford University Press, 2003), p. 48. For the background of this speech, see Martin Gilbert, *"Never Despair": Winston S. Churchill, 1945–1965* (London: Heineman, 1988), pp. 180–206.

17. Joseph M. Jones to Dean Acheson, May 20, 1947, *FRUS: 1947*, III, 229.

18. John Lewis Gaddis, *The Long Peace: Inquiries into the History of the Cold War* (New York: Oxford University Press, 1987), p. 154.

19. Disraeli, *Sybil*, p. 246.

20. Bohlen memorandum, August 30, 1947, *FRUS: 1947*, I, 764.

21. For many examples, see Richard Pipes, ed., *The Unknown Lenin: From the Secret Archive* (New Haven: Yale University Press, 1996).

22. Ronald Grigor Suny, *The Soviet Experiment: Russia, the USSR, and the Successor States* (New York: Oxford University Press, 1998), pp. 226, 228, 266.

23. Catherine Merridale, *Night of Stone: Death and Memory in Russia* (London: Granta, 2000), pp. 196–205.

24. See above, p. 24.

25. William I. Hitchcock, *The Struggle for Europe: The Turbulent History of a Divided Continent 1945–2002* (New York: Doubleday, 2002), p. 105.

26. Vladimir O. Pechatnov and C. Earl Edmondson, "The Russian Perspective," in Ralph B. Levering, *et al.*, eds., *Debating the Origins of the Cold War: American and Russian Perspective* (New York: Rowman & Littlefield, 2002), p. 100.

27. Suny, *The Soviet Experiment*, p. 376.

28. Anne Applebaum, *Gulag: A History* (New York: Doubleday, 2003), pp. xvi, 92. For Stalin's last years, see Yoram Gorlizki and Oleg Khlevniuk, *Cold Peace: Stalin and the Soviet Ruling Circle, 1945–1953* (New York: Oxford University Press, 2004); and Simon Sebag Montefiore, *Stalin: The Court of the Red Tsar* (New York: Knopf, 2004), pp. 585–650.

29. Karl Marx, "Manifesto of the Communist Party," in Robert C. Tucker, ed., *The Marx-Engels Reader*, second edition (New York: Norton, 1978), p. 500.

30. For more on Kennan's reasoning, see Gaddis, *Strategies of Containment*, pp. 30–31.

31. Montefiore, *Stalin*, p. 614.

32. Jonathan Brent and Vladimir P. Naumov, *Stalin's Last Crime: The Plot Against the Jewish Doctors, 1948–1953* (New York: HarperCollins, 2003), pp. 312–22.

33. Amy Knight, *Beria: Stalin's First Lieutenant* (Princeton: Princeton University Press, 1993), pp. 186–91.

34. John Lewis Gaddis, *We Now Know: Rethinking Cold War History* (New York: Oxford University Press, 1997), pp. 125–29.

35. The best account, with documents, is Christian Ostermann, ed., *Uprising in East Germany, 1953* (Budapest: Central European University Press, 2001).

36. For the arrest of Beria and its aftermath, see Knight, *Beria*, pp. 191–224; also Hope M. Harrison, *Driving the Soviets Up the Wall: Soviet–East German Relations, 1953–1961* (Princeton: Princeton University Press, 2003), pp. 12–48.

37. Taubman, *Khrushchev*, p. 274.

38. Dulles speech to Kiwanis International, June 21, 1956, *Department of State Bulletin*, 35 (July 2, 1956), 4.

39. Taubman, *Khrushchev*, p. 290.

40. Andras Hegedus interview, CNN *Cold War,* Episode 7, "After Stalin."

41. Taubman, *Khrushchev,* p. 301.

42. Interview, PBS/BBC *Messengers from Moscow,* Episode 2, "East."

43. See Gaddis, *We Now Know,* pp. 66–68.

44. Li Zhisui, *The Private Life of Chairman Mao: The Memoirs of Mao's Personal Physician,* translated by Tai Hung-chao (New York: Random House, 1994), p. 115.

45. Gaddis, *We Now Know,* p. 214.

46. This figure comes from one of the very few studies of this famine, Jasper Becker, *Hungry Ghosts: Mao's Secret Famine* (New York: Free Press, 1996), pp. 266–74.

47. Stefan Heym interview, CNN *Cold War,* Episode 9, "The Wall."

48. Malenkov remarks at Soviet Communist Party Central Committee Plenum meeting, July 2, 1953, in Ostermann, ed., *Uprising in East Germany, 1953,* p. 158.

49. Harrison, *Driving the Soviets Up the Wall,* pp. 72, 99–100.

50. *Ibid.,* p. 124.

51. David Reynolds, *One World Divisible: A Global History Since 1945* (New York: Norton, 2000), p. 134.

52. Harrison, *Driving the Soviets Up the Wall,* pp. 178–79.

53. *Ibid.,* pp. 20–21, 169, 186.

54. Beschloss, *The Crisis Years,* p. 278.

55. Kennedy Berlin speech, June 26, 1963, *Public Papers of the Presidents of the United States: John F. Kennedy, 1963* (Washington: Government Printing Office, 1964), pp. 524–25.

56. Eric Hobsbawm, *The Age of Extremes: A History of the World, 1914–1991* (New York: Pantheon Books, 1994), pp. 257–67.

57. *Ibid.,* pp. 268–71.

58. *Ibid.,* p. 250.

59. Stéphane Courtois, "Introduction: The Crimes of Communism," in Courtois, *et al., The Black Book of Communism: Crimes, Terror, Repression,* translated by Jonathan Murphy and Mark Kramer (Cambridge, Massachusetts: Harvard University Press, 1999), p. 4.

CHAPTER FOUR: THE EMERGENCE OF AUTONOMY

1. Jonathan Schell, *The Unconquerable World: Power, Nonviolence, and the Will of the People* (New York: Metropolitan Books, 2003), p. 347. I have altered this quotation slightly to make it apply to Cold War empires in addition to the colonial empires Schell focuses on.

2. The quotes, together with this account of Khrushchev's deposition, come from William Taubman, *Khrushchev: The Man and His Era* (New York: Norton, 2003), pp. 13, 15; and from Sergei Khrushchev, *Khrushchev on Khrushchev: An Inside Account of the Man and His Era,* edited and translated by William Taubman (Boston: Little, Brown, 1990), pp. 157–58.

3. For two fine discussions of this, see Jared Diamond, *Guns, Germs, and Steel: The Fates of Human Societies* (New York: Norton, 1997), as well as J. R. McNeill and William H. McNeill, *The Human Web: A Bird's-Eye View of World History* (New York: Norton, 2003).

4. I am especially drawing here on Erez Manela, "The Wilsonian Moment: Self Determination and the International Origins of Anticolonial Nationalism, 1917–1920," Ph.D. Dissertation, Yale University History Department, 2003.

5. See above, p. 15.

6. Taubman, *Khrushchev,* p. 354.

7. Eisenhower press conference, April 7, 1954, *Public Papers of the Presidents of the United States: Dwight D. Eisenhower, 1954* (Washington: Government Printing Office, 1960), p. 383.

8. See Vojtech Mastny, *The Cold War and Soviet Insecurity: The Stalin Years* (New York: Oxford University Press, 1996), pp. 71–74, 102; and Simon Sebag Montefiore, *Stalin: The Court of the Red Tsar* (New York: Knopf, 2004), pp. 631, 635.

9. Taubman, *Khrushchev,* pp. 298–99.

10. The best accounts are Robert J. McMahon, *The Cold War on the Periphery: The United States, India, and Pakistan* (New York: Columbia University Press, 1994); and Andrew J. Rotter, *Comrades at Odds: The United States and India, 1947–1964* (Ithaca: Cornell University Press, 2000).

11. Mohamed Heikal, *The Sphinx and the Commissar: The Rise and Fall of Soviet Influence in the Middle East* (New York: Harper & Row, 1978), p. 58. See also Qiang Zhai, *China and the Vietnam Wars, 1950–1975* (Chapel Hill: University of North Carolina Press, 2000), pp. 65–69.

12. Douglas Little, *American Orientalism: The United States in the Middle East since 1945* (Chapel Hill: University of North Carolina Press, 2002), p. 168.

13. *Ibid.,* pp. 170–72.

14. Keith Kyle, *Suez* (New York: St. Martin's, 1991), p. 314.

15. Little, *American Orientalism,* p. 179.

16. See Diane B. Kunz, *The Economic Diplomacy of the Suez Crisis* (Chapel Hill: University of North Carolina Press, 1991).

17. Salim Yaqub, *Containing Arab Nationalism: The Eisenhower Doctrine and the Middle East* (Chapel Hill: University of North Carolina Press, 2004), p. 178.

18. Minutes, National Security Council meeting, July 31, 1958, *FRUS: 1958–60*, XII, 132. See also John Lewis Gaddis, *We Now Know: Rethinking Cold War History* (New York: Oxford University Press, 1997), p. 175.

19. Fredrik Logevall, *Choosing War: The Lost Chance for Peace and the Escalation of the War in Vietnam* (Berkeley: University of California Press, 1999), pp. 6–8.

20. William Stueck, *The Korean War: An International History* (Princeton: Princeton University Press, 1995), pp. 330–42.

21. Minutes, National Security Council meeting, July 2, 1953, *FRUS: 1952–54*, XV, 1307. Emphasis in the original.

22. Kathryn Weathersby, "New Evidence on North Korea: Introduction," CWIHP *Bulletin*, #14/15 (Winter, 2003–Spring, 2004), p. 5. See also Bernd Schäfer, "Weathering the Sino-Soviet Conflict: The GDR and North Korea, 1949–1989," *ibid.*, pp. 25–85; and Balázs Szalontai, "'You Have No Political Line of Your Own': Kim Il Sung and the Soviets, 1953–1964," *ibid.*, pp. 87–103.

23. Mao speeches to the Supreme State Council, September 5 and 8, 1958, CWIHP *Bulletin*, #6/7 (Winter, 1995–96), pp. 216–19. See also Chen Jian, *Mao's China and the Cold War* (Chapel Hill: University of North Carolina Press, 2001), pp. 185–87.

24. *Ibid.*, pp. 174–76.

25. Dulles conversation with Chinese Nationalist Foreign Minister George Yeh, January 19, 1955, *FRUS: 1955–57*, II, 47.

26. Li Zhisui, *The Private Life of Chairman Mao: The Memoirs of Mao's Personal Physician*, translated by Tai Hung-chao (New York: Random House, 1994), p. 270.

27. Gaddis, *We Now Know*, p. 252.

28. Lawrence Freedman, *Kennedy's Wars: Berlin, Cuba, Laos, and Vietnam* (New York: Oxford University Press, 2000), p. 308.

29. Larry Berman, *Planning a Tragedy: The Americanization of the War in Vietnam* (New York: Norton, 1982), provides a succinct account.

30. Press conference, July 28, 1965, *Public Papers of the Presidents of the United States: Lyndon B. Johnson, 1965* (Washington: Government Printing Office, 1966), p. 794.

31. Lady Bird Johnson tape-recorded diary, July 22 and 25, 1965, in Michael R. Beschloss, ed., *Reaching for Glory: Lyndon Johnson's Secret White House Tapes, 1964–1965* (New York: Simon and Schuster, 2001), pp. 403, 407.

32. Ilya V. Gaiduk, *The Soviet Union and the Vietnam War* (Chicago: Ivan R. Dee, 1996), pp. 55–56. See also Logevall, *Choosing War,* pp. 322–23; and Zhai, *China and the Vietnam Wars,* especially pp. 148–51.

33. Anatoly Dobrynin, *In Confidence: Moscow's Ambassador to America's Six Cold War Presidents (1962–1986)* (New York: Random House, 1995), p. 136.

34. I have borrowed this paragraph, and a few other passages in this section, from *We Now Know,* pp. 149–51.

35. Marc Trachtenberg, *A Constructed Peace: The Making of a European Settlement, 1945–1963* (Princeton: Princeton University Press, 1999), p. 132.

36. *Ibid.,* p. 275.

37. Hope H. Harrison, *Driving the Soviets Up the Wall: Soviet–East German Relations, 1953–1961* (Princeton: Princeton University Press, 2003), p. 74.

38. *Ibid.,* p. 104.

39. See, on this point, Gaddis, *We Now Know,* pp. 252–53.

40. Harrison, *Driving the Soviets Up the Wall,* p. 155.

41. Gaddis, *We Now Know,* pp. 146–47.

42. See, on this last point, Trachtenberg, *A Constructed Peace,* pp. 208–9.

43. Taubman, *Khrushchev,* pp. 336–37; also Chen, *Mao's China and the Cold War,* pp. 61–63; John Wilson Lewis and Xue Litai, *China Builds the Bomb* (Stanford: Stanford University Press, 1988), pp. 35–45.

44. Matthew Connelly, *A Diplomatic Revolution: Algeria's Fight for Independence and the Origins of the Post–Cold War Era* (New York: Oxford University Press, 2002), p. 169.

45. Trachtenberg, *A Constructed Peace,* p. 224.

46. For de Gaulle's nuclear strategy, see Philip H. Gordon, *A Certain Idea of France: French Security Policy and the Gaullist Legacy* (Princeton: Princeton University Press, 1993), pp. 57–64.

47. Dean Rusk, as told to Richard Rusk, *As I Saw It* (New York: Norton, 1990), p. 271.

48. Logevall, *Choosing War,* p. 84.

49. Johnson-Russell telephone conversation, January 15, 1964, in Michael R. Beschloss, ed., *Taking Charge: The Johnson White House Tapes, 1963–1964* (New York: Simon and Schuster, 1997), p. 162.

50. Taubman, *Khrushchev,* p. 337.

51. See, on this point, Thomas J. Christensen, *Useful Adversaries: Grand Strategy, Domestic Mobilization, and Sino-American Conflict, 1947–1958* (Princeton: Princeton University Press, 1996), especially p. 244.

52. Minutes, Mao-Yudin conversation, July 22, 1958, CWIHP *Bulletin,* #6/7, p. 155. See also Chen, *Mao's China and the Cold War,* pp. 73–75.

53. Nikita S. Khrushchev, *Khrushchev Remembers*, translated and edited by Strobe Talbott (New York: Bantam, 1971), p. 519.

54. Chen, *Mao's China and the Cold War*, pp. 73, 82–83.

55. Documented with remarkable thoroughness in Lorenz Lüthi, "The Sino-Soviet Split, 1956–1966," Ph.D. Dissertation, Yale University History Department, 2003.

56. Khrushchev, *Khrushchev Remembers*, p. 270.

57. The metaphor, in a slightly different context, comes from George F. Kennan. See John Lewis Gaddis, *Strategies of Containment: A Critical Appraisal of American National Security Policy During the Cold War* (New York: Oxford University Press, 2005), pp. 73–74.

58. Li, *The Private Life of Chairman Mao*, pp. 488–93.

59. Jeremi Suri, *Power and Protest: Global Revolution and the Rise of Détente* (Cambridge, Massachusetts: Harvard University Press, 2003), p. 1. The paragraphs that follow rely heavily on this path-breaking book.

60. Both quotes are in Matthew J. Ouimet, *The Rise and Fall of the Brezhnev Doctrine in Soviet Foreign Policy* (Chapel Hill: University of North Carolina Press, 2003), pp. 19–20.

61. Suri, *Power and Protest*, pp. 172–81.

62. Allen J. Matusow, *The Unraveling of America: A History of Liberalism in the 1960s* (New York: Harper & Row, 1984), p. 405. For the Chicago convention, see pp. 411–22.

63. Henry Kissinger, *White House Years* (Boston: Little, Brown, 1979), p. 56.

64. Nixon address to the nation, April 30, 1970, *Public Papers of the Presidents of the United States: Richard M. Nixon, 1970* (Washington: Government Printing Office, 1971), p. 143.

65. Stephen Ambrose, *Nixon: The Triumph of a Politician, 1962–1972* (New York: Simon and Schuster, 1989), pp. 354–56.

66. David Reynolds, *One World Divisible: A Global History Since 1945* (New York: Norton, 2000), pp. 137–44.

67. The figures come from Suri, *Power and Protest*, p. 269.

68. Li, *The Private Life of Chairman Mao*, p. 463.

69. Jean-Louis Margolin, "China: A Long March into Night," in Courtois, *et al.*, *The Black Book of Communism*, p. 513.

70. Both quotes are in Suri, *Power and Protest*, pp. 209–10, emphasis added in the latter one.

71. Piero Gleijeses, *Conflicting Missions: Havana, Washington, and Africa, 1959–1976* (Chapel Hill: University of North Carolina Press, 2002), pp. 101–59, documents Guevara's failure in Africa. His overall record and posthumous reputation are succinctly assessed in Alvaro Vargas Llosa,

"The Killing Machine: Che Guevara, From Communist Firebrand to Capitalist Brand," *The New Republic*, 233 (July 11 and 18, 2005), 25–30.

72. Li, *The Private Life of Chairman Mao*, p. 514. For more on Mao's thinking during this period, see Chen, *Mao's China and the Cold War*, pp. 245–49.

73. Kissinger, *White House Years*, pp. 182–83.

74. Ouimet, *The Rise and Fall of the Brezhnev Doctrine*, p. 67.

75. Kissinger, *White House Years*, p. 443. See also Zhai, *China and the Vietnam Wars*, pp. 173–74.

76. *Ibid.*, p. 205.

77. Kissinger, *White House Years*, pp. 750–51; Suri, *Power and Protest*, p. 240.

78. Transcript, Nixon-Mao conversation, Beijing, February 21, 1972, in William Burr, ed., *The Kissinger Transcripts: The Top Secret Talks with Beijing and Moscow* (New York: New Press, 1998), pp. 59–65.

79. Ouimet, *The Rise and Fall of the Brezhnev Doctrine*, pp. 16–17, 21, 43–55, 58; Suri, *Power and Protest*, pp. 202–6.

80. Suri, *Power and Protest*, pp. 220–24. See also Timothy Garton Ash, *In Europe's Name: Germany and the Divided Continent* (New York: Random House, 1991); and M. E. Sarotte, *Dealing with the Devil: East Germany, Détente, and Ostpolitik, 1969–1973* (Chapel Hill: University of North Carolina Press, 2001).

81. Quoted in Richard Nixon, *RN: The Memoirs of Richard Nixon* (New York: Grosset and Dunlap, 1978), p. 715. See also Kissinger, *White House Years*, p. 298.

CHAPTER FIVE: THE RECOVERY OF EQUITY

1. Niccolò Machiavelli, *The Prince*, translated by Harvey C. Mansfield, second edition (Chicago: University of Chicago Press, 1998), p. 61.

2. Anatoly Dobrynin, *In Confidence: Moscow's Ambassador to America's Six Cold War Presidents (1962–1986)* (New York: Random House, 1995), p. 316.

3. Richard M. Nixon, *RN: The Memoirs of Richard Nixon* (New York: Grosset and Dunlap, 1978), p. 1018.

4. Interview with David Frost, May 19, 1977, http://www.landmarkcases.org/nixon/nixonview.html.

5. For a succinct history of the Watergate crisis, see Keith W. Olson, *Watergate: The Presidential Scandal that Shook America* (Lawrence: University Press of Kansas, 2003).

6. "Idea for a Universal History with a Cosmopolitan Purpose," in Hans Reiss, ed., *Kant: Political Writings*, translated by H. B. Nisbet, second edition (Cambridge: Cambridge University Press, 1991), p. 45.

7. Adam Roberts, "Order/Justice Issues at the United Nations," in Rosemary Foot, John Lewis Gaddis, and Andrew Hurrell, eds., *Order and Justice in International Relations* (New York: Oxford University Press, 2003), p. 53. I have also benefited, in the paragraphs that follow, from reading my colleague Paul Kennedy's forthcoming book, *The Parliament of Man: The Past, Present, and Future of the United Nations*.

8. Alonzo L. Hamby, *Man of the People: A Life of Harry S. Truman* (New York: Oxford University Press, 1995), p. 13.

9. Kennan to Dean Acheson, November 14, 1949, *FRUS: 1949*, II, 19.

10. JCS 1769/1, "United States Assistance to Other Countries from the Standpoint of National Security," April 29, 1947, *FRUS: 1947*, I, 748.

11. Roberts, "Order/Justice Issues at the United Nations," pp. 62–63.

12. I have drawn, in this and the following section, on some of the arguments I advanced in *The United States and the End of the Cold War: Implications, Reconsiderations, Provocations* (New York: Oxford University Press, 1992), pp. 48–60.

13. "X" [George F. Kennan], "The Sources of Soviet Conduct," *Foreign Affairs*, 25 (July, 1947), 582.

14. Arnold Wolfers, quoted in Wilson D. Miscamble, C.S.C., *George F. Kennan and the Making of American Foreign Policy, 1947–1950* (Princeton: Princeton University Press, 1992), p. 104.

15. Sallie Pisani, *The CIA and the Marshall Plan* (Lawrence: University Press of Kansas, 1991), p. 70. See also Miscamble, *Kennan and the Making of American Foreign Policy*, pp. 106–11; and James Edward Miller, *The United States and Italy, 1940–1950: The Politics and Diplomacy of Stabilization* (Chapel Hill: University of North Carolina Press, 1986), pp. 243–49.

16. NSC 10/2, "National Security Council Directive on Office of Special Projects," June 18, 1948, *FRUS: 1945–1950: Emergence of the Intelligence Establishment* (Washington: Government Printing Office, 1996), p. 714.

17. "Memorandum of Conversation and Understanding," drafted by Frank G. Wisner and approved by Kennan, August 6, 1948, *ibid.*, p. 720.

18. Anne Karalekas, "History of the Central Intelligence Agency," in U.S. Congress, Senate, Select Committee to Study Government Operations with Respect to Intelligence Activities, *Final Report: Supplementary Detailed Staff Reports on Foreign and Military Intelligence: Book IV* (Washington: Government Printing Office, 1976), p. 31.

19. *Ibid.*, pp. 31–32.

20. For a comprehensive account of these C.I.A. activities, see John Ranelagh, *The Agency: The Rise and Decline of the CIA* (New York: Simon

and Schuster, 1986), pp. 203–28, 246–69. See also, on reconnaissance flights, R. Cargill Hall and Clayton D. Laurie, eds., *Early Cold War Overflights*, two volumes (Washington: National Reconnaissance Office, 2003).

21. Miscamble, *Kennan and the Making of American Foreign Policy*, p. 109. See also George F. Kennan, *Memoirs: 1950–1963* (Boston: Little, Brown, 1972), pp. 202–3.

22. NSC-68, "United States Objectives and Programs for National Security," April 14, 1950, *FRUS: 1950*, I, 243–44.

23. For more on this, see John Lewis Gaddis, *Strategies of Containment: A Critical Appraisal of American National Security Policy During the Cold War*, revised and updated edition (New York: Oxford University Press, 2005), chapters 3–5.

24. Loch K. Johnson, *America's Secret Power: The CIA in a Democratic Society* (New York: Oxford University Press, 1989), p. 10. The report was named for its principal author, Air Force Lieutenant General James Doolittle.

25. Gaddis, *The United States and the End of the Cold War*, p. 55. Emphasis in the original.

26. Johnson, *America's Secret Power*, p. 10.

27. Harold M. Greenberg, "The Doolittle Report: Covert Action and Congressional Oversight of the Central Intelligence Agency in the mid-1950s," Senior Essay, Yale University History Department, 2005.

28. Secretary of State Madeleine K. Albright speech to the American-Iranian Council, Washington, D.C., March 17, 2000; Nicholas Cullather, *Operation PB Success: The United States and Guatemala, 1952–1954* (Washington: Central Intelligence Agency, 1994); *FRUS: 1952–54, Guatemala* (Washington: Government Printing Office, 1993).

29. Robert E. Quirk, *Fidel Castro* (New York: Norton, 1993), especially pp. 87–209.

30. See James A. Bill, *The Eagle and the Lion: The Tragedy of American-Iranian Relations* (New Haven: Yale University Press, 1988).

31. Ranelagh, *The Agency*, pp. 288–96. See also David E. Murphy, Sergei A. Kondrashev, and George Bailey, *Battleground Berlin: CIA vs KGB in the Cold War* (New Haven: Yale University Press, 1997), pp. 205–37.

32. Ranelagh, *The Agency*, pp. 285–88, 307–9.

33. Michael R. Beschloss, *Mayday: Eisenhower, Khrushchev and the U-2 Affair* (New York: Harper & Row, 1986), pp. 173, 372.

34. Lawrence Freedman, *Kennedy's Wars: Berlin, Cuba, Laos, and Vietnam* (New York: Oxford University Press, 2000), pp. 140, 146.

35. Conversation with Senator Richard Russell, May 27, 1964, in Michael R. Beschloss, ed., *Taking Charge: The Johnson White House Tapes, 1963–1964* (New York: Simon and Schuster, 1997), p. 365.

36. Johnson to Rusk, McNamara, and McCone, December 7, 1964, *FRUS: 1964–68*, I, document 440. See also Robert Dallek, *Flawed Giant: Lyndon Johnson and His Times, 1961–1973* (New York: Oxford University Press, 1998), pp. 238–41, 277.

37. *Ibid.*, p. 276.

38. Gaddis, *Strategies of Containment*, pp. 256–58.

39. *Ibid.*, pp. 259–60.

40. Stanley Karnow, *Vietnam: A History* (New York: Viking, 1983), pp. 515–56.

41. Nixon, *RN*, p. 390.

42. *Ibid.*, p. 382.

43. Henry Kissinger, *White House Years* (Boston: Little, Brown, 1979), pp. 252–53; Olson, *Watergate*, p. 12.

44. Nixon radio-television interview, January 4, 1971, *Public Papers of the Presidents of the United States: Richard M. Nixon, 1971* (Washington: Government Printing Office, 1972), p. 12.

45. C.I.A. memorandum, Nixon meeting with Richard Helms, September 16, 1970, in Peter Kornbluh, ed., *The Pinochet File: A Declassified Dossier on Atrocity and Accountability* (New York: New Press, 2004), p. 37.

46. Viron Vaky to Kissinger, September 14, 1970, quoted in *ibid.*, p. 11.

47. Nixon conversation with Robert Haldeman, July 1, 1971, in Stanley I. Kutler, ed., *Abuse of Power: The New Nixon Tapes* (New York: Free Press, 1997), p. 8, emphasis in original. See also Nixon, *RN*, pp. 508–15.

48. Olson, *Watergate*, p. 37.

49. For some possible motives, see *ibid.*, pp. 36–42.

50. Henry Kissinger, *Years of Upheaval* (Boston: Little, Brown, 1982), pp. 307–8.

51. *Ibid.*, pp. 542, 546.

52. Johnson, *America's Secret Power*, pp. 157–59, 208.

53. Ranelagh, *The Agency*, pp. 520–30, 571–72.

54. The fullest recent account, highly critical of Nixon and Kissinger, is Kornbluh, *The Pinochet File.* Kissinger's defense of administration policy is in *Years of Upheaval*, pp. 374–413, and *Years of Renewal* (New York: Simon and Schuster, 1999), pp. 749–60.

55. See especially Christopher Hitchens, *The Trial of Henry Kissinger* (New York: Verso, 2001); William D. Rogers and Kenneth Maxwell, "Fleeing the Chilean Coup," *Foreign Affairs*, 83 (January/February, 2004), 160–65; David Glenn, "'Foreign Affairs' Loses a Longtime Editor and His Re-

placement in Row Over Editorial Independence," *Chronicle of Higher Education*, June 25, 2004, p. A25.

56. Kissinger, *Years of Renewal*, p. 832.

57. Piero Gleijeses, *Conflicting Missions: Havana, Washington, and Africa, 1959–1976* (Chapel Hill: University of North Carolina Press, 2002), pp. 230–396, provides the best account.

58. For more on this, see John Lewis Gaddis, *The Long Peace: Inquiries into the History of the Cold War* (New York: Oxford University Press, 1987), pp. 219–23.

59. Contemporary television interview, CNN *Cold War*, Episode 7, "After Stalin."

60. Dean Rusk, as told to Richard Rusk, *As I Saw It* (New York: Norton, 1990), p. 361. See also Chris Michel, "Bridges Built and Broken Down: How Lyndon Johnson Lost His Gamble on the Fate of the Prague Spring," Senior Essay, Yale University History Department, 2003.

61. Henry A. Kissinger, *A World Restored* (New York: Houghton Mifflin, 1957), pp. 1–2.

62. Kissinger speech to the *Pacem in Terris* III Conference, Washington, October 8, 1973, in Henry A. Kissinger, *American Foreign Policy*, third edition (New York: Norton, 1977), p. 121.

63. *Ibid.*

64. Henry Jackson press conference, September 20, 1974, CNN *Cold War*, Episode 16, "Détente."

65. Kissinger, *Years of Upheaval*, p. 254.

66. Dobrynin, *In Confidence*, p. 268.

67. Kissinger, *Years of Upheaval*, p. 243. See also Henry Kissinger, *Diplomacy* (New York: Simon and Schuster, 1994), pp. 713–14.

68. Robert D. English, *Russia and the Idea of the West: Gorbachev, Intellectuals, and the End of the Cold War* (New York: Columbia University Press, 2000), p. 118.

69. Len Karpinsky, quoted in *ibid.*, 114–15.

70. Timothy Garton Ash, *The Uses of Adversity: Essays on the Fate of Central Europe* (New York: Random House, 1989), p. 10.

71. Politburo minutes, January 7, 1974, in Michael Scammell, ed., *The Solzhenitsyn Files*, translated under the supervision of Catherine A. Fitzpatrick (Chicago: Edition Q, 1995), p. 284.

72. John Lewis Gaddis, *Russia, the Soviet Union, and the United States: An Interpretive History*, second edition (New York: McGraw-Hill, 1990), pp. 283–84.

73. Kissinger, *Years of Renewal*, p. 636.

74. Raymond Garthoff, *Détente and Confrontation: American-Soviet Relations from Nixon to Reagan,* revised edition (Washington: Brookings Institution, 1994), pp. 125–39.

75. For further speculation on Brezhnev's motives, see Kissinger, *Diplomacy,* p. 758.

76. Conference on Security and Co-operation in Europe "Final Act," Helsinki, August 1, 1975, at: http://www.osce.org/docs/English/1990-1999/summits/helfa75e.htm.

77. The negotiations are discussed in William G. Hyland, *Mortal Rivals: Understanding the Hidden Pattern of Soviet-American Relations* (New York: Simon and Schuster, 1987), pp. 114–19. I am also drawing here on an unpublished paper by a Yale University History Ph.D. student, Michael D. J. Morgan, "North America, Atlanticism, and the Helsinki Process."

78. Dobrynin, *In Confidence,* p. 346.

79. Hyland, *Mortal Rivals,* p. 122; Kissinger, *Years of Renewal,* p. 635.

80. *Ibid.,* pp. 648–52, 861–67.

81. *Ibid.,* p. 866; *A Time to Heal: The Autobiography of Gerald R. Ford* (New York: Harper & Row, 1979), pp. 422–25.

82. Dobrynin, *In Confidence,* pp. 345–46.

83. For more on this, see Daniel C. Thomas, "Human Rights Ideas, the Demise of Communism, and the End of the Cold War," *Journal of Cold War Studies,* 7 (Spring, 2005), pp. 111–12.

84. Andrei Sakharov, *Memoirs,* translated by Richard Lourie (New York: Knopf, 1990), pp. 456–57. See also Daniel C. Thomas, *The Helsinki Effect: International Norms, Human Rights, and the Demise of Communism* (Princeton: Princeton University Press, 2001).

85. Garton Ash, *The Uses of Adversity,* p. 64; Gale Stokes, *The Walls Came Tumbling Down: The Collapse of Communism in Eastern Europe* (New York: Oxford University Press, 1993), pp. 24–25.

86. *Ibid.,* p. 24.

87. Václav Havel, *Living in Truth,* edited by Jan Vladislav (London: Faber and Faber, 1989), p. 59. See also Garton Ash, *The Uses of Adversity,* p. 192; and Jonathan Schell, *The Unconquerable World: Power, Nonviolence, and the Will of the People* (New York: Metropolitan Books, 2003), pp. 195–204.

88. George Weigel, *Witness to Hope: The Biography of Pope John Paul II, 1920–2005* (New York: Harper, 2005), pp. 184–85, 279, 301, 304.

89. *Ibid.,* pp. 293, 305–20.

90. The best source for this familiar quotation—even though it is indirect— is Winston S. Churchill, *The Second World War: The Gathering Storm* (New York: Bantam, 1961), p. 121. For the Soviet reaction to John Paul II's

visit, see Matthew J. Ouimet, *The Rise and Fall of the Brezhnev Doctrine in Soviet Foreign Policy* (Chapel Hill: University of North Carolina Press, 2003), pp. 114–16.

CHAPTER SIX: ACTORS

1. On many occasions, but see especially George Weigel, *Witness to Hope: The Biography of Pope John Paul II, 1920–2005* (New York: Harper, 2005), pp. 10, 14, 262.

2. Richard Baum, *Burying Mao: Chinese Politics in the Age of Deng Xiaoping* (Princeton: Princeton University Press, 1994), p. 47.

3. Mikhail Gorbachev, *Memoirs* (New York: Doubleday, 1995), p. 165.

4. See, for example, Kenneth N. Waltz, *Theory of International Politics* (New York: Random House, 1979), pp. 161–83.

5. John Lewis Gaddis, *The Long Peace: Inquiries into the History of the Cold War* (New York: Oxford University Press, 1987), especially pp. 215–45.

6. *Ibid.,* pp. 195–214, 237–43.

7. Address to the Commonwealth Club and the World Affairs Council of Northern California, San Francisco, February 3, 1976, in Henry A. Kissinger, *American Foreign Policy,* third edition (New York: Norton, 1977), p. 305.

8. Tony Smith, *America's Mission: The United States and the Worldwide Struggle for Democracy in the Twentieth Century* (Princeton: Princeton University Press, 1994), especially pp. 146–236.

9. Robert D. English, *Russia and the Idea of the West: Gorbachev, Intellectuals, and the End of the Cold War* (New York: Columbia University Press, 2000), documents this tendency inside the Soviet Union.

10. See, on this phenomenon, David Reynolds, *One World Divisible: A Global History Since 1945* (New York: Norton, 2000), pp. 498–506.

11. For further details, see John Lewis Gaddis, *Strategies of Containment: A Critical Appraisal of American National Security Policy During the Cold War,* revised and updated edition (New York: Oxford University Press, 2005), pp. 322–25; also Gaddis, *The Long Peace,* p. 208.

12. Raymond L. Garthoff, *Détente and Confrontation: American-Soviet Relations from Nixon to Reagan,* revised edition (Washington: Brookings Institution, 1994), pp. 146–223, presents a detailed history of the SALT I negotiations.

13. Henry Kissinger, *Years of Upheaval* (Boston: Little, Brown, 1982), p. 265. For the Jackson resolution, see McGeorge Bundy, *Danger and Survival: Choices About the Bomb in the First Fifty Years* (New York: Random House, 1988), pp. 553–56.

14. Garthoff, *Détente and Confrontation,* pp. 494–505, 596–600.

15. Gaddis Smith, *Morality, Reason, and Power: American Diplomacy in the Carter Years* (New York: Hill and Wang, 1986), pp. 30–31, 67–77; Zbigniew Brzezinski, *Power and Principle: Memoirs of the National Security Adviser, 1977–1981* (New York: Farrar, Straus, Giroux, 1983), p. 157; Jimmy Carter, *Keeping Faith: Memoirs of a President* (New York: Bantam, 1982), pp. 215, 219.

16. Georgi Arbatov, *The System: An Insider's Life in Soviet Politics* (New York: Random House, 1992), pp. 191–92.

17. David Holloway, *The Soviet Union and the Arms Race* (New Haven: Yale University Press, 1983), pp. 49–55.

18. Arbatov, *The System,* pp. 205–6; Anatoly Dobrynin, *In Confidence: Moscow's Ambassador to America's Six Cold War Presidents (1962–1986)* (New York: Random House, 1995), pp. 251–52.

19. Garthoff, *Détente and Confrontation,* p. 880n.

20. *Ibid.,* pp. 913–57.

21. *Department of State Bulletin,* 66 (June 26, 1972), 898–99.

22. Leonid Brezhnev, *On the Policy of the Soviet Union and the International Situation* (Garden City, New York: Doubleday, 1973), pp. 230–31. See also Dobrynin, *In Confidence,* pp. 251–52.

23. Henry Kissinger, *White House Years* (Boston: Little, Brown, 1979), p. 1250.

24. Anwar el-Sadat, *In Search of Identity: An Autobiography* (New York: Harper & Row, 1977), p. 229; Kissinger, *Years of Upheaval,* p. 637.

25. *Ibid.,* p. 638. See also William B. Quandt, *Camp David: Peacemaking and Politics* (Washington: Brookings Institution, 1986). I have learned much about Sadat's strategy and Kissinger's respect for it from supervising two Yale History Department senior essays, Christopher W. Wells, "Kissinger and Sadat: Improbable Partners for Peace" (2004), and Anne Lesley Rosenzweig, "Sadat's Strategic Decision Making: Lessons of Egyptian Foreign Policy, 1970–1981" (2005).

26. Kissinger, *Years of Upheaval,* p. 594; also p. 600.

27. Dobrynin, *In Confidence,* p. 301.

28. *Ibid.,* pp. 404–5. See also Ilya V. Gaiduk, *The Soviet Union and the Vietnam War* (Chicago: Ivan R. Dee, 1996), especially pp. 246–50; Piero Gleijeses, *Conflicting Missions: Havana, Washington, and Africa, 1959–1976* (Chapel Hill: University of North Carolina Press, 2002), pp. 365–72; and Odd Arne Westad, "The Fall of Détente and the Turning Tides of History," in Westad, ed., *The Fall of Détente: Soviet-American Relations during the Carter Years* (Oslo: Scandinavian University Press, 1997), pp. 11–12.

29. Dobrynin, *In Confidence,* pp. 263, 405.

30. Arbatov, *The System,* p. 195.

31. Dobrynin, *In Confidence,* p. 407.

32. Odd Arne Westad, "The Road to Kabul: Soviet Policy on Afghanistan, 1978–1979," in Westad, ed., *The Fall of Détente,* pp. 119–25.

33. Transcript, Kosygin-Taraki telephone conversation, March 17 or 18, 1979, CWIHP *Bulletin,* #8–9 (Winter, 1996/1997), p. 145.

34. Transcript, Kosygin-Taraki meeting, Moscow, March 29, 1979, *ibid.,* p. 147.

35. Quoted in Westad, "The Road to Kabul," p. 132.

36. *Ibid.,* pp. 133–42; Dobrynin, *In Confidence,* pp. 439–40.

37. Carter address to Congress, January 23, 1980, *Public Papers of the Presidents of the United States: Jimmy Carter, 1980–81* (Washington: Government Printing Office, 1982), p. 197; Minutes, Politburo meeting, January 17, 1980, in Westad, ed., *The Fall of Détente,* p. 321. See also John Lewis Gaddis, *Russia, the Soviet Union, and the United States: An Interpretive History,* second edition (New York: McGraw-Hill, 1990), pp. 295–98, 310–12.

38. Gaddis, *Strategies of Containment,* pp. 318–27; Aaron L. Friedberg, *In the Shadow of the Garrison State: America's Anti-Statism and Its Cold War Grand Strategy* (Princeton: Princeton University Press, 2000), pp. 82–84.

39. Kissinger, *White House Years,* p. 62, italics in the original. See also John Lewis Gaddis, "Rescuing Choice from Circumstance: The Statecraft of Henry Kissinger," in Gordon A. Craig and Francis L. Loewenheim, eds., *The Diplomats: 1939–1979* (Princeton: Princeton University Press, 1994), pp. 568–70.

40. M. E. Sarotte, *Dealing with the Devil: East Germany, Détente, and Ostpolitik, 1969–1973* (Chapel Hill: University of North Carolina Press, 2001), pp. 44–54. The quote is on p. 46.

41. Matthew J. Ouimet, *The Rise and Fall of the Brezhnev Doctrine in Soviet Foreign Policy* (Chapel Hill: University of North Carolina Press, 2003), pp. 100–107.

42. *Ibid.,* pp. 87–88.

43. The United States spent 4.9 percent of its gross domestic product ($1,984 billion) on defense in 1977. Soviet figures are much less precise, but a reasonable estimate for the same year is 15–17 percent on a GDP of about $340 billion. [Friedberg, *In the Shadow of the Garrison State,* p. 82n; Gaddis, *Strategies of Containment,* p. 393; International Institute for Strategic Studies, *The Military Balance, 1979–1980* (London: IISS, 1979), p. 9.]

44. Arbatov, *The System,* p. 206.

45. Baum, *Burying Mao,* pp. 11, 56–65; Richard Evans, *Deng Xiaoping and the Making of Modern China* (New York: Penguin, 1997), pp. 184–89, 212–43.

The quote from Mao is in Li Zhisui, *The Private Life of Chairman Mao: The Memoirs of Mao's Personal Physician,* translated by Tai Hung-chao (New York: Random House, 1994), p. 577. I have also benefited from reading Bryan Wong, "The Grand Strategy of Deng Xiaoping," International Studies Senior Essay, Yale University, 2005.

46. "The 'Two Whatevers' Do Not Accord with Marxism," March 24, 1977, http://English.people.com.cn/dengxp/vol2/text/b1100.html.

47. For the relevant statistics, see Baum, *Burying Mao,* p. 391.

48. Mikhail Gorbachev and Zdeněk Mlynář, *Conversations with Gorbachev: On Perestroika, The Prague Spring, and the Crossroads of Socialism,* translated by George Schriver (New York: Columbia University Press, 2002), p. 189.

49. William I. Hitchcock, *The Struggle for Europe: The Turbulent History of a Divided Continent, 1945–2002* (New York: Doubleday, 2002), pp. 328–32. The quote is from Margaret Thatcher, *The Downing Street Years* (New York: HarperCollins, 1993), p. 7.

50. *Ibid.,* pp. 86–87.

51. Radio broadcast of May 29, 1979, in Kiron K. Skinner, Annelise Anderson, and Martin Anderson, eds., *Reagan, In His Own Hand* (New York: Free Press, 2001), p. 47.

52. Radio broadcast of August 7, 1978, in *ibid.,* p. 15.

53. For more on this, see Gaddis, *Strategies of Containment,* pp. 349–53.

54. Radio broadcast, May, 1975, in Skinner, *et al.,* eds., *Reagan, In His Own Hand,* p. 12.

55. Quoted in Paul Lettow, *Ronald Reagan and His Quest to Abolish Nuclear Weapons* (New York: Random House, 2005), p. 30.

56. Radio broadcast, March 23, 1977, in Skinner, *et al.,* eds., *Reagan, In His Own Hand,* p. 118.

57. Timothy Garton Ash, *The Polish Revolution: Solidarity* (London: Granta, 1991), pp. 41–72. See also Weigel, *Witness to Hope,* p. 402.

58. *Ibid.,* pp. 397–98, 422–24; Ouimet, *The Rise and Fall of the Brezhnev Doctrine,* pp. 120–22.

59. *Ibid.,* pp. 187, 189.

60. *Ibid.,* pp. 199–202. See also pp. 95–96.

61. *Ibid.,* pp. 234–35. For more on the Soviet decision not to intervene, see two articles by Mark Kramer, "Poland, 1980–81, Soviet Policy During the Polish Crisis," CWIHP *Bulletin,* #5 (Spring, 1995), pp. 1, 116–23, and "Jaruzelski, the Soviet Union, and the Imposition of Martial Law in Poland, *ibid.,* #11 (Winter, 1998), 5–14.

62. Interview, CNN *Cold War,* Episode 19, "Freeze."

63. I have drawn, in the following two sections, upon arguments developed in further detail in Gaddis, *Strategies of Containment,* pp. 353–79.

64. Speech at Notre Dame University, May 17, 1981, *Public Papers of the Presidents of the United States: Ronald Reagan, 1981* (Washington: Government Printing Office, 1982), p. 434.

65. Speech to members of the British Parliament, London, June 8, 1982, *Reagan Public Papers, 1982,* pp. 744–47. For the drafting of this speech, see Richard Pipes, *Vixi: Memoirs of a Non-Belonger* (New Haven: Yale University Press, 2003), pp. 197–200.

66. Speech to the National Association of Evangelicals, Orlando, Florida, March 8, 1983, *Reagan Public Papers, 1983,* p. 364; Ronald Reagan, *An American Life* (New York: Simon and Schuster, 1990), pp. 569–70.

67. The figures are in Gaddis, *Strategies of Containment,* pp. 393–94.

68. Lettow, *Ronald Reagan,* p. 23; Reagan, *An American Life,* p. 13.

69. Radio-television address, March 23, 1983, *Reagan Public Papers, 1983,* pp. 442–43.

70. *Ibid.,* p. 364. Lettow, *Ronald Reagan,* provides the best discussion of Reagan's nuclear abolitionism.

71. Dobrynin, *In Confidence,* p. 528.

72. *Ibid.,* p. 523.

73. Christopher Andrew and Oleg Gordievsky, *KGB: The Inside Story of Its Foreign Operations from Lenin to Gorbachev* (New York: HarperCollins, 1990), pp. 583–99.

74. Raymond Garthoff, *The Great Transition: American-Soviet Relations and the End of the Cold War* (Washington: Brookings Institution, 1994), pp. 118–31.

75. *Ibid.,* pp. 138–41; Don Oberdorfer, *From the Cold War to a New Era: The United States and the Soviet Union, 1983–1991,* updated edition (Baltimore: Johns Hopkins University Press, 1998), pp. 65–68.

76. Radio-television address, January 16, 1984, *Reagan Public Papers, 1984,* p. 45. See also Oberdorfer, *From the Cold War to a New Era,* pp. 72–73. I have heard the staffer story from two separate well-placed sources.

77. Reagan, *An American Life,* p. 611.

78. Gorbachev, *Memoirs,* p. 165.

79. George Bush and Brent Scowcroft, *A World Transformed* (New York: Knopf, 1998), p. 4; George P. Shultz, *Turmoil and Triumph: My Years as Secretary of State* (New York: Scribner's, 1993), pp. 532–33; Reagan, *An American Life,* p. 635.

80. Chernyaev diary, January 16, 1986, in Anatoly S. Chernyaev, *My Six Years with Gorbachev,* translated and edited by Robert D. English and Eliza-

beth Tucker (University Park, Pennsylvania: Pennsylvania State University Press, 2000), p. 46; Mikhail Gorbachev, *Perestroika: New Thinking for Our Country and the World* (New York: Harper & Row, 1987), pp. 69–70.

81. For more on the movie, see http://www.imdb.com/title/tt0086637/.

82. Lettow, *Ronald Reagan*, pp. 179–86.

83. Chernyaev diary, January 16, 1986, in Chernyaev, *My Six Years with Gorbachev*, pp. 45–46.

84. See Gaddis, *Strategies of Containment*, p. 359.

85. Gorbachev, *Memoirs*, pp. 191, 193.

86. Lettow, *Ronald Reagan*, pp. 217–26; Gaddis, *Strategies of Containment*, p. 366n.

87. Gorbachev, *Memoirs*, p. 419.

88. Remarks on Signing the Intermediate-Range Nuclear Forces Treaty, December 8, 1987, *Reagan Public Papers, 1987*, p. 1208.

89. See the Chernyaev transcript of the Bush-Gorbachev meeting at Malta, December 3, 1989, CWIHP *Bulletin*, #12/13 (Fall/Winter, 2001), p. 236. One SS-20 fragment also made its way, through several hands, to me.

90. Gorbachev, *Memoirs*, pp. 102–3.

91. Shultz, *Turmoil and Triumph*, p. 591; Oberdorfer, *From the Cold War to a New Era*, pp. 133, 223–24, 288.

92. Gorbachev, *Perestroika*, p. 85. See also pp. 138–39.

93. Reagan speech at Moscow State University, May 31, 1988, *Reagan Public Papers, 1988*, p. 684. See also Oberdorfer, *From the Cold War to a New Era*, pp. 299–300.

94. Chernyaev notes, Bush-Gorbachev meeting at Malta, December 2, 1989, CWIHP *Bulletin*, #12/13 (Fall/Winter, 2001), p. 233.

95. Minutes, Politburo meeting, December 27–28, 1988, *ibid.*, p. 25; Chernyaev diary, May, 1989, in Chernyaev, *My Six Years with Gorbachev*, p. 225.

96. Gorbachev and Mlynář, *Conversations with Gorbachev*, p. 160.

97. Reagan, *An American Life*, p. 683. For more on the Reagan Doctrine, see Gaddis, *Strategies of Containment*, pp. 369–73.

98. Gorbachev, *Memoirs*, p. 465. See also Garthoff, *The Great Transition*, pp. 315–18.

99. Gorbachev, *Perestroika*, pp. 138, 221.

100. Joseph Rothschild, quoted in Gale Stokes, *The Walls Came Tumbling Down: The Collapse of Communism in Eastern Europe* (New York: Oxford University Press, 1993), p. 76.

101. *Ibid.*, p. 99. See also pp. 73–75.

102. Minutes, Politburo meeting, December 27–28, 1988, CWIHP *Bulletin*, #12/13 (Fall/Winter, 2001), p. 24.

Chapter Seven: The Triumph of Hope

1. Margaret Thatcher, *The Downing Street Years* (New York: HarperCollins, 1993), p. 753.
2. Timothy Garton Ash, *The Magic Lantern: The Revolution of '89 Witnessed in Warsaw, Budapest, Berlin, and Prague* (New York: Random House, 1990), pp. 141–42.
3. For a scientific analogy, see Per Bak, *How Nature Works: The Science of Self-Organized Criticality* (New York: Oxford University Press, 1997).
4. George Bush and Brent Scowcroft, *A World Transformed* (New York: Knopf, 1998), p. xiii.
5. *Ibid.*, pp. 13–14.
6. Minutes, Politburo meeting, December 27–28, 1988, CWIHP *Bulletin*, #12/13 (Fall/Winter, 2001), pp. 25–26.
7. Bak, *How Nature Works*, especially pp. 1–3. See also, for historical analogies, John Lewis Gaddis, *The Landscape of History: How Historians Map the Past* (New York: Oxford University Press, 2002), pp. 79–81, 84–87.
8. Memorandum, Gorbachev conversation with Egon Krenz, November 1, 1989, CWIHP *Bulletin*, #12/13 (Fall/Winter, 2001), pp. 140–41.
9. Memorandum, Gorbachev-Németh conversation, March 3, 1989, *ibid.*, p. 77. For post-1956 developments in Hungary, see Gale Stokes, *The Walls Came Tumbling Down: The Collapse of Communism in Eastern Europe* (New York: Oxford University Press, 1993), pp. 78–101.
10. *Ibid.*, 99–101, 131; also interviews with Németh, Imre Pozsgay, and Günter Schabowski, CNN *Cold War*, Episode 23, "The Wall Comes Down, 1989."
11. Stokes, *The Walls Came Tumbling Down*, pp. 102–30; Bernard Gwertzman and Michael T. Kaufman, eds., *The Collapse of Communism* (New York: Random House, 1990), p. 132. See also Garton Ash, *The Magic Lantern*, pp. 25–46.
12. Polish transcript, Gorbachev-Jaruzelski meeting, Moscow, May 9, 1989, CWIHP *Bulletin*, #12/13 (Fall/Winter, 2001), p. 113.
13. Mikhail Gorbachev, *Memoirs* (New York: Doubleday, 1995), pp. 287, 290, 292.
14. *Ibid.*, pp. 488–92; Gwertzman and Kaufman, eds., *The Collapse of Communism*, p. 52. See also Richard Baum, *Burying Mao: Chinese Politics in the Age of Deng Xiaoping* (Princeton: Princeton University Press, 1994), pp. 242–74.
15. *Ibid.*, pp. 275–310.
16. Mielke to Heads of Service Units, June 10, 1989, CWIHP *Bulletin*, #12/13 (Fall/Winter, 2001), p. 209.
17. Charles S. Maier, *Dissolution: The Crisis of Communism and the End of East Germany* (Princeton: Princeton University Press, 1997), pp. 125–27.

18. Interview with Birgit Spannaus, CNN *Cold War,* Episode 23, "The Wall Comes Down, 1989." See also Maier, *Dissolution,* pp. 127–31; and Stokes, *The Walls Came Tumbling Down,* pp. 136–38.

19. Interview with Gorbachev, CNN *Cold War,* Episode 23, "The Wall Comes Down, 1989"; Memorandum, Gorbachev-Krenz conversation, November 1, 1989, CWIHP *Bulletin,* #12/13 (Fall/Winter, 2001), pp. 141–43, 151. See also Gorbachev, *Memoirs,* pp. 523–25.

20. Gorbachev-Krenz conversation, November 1, 1989, pp. 147–48. See also Stokes, *The Walls Came Tumbling Down,* pp. 139–40.

21. Transcript, Schabowski press conference, November 9, 1989, CWIHP *Bulletin,* #12/13 (Fall/Winter, 2001), pp. 157–58. See also Hans-Hermann Hertle, "The Fall of the Wall: The Unintended Self-Dissolution of East Germany's Ruling Regime," *ibid.,* pp. 131–40; and Philip Zelikow and Condoleezza Rice, *Germany Unified and Europe Transformed: A Study in Statecraft* (Cambridge, Massachusetts: Harvard University Press, 1995), pp. 98–101.

22. Gorbachev interview, CNN *Cold War,* Episode 23, "The Wall Comes Down, 1989."

23. Stokes, *The Walls Came Tumbling Down,* pp. 141–67, provides a succinct account of these events.

24. Minutes, Gorbachev-Ceauşescu meeting, December 4, 1989, CWIHP *Bulletin,* #12/13 (Fall/Winter, 2001), pp. 220–22.

25. Chernyaev diary, May, 1989, in Anatoly S. Chernyaev, *My Six Years with Gorbachev,* translated and edited by Robert D. English and Elizabeth Tucker (University Park, Pennsylvania: Pennsylvania State University Press, 2000), p. 226; Don Oberdorfer, *From the Cold War to a New Era: The United States and the Soviet Union, 1983–1991,* updated edition (Baltimore: Johns Hopkins University Press, 1998), p. 355.

26. Chernyaev notes, Bush-Gorbachev meeting, Malta, December 2, 1989, CWIHP *Bulletin,* #12/13 (Fall/Winter, 2001), pp. 232–33. See also Bush and Scowcroft, *A World Transformed,* p. 164.

27. Chernyaev notes, Bush-Gorbachev meetings, December 2, 1989, pp. 229, 233, and December 3, 1989, CWIHP *Bulletin,* #12/13 (Fall/Winter, 2001), pp. 237–38.

28. Chernyaev, *My Six Years with Gorbachev,* pp. 114–15; Gorbachev, *Memoirs,* pp. 517–18, 520.

29. Zelikow and Rice, *Germany Unified and Europe Transformed,* p. 83. The poem, written at the time of Bismarck's efforts to unify Germany, was by the Russian poet Fedor Tyutchev.

30. Memorandum, Gorbachev-Krenz conversation, November 1, 1989,

CWIHP *Bulletin*, #12/13 (Fall/Winter, 2001), pp. 144–45; Gorbachev interview, CNN *Cold War*, Episode 23, "The Wall Comes Down, 1989."

31. Bush and Scowcroft, *A World Transformed*, p. 249.

32. *Ibid.*, p. 194. See also Zelikow and Rice, *Germany Unified and Europe Transformed*, pp. 118–25.

33. Gorbachev, *Memoirs*, p. 528; also Zelikow and Rice, *Germany Unified and Europe Transformed*, pp. 160–63.

34. The figures are from Chernyaev, *My Six Years with Gorbachev*, p. 272, and Zelikow and Rice, *Germany Unified and Europe Transformed*, p. 169.

35. Gorbachev, *Memoirs*, p. 532. One source for this idea was John Lewis Gaddis, "One Germany—in Both Alliances," *New York Times*, March 21, 1990. Thatcher's reaction was confirmed for me separately by Gordon Craig and Timothy Garton Ash, both of whom personally witnessed it.

36. Bush and Scowcroft, *A World Transformed*, p. 239. See also James M. Goldgeier, *Not Whether But When: The U.S. Decision to Enlarge NATO* (Washington: Brookings Institution, 1999).

37. Gorbachev, *Memoirs*, pp. 532–33.

38. *Ibid.*, p. 534.

39. Chernyaev, *My Years with Gorbachev*, pp. 269–70.

40. Niccolò Machiavelli, *The Prince*, translated by Harvey C. Mansfield, second edition (Chicago: University of Chicago Press, 1998), p. 66.

41. Ronald Grigor Suny, *The Soviet Experiment: Russia, the USSR, and the Successor States* (New York: Oxford University Press, 1998), pp. 462–63.

42. Gorbachev, *Memoirs*, pp. 572–73.

43. Suny, *The Soviet Experiment*, pp. 478–79.

44. Chernyaev, *My Six Years with Gorbachev*, p. 201.

45. Bush and Scowcroft, *A World Transformed*, pp. 141–43. See also Michael R. Beschloss and Strobe Talbott, *At the Highest Levels: The Inside Story of the End of the Cold War* (Boston: Little, Brown, 1993), pp. 103–4.

46. Bush and Scowcroft, *A World Transformed*, pp. 498, 500.

47. Chernyaev, *My Six Years with Gorbachev*, pp. 360–63; Bush and Scowcroft, *A World Transformed*, pp. 513–14.

48. Beschloss and Talbott, *At the Highest Levels*, pp. 417–18.

49. Chernyaev, *My Six Years with Gorbachev*, p. 369.

50. Suny, *The Soviet Experiment*, pp. 480–82. Gorbachev's account is in his *Memoirs*, pp. 626–45.

51. Suny, *The Soviet Experiment*, pp. 483–84; Bush and Scowcroft, *A World Transformed*, pp. 554–55.

52. Oberdorfer, *From the Cold War to a New Era*, pp. 471–72.

53. Gorbachev, *Memoirs*, p. xxxviii.

Epilogue: The View Back

1. Mikhail Gorbachev, *Memoirs* (New York: Doubleday, 1995), pp. 692–93; also Mikhail Gorbachev and Zdeněk Mlynář, *Conversations with Gorbachev on Perestroika, The Prague Spring, and the Crossroads of Socialism,* translated by George Schriver (New York: Columbia University Press, 2002), pp. 172–74.

2. See Louise Levanthes, *When China Ruled the Seas: The Treasure Fleet of the Dragon Throne, 1405–1433* (New York: Simon and Schuster, 1994).

3. *Public Papers of the Presidents of the United States: Richard Nixon, 1969* (Washington: Government Printing Office, 1971), p. 542.

4. "The Eighteenth Brumaire of Louis Bonaparte," in Robert C. Tucker, ed., *The Marx-Engels Reader,* second edition (New York: Norton, 1978), p. 595.

5. John Mueller, *Retreat from Doomsday: The Obsolescence of Major War* (New York: Basic Books, 1989), makes the argument most convincingly.

6. Kai Bird and Martin J. Sherwin, *American Prometheus: The Triumph and Tragedy of J. Robert Oppenheimer* (New York: Knopf, 2005), p. 348.

7. See, on this point, the essays in John Lewis Gaddis, Philip H. Gordon, Ernest R. May, and Jonathan Rosenberg, eds., *Cold War Statesmen Confront the Bomb: Nuclear Diplomacy since 1945* (New York: Oxford University Press, 1999).

8. Paul Kennedy, *The Rise and Fall of the Great Powers: Economic Change and Military Conflict from 1500 to 2000* (New York: Random House, 1987).

9. See Thomas Cahill, *How the Irish Saved Civilization* (New York: Anchor, 1996).

10. *Democracy's Century: A Survey of Global Political Change in the 20th Century* (New York: Freedom House, 1999), available at: http://www.freedomhouse.org/reports/century.html.

11. Seth Mydans, "At Cremation of Pol Pot, No Tears Shed," *New York Times,* April 19, 1998. See also Jean-Louis Margolin, "Cambodia: The Country of Disconcerting Crimes," in Stéphane Courtois, *et al., The Black Book of Communism: Crimes, Terror, Repression,* translated by Jonathan Murphy and Mark Kramer (Cambridge, Massachusetts: Harvard University Press, 1999), pp. 577–635; and Samantha Power, *"A Problem from Hell": America in the Age of Genocide* (New York: Basic Books, 2002), pp. 87–154.

BIBLIOGRAPHY

DOCUMENTS

Beschloss, Michael R., ed. *Reaching for Glory: Lyndon Johnson's Secret White House Tapes, 1964–1965.* New York: Simon and Schuster, 2001.

———, ed. *Taking Charge: The Johnson White House Tapes, 1963–1964.* New York: Simon and Schuster, 1997.

Burr, William, ed. *The Kissinger Transcripts: The Top Secret Talks with Beijing and Moscow.* New York: New Press, 1998.

Cold War International History Project. *Bulletin.* Washington: Woodrow Wilson International Center for Scholars, 1992–.

Daniels, Robert V., ed. *A Documentary History of Communism.* Revised edition. Hanover, New Hampshire: University Press of New England, 1984.

Etzold, Thomas H., and John Lewis Gaddis, eds. *Containment: Documents on American Policy and Strategy, 1945–1950.* New York: Columbia University Press, 1978.

Ferrell, Robert H., ed. *Off the Record: The Private Papers of Harry S. Truman.* New York: Harper & Row, 1980.

Hanhimäki, Jussi M., and Odd Arne Westad, eds. *The Cold War: A History in Documents and Eyewitness Accounts.* New York: Oxford University Press, 2003.

Jensen, Kenneth M., ed. *Origins of the Cold War: The Novikov, Kennan, and Roberts "Long Telegrams" of 1946.* Revised edition. Washington: United States Institute of Peace, 1993.

Kornbluh, Peter, ed. *The Pinochet File: A Declassified Dossier on Atrocity and Accountability.* New York: New Press, 2004.

Kutler, Stanley I., ed. *Abuse of Power: The New Nixon Tapes.* New York: Free Press, 1997.

May, Ernest R., and Philip D. Zelikow, eds. *The Kennedy Tapes: Inside the White House during the Cuban Missile Crisis.* Cambridge, Massachusetts: Harvard University Press, 1997.

Millis, Walter, ed. *The Forrestal Diaries.* New York: Viking, 1951.

Ostermann, Christian, ed. *Uprising in East Germany, 1953.* Budapest: Central European University Press, 2001.

Pipes, Richard, ed. *The Unknown Lenin: From the Secret Archive.* New Haven: Yale University Press, 1996.

Public Papers of the Presidents of the United States: Dwight D. Eisenhower, 1953–1961. Washington: Government Printing Office, 1960–1961.

————: *Harry S. Truman, 1945–1953.* Washington: Government Printing Office, 1961–1966.

————: *Jimmy Carter, 1977–1981.* Washington: Government Printing Office, 1978–1981.

————: *John F. Kennedy, 1961–1963.* Washington: Government Printing Office, 1962– 1964.

————: *Lyndon B. Johnson, 1963–1969.* Washington: Government Printing Office, 1965–1969.

————: *Richard M. Nixon, 1969–1974.* Washington: Government Printing Office, 1970–1975.

————: *Ronald Reagan, 1981–1989.* Washington: Government Printing Office, 1982–1990.

Reiss, Hans, ed. *Kant: Political Writings.* Translated by H. B. Nisbet. Second edition. Cambridge: Cambridge University Press, 1991.

Rosenman, Samuel I., ed. *The Public Papers and Addresses of Franklin D. Roosevelt.* New York: Random House, 1941–1950.

Scammell, Michael, ed. *The Solzhenitsyn Files.* Translated under the supervision of Catherine A. Fitzpatrick. Chicago: Edition Q, 1995.

Skinner, Kiron K., Annelise Anderson, and Martin Anderson, eds. *Reagan, In His Own Hand.* New York: Free Press, 2001.

Tucker, Robert C., ed. *The Marx-Engels Reader.* Second edition. New York: Norton, 1978.

U.S. Department of State. *Foreign Relations of the United States: 1946–1964/ 68.* Washington: Government Printing Office, 1970–2003.

INTERVIEWS

CNN. *Cold War.* Television documentary, 1998.

PBS/BBC. *Messengers from Moscow.* Television documentary, 1995.

BOOKS

Ambrose, Stephen. *Nixon: The Triumph of a Politician, 1962–1972*. New York: Simon and Schuster, 1989.

Andrew, Christopher, and Oleg Gordievsky. *KGB: The Inside Story of Its Foreign Operations from Lenin to Gorbachev*. New York: HarperCollins, 1990.

Applebaum, Anne. *Gulag: A History*. New York: Doubleday, 2003.

Arbatov, Georgi. *The System: An Insider's Life in Soviet Politics*. New York: Random House, 1992.

Bak, Per. *How Nature Works: The Science of Self-Organized Criticality*. New York: Oxford University Press, 1997.

Baum, Richard. *Burying Mao: Chinese Politics in the Age of Deng Xiaoping*. Princeton: Princeton University Press, 1994.

Becker, Jasper. *Hungry Ghosts: Mao's Secret Famine*. New York: Free Press, 1996.

Berman, Larry. *Planning a Tragedy: The Americanization of the War in Vietnam*. New York: Norton, 1982.

Beschloss, Michael R. *The Crisis Years: Kennedy and Khrushchev, 1960–1963*. New York: HarperCollins, 1991.

———. *Mayday: Eisenhower, Khrushchev and the U-2 Affair*. New York: Harper & Row, 1986.

———, and Strobe Talbott. *At the Highest Levels: The Inside Story of the End of the Cold War*. Boston: Little, Brown, 1993.

Bill, James A. *The Eagle and the Lion: The Tragedy of American-Iranian Relations*. New Haven: Yale University Press, 1988.

Bird, Kai, and Martin J. Sherwin. *American Prometheus: The Triumph and Tragedy of J. Robert Oppenheimer*. New York: Knopf, 2005.

Blight, James G., Bruce J. Allyn, and David A. Welch. *Cuba on the Brink: Castro, the Missile Crisis, and the Soviet Collapse*. New York: Pantheon, 1993.

———, and David A. Welch. *On the Brink: Americans and Soviets Reexamine the Cuban Missile Crisis*. New York: Hill and Wang, 1989.

Bohlen, Charles E. *Witness to History: 1929–1969*. New York: Norton, 1973.

Brent, Jonathan, and Vladimir P. Naumov. *Stalin's Last Crime: The Plot Against the Jewish Doctors, 1948–1953*. New York: HarperCollins, 2003.

Brezhnev, Leonid. *On the Policy of the Soviet Union and the International Situation*. Garden City, New York: Doubleday, 1973.

Brodie, Bernard, ed. *The Absolute Weapon: Atomic Power and World Order*. New York: Harcourt, 1946.

Brzezinski, Zbigniew. *Power and Principle: Memoirs of the National Security Adviser, 1977–1981*. New York: Farrar, Straus, Giroux, 1983.

Bullock, Alan. *Hitler and Stalin: Parallel Lives.* New York: Knopf, 1992.

Bundy, McGeorge. *Danger and Survival: Choices About the Bomb in the First Fifty Years.* New York: Random House, 1988.

Bush, George, and Brent Scowcroft. *A World Transformed.* New York: Knopf, 1998.

Cahill, Thomas. *How the Irish Saved Civilization.* New York: Anchor, 1996.

Carr, Edward Hallett. *The Twenty Years' Crisis, 1919–1939: An Introduction to the Study of International Relations.* London: Macmillan, 1940.

Carter, Jimmy. *Keeping Faith: Memoirs of a President.* New York: Bantam, 1982.

Chace, James. *Acheson: The Secretary of State Who Created the Modern World.* New York: Simon and Schuster, 1998.

Chen Jian. *China's Road to the Korean War: The Making of the Sino-American Confrontation.* New York: Columbia University Press, 1994.

———. *Mao's China and the Cold War.* Chapel Hill: University of North Carolina Press, 2001.

Chernyaev, Anatoly S. *My Six Years with Gorbachev.* Translated and edited by Robert D. English and Elizabeth Tucker. University Park, Pennsylvania: Pennsylvania State University Press, 2000.

Christensen, Thomas J. *Useful Adversaries: Grand Strategy, Domestic Mobilization, and Sino-American Conflict, 1947–1958.* Princeton: Princeton University Press, 1996.

Churchill, Winston S. *The Second World War: The Gathering Storm.* New York: Bantam, 1961.

Clausewitz, Carl von. *On War.* Edited and translated by Michael Howard and Peter Paret. Princeton: Princeton University Press, 1976.

Connelly, Matthew. *A Diplomatic Revolution: Algeria's Fight for Independence and the Origins of the Post–Cold War Era.* New York: Oxford University Press, 2002.

Courtois, Stéphane, *et al. The Black Book of Communism: Crimes, Terror, Repression.* Translated by Jonathan Murphy and Mark Kramer. Cambridge, Massachusetts: Harvard University Press, 1999.

Craig, Campbell. *Destroying the Village: Eisenhower and Thermonuclear War.* New York: Columbia University Press, 1999.

Craig, Gordon A., and Francis L. Loewenheim, eds. *The Diplomats: 1939–1979.* Princeton: Princeton University Press, 1994.

Cullather, Nicholas. *Operation PB Success: The United States and Guatemala, 1952–1954.* Washington: Central Intelligence Agency, 1994.

Dallek, Robert. *Flawed Giant: Lyndon Johnson and His Times, 1961–1973.* New York: Oxford University Press, 1998.

———. *Franklin D. Roosevelt and American Foreign Policy, 1932–1945.* New York: Oxford University Press, 1979.

Diamond, Jared. *Guns, Germs, and Steel: The Fates of Human Societies.* New York: Norton, 1997.

Disraeli, Benjamin. *Sybil; or, The Two Nations.* New York: Oxford University Press, 1991; first published in 1845.

Djilas, Milovan. *Conversations with Stalin.* Translated by Michael B. Petrovich. New York: Harcourt, Brace & World, 1962.

Dobrynin, Anatoly. *In Confidence: Moscow's Ambassador to America's Six Cold War Presidents (1962–1986).* New York: Random House, 1995.

English, Robert D. *Russia and the Idea of the West: Gorbachev, Intellectuals, and the End of the Cold War.* New York: Columbia University Press, 2000.

Evans, Richard. *Deng Xiaoping and the Making of Modern China.* New York: Penguin, 1997.

Foot, Rosemary, John Lewis Gaddis, and Andrew Hurrell, eds. *Order and Justice in International Relations.* New York: Oxford University Press, 2003.

Ford, Gerald R. *A Time to Heal: The Autobiography of Gerald R. Ford.* New York: Harper & Row, 1979.

Fox, Richard Wightman. *Reinhold Niebuhr: A Biography.* New York: Pantheon, 1985.

Freedman, Lawrence. *The Evolution of Nuclear Strategy.* New York: St. Martin's Press, 1983.

———. *Kennedy's Wars: Berlin, Cuba, Laos, and Vietnam.* New York: Oxford University Press, 2000.

Freedom House. *Democracy's Century: A Survey of Global Political Change in the 20th Century.* New York: Freedom House, 1999.

Friedberg, Aaron L. *In the Shadow of the Garrison State: America's Anti-Statism and Its Cold War Grand Strategy.* Princeton: Princeton University Press, 2000.

Fursenko, Aleksandr, and Timothy Naftali. *"One Hell of a Gamble": Khrushchev, Castro, and Kennedy, 1958–1964.* New York: Norton, 1997.

Gaddis, John Lewis. *The Landscape of History: How Historians Map the Past.* New York: Oxford University Press, 2002.

———. *The Long Peace: Inquiries into the History of the Cold War.* New York: Oxford University Press, 1987.

———. *Russia, the Soviet Union, and the United States: An Interpretive History.* Second edition. New York: McGraw-Hill, 1990.

———. *Strategies of Containment: A Critical Appraisal of American National Security Policy During the Cold War.* Revised and updated edition. New York: Oxford University Press, 2005.

————. *The United States and the End of the Cold War: Implications, Reconsiderations, Provocations.* New York: Oxford University Press, 1992.

————. *The United States and the Origins of the Cold War, 1941–1947.* New York: Columbia University Press, 1972.

————. *We Now Know: Rethinking Cold War History.* New York: Oxford University Press, 1997.

————, Philip H. Gordon, Ernest R. May, and Jonathan Rosenberg, eds. *Cold War Statesmen Confront the Bomb: Nuclear Diplomacy since 1945.* New York: Oxford University Press, 1999.

Gaiduk, Ilya V. *The Soviet Union and the Vietnam War.* Chicago: Ivan R. Dee, 1996.

Garthoff, Raymond. *Détente and Confrontation: American-Soviet Relations from Nixon to Reagan.* Revised edition. Washington: Brookings Institution, 1994.

————. *The Great Transition: American-Soviet Relations and the End of the Cold War.* Washington: Brookings Institution, 1994.

Garton Ash, Timothy. *In Europe's Name: Germany and the Divided Continent.* New York: Random House, 1991.

————. *The Magic Lantern: The Revolution of '89 Witnessed in Warsaw, Budapest, Berlin, and Prague.* New York: Random House, 1990.

————. *The Polish Revolution: Solidarity.* London: Granta, 1991.

————. *The Uses of Adversity: Essays on the Fate of Central Europe.* New York: Random House, 1989.

Gilbert, Martin. *"Never Despair": Winston S. Churchill, 1945–1965.* London: Heineman, 1988.

Gleijeses, Piero. *Conflicting Missions: Havana, Washington, and Africa, 1959–1976.* Chapel Hill: University of North Carolina Press, 2002.

Goldgeier, James M. *Not Whether But When: The U.S. Decision to Enlarge NATO.* Washington: Brookings Institution, 1999.

Goncharov, Sergei N., John W. Lewis, and Xue Litai. *Uncertain Partners: Stalin, Mao, and the Korean War.* Stanford: Stanford University Press, 1993.

Gorbachev, Mikhail. *Memoirs.* New York: Doubleday, 1995.

————. *Perestroika: New Thinking for Our Country and the World.* New York: Harper & Row, 1987.

————, and Zdeněk Mlynář. *Conversations with Gorbachev: On Perestroika, The Prague Spring, and the Crossroads of Socialism.* Translated by George Schriver. New York: Columbia University Press, 2002.

Gordon, Philip H. *A Certain Idea of France: French Security Policy and the Gaullist Legacy.* Princeton: Princeton University Press, 1993.

Gorlizki, Yoram, and Oleg Khlevniuk. *Cold Peace: Stalin and the Soviet Ruling Circle, 1945–1953.* New York: Oxford University Press, 2004.

Gwertzman, Bernard, and Michael T. Kaufman, eds. *The Collapse of Communism.* New York: Random House, 1990.

Hall, R. Cargill, and Clayton D. Laurie, eds. *Early Cold War Overflights.* Two volumes. Washington: National Reconnaissance Office, 2003.

Hamby, Alonzo L. *Man of the People: A Life of Harry S. Truman.* New York: Oxford University Press, 1995.

Hammond, Thomas T., ed. *Witnesses to the Origins of the Cold War.* Seattle: University of Washington Press, 1982.

Harriman, W. Averell, and Elie Abel. *Special Envoy to Churchill and Stalin, 1941–1946.* New York: Random House, 1975.

Harrison, Hope M. *Driving the Soviets Up the Wall: Soviet–East German Relations, 1953–1961.* Princeton: Princeton University Press, 2003.

Hasegawa, Tsuyoshi. *Racing the Enemy: Stalin, Truman, and the Surrender of Japan.* Cambridge, Massachusetts: Harvard University Press, 2005.

Haslam, Jonathan. *No Virtue Like Necessity: Realist Thought in International Relations since Machiavelli.* New Haven: Yale University Press, 2002.

Havel, Václav. *Living in Truth.* Edited by Jan Vladislav. London: Faber and Faber, 1989.

Heikal, Mohamed. *The Sphinx and the Commissar: The Rise and Fall of Soviet Influence in the Middle East.* New York: Harper & Row, 1978.

Hitchcock, William I. *The Struggle for Europe: The Turbulent History of a Divided Continent 1945–2002.* New York: Doubleday, 2002.

Hitchens, Christopher. *The Trial of Henry Kissinger.* New York: Verso, 2001.

Hobsbawm, Eric. *The Age of Extremes: A History of the World, 1914–1991.* New York: Pantheon Books, 1994.

Holloway, David. *The Soviet Union and the Arms Race.* New Haven: Yale University Press, 1983.

———. *Stalin and the Bomb: The Soviet Union and Atomic Energy, 1939–1956.* New Haven: Yale University Press, 1994.

Hull, Cordell. *The Memoirs of Cordell Hull.* New York: Macmillan, 1948.

Hyland, William G. *Mortal Rivals: Understanding the Hidden Pattern of Soviet-American Relations.* New York: Simon and Schuster, 1987.

James, D. Clayton. *The Years of MacArthur: Triumph and Disaster, 1945–1964.* Boston: Houghton Mifflin, 1985.

Jenkins, Roy. *Churchill: A Biography.* New York: Farrar, Straus and Giroux, 2001.

Jervis, Robert. *Perception and Misperception in International Politics.* Princeton: Princeton University Press, 1976.

Johnson, Loch K. *America's Secret Power: The CIA in a Democratic Society.* New York: Oxford University Press, 1989.

Karnow, Stanley. *Vietnam: A History.* New York: Viking, 1983.

Keegan, John. *The Face of Battle: A Study of Agincourt, Waterloo, and the Somme.* New York: Viking, 1976.

Kennan, George F. *Memoirs: 1925–1950.* Boston: Atlantic-Little, Brown, 1967.

———. *Memoirs: 1950–1963.* Boston: Little, Brown, 1972.

Kennedy, Paul. *The Rise and Fall of the Great Powers: Economic Change and Military Conflict from 1500 to 2000.* New York: Random House, 1987.

Kersten, Krystyna. *The Establishment of Communist Rule in Poland, 1943–1948.* Translated by John Micgiel and Michael H. Barnhart. Berkeley: University of California Press, 1991.

Khrushchev, Nikita S. *Khrushchev Remembers.* Translated and edited by Strobe Talbott. New York: Bantam, 1971.

———. *Khrushchev Remembers: The Last Testament.* Translated and edited by Strobe Talbott. Boston: Little, Brown, 1974.

Khrushchev, Sergei. *Khrushchev on Khrushchev: An Inside Account of the Man and His Era.* Edited and translated by William Taubman. Boston: Little, Brown, 1990.

Kimball, Warren F. *The Juggler: Franklin Roosevelt as Wartime Statesman.* Princeton: Princeton University Press, 1991.

Kissinger, Henry A. *American Foreign Policy.* Third edition. New York: Norton, 1977.

———. *Diplomacy.* New York: Simon and Schuster, 1994.

———. *White House Years.* Boston: Little, Brown, 1979.

———. *A World Restored.* New York: Houghton Mifflin, 1957.

———. *Years of Renewal.* New York: Simon and Schuster, 1999.

———. *Years of Upheaval.* Boston: Little, Brown, 1982.

Knight, Amy. *Beria: Stalin's First Lieutenant.* Princeton: Princeton University Press, 1993.

Kunz, Diane B. *The Economic Diplomacy of the Suez Crisis.* Chapel Hill: University of North Carolina Press, 1991.

Kyle, Keith. *Suez.* New York: St. Martin's, 1991.

Leffler, Melvyn P., and David S. Painter, eds. *Origins of the Cold War: An International History.* Second edition. New York: Routledge, 2005.

Lettow, Paul. *Ronald Reagan and His Quest to Abolish Nuclear Weapons.* New York: Random House, 2005.

Levanthes, Louise. *When China Ruled the Seas: The Treasure Fleet of the Dragon Throne, 1405–1433.* New York: Simon and Schuster, 1994.

Levering, Ralph B., Vladimir O. Pechatnov, Verena Botzenhart-Viehe, and C. Earl Edmondson. *Debating the Origins of the Cold War: American and Russian Perspectives.* New York: Rowman & Littlefield, 2002.

Lewis, John Wilson, and Xue Litai. *China Builds the Bomb.* Stanford: Stanford University Press, 1988.

Li Zhisui. *The Private Life of Chairman Mao: The Memoirs of Mao's Personal Physician.* Translated by Tai Hung-chao. New York: Random House, 1994.

Lilienthal, David E. *The Journals of David E. Lilienthal: The Atomic Energy Years, 1945–1950.* New York: Harper & Row, 1964.

Little, Douglas. *American Orientalism: The United States in the Middle East since 1945.* Chapel Hill: University of North Carolina Press, 2002.

Logevall, Fredrik. *Choosing War: The Lost Chance for Peace and the Escalation of the War in Vietnam.* Berkeley: University of California Press, 1999.

Machiavelli, Niccolò. *The Prince.* Translated by Harvey C. Mansfield. Second edition. Chicago: University of Chicago Press, 1998.

McMahon, Robert J. *The Cold War on the Periphery: The United States, India, and Pakistan.* New York: Columbia University Press, 1994.

Macmillan, Margaret. *Paris 1919: Six Months That Changed the World.* New York: Random House, 2001.

McNeill, J. R., and William H. McNeill. *The Human Web: A Bird's-Eye View of World History.* New York: Norton, 2003.

Maier, Charles S. *Dissolution: The Crisis of Communism and the End of East Germany.* Princeton: Princeton University Press, 1997.

Martel, Yann. *Life of Pi.* New York: Harcourt, 2002.

Mastny, Vojtech. *The Cold War and Soviet Insecurity: The Stalin Years.* New York: Oxford University Press, 1996.

———. *Russia's Road to the Cold War: Diplomacy, Warfare, and the Politics of Communism, 1941–1945.* New York: Columbia University Press, 1979.

Matusow, Allen J. *The Unraveling of America: A History of Liberalism in the 1960s.* New York: Harper & Row, 1984.

Mayer, Arno J. *Wilson vs. Lenin: Political Origins of the New Diplomacy, 1917–1918.* New Haven: Yale University Press, 1959.

Merridale, Catherine. *Night of Stone: Death and Memory in Russia.* London: Granta, 2000.

Merrill, Dennis, and Thomas G. Paterson, eds. *Major Problems in American Foreign Policy.* Sixth edition. New York: Houghton Mifflin, 2005.

Miller, James Edward. *The United States and Italy, 1940–1950: The Politics and Diplomacy of Stabilization.* Chapel Hill: University of North Carolina Press, 1986.

Miscamble, Wilson D., C.S.C. *George F. Kennan and the Making of American Foreign Policy, 1947–1950.* Princeton: Princeton University Press, 1992.

Montefiore, Simon Sebag. *Stalin: The Court of the Red Tsar.* New York: Knopf, 2004.

Mueller, John. *Retreat from Doomsday: The Obsolescence of Major War.* New York: Basic Books, 1989.

Murphy, David E., Sergei A. Kondrashev, and George Bailey. *Battleground Berlin: CIA vs KGB in the Cold War.* New Haven: Yale University Press, 1997.

Naimark, Norman M. *The Russians in Germany: A History of the Soviet Zone of Occupation, 1945–1949.* Cambridge, Massachusetts: Harvard University Press, 1995.

Nixon, Richard M. *RN: The Memoirs of Richard Nixon.* New York: Grosset and Dunlap, 1978.

Oberdorfer, Don. *From the Cold War to a New Era: The United States and the Soviet Union, 1983– 1991.* Updated edition. Baltimore: Johns Hopkins University Press, 1998.

Olson, Keith W. *Watergate: The Presidential Scandal that Shook America.* Lawrence: University Press of Kansas, 2003.

Orwell, George. *1984.* New York: Harcourt Brace, 1949.

Oshinsky, David M. *A Conspiracy So Immense: The World of Joe McCarthy.* New York: Free Press, 1983.

Ouimet, Matthew J. *The Rise and Fall of the Brezhnev Doctrine in Soviet Foreign Policy.* Chapel Hill: University of North Carolina Press, 2003.

Overy, Richard. *Why the Allies Won.* New York: Norton, 1996.

Pipes, Richard. *Vixi: Memoirs of a Non-Belonger.* New Haven: Yale University Press, 2003.

Pisani, Sallie. *The CIA and the Marshall Plan.* Lawrence: University Press of Kansas, 1991.

Power, Samantha. *"A Problem from Hell": America in the Age of Genocide.* New York: Basic Books, 2002.

Quandt, William B. *Camp David: Peacemaking and Politics.* Washington: Brookings Institution, 1986.

Quirk, Robert E. *Fidel Castro.* New York: Norton, 1993.

Ranelagh, John. *The Agency: The Rise and Decline of the CIA.* New York: Simon and Schuster, 1986.

Reagan, Ronald. *An American Life.* New York: Simon and Schuster, 1990.

Resis, Albert, ed. *Molotov Remembers: Inside Kremlin Politics: Conversations with Felix Chuev.* Chicago: Ivan R. Dee, 1993.

Reynolds, David. *One World Divisible: A Global History Since 1945.* New York: Norton, 2000.

Rhodes, Richard. *Dark Sun: The Making of the Hydrogen Bomb.* New York: Simon and Schuster, 1995.

Rotter, Andrew J. *Comrades at Odds: The United States and India, 1947–1964.* Ithaca: Cornell University Press, 2000.

Rusk, Dean, as told to Richard Rusk. *As I Saw It.* New York: Norton, 1990.

Sadat, Anwar el-. *In Search of Identity: An Autobiography.* New York: Harper & Row, 1977.

Sakharov, Andrei. *Memoirs.* Translated by Richard Lourie. New York: Knopf, 1990.

Sarotte, M. E. *Dealing with the Devil: East Germany, Détente, and Ostpolitik, 1969–1973.* Chapel Hill: University of North Carolina Press, 2001.

Schell, Jonathan. *The Unconquerable World: Power, Nonviolence, and the Will of the People.* New York: Metropolitan Books, 2003.

Shelden, Michael. *Orwell: The Authorized Biography.* New York: Harper-Collins, 1991.

Shultz, George P. *Turmoil and Triumph: My Years as Secretary of State.* New York: Scribner's, 1993.

Smith, Gaddis. *Morality, Reason, and Power: American Diplomacy in the Carter Years.* New York: Hill and Wang, 1986.

Smith, Tony. *America's Mission: The United States and the Worldwide Struggle for Democracy in the Twentieth Century.* Princeton: Princeton University Press, 1994.

———. *Thinking Like a Communist: State and Legitimacy in the Soviet Union, China, and Cuba.* New York: Norton, 1987.

Stokes, Gale. *The Walls Came Tumbling Down: The Collapse of Communism in Eastern Europe.* New York: Oxford University Press, 1993.

Stueck, William. *The Korean War: An International History.* Princeton: Princeton University Press, 1995.

———. *Rethinking the Korean War: A New Diplomatic and Military History.* Princeton: Princeton University Press, 2002.

Suny, Ronald Grigor. *The Soviet Experiment: Russia, the USSR, and the Successor States.* New York: Oxford University Press, 1998.

Suri, Jeremi. *Power and Protest: Global Revolution and the Rise of Détente.* Cambridge, Massachusetts: Harvard University Press, 2003.

Taubman, William. *Khrushchev: The Man and His Era.* New York: Norton, 2003.

Thatcher, Margaret. *The Downing Street Years.* New York: HarperCollins, 1993.

Thomas, Daniel C. *The Helsinki Effect: International Norms, Human Rights, and the Demise of Communism.* Princeton: Princeton University Press, 2001.

Thucydides. *History of the Peloponnesian War.* Translated by Rex Warner. New York: Penguin, 1972.

Trachtenberg, Marc. *A Constructed Peace: The Making of a European Settlement, 1945–1963.* Princeton: Princeton University Press, 1999.

Vonnegut, Kurt. *Slaughterhouse-Five.* New York: Delacorte Press, 1969.

Waltz, Kenneth N. *Theory of International Politics.* New York: Random House, 1979.

Weigel, George. *Witness to Hope: The Biography of Pope John Paul II, 1920–2005.* New York: Harper, 2005.

Werth, Alexander. *Russia at War: 1941–1945.* New York: E. P. Dutton, 1964.

Westad, Odd Arne, ed. *The Fall of Détente: Soviet-American Relations during the Carter Years.* Oslo: Scandinavian University Press, 1997.

Yaqub, Salim. *Containing Arab Nationalism: The Eisenhower Doctrine and the Middle East.* Chapel Hill: University of North Carolina Press, 2004.

Zaloga, Stephen J. *The Kremlin's Nuclear Sword: The Rise and Fall of Russia's Strategic Nuclear Forces, 1945–2000.* Washington: Smithsonian Institution, 2002.

Zelikow, Philip, and Condoleezza Rice. *Germany Unified and Europe Transformed: A Study in Statecraft.* Cambridge, Massachusetts: Harvard University Press, 1995.

Zhai, Qiang. *China and the Vietnam Wars, 1950–1975.* Chapel Hill: University of North Carolina Press, 2000.

Zhang, Shu Guang. *Mao's Military Romanticism: China and the Korean War, 1950–1953.* Lawrence: University Press of Kansas, 1995.

ARTICLES

Armitage, John A. "The View from Czechoslovakia." In Thomas T. Hammond, ed., *Witnesses to the Origins of the Cold War.* Seattle: University of Washington Press, 1982, pp. 210–30.

Brodie, Bernard. "War in the Atomic Age." In Bernard Brodie, ed., *The Absolute Weapon: Atomic Power and World Order.* New York: Harcourt, 1946, pp. 21–69.

Broscious, S. David. "Longing for International Control, Banking on American Superiority: Harry S. Truman's Approach to Nuclear Weapons." In John Lewis Gaddis, Philip H. Gordon, Ernest R. May, and Jonathan Rosenberg, eds., *Cold War Statesmen Confront the Bomb: Nuclear Diplomacy since 1945.* New York: Oxford University Press, 1999, pp. 15–38.

Courtois, Stéphane. "Introduction: The Crimes of Communism." In Stéphane Courtois, *et al.*, *The Black Book of Communism: Crimes, Terror, Repression,* translated by Jonathan Murphy and Mark Kramer. Cambridge, Massachusetts: Harvard University Press, 1999, pp. 1–31.

Dingman, Roger. "Atomic Diplomacy During the Korean War." *International Security,* 13 (Winter, 1988/89), 50–91.

Erdmann, Andrew P. N. "'War No Longer Has Any Logic Whatever': Dwight D. Eisenhower and the Thermonuclear Revolution." In John Lewis Gaddis, Philip H. Gordon, Ernest R. May, and Jonathan Rosenberg, eds., *Cold War Statesmen Confront the Bomb: Nuclear Diplomacy since 1945.* New York: Oxford University Press, 1999, pp. 87–119.

Gaddis, John Lewis. "One Germany—in Both Alliances." *New York Times,* March 21, 1990.

———. "Rescuing Choice from Circumstance: The Statecraft of Henry Kissinger." In Gordon A. Craig and Francis L. Loewenheim, eds., *The Diplomats: 1939–1979.* Princeton: Princeton University Press, 1994, pp. 564–92.

Glenn, David. "'Foreign Affairs' Loses a Longtime Editor and His Replacement in Row Over Editorial Independence." *Chronicle of Higher Education,* June 25, 2004, p. A25.

Hertle, Hans-Hermann. "The Fall of the Wall: The Unintended Self-Dissolution of East Germany's Ruling Regime." Cold War International History Project *Bulletin,* #12/13 (Fall/Winter, 2001), 131–40.

James, Harold, and Marzenna James. "The Origins of the Cold War: Some New Documents." *Historical Journal,* 37 (September, 1994), 615–22.

Karalekas, Anne. "History of the Central Intelligence Agency." In U.S. Congress, Senate, Select Committee to Study Government Operations with Respect to Intelligence Activities, *Final Report: Supplementary Detailed Staff Reports on Foreign and Military Intelligence: Book IV.* Washington: Government Printing Office, 1976.

[Kennan, George F.] "X." "The Sources of Soviet Conduct." *Foreign Affairs,* 25 (July, 1947), 566–82.

Kramer, Mark. "Jaruzelski, the Soviet Union, and the Imposition of Martial Law in Poland." Cold War International History Project *Bulletin,* #11 (Winter, 1998), 5–14.

———. "Poland, 1980–81, Soviet Policy During the Polish Crisis." Cold War International History Project *Bulletin,* #5 (Spring, 1995), 1, 116–23.

Mal'kov, Viktor L. "Commentary." In Kenneth M. Jensen, ed., *Origins of the Cold War: The Novikov, Kennan, and Roberts "Long Telegrams" of 1946,* revised edition. Washington: United States Institute of Peace, 1993, pp. 73–79.

Margolin, Jean-Louis. "Cambodia: The Country of Disconcerting Crimes." In Stéphane Courtois, *et al., The Black Book of Communism: Crimes, Terror, Repression,* translated by Jonathan Murphy and Mark Kramer. Cambridge, Massachusetts: Harvard University Press, 1999, pp. 577–635.

———. "China: A Long March into Night." In Stéphane Courtois, *et al., The Black Book of Communism: Crimes, Terror, Repression,* translated by Jonathan Murphy and Mark Kramer. Cambridge, Massachusetts: Harvard University Press, 1999, pp. 463–546.

Mark, Eduard. "The Turkish War Scare of 1946." In Melvyn P. Leffler and David S. Painter, eds., *Origins of the Cold War: An International History,* second edition. New York: Routledge, 2005, pp. 112–33.

Mydans, Seth. "At Cremation of Pol Pot, No Tears Shed." *New York Times,* April 19, 1998.

"NRDC Nuclear Notebook: Global Nuclear Stockpiles." *Bulletin of the Atomic Scientists,* 58 (November/December, 2002), 102–3.

Niebuhr, Reinhold. "Russia and the West." *The Nation,* 156 (January 16, 1943), 83.

Pechatnov, Vladimir O., and C. Earl Edmondson. "The Russian Perspective." In Ralph B. Levering, Vladimir O. Pechatnov, Verena Botzenhart-Viehe, and C. Earl Edmondson, *Debating the Origins of the Cold War: American and Russian Perspectives.* New York: Rowman & Littlefield, 2002, pp. 85–151.

Raine, Femande Scheid. "The Iranian Crisis of 1946 and the Origins of the Cold War." In Melvyn P. Leffler and David S. Painter, eds., *Origins of the Cold War: An International History,* second edition. New York: Routledge, 2005, pp. 93–111.

Roberts, Adam. "Order/Justice Issues at the United Nations." In Rosemary Foot, John Lewis Gaddis, and Andrew Hurrell, eds., *Order and Justice in International Relations.* New York: Oxford University Press, 2003, pp. 49–79.

Roberts, Geoffrey. "Stalin and Soviet Foreign Policy." In Melvyn P. Leffler and David S. Painter, eds., *Origins of the Cold War: An International History,* second edition. New York: Routledge, 2005, pp. 42–57.

Rogers, William D., and Kenneth Maxwell. "Fleeing the Chilean Coup." *Foreign Affairs,* 83 (January/February, 2004), 160–65.

Rosenberg, Jonathan. "Before the Bomb and After: Winston Churchill and the Use of Force." In John Lewis Gaddis, Philip H. Gordon, Ernest R. May, and Jonathan Rosenberg, eds., *Cold War Statesmen Confront the Bomb: Nuclear Diplomacy since 1945.* New York: Oxford University Press, 1999, pp. 171–93.

Schäfer, Bernd. "Weathering the Sino-Soviet Conflict: The GDR and North Korea, 1949–1989." Cold War International History Project *Bulletin*, #14/15 (Winter, 2003–Spring, 2004), 25–38.

Szalontai, Balázs. "'You Have No Political Line of Your Own': Kim II Sung and the Soviets, 1953–1964." Cold War International History Project *Bulletin*, #14/15 (Winter, 2003–Spring, 2004), 87–103.

Thomas, Daniel C. "Human Rights Ideas, the Demise of Communism, and the End of the Cold War." *Journal of Cold War Studies*, 7 (Spring, 2005), 110–41.

Vargas Llosa, Alvaro. "The Killing Machine: Che Guevara, From Communist Firebrand to Capitalist Brand." *The New Republic*, 233 (July 11 and 18, 2005), 25–30.

Weathersby, Kathryn. "New Evidence on North Korea: Introduction." Cold War International History Project *Bulletin*, #14/15 (Winter, 2003–Spring, 2004), 5–7.

———. "Stalin and the Korean War." In Melvyn P. Leffler and David S. Painter, eds., *Origins of the Cold War: An International History*, second edition. New York: Routledge, 2005, pp. 265–81.

Westad, Odd Arne. "The Fall of Détente and the Turning Tides of History." In Odd Arne Westad, ed., *The Fall of Détente: Soviet-American Relations during the Carter Years*. Oslo: Scandinavian University Press, 1997, pp. 3–33.

———. "The Road to Kabul: Soviet Policy on Afghanistan, 1978–1979." In Odd Arne Westad, ed., *The Fall of Détente: Soviet-American Relations during the Carter Years*. Oslo: Scandinavian University Press, 1997, pp. 118–48.

Zubok, Vladislav M. "Stalin and the Nuclear Age." In John Lewis Gaddis, Philip H. Gordon, Ernest R. May, and Jonathan Rosenberg, eds., *Cold War Statesmen Confront the Bomb: Nuclear Diplomacy since 1945*. New York: Oxford University Press, 1999, pp. 39–61.

UNPUBLISHED MATERIAL

Greenberg, Harold M. "The Doolittle Report: Covert Action and Congressional Oversight of the Central Intelligence Agency in the mid-1950s." Senior Essay, Yale University History Department, 2005.

Kennedy, Paul. *The Parliament of Man: The Past, Present, and Future of the United Nations*. Draft Manuscript.

Lüthi, Lorenz. "The Sino-Soviet Split, 1956–1966." Ph.D. Dissertation, Yale University History Department, 2003.

Manela, Erez. "The Wilsonian Moment: Self Determination and the International Origins of Anticolonial Nationalism, 1917–1920." Ph.D. Dissertation, Yale University History Department, 2003.

Michel, Chris. "Bridges Built and Broken Down: How Lyndon Johnson Lost His Gamble on the Fate of the Prague Spring." Senior Essay, Yale University History Department, 2003.

Morgan, Michael D. J. "North America, Atlanticism, and the Helsinki Process." Draft Manuscript.

Rosenzweig, Anne Lesley. "Sadat's Strategic Decision Making: Lessons of Egyptian Foreign Policy, 1970–1981." Senior Essay, Yale University History Department, 2005.

Selverstone, Marc. "'All Roads Lead to Moscow': The United States, Great Britain, and the Communist Monolith." Ph.D. Dissertation, Ohio University History Department, 2000.

Wells, Christopher W. "Kissinger and Sadat: Improbable Partners for Peace." Senior Essay, Yale University History Department, 2004.

Wong, Bryan. "The Grand Strategy of Deng Xiaoping." Senior Essay, Yale University International Studies Program, 2005.

PHOTOGRAPH CREDITS

Insert page 1, *top:* Bettmann/Corbis; *bottom:* Corbis.

Page 2, *top:* Bettmann/Corbis; *bottom:* Hulton-Deutsch Collection/Corbis.

Page 3, *top:* Corbis; *middle:* Bettmann/Corbis; *bottom:* Corbis.

Page 4, *top:* Bettmann/Corbis; *bottom left:* Hulton | Archive/Getty Images; *bottom right:* Bettmann/Corbis.

Page 5, *top:* Carl Mydans/Time & Life Pictures/Getty Images; *middle:* Thomas D. Mcavoy/Time & Life Pictures/Getty Images; *bottom:* Robert Lackenbach/Time & Life Pictures/Getty Images.

Page 6, *top:* Bettmann/Corbis; *middle:* Keystone/Hulton | Archive/Getty Images; *bottom:* Bettmann/Corbis.

Page 7, *top left:* Bettmann/Corbis; *top right:* Hulton-Deutsch Collection/Corbis; *bottom left:* Hulton-Deutsch Collection/Corbis; *bottom right:* Hulton-Deutsch Collection/Corbis.

Page 8, *top left:* Hulton | Archive/Getty Images; *top right:* Central Press/Hulton | Archive/Getty Images; *bottom:* Bettmann/Corbis.

Page 9, *top:* Corbis; *bottom:* Bettmann/Corbis.

Page 10, *top:* SOBI/Corbis Sygma; *middle:* Jacques Pavlovsky/Sygma/Corbis; *bottom:* Bettmann/Corbis.

Page 11, *top:* Corbis; *bottom:* Wally McNamee/Corbis.

Page 12, *top:* AP/Wide World Photos; *bottom:* Reuters/Corbis.

Page 13, *top left:* Wally McNamee/Corbis; *top right:* Owen Franken/Corbis; *bottom:* Reuters/Corbis.

Page 14, *top left:* Corbis; *top right:* Peter Turnley/Corbis; *bottom:* AP/Wide World Photos.

Page 15, *top:* Peter Turnley/Corbis; *bottom:* Regis Bossu/Sygma/Corbis.

Page 16, *top:* Miroslav Zajíc/Corbis; *middle:* Pascal Le Segretain/Corbis Sygma; *bottom:* AP/Wide World Photos.

MAP SOURCES

"European Territorial Changes, 1939–1947," p. 13, after John Lewis Gaddis, *Russia, the Soviet Union, and the United States: An Interpretive History*, second edition (New York: McGraw-Hill, 1990), p. 162.

"Divided Germany and Austria," p. 23, after Gaddis, *Russia, the Soviet Union, and the United States*, p. 192.

"The Korean War, 1950–1953," p. 44, after David Reynolds, *One World Divisible: A Global History Since 1945* (New York: Norton, 2000), p. 48.

"U.S. and U.S.S.R. Alliances and Bases, Early 1970s," pp. 96–97, after Walter LaFeber, *America, Russia, and the Cold War, 1945–1990*, sixth edition (New York: McGraw-Hill, 1991), pp. xii–xiii.

"The Middle East, 1967, 1979," p. 205, after LaFeber, *America, Russia, and the Cold War*, p. 276.

"The Near East in Upheaval, 1980," p. 209, after LaFeber, *America, Russia, and the Cold War*, p. 295.

"A 1980s Soviet View," p. 220, after LaFeber, *America, Russia, and the Cold War*, p. 270.

"Post–Cold War Europe," p. 258, after Richard Crockatt, *The Fifty Years War: The United States and the Soviet Union in World Politics, 1941–1991* (New York: Routledge, 1995), p. xxi.

INDEX

Able Archer crisis, 227–28
Acheson, Dean, 33, 37, 38, 42
Adams, John Quincy, 15–16
Adenauer, Konrad, 105, 135–36, 138, 140
Afghanistan, 203, 224, 235, 257, 261
    Marxist coup in, 208–10
    Soviet invasion of, 203, 210–11, 212, 214, 216
Ağca, Mehmet Ali, 218–19
Algeria, 139
Allen, Woody, 230
Allende, Salvador, 173–74, 178

America House, Berlin, 144
American Revolution, 7
Amin, Hafizullah, 210–11
Andropov, Yuri, 221, 224, 230, 248, 264
    concerns over dissent in Soviet bloc, 186, 190, 219
    and election of Pope John Paul II, 192
    and Reagan, 227, 231
    U.S. attack on Soviet Union predicted by, 227–28, 231
Angola, 179, 206–8

Anti-Ballistic Treaty of 1972, 81, 226
Arab-Israeli wars, 261
    of 1967, 204
    of 1973, 204–6, 212
    Suez crisis and, 70, 127–28
Arbatov, Georgi, 202, 207, 213–14
Arbenz Guzmán, Jacobo, 164, 166
Armenia, 253, 256
Aswan High Dam, 127
Atlantic Charter, 20
atomic bomb, 24–26, 40, 47, 61
    Soviet acquisition of, 35–36, 57,
        105
    see also nuclear weapons
Attlee, Clement, 10, 28
Austria, 241, 243
Azerbaijan, 253

baby boom, 146–47
Baker, James, 251
Baltic States, 11, 19, 21, 253, 256
Bandung conference of 1955, 126–27
Baruch, Bernard, 54
Baruch Plan, 54, 56
"Basic Principles" statement of
    1972, 203–4
Bay of Pigs invasion, 74, 76, 166,
    168, 171, 177
Begin, Menachem, 204
Beria, Lavrentii, 104–7
Berlin, *see* East Berlin; West Berlin
Berlin blockade of 1948, 33–34,
    56, 71
Berlin crisis of 1958–61, 112–14
Berlin Wall, 74, 120, 198, 248, 250
    building of, 114–15
    fall of, 245–46
Bierut, Boleslaw, 108
Bismarck, Otto von, 86, 155, 196
Blair, Eric, *see* Orwell, George
Bohlen, Charles E., 83, 98, 117

Bolivia, 148
Bolshevik Revolution of 1917, 8, 18,
    38, 87, 121, 237–38, 257
Brandt, Willy, 154, 187, 213
    at Erfurt meeting, 213
BRAVO nuclear test, 64–65, 66
Brezhnev, Leonid, 120, 134, 181,
    183–84, 200, 201–2, 204, 214,
    230, 242, 248, 264
    Afghanistan invasion and,
        210–11
    Czechoslovakia invasion and,
        144, 150, 152–53
    death of, 224
    Helsinki Accords and, 186–88,
        189, 190, 192, 193
Brezhnev Doctrine, 150, 153, 185, 188,
    212, 213, 221, 234, 247
Britain, Battle of, 17
Brodie, Bernard, 51
Bulgaria, 20, 99, 219, 246
Bush, George H. W., 229, 233–34,
    239–40, 251, 254, 257
    "chicken Kiev" speech of, 255–56
    Cold War seen as permanent
        by, 222
    at Malta summit, 248–249, 259
    review of U.S.-Soviet relations
        ordered by, 239
Byelorussia, 253, 256

Cambodia, 145–46, 173, 266
Canada, 188
capitalism, 91–92, 94, 95, 98, 197, 217,
    261, 264
    in Lenin's theory, 87–89
    in Marx's theory, 85–86
    and occupation of Germany
        and Japan, 101–3
    postwar success of, 115–17
    World War I and, 86–89

Carter, Jimmy, 189, 210, 211–12, 218,
219, 225, 234
    Middle East peace mediated
        by, 204
    Moscow Olympic boycott
        ordered by, 211
    SALT II and, 201–3, 211
Castlereagh, Robert Stewart
    Viscount, 155, 183
Castro, Fidel, 74, 76–78, 114, 144,
    148, 166, 168, 207
Ceaușescu, Elena, 247
Ceaușescu, Nicolai, 247, 257,
    259
Central Intelligence Agency
    (C.I.A.), 72, 112, 128, 148,
        169, 172, 174
    Chile coup of 1973 and, 173–74,
        177–78
    congressional investigation of,
        177–79
    covert operations of, 163–67
    domestic surveillance program
        of, 177–78
    Doolittle Report and,
        166–67
    Italy's 1948 election and, 162
    N.S.C. and expanded role of,
        162–63
Central Treaty Organization
    (CENTO), 125
Charter 77, 191
Chernenko, Konstantin, 228–30,
    248, 264
Chernobyl nuclear disaster, 231
Chernyaev, Anatoly, 229, 230–31,
    234, 247, 254–56
Chiang Kai-shek, 37, 38, 126, 129,
    131, 132, 159
Chile, 160
    1973 coup in, 173–74, 177–78

China, People's Republic of, 36–38,
    40, 123, 125, 126, 153, 163, 179,
    180, 217, 234, 263–65
    Cultural Revolution in, 147–48,
        151, 215
    Egypt's recognition of, 127
    Great Leap Forward in, 111–12,
        141, 142, 161
    Korean War and, 42, 45–46, 60,
        105, 109–10
    Mao's cult of personality in,
        110–11
    market economy of, 214–16
    offshore islands crisis and, 131–
        32, 136–37, 141
    Soviet Union's relations with,
        see Sino-Soviet relations
    Tiananmen Square massacre in,
        242–43
    U.S. relations with, *see* Sino-
        American relations
    Vietnam War and, 150–51
China, Republic of, 17, 37, 159
China Lobby, 37–38
Christian Democratic Party,
    German, 135
Christian Democratic Party, Italian,
    162
Churchill, Winston, 5–6, 10, 14, 17–
    20, 24, 26–27, 54, 65, 66, 80,
    81, 146, 216
    "Iron Curtain" speech of, 94–95,
        223
    Stalin's 1944 deal with, 20
C.I.A., *see* Central Intelligence
    Agency
Civil War, U.S., 53
Clausewitz, Carl von, 51, 52, 55, 63,
    67, 68
Clinton, Bill, 251
Colby, William, 177

colonialism, 89, 121–24
    demise of, 121
    rise of nationalism and, 123–24
    superpowers and, 122–23
Columbus, Christopher, 260
Cominform, 32, 33
Comintern, 32
Commonwealth of Independent
        States, 256–57
communism, 94, 95, 98, 101, 107, 217
    failure of, 263–64
    as historically determined,
        84–85, 87
    in Marxist theory, 86
    see also Marxism-Leninism
Communist Manifesto (Marx), 8
Communist Party, Bulgarian, 246
Communist Party, Chinese, 111,
        214–15, 243
Communist Party, Polish, 108, 192
Communist Party, Soviet, 107, 186,
        207, 229, 242, 253, 254
    abolition of, 256
Conference on Security and
        Cooperation in Europe,
        187–88
    see also Helsinki Accords
Congress, U.S., 34, 166, 167–68, 169,
        172, 200
    "China Lobby" in, 37
    C.I.A. investigated by, 177–79
    Jackson-Vanik amendment
        passed by, 182–83, 184,
        200–201
    War Powers Act passed by,
        176–77
    see also House of
        Representatives, U.S.;
        Senate U.S.
Congress of People's Deputies,
        Soviet, 242, 256

Constitution, U.S., 171
containment policy, U.S., 28–29, 32,
        46, 154, 212
Cuba, 74, 114, 160, 166, 179, 203, 207
Cuban missile crisis, 75–78, 80, 82,
        134, 203, 228
Cultural Revolution, 147–48, 151, 215
Czechoslovakia, 21, 99, 100, 127, 160,
        191, 211, 221, 243, 244
    communist coup in, 32–34
    1989 revolution in, 246
    Soviet invasion of, 144, 150,
        152–53, 162, 180–81, 185

D-Day, 14, 19
Declaration of Independence, 15
Defense Department, U.S., 54, 172,
        201, 225
de Gaulle, Charles, 138–40, 142, 143
democracy, 87, 91, 92, 94, 95, 98, 199,
        217
    globalization of, 264–65
    Marshall Plan and, 100, 102–4
Democratic National Committee,
        156–57, 175
Democratic Party, U.S., 145, 189, 202
Deng Xiaoping, 195, 197, 222, 234,
        240, 245, 257, 259
    achievement of, 214–15
    Tiananmen Square massacre
        and, 242–43
Depression, Great, 12, 90, 116
détente, 153, 180–84, 210, 211
    Arab-Israeli war of 1973 and,
        204–6
    decline of, 213–14
    Helsinki Accords and, 187–88, 189
    Kissinger on, 183–84
    morality and, 180–82
    as Reagan's target, 217–18, 225
    shortcomings of, 197–99

Soviet Union as affected by,
    184–87
Soviet Union's third-world
    involvement and, 206–8
Thatcher on, 216
dictatorship of the proletariat, 88,
    98, 100
Disraeli, Benjamin, 83, 85–88, 98, 117
Dobrynin, Anatoly, 134, 156, 183,
    190, 194, 202, 206–8, 211, 227
domino theory, 123-24
Doolittle Report, 165–66
Dubček, Alexander, 246
Dulles, John Foster, 63, 67, 107–8,
    127, 131, 180
Dutschke, Rudi, 144

East Berlin, 113–15, 167, 246
East Germany, *see* Germany,
    Democratic Republic of
Eden, Anthony, 127
Egypt, 70, 126–27, 204-6
Eisenhower, Dwight D., 63, 65, 69,
    71, 72–74, 79–81, 136, 139, 166,
    170, 171, 172
    domino theory of, 123–24
    Khrushchev's meetings with,
        72, 74
    nuclear weapons policy of, 66–68
    Suez crisis and, 70, 127–28
    U-2 incident and, 73–74, 167–68
Eisenhower administration, 74, 76,
    114, 163, 164
Eisenhower Doctrine, 128
elections, U.S.:
    of 1964, 133, 168–69
    of 1968, 145, 170
    of 1972, 155
    of 1976, 189, 201
    of 1980, 218
Ellsberg, Daniel, 174

Engels, Friedrich, 86, 87, 107
Estonia, 253, 254
Ethiopia, 89, 206, 207–8
European Economic Community,
    140
European Recovery Plan,
    see Marshall Plan
Export-Import Bank, 182

Farouk I, king of Egypt, 126
Federal Bureau of Investigation
    (F.B.I.), 173, 174
Finland, 11, 19, 21
flexible responsive strategy, 67
    NSC-68 and, 164–65
Ford, Gerald, 177, 179, 188, 189, 201
Forrestal, James, 35
Foster, Jodie, 222
Fourteen Points, 87, 121
France, 14, 16, 17, 42, 49, 52, 71, 104,
    122, 123, 132, 159, 200
    de Gaulle's policies and, 138–40
    occupation of Germany and,
        22, 24
    Suez crisis and, 70, 77, 127–28
Free University, 144
French Revolution, 237–38, 266
Fuchs, Klaus, 39–40

Gandhi, Mohandas K., 121
Garton Ash, Timothy, 186, 237
Geneva Conference on Indochina,
    1954, 131, 132
Geneva summit of 1955, 72–73
Geneva summit of 1985, 229–30
Georgia, 253
Gerasimov, Gennadi, 247
Germany, Democratic Republic of
    (East Germany), 71, 74, 99,
    105–6, 108, 135, 144, 153, 160,
    213, 221, 241, 259

Germany, Democratic Republic
of (*cont.*)
emigration issue and, 113–15,
136–37
reunification issue and, 248–52
revolution of 1989 and, 243–46
Germany, Federal Republic of
(West Germany), 34, 136,
138, 140, 148, 213, 244, 246
Berlin crisis and, 112–14
NATO and, 134–35
Ostpolitik strategy of, 153–54
reunification issue and, 248–52
Germany, Imperial, 16, 52, 86, 87, 89
Germany, Nazi, 5, 7, 8, 10, 12, 17, 18,
19, 21, 25, 46, 89, 90, 92, 99,
263, 265
occupation of, 101–2
Gierek, Edward, 193
glasnost (publicity), 231, 253
Goldwater, Barry, 133, 169
Gomulka, Wladyslaw, 100, 108
Gorbachev, Mikhail, 95, 197, 216,
252, 255
assessment of, 257
Bush administration's distrust
of, 239–40
Chernobyl disaster and, 231
domestic contempt for, 252–53
German reunification issue
and, 248–51
at Malta summit, 248–49, 259
Reagan and, 230–36
revolution of 1989 and, 239, 241–
45, 247–48
at Reykjavik summit, 231–32
Yeltsin's replacement of, 256–57
Gorbachev, Raisa, 229
Gorbachev Foundation, 259–60
Great Britain, 8, 9, 12, 14, 15–18, 20,
25, 30, 31, 46, 49, 52, 71, 76,
85, 86, 89–90, 94, 123,
125, 139, 140, 159, 197,
200, 228
Egypt's non-alignment strategy
and, 126–27
Fuchs spy case in, 39–40
occupation of Germany and,
22, 24
Suez crisis and, 70, 77, 127–28
Thatcher government in, 197,
216
World War II objectives of,
17–18
Great Depression, 12, 90, 116
Great Leap Forward, 111–12, 141,
142, 161
Great Society, 169–70
Greece, 20, 31, 95
Gribkov, Anatoly, 221
Gromyko, Andrei, 188, 211, 212, 228
Guatemala, 160, 166, 178
Guevara, Che, 148, 166

Havel, Václav, 191–92, 246, 257, 263
Helsinki Accords of 1975, 186–91,
214, 265
Soviet Union as affected by,
190–91
Hinckley, John W., 222
Hiss, Alger, 39–40
Hitler, Adolf, 5, 7, 9–10, 14, 19, 89,
90, 92, 250, 254
Hobsbawm, Eric, 116–17
Ho Chi Minh, 42, 121–22, 129, 132
Honecker, Erich, 243–45, 259
Hongxi, emperor of China, 260
Hopkins, Harry, 6
House of Commons, British, 65
House of Representatives, U.S., 175,
177, 178
Hull, Cordell, 93

human rights, 182, 201
    Helsinki Accords and, 187–91
    U.N. and, 158, 160–61
Humphrey, Hubert, 70, 145
Hungary, 20, 70, 99, 127, 136, 144, 153,
    160, 167, 259, 262
    1956 uprising in, 108–9, 114–15,
        124–25, 180, 221, 240–41
    1989 thaw in, 240–41, 243,
        247–48
Hussein, Saddam, 262
Hu Yaobang, 242
hydrogen bomb, 36, 39, 47
    BRAVO test of, 64–65, 66
    development of, 61–62
    Eisenhower's policy on, 63–64,
        66–68
    flexible response strategy and,
        66–67
    rational use of, 62–63
    see also nuclear weapons

imperialism, 123
India, 121
    non-alignment strategy of,
        125–26, 128
India-Pakistan wars, 261
Indochina, 42, 121–22, 131, 132
industrial revolution, 85
Intermediate-Range Nuclear
    Forces Treaty of 1987, 235
International Monetary Fund,
    93–94
Iran, 11, 28, 160, 164, 166–67,
    178
    1979 hostage crisis in, 212
Iran-Iraq war, 261
Iraq, 128
    Kuwait invaded by, 262
Israel, 204-6, 261
    see also Arab-Israeli wars

Italy, 19–20, 28, 76, 89, 92, 219
    C.I.A. and 1948 election of,
        162

Jackson, Henry M., 182–83, 200–201
Jackson-Vanik amendment, 182–83,
    200–201
Japan, 7, 8, 17, 37, 46, 58, 89, 92, 95,
    121, 263
    atomic bombing of, 25–26,
        48–49, 50, 54
    and Korea, 40–41
    occupation of, 101–2
Jaruzelski, Wojciech, 221–22, 241,
    242, 250
Jews, 52
    Soviet, 182–83
John Paul II, pope, 192–96, 214, 217,
    220, 222–23, 230, 240, 257,
    263–64
    attempted assassination of,
        218–19
Johnson, Lady Bird, 133, 169
Johnson, Lyndon B., 133, 140, 145,
    154, 174
    Great Society programs of,
        169–70
    Vietnam War and, 168–70,
        173
Johnson administration, 170–71, 172,
    177, 181
Joint Chiefs of Staff, U.S., 46, 54,
    67, 160
Justice Department, U.S., 173

Kádár, János, 114–15, 240
Kant, Immanuel, 158, 182
Katyn Wood massacre, 21
Kazakhstan, 253, 256
Kennan, George F., 32, 46–47, 61,
    101, 171

Kennan, George F. (*cont.*)
  "long telegram" of, 29–31
  on role of C.I.A., 161–64
  on U.N., 160
Kennedy, John F., 79, 84, 115, 132, 137, 166, 168, 170, 171, 172, 203
  Cuban missile crisis and, 76–78
  U.S.-Soviet relations and, 74–75
Kennedy, Robert F., 145
Kent State incident, 146
K.G.B., 186, 192, 227, 228
Khmer Rouge, 266
Khomeini, Ayatollah Ruhollah, 167, 208
Khrushchev, Nikita, 65, 72–75, 80, 117, 119, 122, 130, 132, 134, 185, 203, 248
  background and personality of, 68–69
  Berlin Wall and, 113–14, 120
  Cuban missile crisis and, 76–78
  East German alliance and, 136–38
  Eisenhower's meetings with, 72, 74
  Hungarian uprising and, 108–9, 124–25, 240
  nuclear weapons policy of, 69–70
  ouster of, 119–20
  rise of, 106–7
  Sino-Soviet relations and, 140–42
  Stalin denounced by, 107–8, 111, 167
  Suez crisis and, 70
  Tito visited by, 124–25
  U.S. visited by, 71–72
  U-2 incident and, 73–74, 168
  "We will bury you" remark of, 84

Khrushchev, Sergei, 69, 71
Kim Il-sung, 41–42, 45, 109–10, 122
King, Martin Luther, Jr., 145
Kirghizia, 253
Kissinger, Henry, 67, 145, 150, 151, 154, 155, 172, 173, 174, 176–88, 187, 188, 189, 198, 201, 212
  on détente, 183–84
  and Israeli-Egyptian peace deal, 204–6
  morality in policy of, 181–83
Kohl, Helmut, 250, 251–52
Korea, Democratic Republic of (North Korea), 40–43, 60, 105, 129, 130–31, 159
Korea, Republic of (South Korea), 40–43, 122, 123, 129–30, 159, 265
Korean War, 40–46, 48–50, 63, 122, 123, 130–31, 169, 261
  armistice negotiations in, 59–60
  casualties in, 50
  Chinese intervention in, 45–46, 60, 105, 109–10
  Inchon landings in, 42–43
  non-use of nuclear weapons in, 58–59, 63
  prelude to, 40–42
  proposed use of atomic weapons in, 48–50
  Soviet Union and, 42–45, 49, 54, 60, 130–31
  U.N. and, 41, 43, 49, 159
Kosygin, Alexei, 134, 208–10
Krenz, Egon, 245–46, 250
Kryuchkov, Vladimir, 250
kulaks, 99
Kurile Islands, 24
Kuwait, 262

Labour Party, British, 10
Laos, 173
Latvia, 253, 254
League of Nations, 16, 27, 89, 158
Lebanon, 128, 131
Le Duc Tho, 151
Lend-Lease, 6
Lenin, V. I., 8, 12, 31, 76, 77, 94, 98,
        99, 103–4, 116, 117, 121, 185,
        229, 238, 253, 261, 264
    capitalism in theory of, 87–89
    New Economic Policy of, 110
    World War II and vision of,
        89–90
Life of Pi (Martel), 82
Limited Test Ban Treaty of 1963, 81
Lincoln, Abraham, 53, 157
Lithuania, 253, 254
Li Zhisui, 149
Locksley Hall (Tennyson), 159
"long telegram" (Kennan), 29–31

MacArthur, Douglas, 41, 43, 45–46,
        48, 60
McCarthy, Joseph, 40
McCarthyism, 46
McGovern, George, 155
Machiavelli, Niccolò, 156, 252, 257
Macmillan, Harold, 84
McNamara, Robert S., 79–80, 174
MAD, *see* Mutual Assured
        Destruction
Malenkov, Georgii, 64–65, 66, 69,
        105, 107, 113, 125
Malta summit of 1989, 248–49, 250,
        259
Manchuria, 24, 40, 89
Manhattan Project, 25, 39, 52, 56, 61
Mao Zedong, 36–39, 40, 42, 45, 60,
        71, 109, 117, 121, 138, 144, 161,
        180, 197, 214, 215, 245, 264

    cult of personality and, 110–11
    Cultural Revolution and,
        147–48
    Great Leap Forward of, 111–12,
        141, 142, 161
    Korean War and, 109–10
    offshore islands crisis and,
        131–32, 136–37
    Sino-American relations and,
        149–52
    Sino-Soviet relations and,
        140–42, 143
    Soviet Union visited by, 39
    Stalin as model for, 109–10, 111
Marshall, George C., 30–31, 98,
        101
Marshall Plan, 30–32, 34, 36, 112
    democracy and, 100, 102–4
    premises and goals of, 32, 35,
        95–98, 162
Martel, Yann, 82
Marx, Karl, 8, 22, 75–76, 87, 89,
        92–93, 98, 101, 104, 107, 117,
        123, 224, 238, 261, 264
    capitalism in theory of,
        85–86
Marxism-Leninism, 85, 93, 99, 104,
        109, 130, 212, 215, 263, 265
    double life required by, 185–86,
        192, 196
    failure of, 106, 153, 185–86, 229,
        238
    Maoist version of, 111–12
    Marxist coup in Afghanistan
        and, 210
    postwar reconstruction and,
        90–91
Masaryk, Jan, 33
Masaryk, Thomas, 33
Masur, Kurt, 245
Mazowiecki, Tadeusz, 242

Metternich, Klemens von, 155, 183, 196

Mexico, 99

Mielke, Erich, 243–44

Mikoyan, Anastas, 76, 114

"missile gap," 74, 76

Mitchell, John, 175

Mitterrand, François, 250

Modrow, Hans, 250

Mohammad Reza Shah Pahlavi, 167, 208, 212

Moldavia, 253

Molotov, Vyacheslav, 21, 28, 30, 31, 42, 105, 107, 114, 187

Mondale, Walter, 228

moon landings, 260

Moscow Olympics, see Olympic Games of 1980

Moscow summit of 1972, 182, 200

    "Basic Principles" statement in, 203–4

Moscow summit of 1989, 255

Mossadegh, Mohammed, 164

Mussolini, Benito, 89

Mutual Assured Destruction (MAD), 80–81, 180, 198, 200, 225, 226

Nagy, Imre, 109, 241

Napoleon I, emperor of France, 84, 183

Nasser, Gamal Abdel, 70, 204

    non-alignment strategy of, 126–28

National Association of Evangelicals, 224

National Front for the Liberation of Angola, 179

nationalism, 125, 128, 234

    colonialism and rise of, 123–24

National Security Council, 42

    C.I.A.'s role expanded by, 162–63

National Student Association, 177

National War College, 46

NATO, see North Atlantic Treaty Organization

Nazi-Soviet Pact of 1939, 11, 19, 21, 90, 254

Nehru, Jawaharlal, 125–26, 128

Németh, Miklós, 240–41

Netherlands, 123

New Deal, 91, 169

New Economic Policy, 110

New York Times, 3, 157, 173, 174, 255–56

Ngo Dinh Diem, 129, 132–33

Nicaragua, 212

Nicholas II, tsar of Russia, 87

Niebuhr, Reinhold, 91

1984 (Orwell), 1–2, 47, 263

Nitze, Paul, 164–65

Nixon, Richard M., 145–46, 154, 155, 166–67, 171–78, 181–84, 186, 200, 204, 206, 260

    China opening and, 149–52, 215

    credibility gap of, 172–74

    Plumbers unit of, 174–75

    resignation of, 157, 175–76

    on secrecy, 172–73

    taping system of, 173, 175–76

    Vietnam War and, 150–51

    Watergate affair and, 155–58, 175, 176

Nixon administration, 158, 177, 183, 200

Nobel Peace Prize, 204, 257

"no cities" doctrine, 79–80

non-alignment strategy, 124–28

non-intervention, principle of,
160–61
North Atlantic Treaty of 1949, 143
North Atlantic Treaty Organization
(NATO), 34, 35, 39, 49, 59,
69, 104, 105, 109, 124, 127, 153,
187, 200, 202, 203, 210, 211
and Able Archer crisis, 227–28
France and, 139–40
German reunification issue
and, 250–51
West Germany question and,
134–35
North Korea, see Korea,
Democratic Republic of
North Vietnam, see Vietnam,
Democratic Republic of
Novikov, Nikolai, 30–31
NSC-68, 164–65, 170–71
nuclear freeze movement, 225–26
Nuclear Non-Proliferation Treaty
of 1968, 81
nuclear weapons, 196, 199–203, 238
Baruch Plan and, 54, 56
Eisenhower's policy on, 66–68
France's testing of, 139–40
Jackson resolution on,
200–201
Khrushchev's policy on, 69–70
in Korean War, 48–50, 58–59, 63
MAD strategy and, 80–81
nature of warfare and, 50–52, 58,
262–63
"no cities" doctrine of, 79–80
proposed abolition of, 230–31
in SALT agreements, 172,
199–202, 210–12
SS-20 missile crisis and,
202–3
Stalin's policy on, 56–58
Truman's policy on, 54–56
U.S. monopoly of, 34–36, 54,
56–58
see also atomic bomb; hydrogen
bomb
Nuclear Weapons and Foreign Policy
(Kissinger), 67

oil embargo, 212
Okinawa, 41, 58
Olympic Games of 1980, 210, 211
"open skies," 72–73, 81
Oppenheimer, J. Robert, 61, 262
Orwell, George, 1–3, 47, 101, 228, 263
Ostpolitik, 153–54, 187, 213

Pahlavi, Mohammad Reza Shah,
167, 208, 212
Paine, Thomas, 15, 122
Pakistan, 125
Paul VI, pope, 192
"peaceful coexistence," 70
Pearl Harbor attack, 7, 8, 17, 92
Peloponnesian War, 51
Pentagon Papers, 157, 174–75
People's Daily, 148
perestroika (restructuring), 231, 253,
254
Perestroika (Gorbachev), 233, 235
Pershing II missiles, 202–3, 211, 225,
232
Pervukhin, Mikhail, 113
Philby, Kim, 72
Philippines, 41, 122, 164
Pinochet, Augusto, 178
"Plastic People of the Universe," 191
Plumbers, 175, 177
Poland, 11, 19, 21–22, 90, 99, 100, 127,
136, 144, 153, 167, 213, 223,
224, 247–48, 259
John Paul II and, 192–94, 195
1989 election in, 241–42, 244

Poland (*cont.*)
  rise of Solidarity in, 219–22
  Soviet non-intervention in,
    219–22, 235
Politburo, Soviet, 186, 188, 202, 207,
    210, 211, 221, 229, 231, 234,
    235, 236, 239–40, 242
Pol Pot, 266
Portugal, 121, 123
Potsdam Conference of 1945, 25
Powers, Francis Gary, 73, 167
Prague spring, 152, 185, 188, 246
Pravda, 105, 190
Public Group to Promote
    Observance of the Helsinki
    Accords, 190–91

Quemoy and Matsu crises, 131–32,
    136–37

Radio Free Europe, 167
Rákosi, Mátyás, 108
Reagan, Ronald, 2–3, 189, 197,
    216–18, 239, 240, 248, 257
  abolition of nuclear weapons
    proposed by, 232–33
  attempted assassination of, 222
  détente as target of, 217–18, 225
  "evil empire" speech of, 224–25,
    227
  Gorbachev and, 230–36
  at Reykjavik summit, 231–32
  rise of, 217
  SDI concept and, 226–27
  Soviet Union visited by, 233–34
  "tear down this wall" speech of,
    235
  U.S.-Soviet relations and,
    222–28
Reagan Doctrine, 234, 236
Red Guards, 143, 147–48, 215

Republican Party, U.S., 189, 202
Reykjavik summit of 1986, 231–32
Rhee, Syngman, 41, 121, 129–30, 132
Rice, Condoleezza, 255
Ridgway, Matthew B., 59
Romania, 11, 19, 20, 99, 153
  1989 Revolution in, 247
Roosevelt, Franklin D., 5–6, 9–10,
    14, 16–22, 24, 54, 55, 91, 157,
    234, 250
  postwar settlement as seen by,
    26–27
  U.S.-Soviet alliance and, 93
Rostow, Walt, 132–33
Rusk, Dean, 140, 181
Russell, Richard, 140
Russia, Imperial, 87, 121, 238
Russo-Japanese War of 1904–5, 24,
    121

Sadat, Anwar-el, 204–6
Safire, William, 255–56
Sakhalin Island, 24
Sakharov, Andrei, 186, 190–91, 201,
    263
SALT, *see* Strategic Arms
    Limitation Talks
SALT II, 200–203, 210–11, 225
Sandinistas, 212
Saudi Arabia, 160
Schabowski, Günter, 245–46
Schell, Jonathan, 119
Schneider, René, 174
Schumacher, Kurt, 135
Scowcroft, Brent, 239, 254
SDI, *see* Strategic Defense
    Initiative
SEATO, *see* Southeast Asian Treaty
    Organization
Senate, U.S., 175, 177, 179
  SALT II treaty in, 202–3, 211

Shelest, Petr, 144
Shi Zhe, 110
Shultz, George, 229, 233
Siberia, 16
Sicily, 19
Sieyès, Abbé, 266
Singapore, 265
Sino-American relations, 171
    Deng and, 215
    Mao and, 149–52
    in Quemoy and Matsu crises,
      131–32
    Taiwan and, 130–31
Sino-Soviet relations, 138
    border warfare and, 149
    Khrushchev and, 140–42
    Mao and, 140–43
    Treaty of 1950 and, 39, 109, 126
    U.S.-China détente and, 150–52,
      154
Six Crises (Nixon), 152
Six-Day War, 204
Sixth Fleet, U.S., 28–29, 124
Smith, Adam, 89
Solidarity (Solidarność), 197, 218–19,
    221–22, 241, 259
Solzhenitsyn, Aleksandr, 186, 189,
    190, 263
Somalia, 206, 207–8
Somme, Battle of the, 53
Somoza, Anastasio, 212
Sonnenfeldt, Helmut, 189
South Africa, 160
Southeast Asian Treaty
    Organization (SEATO),
    125
South Korea, *see* Korea, Republic of
South Vietnam, *see* Vietnam,
    Republic of
Soviet Union, 2, 6, 11, 17–22, 46, 66,
    67, 84, 93, 102, 103, 110, 120,

123, 147, 148, 152–53, 159, 163,
    230, 236, 244, 251, 261, 262,
    264
    Able Archer crisis and, 227–28
    Afghanistan invaded by, 203,
      210–11, 212, 214, 216
    atomic bomb acquired by,
      35–36, 57, 105
    atomic bomb policy of, 56–58
    and attempted assassination of
      John Paul II, 219
    August coup in, 256
    Chernobyl nuclear disaster in,
      231
    China's relations with, *see* Sino-
      Soviet relations
    Chinese Revolution and, 37–38
    collapse of, 3, 238, 242, 252–57,
      263
    Cuban Revolution and, 75–76
    Czechoslovakia invaded by, 144,
      150, 152–53, 162, 180–81, 185
    détente and, *see* détente
    Eastern European sphere of
      influence of, 20–22
    economy of, 212–14, 216, 219–21,
      224, 252
    German invasion of, 7, 90
    Helsinki Accords' effect on,
      190–91
    Hungarian uprising and, 108–9
    hydrogen bomb and, 62
    Khrushchev's de-Stalinization
      speech and, 107–8
    Korean War and, 42–45, 49, 54,
      60, 130–31
    Mao's visit to, 39
    Marxism-Leninism and life in,
      185–86
    and non-intervention in
      Poland, 219–22

Soviet Union (*cont.*)
    non-Russian republics of, 253
    postwar goals of, 10–14
    postwar settlement and, 9–10
    Reagan's visit to, 233–34
    SDI reaction of, 227–28
    Sputnik program of, 68
    SS-20 deployment decision of,
        202
    Stalin's dictatorship in, 98–101
    U.S. contrasted with, 7–8
    U.S. relations with, *see* United
        States–Soviet relations
    Watergate reaction of,
        156–57
    in World War II, 9
    Yeltsin's emergence in,
        255–56
    Yugoslavia's rift with, 33
Spain, 121
Sputnik, 68
SS-20 missiles, 202, 211, 214, 225, 232
Stalin, Josef, 5, 8–14, 18, 24, 35, 54, 61,
    69, 77, 84, 90, 102, 103, 109,
    112, 116, 117, 122, 141, 161, 185,
    194, 250, 254, 264
    atomic bomb policy of, 25–26,
        56–58, 63
    Berlin blockade and, 33–34
    China policy and, 36–37
    Churchill's 1944 deal with, 20
    Czech coup and, 32–33, 34
    description of, 10–11
    dictatorship of, 98–101, 105
    German reunification initiative
        of, 105–6
    Khrushchev's denunciation of,
        107–8, 111, 167
    Korean War and, 42–45
    Marshall Plan and, 32–34
    as model for Mao, 109–10

    personality of, 10–11
    postwar goals of, 10–14, 20–22,
        27
    successors to, 104–5, 106
    U.S.-Soviet alliance and, 93–94
State Department, U.S., 29, 37, 162,
    163, 164, 168, 172
Strategic Arms Limitation Interim
    Agreement of 1972, 81
Strategic Arms Limitation Talks
    (SALT), 172, 199–202, 212
    see also SALT II
Strategic Arms Reduction Talks
    (START), 225, 235, 255
Strategic Defense Initiative (SDI),
    226–27, 230, 231–32
Suez Canal, 70, 77, 126, 127–28
Supreme Court, U.S., 175
Suslov, Mikhail, 221
Sybil: The Two Nations (Disraeli),
    85, 98

Tadzhikistan, 253
Taiwan, 37, 41, 126, 129, 130–31, 265
Taraki, Nur Mohammed, 210
Teheran Conference of 1943, 5–6, 9
Tennyson, Alfred, 159
Tet Offensive, 170
Thatcher, Margaret, 197, 216–17, 222,
    223, 230, 237, 240, 250, 251,
    257
third world, 122–23, 180, 187, 199,
    207, 235
    non-alignment strategy of,
        124–28
    threat of collapse strategy of,
        129–34
Thucydides, 51, 52
Tiananmen Square massacre,
    242–43
Timoșoara, 247

Tito (Josip Broz), 33–34, 37, 38,
    99–100, 134
  non-alignment strategy of,
    124–25
Tocqueville, Alexis de, 237
totalitarianism, 2, 50
Trade Reform Act, 182–83
Triumph and Tragedy (Churchill), 6
Trotsky, Leon, 99, 224
Truman, Harry S., 10, 26, 35–37, 53,
    57, 58, 94, 103, 180
  hydrogen bomb decision of,
    61–62
  nuclear weapons policy of, 48,
    50, 54–56, 63
  onset of Korean War and, 43,
    45, 159
  Truman Doctrine speech of, 95
Truman administration, 25, 35, 38,
    40, 47, 49, 58–59, 131, 159, 164
Truman Doctrine, 31, 95, 102
Turkey, 11, 28, 31, 76, 95
Turkmenistan, 253

Ukraine, 99, 253, 255, 256
Ulbricht, Walter, 105–6, 114, 136–38
United Nations, 27–28, 54, 56,
    93–94, 101, 184, 188, 236
  human rights and, 158, 160–61
  Kennan on, 160
  Korean War and, 41, 43, 49, 159
  non-intervention principle of,
    160–61
  veto power in, 159
  Wilsonian ideas and, 158–59
United States, 2, 46, 86, 87, 94, 98,
    103, 148, 161
  anti-war movement in, 144–46
  atomic bomb policy of, 55–56
  atomic monopoly of, 34–36, 54,
    56–58

authoritarian regimes and, 161
China's relations with, *see*
    Sino-American relations
colonialism and, 122–23
Cuban missile crisis and, 75–78
decline of détente and, 213–14
de Gaulle's relations with,
    139–40
elections in, *see* elections, U.S.
Hiss spy case in, 39–40
isolationism of, 15–17, 91–92
Kent State incident in, 146
Khrushchev's visit to, 71–72
moral standards in foreign
    policy OF, 179–82
non-aligned countries and, 125,
    127
origins of World War II and,
    89–90
postwar objectives of, 15–17
postwar settlement and, 9, 17
Soviet Union contrasted with,
    7–8
Soviet Union's relations with,
    see United States–Soviet
    relations
in Stalin's postwar plans, 12–14
in World War II, 8–9
United States–Soviet relations:
  Angola conflict and, 179
  Arab-Israeli war of 1973 and,
    204–6, 212
  arms race and, *see* nuclear
    weapons; SALT
  atomic bomb and, 55–58,
    69–70, 81
  "Basic Principles" statement
    and, 203–4
  Berlin blockade and, 33–34
  Bush administration's review of,
    239

United States–Soviet relations (*cont.*)
  collapse of Soviet Union and,
      255–56
  Cuban missile crisis and, 75–78
  emigration issue and, 182–84
  German reunification issue
      and, 248–51
  justice and, 159–61
  Kennedy and, 74–75
  Khrushchev's U.S. visit and,
      71–72
  "long telegram" and, 29–31
  Marshall Plan and, 30–34
  moral ambivalence in, 180–82
  non-aligned nations and,
      124–28
  occupation of Germany and,
      22–23
  origins of Cold War and, 27–28
  Ostpolitik and, 153–54
  postwar Germany policy and,
      134–38
  postwar settlement and, 9–17,
      20–22, 28–29
  Reagan's policies and, 222–28
  rule of law and, 158–59
  Soviet unilateralism and, 24–25
  SS-20 missile crisis and,
      200–203
  U-2 incident and, 73–74,
      167–68, 171, 177
  see also capitalism; communism;
      détente
Universal Declaration of Human
      Rights, 160, 184, 188
U-2 incident, 73–74, 167–68, 171, 177
Uzbekistan, 253

Vanik, Charles, 182–83
Versailles Treaty of 1919, 16, 89
Vienna summit of 1961, 74, 84, 137

Vienna summit of 1979, 202, 210–11
Viet Minh, 42
Vietnam, Democratic Republic of
      (North Vietnam), 129, 151,
      172, 177, 206–7
Vietnam, Republic of (South
      Vietnam), 129, 168, 173,
      177
  Diem's regime in, 132–33
Vietnam War, 133–34, 140, 157, 172,
      173, 206–7, 212, 261, 266
  anti-war movement and,
      144–46, 154–55
  Cambodia invasion in, 145–46
  Johnson's credibility in,
      168–71
  Pentagon Papers and, 174–75
  Sino-American relations and,
      150–51
  Tet Offensive in, 170
  War Powers Act and, 176–77
Vonnegut, Kurt, 49, 82

Wałęsa, Lech, 196–97, 218, 222, 230,
      241, 257
Wallace, Henry A., 91
warfare, nuclear weapons and
      nature of, 50–52, 58, 262–63
War Powers Act of 1973, 176–77
Warsaw Pact, 108–9, 134–35, 187, 235,
      236, 250
Warsaw uprising, 21
Washington Summit of 1987,
      232–33, 235
Watergate affair, 155, 156–58, 175–77,
      212
Weizsäcker, Richard von, 249
welfare state, 86, 216
West Berlin, 112–13, 115, 138, 144, 167
West Germany, *see* Germany,
      Federal Republic of

Wilson, Woodrow, 16–17, 20, 27, 87,
    92–95, 158
  Fourteen Points of, 87, 121
  relevance of, 92–93
  World War II and vision of,
    90–91
World Bank, 93–94
World War I, 12, 16, 33, 50, 52, 53, 92,
    94, 262
  capitalism and, 86–89
  colonialism and, 121
World War II, 7, 12, 14, 15, 17, 26–27,
    43, 46, 48–49, 50, 52, 69, 79,
    87, 89–90, 94, 139, 157, 238,
    248, 250, 262
  colonialism and, 121–22

second front in, 18–20
separate peace issue in, 18–20
strategic bombing, 53–54

Yalta Conference of 1945, 5–6, 21, 22
Yeltsin, Boris, 254–56
Yugoslavia, 37, 99–100, 126, 153
  non-alignment strategy of,
    124–25
  Soviet Union's rift with, 33

Zelig (film), 230
"zero option," 225, 231
Zhdanov, Andrei, 32
Zhivkov, Todor, 246
Zhou Enlai, 125, 151